D1029338

RELIGION
AND
THE HUMAN IMAGE

Carl A. Raschke
University of Denver

James A. Kirk
University of Denver

Mark C. Taylor
Williams College

PRENTICE-HALL, INC., Englewood Cliffs, New Jersey 07632

Library of Congress Cataloging in Publication Data

Raschke, Carl A
   Religion and the human image.

   Includes bibliographies.
   1. Religion. 2. Religions. I. Kirk, James A., joint author. II. Taylor, Mark C.,
1945– joint author. III. Title.
BL48.R29   291   76-43047
ISBN 0-13-773424-7   Jan 25 '78

© 1977 by
PRENTICE-HALL, INC.
Englewood Cliffs, New Jersey 07632

10 9 8 7 6 5 4 3 2 1

PRENTICE-HALL INTERNATIONAL, INC., *London*
PRENTICE-HALL OF AUSTRALIA PTY. LIMITED, *Sydney*
PRENTICE-HALL OF CANADA, LTD., *Toronto*
PRENTICE-HALL OF INDIA PRIVATE LIMITED, *New Delhi*
PRENTICE-HALL OF JAPAN, INC., *Tokyo*
PRENTICE-HALL OF SOUTHEAST ASIA PTE. LTD., *Singapore*
WHITEHALL BOOKS LIMITED, *Wellington, New Zealand*

Contents

Foreword

In the past decade or two the academic study of religion has matured from a preoccupation with theology and Christian apologetics to a broad-brush concern with the rich data of man's total religious life. Numerous theories and models intended to explicate the many faces of the world's sacred traditions have been proposed, even while at the same time there has emerged among certain scholars the use of a methodology called the "scientific study of religion." Introductory textbooks in religion, however, more often than not have not cued to this trend. The general stress in most such textbooks is apt to fall on the purely descriptive, experiential, or phenomenological approach to the subject. Religious phenomena are presented as bare givens that require appreciation but not careful explanation. No serious attempt is made to build a comprehensive framework of theory for interpreting a hodgepodge of religious beliefs and practices. On the other hand, those few texts that do offer theoretical paradigms for the study of religion frequently tend to do so in an abbreviated and haphazard manner. Snippets and selections from the famous published theories of religion are tossed together without any appreciable effort to furnish a body of information that might bolster the theoretical material.

The following textbook is intended for general introductory courses in the study of religion, primarily at the college level. The material embodies what the authors have termed a "constructionist" approach, which rests on the premise that religion can best be understood as a complex artifact of human symbol making and culture.

The constructionist approach draws in large part upon the theories and methods of the *Religionswissenschaft* school for dealing with religious phenomena. It views religion as the product of various cultural elements: social, historical, and psychological. In religion the human species fashions a set of master *images* of itself and of its situation in the universe, it engages in what Peter Berger has termed the "construction of reality."

A comprehensive discussion of the nature of religion along these lines is undertaken in the first chapter. Subsequent chapters are intended to develop and analyze particular images and to explore their context within the Eastern and Western religious traditions. Chapter 2 looks at the human image as it evolved in ancient Hebrew thought with reference to biblical passages from the time of Moses up through the beginnings of Christianity and the writing of the New Testament. Chapter 3 examines the development of the Christian image against the backdrop of the late Roman Empire, the Middle Ages, and the Reformation. Chapters 4 and 5 look at the images carved from Oriental religious experiences, beginning in India and spreading eastward to China and Japan. Chapter 6 deals with the breakdown of the traditional images under the impact of science and secularization in the nineteenth and twentieth centuries and the attempt to redefine the religious condition of humanity. Chapter 7 inspects some recent trends in Western religion and culture, including the use of psychedelic drugs, the fusion of religion and politics, and the growth of non-Western sects and cults, under the larger rubric of the "search for transcendence."

The text, however, is not designed as an overview of all issues in religious studies. Nor is it targeted necessarily for specialized courses. It is not, for example, a text in the history of religions and does not pretend to cover all the different religious expressions of mankind, nor to survey each tradition in its historical entirety. It is not a text for the sociology or the psychology of religion, although material and insights from such disciplines are cited.

The relative brevity of the book should make it useful, however, as basic reading for introductory classes, either in departments of religious studies, philosophy, or general humanities. It is hoped that the instructor will be able to supplement such material with whatever readings he deems valuable for arranging the course in accordance with his own interests. Too often textbooks pretend to do too much, to be all things to all people. Definitive textbooks in religious studies, however, are virtually impossible, because of the intricacy of the subject and the fluidity of methodologies. *Religion and the Human Image* aims to distill a number of these methodologies into a single, elementary approach and to apply them to those themes, contemporary as well as historical, that are alive for students today.

Carl A. Raschke

James H. Kirk

Mark C. Taylor

Acknowledgments

The authors wish to express gratitude to the following persons and organizations for consideration and assistance in the preparation of the completed manuscript of this book.

Our greatest token of thanks goes to Mrs. Gretchen Hawley, Administrative Assistant to the Department of Religion at the University of Denver, for her long hours and tireless typing and editing of the several versions of the manuscript prior to publication. Without her critical eye and helpful comments, many mistakes or gaffes might have passed unnoticed.

Mention of appreciation is due to Williams College for a grant to help defray part of the cost of preparation as well as to the University of Denver, whose general resources were utilized in various ways. Also a note of thanks to Prof. Roger Johnson of Wellesley College for his helpful comments on the manuscript during its final stage; to Miss Aletha Kirk for her invaluable babysitting services during the summer of 1975, without which the final version might have been stillborn; to Ms. Tracy Surber for clerical assistance; to Ms. Rosemary Lane for assistance in typing; to Mrs. Grace Raschke, for her long labors in indexing this book; and to Mr. Norwell Therien and Mrs. Teru Uyeyama for invaluable editorial help and consultation.

Finally, acknowledgment is given to the following publishers:

Excerpt from Augustine, *The City of God,* Vol. 14, from Father of the Church series translated by G. G. Walsh and G. Monahan (Washington, D. C.: Catholic University of America Press, 1952). Reprinted by permission.

Excerpts from Karl Barth, *The Epistle to the Romans,* trans. E. C. Hoskyns. Oxford University Press, 1968. Reprinted by permission.

Excerpt from *Endgame,* Samuel Beckett. Reprinted by permission of Grove Press, Inc. Copyright © 1958 Grove Press, Inc.

x   *Acknowledgments*

Excerpts from *A Rumor of Angels* by Peter Berger. Copyright © 1969 by Peter L. Berger. Reprinted by permission of Doubleday & Company, Inc.

Excerpts from *The Sacred Canopy* by Peter L. Berger. Copyright © 1967 by Peter L. Berger. Reprinted by permission of Doubleday & Company, Inc.

Excerpt from *Love Songs of Vidyapati* by Deben Bhattacharya, translated and edited by W. G. Archer. Copyright © 1963, 1969 by UNESCO. Reprinted by permission of Grove Press, Inc. and George Allen & Unwin Ltd.

Excerpt from John Bowker, *The Sense of God.* Oxford: The Clarendon Press, 1973.

Excerpts from *Origen, on First Principles,* translated by G. W. Butterworth. First published by SPCK 1936, reprinted by Harper Torchbooks 1966. Reproduced by permission of SPCK.

Excerpts from *The Myth of Sisyphus and Other Essays,* by Albert Camus, trans. Justin O'Brien. Copyright © 1955, Alfred A. Knopf, Inc. Used by permission.

Excerpt from *The Plague* by Albert Camus. Copyright © 1948 by Gallimard, translated by Stuart Gilbert. Reprinted by permission of Hamish Hamilton, Ltd. and Mme. W. A. Bradley.

Excerpts from *The Philosophy of the Enlightenment,* by Ernst Cassirer, trans. Fritz C. A. Koelln and James P. Pettegrove (copyright 1951 by Princeton University Press).

Excerpt from *The Buddhist Teaching of Totality* by Garma C. C. Chang. Copyright 1971 Pennsylvania State University Press. Reprinted by permission.

Excerpts from *Martin Luther: A Commentary on St. Paul's Epistle to the Galatians.* James Clarke and Co. Ltd. (© James Clarke and Co. Ltd. 1953).

Bob Dylan, "Like a Rolling Stone," © 1965 Warner Bros. Inc. All Rights Reserved. Used by permission.

Excerpts from *Writings of the Young Marx on Philosophy,* edited and translated by Loyd D. Easton and Kurt H. Guddat. Copyright © 1967 by Loyd D. Easton and Kurt H. Guddat. Reprinted by permission of Doubleday & Company, Inc.

Excerpts from *The Bhagavad Gita,* translated by Franklin Edgerton (© Harvard University Press, 1944), reprinted by permission.

Excerpt from "The Waste Land" in *Collected Poems 1909-1962* by T. S. Eliot, copyright, 1936, by Harcourt Brace Jovanovich, Inc.; copyright, 1963, 1964, by T. S. Eliot. Reprinted by permission of the publishers and Faber and Faber Ltd.

Excerpts from *The Future of an Illusion* by Sigmund Freud. Translated and edited by James Strachey. Copyright © 1961 by James Strachey. Reprinted by permission of W. W. Norton & Company, Inc., and the Hogarth Press Ltd.

Excerpt from *Thespis* by Theodor H. Gaster. Copyright © 1950, 1961 by Theodor H. Gaster. Reprinted by permission of Doubleday & Company, Inc.

Excerpt from Hegel, *The Encyclopaedia of the Philosophical Sciences, Logic,* trans. E. B. Spiers and J. B. Sanderson. New York: Humanities Press, 1968. Reprinted by permission of Humanities Press and George Allen & Unwin Ltd.

Excerpt from *Søren Kierkegaard's Journals and Papers,* trans. Howard and Edna Hong. Bloomington: Indiana University Press, 1967. Reprinted by permission.

Excerpts from *Dialogues Concerning Natural Religion* by David Hume, edited by H. D. Aiken. Copyright 1966 Macmillan Publishing Co., Inc. Reprinted by permission.

Excerpts from *The Thirteen Principal Upanishads,* translated by Robert Ernest Hume and published by Oxford University Press, Indian Branch.

Excerpt from *The Undiscovered Self* by C. G. Jung, reprinted by permission of Little, Brown and Company in association with The Atlantic Monthly Press.

Excerpt from *Training in Christianity,* by Søren Kierkegaard, trans. Walter Lowrie (Princeton University Press, 1967; Princeton Paperback, 1967); and from *Fear and Trembling* and *The Sickness unto Death,* by Søren Kierkegaard, also trans. Walter Lowrie (Princeton University Press, 1941, 1954; Princeton Paperback 1968). Reprinted by permission.

Excerpts from *The Politics of Experience and the Bird of Paradise* by R. D. Laing. Copyright © 1967 by R. D. Laing. Reprinted by permission of Penguin Books Ltd.

Excerpts from *Calvin: Institutes of the Christian Religion,* The Library of Christian Classics, Volumes XX and XXI, edited by John T. McNeill and translated by Ford Lewis Battles. Published simultaneously in the U.S.A. by The Westminster Press, Philadelphia, and in Great Britain by S. C. M. Press Ltd., London. Copyright © 1960, by W. L. Jenkins. Used by permission.

Excerpt from *The Varieties of Psychedelic Experience* by R. E. L. Masters and Jean Houston. Copyright © 1966 by R. E. L. Masters and Jean Houston. Reprinted by permission of Holt, Rinehart and Winston, Publishers.

Excerpt from "Appeal from the Sorbonne—June 13-14, 1968," in Carl Oglesby, ed., *The New Left Reader* © by Carl Oglesby 1969. Reprinted by permission of Grove Press, Inc.

Excerpt from *Catholics and Unbelievers in Eighteenth-Century France,* by Robert R. Palmer (copyright 1939 © 1967 by Princeton University Press). Reprinted by permission of Princeton University Press.

Excerpt from *Theology and the Kingdom of God,* by Wolfhart Pannenberg. Copyright © MCMLXIX, The Westminster Press. Used by permission.

Excerpt from *Luther: Lectures on Romans,* The Library of Christian Classics, Volume XV, newly translated and edited by Wilhelm Pauck. Copyright © MCMLXI, W. L. Jenkins. Used by permission of The Westminster Press.

Excerpt from *Reality and Ecstasy: A Religion for the 21st Century,* by Harvey Seifert. Copyright © 1974, The Westminster Press. Used by permission.

Excerpt from *Krishna: Myths, Rites, and Attitudes,* edited by Milton Singer and translated by T. K. Venkateswaran. Copyright © 1966 by East-West Center Press (since 1971 The University Press of Hawaii).

Excerpt from *Zen and Japanese Culture,* by Daisetz T. Suzuki, Bollingen Series LXIV (copyright © 1959 by Bollingen Foundation), reprinted by permission of Princeton University Press.

Excerpts from *Early Christian Fathers,* Volume I, The Library of Christian Classics, newly translated and edited by Cyril C. Richardson. Published in the U.S. by The Westminster Press, 1953. Used by permission.

Excerpt from *Vedic Hymns,* trans. Edward J. Thomas, Wisdom of the East Series. London: John Murray, 1923.

Excerpts from *The Analects of Confucius,* trans. and annotated by Arthur Waley. Copyright 1938 by Allen & Unwin Ltd in England and Barnes & Noble in the U.S.A.

Excerpts from *The Confessions of Saint Augustine,* translated by Rex Warner. Copyright © 1963 by Rex Warner. Reprinted by permission of The New American Library, Inc., New York, N.Y.

Reprinted with the permission of Farrar, Straus & Giroux, Inc., from *Night* by Elie Wiesel, translated by Stella Rodway. Translation copyright © 1960 by MacGibbon & Co.

Excerpt from *The I Ching: Or Book of Changes,* trans. Richard Wilhelm, rendered into English by Cary F. Baynes, Bollingen Series XIX (copyright © 1950 and 1967 by Bollingen Foundation), reprinted by permission of Princeton University Press.

Excerpt from *Myths and Symbols in Indian Art and Civilization* by Heinrich Zimmer, ed. Joseph Campbell, Bollingen Series VI (copyright 1946 by Bollingen Foundation), reprinted by permission of Princeton University Press.

Introduction:

A Gallery of Images

Who has not wandered through an art museum in a large city and marveled at the multitude of images in stone and on canvas, the collective handiwork of untold visionaries and geniuses, reaching far back through time? Browsing among Titians, Whistlers, or perhaps Van Goghs, one is drawn into the lives and minds of their creators, wondering what clues the work of art might yield about the artist's own values, world view, even his own understanding of himself. The virtue of a good painting or sculpture is that the mere image does not speak only for itself; it is a visible hint of something more vast and intriguing. Whoever truly appreciates art cannot help but be enticed into the story behind the image and attracted to the greater reality beyond what first strikes the senses.

What if man's religions were also gathered together in something like an art museum? Obviously, religions are forms of life and expression that cannot be displayed on walls, in corners, or on shelves. Yet religion does provide a host of images—images in the sense of finely delineated symbol-pictures of the universe and its inhabitants. We can puzzle over their obvious or not so obvious meanings. We can speculate about the lives that found expression in them. We can discern in each one an image of humanity.

Let us begin our tour with some random offerings on exhibit.

In the foreground is a dark-skinned desert nomad clad in camel hides. He is alone in a vast barrens of rock, sand, and shadow. Above him a shimmering and vacant blue sky stretches out toward infinity. The scene evokes feelings of both majesty and terror—the grandeur of space, the anxiety of isolation, and the sense of nothingness in the midst of a perilous wilderness. Wherever the eye travels, it beholds only vastness and emptiness. The eye retires and bows to the ear, which

1

strains within the boundless hush to catch the low moan of the rising wind or possibly even the cry of a human voice. The ear picks up sounds so subtle in the desert. Our nomad seems to have his ear cocked for sound. He is kneeling in a posture of fright, gazing with awe toward the sky. His lips tremble as if they were struggling to give forth words. With whom is he attempting to communicate? Perhaps with a presence only he is aware of, a presence that seems so transitory, yet that overwhelms his sensibilities and fills him with amazement.

Next there is a man with sorrowful, yet triumphant visage, in agony, his arms spread out from his side and nailed to a rough wooden cross. Beside him is a crowd of ordinary people, some sneering at him, some weeping, some going about their business as if this were merely another public execution of a criminal. Blurred in the background of the picture are dim masses of humanity, masses that seem to rise up like mist from the ground. They are the masses of all human history. To the right shambles an old monk in a black cowl. To the left armies tangle with flailing swords and banners. In the center a young girl kneels with hands folded in prayer before an altar.

Then we see the evening sun setting over the scorching plains of northern India. A great river meanders across the land, as slowly and unalterably as time itself. In the shallows and side pools of the river swarthy and ragged people of the nearby villages are bathing. Even the cattle come to bathe. Some are washing themselves with ritual solemnity; others intone a monotonous, but haunting chant. The picture has an air of timelessness. The figures in the immense landscape are specks and shadows. The sky seems to swallow up the earth. And the great river flows on from one dusky horizon to the next.

Now, look on as a little motorbike whirs to a stop before an unpretentious wood and stucco building. The riders, a boy and a girl, dismount. At the entry way they step inside a low gate, slip off their shoes, and set them neatly on a rack along the entrance wall. The boy speaks briefly with the gatekeeper, an unsmiling old woman, and pays her a fee. The young couple then make their way into the Buddhist temple they have come to visit.

It is a small, traditional temple. The boy and girl wander slowly through the rooms. A faded screen with a solitary flower painted on it stands in the Butsudan, or Buddha-hall, where three images on the altar are illuminated by several candles.

The pair moves on. Outside the mellow sunlight bathes a clump of trimmed azaleas. A tiny stream of water gurgles out of a bamboo sprout and overflows a rock basin. They are in a garden with clusters of rocks inlaid along a gentle hillside and bordered with neatly raked sand. They sit down on a nearby bench, chatting softly, and looking upon each other with tenderness.

The setting is contemporary Japan. The couple has come to the garden to escape the hurly-burly of the streets and the press of the crowds. Yet they cherish the garden solely as a retreat. Its ancient symbols—on rock and water, sand and bush—are known to them only casually or not at all. Their real lives are swept up in the mundane struggle for education and economic security, in their families, in the contest of wills with the older generation over the new styles of living. They see Buddhism, like other traditional faiths, as remote from the events of life that genuinely concern them. Yet many of their attitudes—their stances in the face of the hazards of street traffic, of earthquake or typhoon, of growing old and dying, their feeling for the fragile loveliness of the things of nature— are all shaped by Japanese Buddhism. Their sense of responsibility to others, their shame and pride, their identity as Japanese grow out of the ancient Shinto tradition.

Beneath the surface of this picture lies a suggestion of both continuity and change. The garden reposes in its archaic dignity, still and hardly disturbed by the momentary intrusion of some moderns inattentive to the spiritual messages from a flower or a bird chirping in the treetops. The garden remains, but the couple gets up and goes away.

The next pictures are historical. The year is 1791, the place a village in France. A furious mob is sacking a country church and is leading the humiliated priest away with a rope about his neck. The priest's crime is that of belonging to the past, to the now moribund social and religious order. Like all partisans of the past, he will perish on the guillotine before the assembled crowd who thunders for more heads to roll. In the village square, by a trickling fountain a statue of the helmeted goddess Minerva, an emblem of nationalism, has been raised. A rudely scrawled banner, draped from a balcony, reads "To the new god Reason."

We leap ahead to the year 1969. A throng of young people in cheap, disheveled clothing is gathered about the Washington Monument. They are chanting, like the Indian peasants at the river, but their song is political: it talks of "peace" and "ending the war." Black against the marquetry of bodies and faces is the profile of a priest. He is chanting along with the crowd. At the edge of the gathering a small circle of young men with shaved heads and orange robes dance and sing a different song, the song of praise to Krishna, in time with the steady jangle of a tambourine.

Here is our last sequence of images. An old woman shuffles through the dusty streets of a Spanish village toward a bell that is loudly clanging from atop a church steeple, calling the faithful to Mass. In wintry Moscow a troop of school children file into a so-called atheist museum, set up by the Soviet state to put on exhibition the discarded relics of orthodox religion that the Bolsheviks suppressed after the Revolution of 1917. The children are lectured on the evils of religion as it was practiced in the old days, about how the church allied itself with the reactionary Tsarist regimes to keep the workers and peasants in bondage, about how the new socialist order has replaced the vision of God with the earthly glories of the revolutionary proleteriat. On a mountainside in the western

United States a large circular wooden platform is built beneath a canvas canopy to face the rising sun. It is a cold February morning. Dressed in an old army parka, a young man with a full beard and flowing hair sits cross-legged on the platform, his eyes shut in serene meditation. The rustle of a slight breeze through the overhanging pines barely breaks the quiet. In a large, modern sanctuary of a suburban church a minister delivers an Easter sermon on the resurrection of Christ. The adults listen attentively. An adolescent fidgets a bit and lets out a tired yawn.

These are vignettes of the human situation. They are also illustrations from the pageless picture book of religion. The images of humanity that they evoke are bound up with the very religious images that we fashion for ourselves. But one cannot simply muse over the pictures themselves. One must go beyond glimpses, beyond bare slices of life, to comprehend the entire fabric of symbols and images that inform the various traditions and cultures of the world. In the ensuing pages we look at these images on a more theoretical plane. We seek to understand their implications. We explore how religion and the human image are wrapped together by common threads in the complex tapestry of human existence.

Religion as a Mirror of Humanity:

Self, Society, and Cosmos

1

MAN AS A RELIGIOUS ANIMAL

"Man," wrote the English philosopher Edmund Burke, "is by his constitution a religious animal." Although more than a few scientists and social researchers would refute such a claim today, the historical record is apt to argue against them. Only until the so-called Age of Reason beginning in the late seventeenth century, scarcely any European intellectual, no matter how impious or unorthodox his views on other people's faith, would have questioned the premier role that religion performs in the conduct of human life. Even in the modern period, with the advent of popular atheism and the loss of control by the churches over the habits of acting and thinking for masses of individuals, the contention that religion still survives as an integral and necessary human enterprise, both psychologically and sociologically speaking, can hardly be dismissed out of hand.

For a number of years now media commentators have been trumpeting a revived and widespread interest in religion throughout Western culture. The German sociologist Thomas Luckmann has underscored this trend by describing the persistence of an "invisible religion" concealed beneath the bony shield of secular consciousness—a hidden pool of sacred feelings and values that lie locked within our profane universe of science and technology.[1] Similarly, Peter Berger, another sociologist of religion, deems the current climate of materialistic and utilitarian culture not as relentlessly inhospitable to the religious perspective, but as an implicit opportunity for a renaissance of religious meanings. Within our workaday situation it is possible, according to Berger, to monitor distinct "signals of transcendence." By signals of transcendence he means a particular body

5

of clues given within our ordinary experience that point to a higher purpose for our existence.[2]

Although contemporary people may have lost trust in the traditional beliefs and symbols that for past epochs served to mediate between earth and heaven, between the known and murky unknown that prowls at the edges of their life-world, nonetheless they have not surrendered the innate desire to contemplate or commune with a higher reality. John Bowker has aptly named this radical disposition to find confirmation of religious truth "the sense of God."[3] Indeed, the recent resurgence of interest in occultism, spiritualism, and altered states of consciousness through hallucinogenic drugs, even among persons who are habitually unreligious in the usual sense of "religious," furnishes some evidence for an enduring sense of God as native to the human mind.

Whether or not a contemporary observer chooses to admit the religious *option* as a means for comprehending the predicament in which he finds himself, he yet remains confronted with the unshakeable fact that religion continues to hold great sway over the aims and policies of millions around the globe. Religion looms as a pervasive phenomenon with which believer and nonbeliever alike must reckon. It matters little if we are looking primarily at the many colored myths, rites, and customs of archaic societies or at the disguised forms of worship that characterize new religious postures. Countless efforts have been made to explain just *why* man survives as a religious animal. Yet all such efforts seem to converge on the presumption that there is something in human nature that impels us to create a *sacred cosmos*—a knotted, yet finely stitched fabric of symbols, morals, and meanings that allow us to feel at home in an otherwise terrifying and unfathomable universe.

The great Christian theologian Paul Tillich put the matter this way: religion answers to humanity's "ultimate concerns." That is, human beings essentially are creatures who seek and probe toward the ultimate limits of their knowledge and experience. They thirst for solutions to problems that *ultimately matter*, problems with literally life-and-death importance. And they direct themselves toward whatever solutions may be offered with *ultimate interest and passion*. A precise formula for the manner in which religion serves to organize human life around this attention to the outer boundaries of experience comes from the sociologist Robert Bellah. Religion, Bellah says, is "a set of symbolic forms and acts that relate man to the ultimate conditions of his existence."[4] Because religion provides motives as well as meanings, it succeeds in bringing about profound changes in the way man relates to himself, his fellows, and his surroundings. Religion, therefore, involves not only ultimate concern but also, in the words of Frederick Streng, a "means toward ultimate transformation."[5] Religious man endeavors to regulate and pattern his style of living in conformity with the sacred cosmos he constructs.

As the anthropologist Clifford Geertz has phrased the matter, religion produces both "models *of*" the larger reality in which man participates and "models *for*" the techniques by which he carries through his daily routines in keeping with his sense of that reality.[6] Humanity is far from content merely to erect a structure of religious meanings and aspirations for sheerly disinterested or theoretical ends. Human beings choose also *to dwell inside that structure* and comport themselves in a manner appropriate to their domicile. Religion is thus something like a house built according to the specifications that fit the life-needs of the builder. Humanity constructs religion in harmony with its own perceptions of how one ought to live and of what one feels should be the order of things that renders his form of life coherent and purposeful. Yet at the same time man submits to the discipline of his religious vision as an order that commands unassailable authority. This human tendency to construct a religious world view and still act as though the construction is external and normative points to the *reflexive* dimension of religious experience. By the reflexivity of religion is meant the fact that religion both shapes and is simultaneously shaped by humanity.

Man, therefore, is the creature who does not merely adapt *passively* through natural selection or instinct to the forces of the environment that constantly encroach upon him, but also contrives his own patterns of order as he sees fit and conducts himself according to rules that he imagines as inscribed in the very nature of things. The saying *Deus vult*—"God wills it"—gives hint also of human will. Yet the will of God can only have a binding influence on mortal wills so long as it appears to be *more than* human. This is perhaps one of the great paradoxes of religious thought and behavior.

In fine, religion serves as a mirror to the human face, as a polished and resplendent looking glass in which humanity beholds its own image, its ideal portrait of itself, its highest intentions, its destiny. But the factor that makes religion such a powerful and traansfigurative force in human affairs is that man tends to accept the reflection of himself in the religious mirror as an *objective* state of affairs and not merely as an arbitrary artifact of the mind. Geertz notes that most religious concepts are bedecked "with such an aura of factuality that the moods and motivations seem uniquely realistic."[7] The image which appears in the mirror is construed by the ordinary religious devotee as one among certain higher order truths about the cosmos. *Homo religiosus* finds himself not unlike the dog in Aesop's fable who could not differentiate between himself and his own reflection in the water of a pond. The moral of such a tale, of course, has to do with the human race's universal capacity for self-deception. And certain learned critics of religion never tire of seeking to disabuse believers of the religious "illusion." Whether the fact that man fashions a likeness of himself in the lore of religion and then turns right around to worship his own likeness should be viewed as plain testimony to his preference for living in a fool's paradise has been long and heatedly debated and still must remain open to question. Followers of Karl Marx and Sigmund Freud have frequently adopted the stance that religion diverts human attention from the reality of its ambiguous and perhaps unpleasant place in civilization. Religion generates fantasy worlds that supply mental security and ease, but that in the final assessment are merely strategies for avoiding the overwhelming challenges and responsibilities of being human.

On the other hand, others such as Peter Berger suggest that *all* of man's grasps of reality, religious or otherwise, are in some sense "constructed" and hence artificial. Thus the criteria according to which an outsider should judge religion must not reside in the purported reality or unreality of religious images, but in the degree to which religious man puts together an intelligible system of symbols which continue to be adequate to his existence in the world. Is the religious image truly tailored to answer the pressing questions that he poses in his life-situation? Does it represent faithfully his goals and projects, or is it a distorted and deceptive image, as in a funhouse mirror? Does the image serve to compel action that enhances or degrades the quality of human existence? These are the kinds of questions, rather than questions of the truth of cognitive claims, which one ought properly address to a particular form of religious expression.

The first modern thinker to clearly pronounce the fundamental insight that religion is a function of the human condition was the German philosopher Ludwig Feuerbach (1804–1872). In his epochal and provocative treatise *The Essence of Christianity* Feuerbach laid down the fundamental premises from which the major share of philosophical and scientific interpretation of religion would proceed. "The absolute is to man his own nature," Feuerbach wrote.[8] At the core of all religious representations of God are inverted human images projected, as in a Chinese lantern, onto the vast heavens. But humanity does not realize the nature of its projections. In its naïveté and preoccupation with the sense of divine presence humanity fails to acknowledge the true author of its religious objects. Humanity is either unwilling or unable to recognize that religion is merely "the relation of man to himself, or more correctly to his own nature."[9] Feuerbach thought that, insofar as man fails to discern that he is the source of religious representations, he deprives himself of his natural dignity and integrity. "To enrich God, man must become poor; that God may be all, man must be nothing."[10] Because of religion man grows grievously alienated from his authentic self. Unwittingly, he enslaves himself to the handiwork of his own imagination. Since what man adores is really nothing more than what he has created alone, all religion constitutes, for Feuerbach, a species of idolatry.

Without wholeheartedly endorsing Feuerbach's harsh dictum about the alienating features of religion, it is possible nevertheless to make use of his theory of projection. By examining a primitive icon an anthropoligist or archaeologist may discover something telling and profound about its maker. Similarly, the student of religion may learn that the religious symbol set bears a distinctive impress of the symbol maker. Evaluation of the projection gives revealing evidence as to the character of the projector. On the one hand, the religious image furnishes information about the total life-context in which the man of faith wrestles with problems of survival and meaning. Invariably, the language of religious myth discloses in some measure the contours of the mundane surroundings perceived by the mythifier. Yahweh, the God of the ancient Hebrews, is portrayed as a "man of war" in one passage of the Old Testament (Exodus 15:3), because warring was a habit among ancient nomadic peoples. Likewise, in most patriarchal societies, the Deity is usually conceived as maculine in some form. On the other hand, religious images also tell us much, not just about the way in which man interprets his *actual* situation, but about his feeling for what is *possible* as well. Religion constructs an imaginative scaffolding of signs and codes which indicates what man both *is* and *wants to be*.[11] This dual intention of religious symbols was first recognized by Feuerbach. Feuerbach saw that religion sketches the lights and shadows of humanity's ideal self-image as well as its empirical character. Religion composes a universe in which the supreme values and goals of a particular community of individuals are transformed into real elements of cosmic order. An example is the New Testament claim that "God is love" (I John 4:8). To say that God is love affirms not necessarily the fact that man experiences love as active in the world, but mainly that man hopes and strives to realize a world suffused with love.

In short, religion supplies a paradigm of a truly humanized world, wherein the "will of the gods" comes to betoken man's will to overcome his natural limitations, to set before himself potentials and purposes that go beyond his average expectations about himself, his society, and his world. Whether the "will of the gods" does correspond also to something absolute and mysterious in itself beyond the edge of human influence or comprehension is a theological problem that our method of constructionism does not seek finally to tackle. Philosophers of religion and theologians have debated endlessly over whether there ever can be ample evidence to demonstrate the existence of a divine reality over and above the symbols and images that human beings create for their worship of the ultimate. The evidence has never been conclusive, and the force of any proof usually amounts to arguments based on probability, what William James called "the will to believe," or what Søren Kierkegaard dubbed "the leap of faith." To infer or deny the reality of something that lies behind the images requires a careful evaluation of the data at hand. Our purpose is primarily to describe that data and to show certain relationships between the different levels—between the factual and the symbolic, between the observable universe and the notions that reflect like a mirror, or refract like a prism, that universe. To employ an analogy from physics, one can explain the relationship between matter and energy without seriously asking what energy and matter ultimately *are*, or to what, besides being constructs of science, they really refer. It may very well be that the image in the mirror is not merely a pattern of light waves rebounding off a glossy surface, but a living entity as in the often used joke about the person who goes to admire himself in a looking glass and discovers his double is making faces at him. If the religious image of man is something more than human, it still has a human face, and it is the contours and furrows of that face on which we shall concentrate our attention.

THE DIALECTIC OF SELF AND SOCIETY

The cluster of meanings which emerge as a particular religious world-view derive from a dialectic or constant interaction between the aims of the self, the demands of a society, and the pressures of an impersonal universe. In other words, the gallery of religious images proves to be as diverse and intricate as human culture. Some cultures tend to stress the worth and integrity of the individual personality. In such instances a personal god—a being who at once loves, wills, and cares for human persons—arises as the master image or root metaphor for the divine nature. This sovereign estimation at both the social and cosmic plane has loomed large behind the Judaeo-Christian religious images for millennia. In contrast, Hinduism tends to view the individual as a specific manifestation of the cosmic order, as the bearer of species traits that have meaning only as elements in the universal whole. Thus Hinduism fashions an idea of the absolute as ultimately impersonal. For Hinduism, the realization of the self in the gigantic ocean of being requires its divorce from ego and individuality and becomes the dominant image of salvation, an image that is mirrored in social relations governed by typological considerations. At all events, the full religious picture of the cosmos depends on the manner in which certain persons in a given orbit of social experience discern the kinds of parts they must play as agents in the web of life.

Peter Berger and Thomas Luckmann have classified the process of symbolization according to the interests of a group as "the social construction of reality."[12] The real world—both the sacred and profane—is mapped in human consciousness alongside the self's patterns of knowing and doing within the social order. Religious myths and meanings, therefore, function as ultimate reference points against which the ordinary person can measure his everyday attitudes, intuitions, and judgments, even though the ultimate force of the religious symbol may translate, from the vantage point of the neutral observer, into the unconditional norms of the culture in question. The individual member of that culture may be disposed either to adopt these norms or oppose them. When the self identifies its own norms with the norms of the social order under the guise of religious authority, the process of *legitimation* takes place. Legitimation is the tendency inherent in religion to make certain finite and culture-based values appear as though they were the court of last appeal. According to Berger, "religion legitimates so effectively because it relates the precarious reality constructions of empirical societies with ultimate reality."[13] A perfect illustration of the legitimating mechanism can be found in Hinduism, where the lawful order of *dharma* of a hierarchical society (the tight regimen of caste responsibilities and duties) is thought to coincide with the cosmic *dharma* that lies embedded in the very fabric of creation. The god-man Krishna says in the *Bhagavad-Gita:*

> The four-caste-system was created by Me
> With distinctions of Strands and actions
> (appropriate to each)
>
> [IV.13]

In those instances where the self enters into conflict with the entrenched norms of a society—as, for example, in Reformation Protestantism's assertion of private religious conscience over the sacramental authority of Roman Catholicism—the reverse process goes forth. The source of value and truth is located within the person's own original insights rather than in the de facto public authority. Yet here too the alternative reality that the religious innovator chooses still must be interpreted by him as divinely sanctioned in some sense. The rebel proclaims that God is on his side in his assault on the institutions and habituations of his culture. Thus the Hebrew prophet Amos inveighs in the name of Yahweh against the social abuses of his time.

> Woe to those who are at ease in Zion,
>   and to those who feel secure on the
>   mountain of Samaria,
>   the notable men of the first of the
>   nations,
>   to whom the house of Israel come!
>
> (Amos 6:1)

The prophet calls upon a transcendent standard of right and justice to legitimate his protest against the status quo, against the "notable men." The prophet's image of the divine will stands in counterpoise to the comfortable religious beliefs of a decadent society, and the self which affirms its own definitions of reality in resistance to the apparently false models of that society feels itself the bearer of the heavenly purpose.

Nevertheless, the private intuitions of the prophet, in contrast with the orthodox conceptions of certain religious functionaries or priests, must always find expression through the routine symbols of the culture, lest there be no effective communication of the new revelation. Not only must the religious innovator resort to the same language as his adversaries to get his point across, he must also show how his radical perspective on the cosmos is more genuinely in concert with traditional notions about justice. It is for such a reason that prophets have frequently wound up claiming to conserve or restore older moral and religious ideals while unconsciously essaying a sweeping reinterpretation of those ideals. The prophets of Israel, for example, intended mainly to rehabilitate loyalty to the Mosaic covenant and the faith of their fathers, yet in actuality they hammered out an altogether unprecedented list of prescriptions for the righteous and holy life. The religious vision, therefore, draws upon the standard symbols and conceptions shared within a community of men as well as the inspirations of the lonely seer. The fashion in which self and society are at last integrated determines the texture of the religious image. Yet, regardless of the degree of integration, religion operates chiefly as an absolute rationale for the rules of experiencing and acting that one has incorporated into his life style.

THEORIES OF RELIGION: FUNCTIONAL OR DYSFUNCTIONAL?

The fundamental human needs that religions seek to fill, whether it be the need for social stability or for personal autonomy and integrity, have been explored and weighed at varying lengths by numerous theorists since Feuerbach. Some thinkers have stressed the social importance of religious expression. Others have remained more concerned with the role of religion in personal self-discovery. The former concerns have generally worked their way into the sociology of religion, the latter into the psychology of religion. However, within all these approaches, divergent opinions on how useful religion may be for maintaining the well-being of the human race can be found. In the main, this body of opinion divides itself into two camps, which we call *functionalists* and *dysfunctionalists*. Together these two schools of thought agree on the point that religion is a complex construction of human consciousness in the effort to wrest order from an ambiguous universe. But they part company on the issue of whether the symbolic order religion imposes truly enables man to fulfill himself in the highest manner. The dysfunctionalists argue that religion seduces humanity away from its true tasks and challenges, that it conjures up figments and illusions about the world which render people powerless to cope with their real situation. Religion serves, therefore, no worthwhile function in human affairs. The functionalists, on the other hand, maintain that religion persists as a critical vehicle for humanity to attain its evolutionary goals as a species. The functionalists regard religion as the consummate heightening of all the human faculties, both conscious and unconscious. The dysfunctionalists contend that man can readily dispense with religion and would discover himself much better off if he did so. In contrast, the functionalists suggest that religiosity is as natural to *homo sapiens* as his erect posture. Man most explicitly manifests his talents and capacities through religious activity.

Dysfunctionalism: Marx and Freud

As mentioned earlier, Marx and Freud discredited religion as a fantastic smokescreen that conceals from the pious certain unpalatable truths about their condition. Marx and Freud criticized religion severely for exploiting humanity's worst instincts, for creating subterfuges that allow people to avoid dealing constructively with pain, stress, and injustice. Marx and Freud construed religion as a kind of pathology or sickness. Thus they saw religion as a warped use of man's capacity for projecting an image at himself.

Marx advanced the view that religion only comes into existence when society oppresses certain classes of people and prohibits them from developing their natural human aptitudes. It is those aspects of human feeling and expression which are thwarted by a dehumanizing system of social relations that seek symbolic outlet in religious imagery. As Marx said,

> The basis of irreligious criticism is: *Man makes religion*, religion does not make man. In other words, religion is the self-consciousness and self-feeling of man who has either not yet found himself or has already lost himself again. But man is no abstract being squatting outside the world. Man is the *world* of man, the state, society. This state, this society, produce religion, a reversed *world-consciousness*, because they are a *reversed world*. Religion is the general theory of that world, its encyclopaedic

compendium, its logic in a popular form, its spiritualistic *point d'honneur*, its enthusiasm, its moral sanction, its solemn completion, its universal ground for consolation and justification. It is the *fantastic realization* of the human essence because the *human essence* has no true reality.[14]

According to Marx, were the "reversed world" of alienated labor and capitalist exploitation to vanish suddenly, so the need for religion would evaporate in the same breath. The human essence has no reality because it is distorted by the stifling and brutalizing impact of capitalist economic practices. Under such dehumanizing circumstances, man's suppressed nature takes on a fictional form in the toiling masses' dreams of an eternal paradise. But the inability of the masses to understand their dreams as a fiction instead of a reality bars them from recognizing deprivation and exploitation as naked facts of life under capitalism and from taking concrete revolutionary steps that would allay their misery. Thus Marx wrote:

> *Religious* distress is at the same time the *expression* of real distress and the *protest* against real distress. Religion is the sigh of the oppressed creature, the heart of the heartless world, just as it is the spirit of a spiritless situation. It is the *opium* of the people.
>
> The abolition of religion as the *illusory* happiness of the people is required for their *real* happiness. The demand to give up the illusions about its condition is the *demand to give up a condition which needs illusions*. The criticism of religion is therefore in *embryo the criticism of the vale of woe*, the *halo* of which is religion.[15]

To the impoverished worker suffering from the filth and crowding of the urban slum, religion is what drugs are to the drug addict; it softens the anguish of day-to-day begging and scraping while numbing his senses to the sordid environment in which he dwells. Thus Marx in a celebrated aphorism described religion as "the opium of the people."[16] Religion is the narcotic that keeps human beings passively absorbed in their self-willed fool's paradise and unwittingly "hooked" on an unjust society.

One can certainly visualize the type of situation Marx is talking about. The ragged, black sharecropper in the South of several generations past could neither understand nor articulate the complex social arrangements by which he was compelled to eke out a living at the mercy of his landlord and in dread of lynch mobs who might single him out as a scapegoat in times of trouble. As compensation he learned to symbolize his misery in terms of the Christian image of this life as a vale of tears and to anticipate some heavenly reward which would make over his present sufferings. Thus arose the familiar sayings which capture the pathos of the black religious experience: "all God's children got shoes" and "pie in the sky by and by."

For Marx, the postponed happiness that religion offers in an afterlife or on some "higher" plane of reality is a distraction from the fundamental human need to have happiness here and now. Religion also violated people's dignity by giving them a false feeling of powerlessness in contexts where they could assume control if they understood what was going on and how to prepare themselves. Thus the Bengali man whose son dies from starvation in a great famine wails that his misfortune is the punishment of Allah for some unspecified transgression. A Marxist would say that the Bengali man needs to have his consciousness raised, to realize that his family would not have gone hungry if there had been adequate land distribution and sharing of food in his society. The passive submission to religious dogma on Marxist grounds must give way to a thorough critique of social injustice and the will to take concrete steps to make human life decent. The addiction of religion must be kicked by going through the "cold turkey" of a new political awareness.

While not employing Marx's "opium" metaphor precisely, Freud still denigrated religion as a kind of thought disruption—we might even say mental illness. "Religion," Freud wrote, is the "universal obsessional neurosis of humanity."[17] Humanity contrives religion in order to handle its own deep-rooted sense of helplessness in the teeth of mysterious and menacing cosmic forces. Religion acts as psychic insulation against dim and confusing threats to existence that emanate from all angles of man's encounter with the world. Religion, therefore, becomes institutionalized as a socially acceptable form of reality and displacement. As with all neuroses, religion flourishes when man fails in reconciling his wishes and aspirations with the hard facts that confront him, in particular with the fact of his lack of importance in the universe as a whole. The best cure, therefore, for religion involves *reality therapy*, the use of probing and careful analysis of the actual situation according to the methods of science. As Freud put it:

> Perhaps those who do not suffer from the neurosis will need no intoxicant to deaden it. They will, it is true, find themselves in a difficult situation. They will have to admit to themselves the full extent of their helplessness and their insignificance in the machinery of the universe; they can no longer be the centre of creation, no longer the object of tender care on the part of a beneficent Providence. They will be in the same position as a child who has left the parental house where he was so warm and comfortable. But surely infantilism is destined to be surmounted. Men cannot remain children for ever; they must in the end go out into "hostile life." We may call this *"education to reality."*[18]

In comparison with Marx, Freud did not trace the origins of religion to the tension simply between man and society. Freud spotted the beginnings of religion in the early conflict of the child with his parents, especially with his father. The key to the religious drive lies in what Freud labeled the Oedipus complex— the child's simultaneous lust for his mother to whom he is sexually attracted and his aversion toward his father who competes for maternal affections. Though the child feels thwarted and constricted by his father's dominance, he nonetheless cannot renounce his attachment to this stronger personality who also protects him from the perils and privations of life. Thus, the child's attitude to its father is coloured by a peculiar ambivalence. The father himself constitutes a danger for the child, perhaps because of its earlier relation to its mother. Thus it fears him no less than it longs for him and admires him. The indications of this ambivalence in the attitude to the father are deeply imprinted in every religion.[19]

It is an ambivalence that harbors love, hatred, and fear for the omnipotent father, God.

Freud thought that the structures of patriarchal control in civilization have served to keep in check every individual's promiscuous desires for forbidden sex objects, such as an incestuous union with the mother, and the antisexual masculine religious authorities that accompanied the rise of civilization merely comprised an illusory shadow of the concrete fatherly authorities that loom large in every person's daily human relationships. Freud insisted that religious adoration of the divine father indicates man's lack of power to consciously and logically resolve "the helplessness of his own childhood." Religion, henceforth, remains a memento of the "childhood of the human race."[20]

In his book *Totem and Taboo* Freud undertook to find the historical event by which the conflict between father and child was established as the source of religious ideas. Freud conjectured that this event was recollected within every individual's unconscious activities and served to shape contemporary religious attitudes and behavior. Way back in prehistory, Freud thought, human beings lived together in a "primal horde," a small band with a dominant male in charge, much like ape and monkey societies that have been observed in nature. The dominant male, or "father," tended to monopolize the sexual favors of the females, causing jealousy among the younger sons. One day the sons rose up, slew the father, and ate him. Their suppressed fury against him for barring their own sexual enjoyment was therefore given vent. On the other hand, the sons still recognized the authority of the dead patriarch and suffered guilt feelings about their rebellion. They allayed their guilt by venerating the memory of the slain one and by restricting their own sexual appetites in conformance with the system of authority that had existed before. Freud believed that the vicarious worship of the dead father persisted in the primitive religion of totemism, or the cult of a certain animal embodying the spirit of the community. The totem animal, too sacred to be killed or eaten, stood as a symbolic substitute for the father. The restrictions on promiscuity and the rules of intermarriage enforced by totemic religion tend to have the same function as the direct controls on the sexuality of the tribe by the dominant male. Tribal taboos or religious prohibitions against eating or harming the totem serve to keep individual desires within socially acceptable bounds in the same way that the primal father did by his immediate authority and power.

It was Freud's view, however, that man's attitudes toward authority is always *ambivalent*. People cannot handle their own passions and submit to discipline, yet inwardly resent that discipline. Freud reasoned that the regular totemic feast—a holiday occasion when the sacred animal could be eaten and all sorts of social rules suspended for a short time, not unlike the celebration of Mardi Gras in New Orleans—served as a kind of safety valve for pent-up instinctual pressures. By the same token, the consumption of the totem animal could be construed as a ritual reenactment of the original murder of the father, an opportunity for guilt to be set aside and the rage against authority given legitimate expression.

Out of totem worship, according to Freud, evolved the submission of humanity to a distant, heavenly deity. The totem animal was gradually transformed into the remote and invisible Yahweh of Hebraic tradition. The new God demanded obedience and kept sexuality in check, but more fiercely and rigorously than ever before. Finally, God's authority became too tyranical for his subjects to endure. Like the sons of old, they revolted against him and "killed him," although on the level of myth and symbol. The "death" of God on the cross in Christian mythology represents such a repetition of the primeval murder in a later age. The eating of the "body" and the drinking of the "blood" of Christ in the sacrament of the Catholic Mass constitute a reiteration of the totem feast and ultimately of the devouring of the father's flesh. Religion, therefore, in Freud's estimate, invariably centered on unresolved conflicts between the individual's sexual drive and external restraints, between the authority of the father which was also embodied in society and the childhood demand to satisfy basic instincts.

Freud, of course, can easily be faulted for making sweeping and undocumented generalizations about the meaning of religious symbols, particularly when it becomes evident that the data by which he buttresses his theories come almost exclusively from his own acquaintance with Victorian Christianity and orthodox Judaism. The same complaint can be laid against Marx, who built his model of religion *in toto* from his limited experience with the neo-feudal brand of Lutheranism prevalent in Germany during the first half of the nineteenth century. Even if we reject Marx and Freud's condemnation of religion as not applicable to all forms of religious expression, we can still learn a great deal from them in respect to the connection between symbolic images and man's existential needs. On the other hand, it may very well be that certain needs vital to humanity can *only* be satisfied through religion and not through social revolution or psychoanalysis. Religion would then turn out to be highly instrumental in raising humanity's estimation of itself in the cosmos.

One of the striking difficulties with dysfunctionalism is its implicit rejection of religion mainly on the grounds of its suspicious origins in many documented instances. According to the dysfunctionalists, religion would seem to constitute a failure to cope correctly with the real challenges of being a psychically balanced person or a worthy member of society. Nevertheless, such criticisms presuppose certain unstated value judgments concerning the merits of any set of symbols, religious or otherwise. Freud's dismissal of the "neurotic" core of religion is predicated on his materialism, the idea that if a particular way of looking at events does not conform to tough-minded, common sense realism, it must be put out of court. But there remain many forms of human activity and self-expression that obviously do not meet Freud's narrow requirements. For example, man's love for art and for the work of the creative imagination would, in Freud's view, tend to sustain his enchantment with illusions of a special variety: it is no wonder that Freud had the same prejudice toward humanity's aesthetic side as toward its religiosity.

Second, a wholehearted acceptance of real life may be just as defeating, if not more so, to man's quest for genuine selfhood. The Scottish psychiatrist and author R. D. Laing, an opponent of Freud, has emphasized how deference to the real world—in particular, the world of war, exploitation, murder, and the like—may actually be a recipe for madness. As Laing wrote: "What we call 'normal' is a product of repression, denial, splitting, projection, introjection and other forms of destructive action on experience."[21] "Sanity today appears to rest very largely on a capacity to adapt to the external world—the interpersonal world, and the realm of human collectivities."[22] For Laing, religion, even if it be a form of madness, may have a therapeutic effect.

> Certain transcendental experiences seem to me to be the original well-spring of all religions. Some psychotic people have transcendental experiences. Often (to the best of their recollection), they have never had such experiences before, and frequently they will never have them again. I am not saying, however, that psychotic experience necessarily contains this element more manifestly than sane experience.
>
> We experience in different modes. We perceive external realities, we dream, imagine, have semi-conscious reveries. Some people have visions, hallucinations, experience faces transfigured, see auras, and so on. Most people most of the time experience themselves and others in one or another way that I shall call egoic. That is, centrally or peripherally, they experience the world and themselves in terms of a consistent identity, a me-here over against a you-there, within a framework of certain ground structures of space and time shared with other members of their society.[23]

Similarly, the "left-wing" Freudian social philosopher, Herbert Marcuse, challenged the tendency of orthodox Marxism and psychoanalysis to disparage the use of fantasy. Fantasy, Marcuse claimed, can strike a liberating blow in the face of the narrow and stultifying definitions of what is normal or real foisted on the individual by an oppressive social system.[24] Fantasy thus gives birth to visions of a more humane social order, as in utopian speculation, which makes possible the rise of revolutionary sentiments. An illustration of Marcuse's thesis, in connection with religion, is found in Vittorio Lanternari's study of revolutionary messianism among the American Indians and nonwhite colonial peoples of the so-called Third World. Lanternari has demonstrated how revolutionary messianism draws upon certain fantastic symbols, such as the coming of the redeemer on the clouds or in the whirlwind and his vanquishing of the imperialist rulers, in order to supply powerful incentives to political action.[25]

In consequence, it is often the dysfunctional character of religion that

makes it creative and vital. Many leaders of the great cultural and political upheavals in human history, from Jesus to Gandhi, were in a sense out of step with
their environment. But their estrangement from their times and society did not
make them hopeless neurotics, as Freud might have it, or conservatives and
quietists, in Marxist terms. Rather, their disenchantment with customary standards of reality drove them toward transforming the world around them. The
image of humanity that religion projects may become a blueprint for the meta-
morphosis of human life.

Functionalist Perspectives

In contrast with dysfunctionalism, there is a major school of research that
esteems religion as enhancing humanity's sense of belonging in the cosmos. Religion, for these scholars, is quite functional insofar as the maintenance of an
authentic human image is concerned. Hence arises the general designation for
this way of treating religion—"functionalism." The exact connotations of the
term "functionalism," especially as invoked in sociological theory, are somewhat
difficult to pin down, as Robert Merton has shown.[26] However, for our purposes,
we may consider religion as functional in some manner of speaking, *if* it enables
people to interact purposefully and creatively with nature and society. During
the last generation or so, the functionalist orientation has gained ground in many
academic circles and has nosed out the hard-boiled, uncompromising enmity
toward religion that was evident in Freud and Marx. The viewpoint of the latter
may, in hindsight, be downgraded as merely a vestige of eighteenth-century
anticlericalism and dogmatic nineteenth-century positivism. Certainly the
functionalist approach has allowed many scientists and humanists, let alone
theologians, to appreciate the intricate strands through which religion is bound
up with all areas of human intercourse, no matter whether such theorists may
themselves be personally devout. A toning down of the older disposition toward
rejecting religious phenomena out of hand has led, perhaps ironically, to a finer
and richer understanding of how religion is in fact both temporal and constructed in human consciousness. The very relativity of religious modes and ideas
to changing constellations of social and psychic facts about man has made possible the development of a new and promising theoretical framework in which
researchers can closely inspect and appraise the significance of seemingly non-
sensical attitudes, beliefs, rites, moral strictures, and so on.

Tillich comments that the vital clue to the study of religious symbols lies
in the sundry historical meshes of experience and behavior that we call *cultures.*
"Religion as ultimate concern is the meaning-giving substance of culture, and
culture is the totality of forms in which the basic concern of religion expresses
itself."[27] This account tallies with much of what we have been saying up to now.
Religion constitutes the axis of meaning upon which a people's many dimen-
sional interpretations of things and events rotate. It is foolish to separate religious meanings from ordinary cultural meanings; for each is the source and

guarantee of the other. The great Gothic churches of the thirteenth century were culturally analogous in both form and meaning to the "cathedrals of intellect" displayed in the theological systems of Thomas Aquinas and the Schoolmen, which in turn embodied the robust confidence of a popular faith and the quest for communion with the Creator as the underlying values of society at that time. Conversely, these visible tokens of the spirit worked as the very compasses of meaning by which the man in the street navigated the course of his life.

The nineteenth-century American philosopher and master of letters Ralph Waldo Emerson voiced a similar sentiment when he wrote, "Small and mean things serve as well as great symbols."[28] In a religiously animated culture it becomes inappropriate to consign the sacred to some remote and unfamiliar compartment of human awareness. Religion permeates the average man's habits of evaluating and deciding how to deal with the issues and items of ordinary experience. The Japanese Buddhist may finger his prayer beads in hopes of gaining spiritual power as perfunctorily as the modern-day shopkeeper punches his adding machine. The long-haired resident of a religious commune in New Mexico chants to the rising sun every morning before breakfast with the aim of purifying his mind and being filled with a holy presence.

Of course, it can be, and frequently is, argued that contemporary secular culture has rid itself for the most part of religious practices and messages, except for those of traditional remnants of most of the world's religions that may soon become mere museum curiosities, like the alleged bones of Saint Joseph. Certainly, it can hardly be denied that many long-standing ways of being religious have tended to melt slowly away in the contemporary era. On the other hand, the eclipse of traditional piety within the secular order has not incontestably resulted in the demise of religion itself. Tillich's definition of religion as the "form of culture" still holds up during this twilight period of the older faiths. Peter Berger attacks as a misconception the conventional wisdom that we now have moved forward into an age when "God is dead" and the religious factor has gone altogether. In his short book, *Rumor of Angels*, Berger remarks about the persistence of transcendent elements in human experience—what he calls "prototypical human gestures"—which subsist apart from any intense participation in a traditional body of rites and beliefs.[29] Berger cites such prototypical gestures as man's universal refusal to consent to death, his will to affirm the power and sublimity of love in the face of mass atrocities like the Nazi slaughter of the Jews. These utterly worldly and human modes of being and acting take on a distinctively religious hue, even when formal religious observances have lost their public context. Man's ultimate concern for the solutions to the riddles of existence does not lapse over time. Only a particular configuration of images and symbols, which may have at one time answered to an ultimate concern, grow timeworn and obsolete.

Religion can be seen, therefore, as functionally indispensable for man in regard to both his life in society and his individual personality. The French sociologist Emile Durkheim (1858–1917) was one of the first to fully elaborate the functional value of religion for the social order. Religion, Durkheim stated, consists primarily in a system of "collective representations" (such as concepts of God, notions about sin and evil, and so forth) that are patterned essentially after the structure of community life. For example, the allocation of roles among the gods in a particular pantheon for preserving the economy of the cosmos may correspond to the division of labor in society. Just as there are farmers and huntsmen in an archaic culture, so there will also be patron dieties of farmers and hunters or divinities that do farming and hunting themselves. This illustration may appear a bit crude and not necessarily typical of real social and religious setups, yet it is the kind of thesis that Durkheim thought he could demonstrate adequately as the first plank in a general theory of religion. Unfortunately, Durkheim devoted nearly all his energies to dissecting the totemistic religion of the Australian Arunta in developing his models, and therefore the applicability of his theory to more historically complex traditions remains problematic. At any event, in analyzing the importance of religious pictures of the world, Durkheim dealt with more than the simple projective character of such pictures. Above all, he recognized the role of religious images in upholding the unity and stability of society. The "essential task" of even the "most simple religions," Durkheim declared, "is to maintain, in a positive manner, the normal course of [social] life."[30] Religious symbols accomplish this aim by casting a sacral aura around common persons, places, or things. A small animal is symbolically transformed into a venerable totem which then endures as the focus of a people's religious commitment. An influential tribal chief is said not merely to possess prestige and authority, but also *mana*—the awesome spiritual and creative energy of the universe.

The source of all sacred attributions, Durkheim said, is society itself. Society is "constantly creating sacred things out of ordinary ones."[31] And the reason society confers sacred status on the commonplaces of its environment is its need to give some objective guise to its own intangible moral values. Extrapolating from Durkheim's argument, for example, we have the hypothetical case of a "holy man" who is revered for his divine gifts of magic and spiritual healings. In Durkheim's estimate, it is irrelevant from the standpoint of functionalist theory whether the holy man has supernatural talents. The important point is that he enjoys extraordinary respect, and his sacred distance from other members of the tribe is due to the fact that "public opinion" or social consensus puts him there. The "religious" qualities of the man are simply ciphers for the social norms and cherished values that he symbolically manifests. Everything that conforms to social conventions is *ipso facto* holy. Durkheim shows how this process of making things sacred occurs even in the modern secular world.

> The aptitude of society for setting itself up as a god or for creating gods was never more apparent than during the first years of the French Revolution. At this time, in fact, under the influence of general enthusiasm, things purely laical by nature were transformed by public opinion into sacred things: these were the Fatherland, Liberty, Reason.[32]

Religion is a device of legitimation, of sustaining social equilibrium; for religious images are the forms of social organization incarnate.

A more recent and comprehensive profile of how religion functions in the maintenance of life and experience has been sketched by Peter Berger, who has updated Durkheim's theories and made them more historically precise. Religion carries through the dialectic of self and society, according to Berger, by creating a system of symbolic order that resolves all potential conflicts of the individual with the norms and intentions of those to whom he must remain trustworthy and loyal. Religion does double duty of both "world building" and "world maintenance," that is, it expresses what members of a culture take to be binding rules of experience and behavior as a set of objective facts about things in general, and it acts to solidify these facts as holy and inviolable. Man's religious world is always the familiar social setting magnified to the dimensions of a "totalizing *nomos*," a monolithic complex of laws, institutions, meanings, prohibitions, and injunctions that literally have divine force behind them. Moreover, this world remains eternally valid and sacred, Berger tells us, because religious myth and belief gives humanity the overwhelming sense that it may resist the divine plan for life only at great peril. "Man produces values and discovers that he feels guilt when he contravenes them."[33] The stark "factuality" of religious artifacts is illustrated through the legend of the sorcerer's apprentice.

> The mighty buckets, magically called out of nothing by human *fiat*, are set in motion. From that point on they go about drawing water in accordance with an inherent logic of their own being that, at the very least, is less than completely controlled by their creator.[34]

Berger goes on to explain how religion further renders the objective order of the world that man constructs as *subjectively* real through the mechanism of "internalization." Once religious symbols and values have been internalized, they become self-evident from the standpoint of individual consciousness. They become fundamental assumptions about reality, held by all participants in a given religion and culture, which prove to be impervious to questioning and criticism. For instance, it would be an irrefutable datum of experience for a pious Catholic that the Pope in Rome is right when he interprets the Church's teaching on birth control as decreed by God. Religion makes the human self secure in the precarious balance between one's own desires, the demands of social life, and the limits imposed by nature, inasmuch as it restricts not only outward actions, but also perception of what is ultimately possible. Religion functionally integrates all human experience of the universe in concert with a traditional pattern of feeling, reflecting, and doing. Through religion the human image emerges as a fixed point of orientation. In short,

> It can thus be said that religion has played a strategic part in the human enterprise of world-building. Religion implies the farthest reach of man's self-externalization, of his infusion of reality with his own meanings. Re-

ligion implies that human order is projected into the totality of being. Put differently, religion is the audacious attempt to conceive of the entire universe as being humanly significant.[35]

A third representative of functionalism on the sociological side, who should not be passed by in our discussion, is Max Weber. Weber's investigations into religious phenomena have had an enormous impact, both directly and indirectly, on the modern study of religion. While the countless lanes and pathways of Weber's life and work cannot be summarized here, it is instructive to point out how he identified the chief economic factors that figure in the social function of religion. In *The Sociology of Religion* Weber remarked that "the ends of religious and magic actions are predominantly economic."[36] Religious beliefs and symbols spring from the rationally organized economic activities of people in society. "A certain god may have achieved eminence because he was originally a natural object of importance for economic life."[37] Thus the primitive worship of Mother Earth presupposes the reliance of a people on agriculture for their livelihood, and the veneration of the cow by the peasant culture of India is due mainly to the invaluable service such a beast of burden performs in helping to till the soil.

Nonetheless, Weber did not want to say outright that religious categories are inseparable from economic activity. Weber sought to set aright Marx's theory that the structure of economic relationships between individuals and groups in a society is of decisive weight, and that religious images have virtually no meaning aside from this structure. In Weber's view the larger economic context in which religion arises only stands as a framework in which the internal significance of religious meanings and acts can be interpreted. "The external courses of religious behavior are so diverse that an understanding of this behavior can only be achieved from the viewpoint of the subjective experiences, ideas, and purposes of the individuals concerned—in short, from the viewpoint of the religious behavior's 'meaning' (*Sinn*)."[38] Religion is joined to economic activity, not as the consequence of the latter, but as system of meaning and purpose whereby such activity attains validity in the eyes of certain members of society. Without religion certain kinds of economic behavior would not seem rational and consistent. In addition, religion grows primarily out of its own resources and secondarily may become a body of ideas that legitimates worldly concerns. Thus Weber dismissed as crude Marx's notion that religion only flourishes under conditions of social and economic injustice. Religion is necessary to impart "soul," we might say, to the various forms of work and financial transactions in which people of all classes and professions engage.

Weber cited copious evidence to document his theory. For example, Weber observed that people with economically important offices as well as useful objects are believed by the religious person to possess *charisma*—a supernatural power that distinguishes them from mere mortals or commonplace things. Those who are deprived of wealth or power tend to deny the charisma inherent in the traditional holy men or shrines of society, but will invest it in a prophet who speaks for the oppressed and promises a reordering of economic priorities. Prophets are apt to transfer sacred meaning or charisma from the privileged groups of society and their spokesmen to the disinherited and downtrodden. Prophets often are allowed to wear the mantle of the divine precisely because they live an austere life and abstain from superfluous riches. Weber also noted that the lower economic classes are prone to symbolize their religious aspirations in terms of worldly goods. An example would be the hackneyed expression "pie in the sky by and by" or the poignant lines from the black slave spiritual: "All God's children got shoes." From the standpoint of the reformer or critic, such sentiments may amount to an opiate, but at least they genuinely reflect the economic circumstances of the people who evoke them and in that sense should be appreciated. Finally, in his epochal work *The Protestant Ethic and the Spirit of Capitalism* Weber showed how the leading theological tenets of Protestant Christianity—such as individualism, the distrust of human authority, and the idea of hard work as a divine calling—arose primarily from religious considerations, yet in the long run contributed to the growth of a pattern of economic and social life that was the basis of the modern industrial state. The Protestant ethic thus made possible the rise of capitalism as an economic system.

In essence, Weber aids in clarifying the exact relationship between religion and society. Society, for Weber, is not a vague and abstract entity that somehow has religion as its legitimating tool, but a complex process that involves political and economic behavior in which religious self-understanding plays a part. Economic activity is the practical source of the need for religious justification, for it is what keeps society intact and thus raises the need for a symbolic mode in which it can be understood and affirmed.

The approach exhibited by Durkheim, Berger, and Weber has often been accused of making too much of the social function of religion and of giving short shrift to the manner in which religion relates to the individual mind or psyche. Possibly the most influential among those thinkers who stress the role of religion in the realization of human personality or selfhood has been the twentieth-century architect of analytical psychology, C. G. Jung. More than any other psychologist, including Freud, Jung revolutionized the study of religion in the past thirty years. Jung argued that religion is that faculty of human personality which leads one back into touch with the unconscious impulses of the species. "Religion means dependence on and submission to the irrational facts of experience."[39] That is "because the religious impulse rests on an instinctive basis and is therefore a specifically human function. You can take away a man's gods, but only to give him others in return."[40] Without delving into the nuances of his thought, we should note that Jung looked upon rationality and conscious reflection as only minor parts of man's sentient processes. Science, common sense, and inductive reasoning are only the barren tip of a primeval iceberg of unconscious memories, dream materials, and collective symbols that belong to the race as a "collective unconscious." Jung believed that as modern man gradually cut himself off from and denied the reality and power of these shadowy, subterranean promptings, he forfeited his essential humanity and became virtually neurotic. In Jung's words, modern man has "lost his soul." It was Jung's overriding thesis that religion, rather than lying at the root of neurosis, could actually help salvage the neurotic personality which had suppressed its natural unconscious feelings for the sake of logic and reason. There are places in Jung's works where he seems to identify the collective unconscious with man's relationship to the natural order. Thus religion serves, for Jung, to integrate man's personality with the very rhythms and energies of the whole universe. Indeed, the pace of secularization in the modern epoch, along with the fading of religious sentiment, has upset man's psychic harmony. "Man feels himself isolated in the cosmos, because he is no longer involved in nature and has lost his emotional 'unconscious identity' with natural phenomena."[41] Religion is a precondition, according to Jung, for restoring that unconscious identity—an identity that must be forged through introspection at the level of individual awareness.

Functionalist psychology of religion takes its cue from the position first hammered out by William James in *Varieties of Religious Experience*. James observed that every personality type "reacts" differently upon the universe and thus constructs its own singular image of divine matters. Numerous neo-Freudians, followers of Jung, and others during the past few decades have brought us to appreciate the fact that religion is a multifaceted phenomenon that performs an assortment of tasks in meeting the requirements of psychic health and wholeness. Rather than defeating the natural inclinations of man, religion aids in the formation of well-balanced personalities in various forms.

For example, many ordinary Americans will testify that a habit of constant prayer enriches their lives; it gives them confidence, self-understanding, dedication to tasks, and an overall feeling of well-being in a manner that might have been lacking in the past. Since the Second World War numerous clinical psychologists have suggested an affinity with religious faith and mental health, though in many cases the latter phrase is often loosely specified. Many of the new religious cults that emerged in the early 1970s, such as the so-called Jesus freaks and Eastern meditation cults (see Chapter 7), had the salutary effect of drawing confused and potentially psychotic young people away from drugs and into more lasting and positive paths of self-inquiry.

On the other hand, functionalist perspectives, whether they stem principally from sociological or psychological interests, tend to suffer many of the same shortcomings as dysfunctionalist analysis, although for different reasons. Like Marxism or Freudianism, the conclusions adduced in the writings of Durkheim, Berger, Jung, and so on, have the effect of narrowing too far the rich complexity of religious expression and meaning. They stress too incautiously what we might term the "adaptive" purpose of religious activity. They give exclusive weight to the incidents whereby religious man relaxes all tensions with the world as he encounters it, just as the dysfunctionalists overemphasize the cases in which religion manifests itself as a sign of tension. But, gathering as many historical instances of religion as is feasible, we come to see that both models are insufficient to exhaust the entirety of examples. There are times when Berger's theory is appropriate, especially with regard to the religions of archaic or feudal societies, but his functionalist considerations fall apart when we are pressed to account for character of religious sects and cults in the pluralistic culture of contemporary America. In the present case, religion, more often than not, sets men at variance with the secular order of science and technology. Most individuals today do not justify their allegiance to the status quo, to free enterprise, or the Republican party simply by appeal to a sacred cosmos in exactly the same sense as Berger implies. By the same token, it is clear that a Freudian would be partially correct in his assimilation of religious belief to neurosis were he *only* to cite as evidence clinical records of young men or women who imagined God after the likeness of an authoritarian father. But what can a Freudian do with another young person who converts to one of the new forms of Western Buddhism, which not only sustains no symbol of a personal god, but also encourages the initiate to cut through all prejudices, projections, and illusions in order to behold the "suchness" of the world in its reality? Indeed, Buddhism offers a form of reality therapy that is perhaps even more poignant and convincing (and less expensive) than psychoanalysis. Both functionalism and dysfunctionalism by themselves can provide only a restricted picture of the ways in which religion works as a mirror of humanity.

MYTH AND RITUAL: THE MEDIA OF RELIGIOUS MEANING

So far we have discussed how religion serves as a set of images man fashions of himself and have surveyed the major thinkers who have adopted, to a certain extent, a point of view that looks upon religion as a construction of the world reflecting the human image, even though we appreciate the problems in classifying religion as being completely functional or dysfunctional in its performance. Just as there are many styles of architecture, so there must be a diversity of modes in which humanity erects a religious dwelling for itself amidst the mysteries of existence. Perhaps further investigation will allow us to look not at the separate uses to which religious houses are put, or at the different designs that reflect his self-image, but rather at the universal building materials that enter into the final construction of all religious systems. In other words, let us now inspect the media through which religious images are universally experienced as vital, actual, and concrete, regardless of their peculiar mass and shape.

Through the media of myth and ritual the forms of religious meaning take on a life of their own. Like the tale of Pygmalion whose statue was miraculously transfigured into flesh and blood, the record of religious man is that of the unconscious artificer who changes inert symbols into dynamic events. The principal instruments by which this alteration takes place in religious experience are myth and ritual. Etymologically, a myth can be defined as a story about the deeds of the gods. But more significantly, a myth is an organic unity of meaningful images that supply a pattern of ultimate meaning for the ways in which religious individuals carry out their everyday affairs. Ritual, on the other hand, consists of man's undertaking to make this pattern visible and present through sacred gestures and mimetic actions. Ritual is a kind of powerful play or drama, wherein men act out an ancient script, which is the myth. In fact, many historians have contended that classical drama originally grew out of certain religious rituals dramatizing mythical themes. For example, the Greek comedy may be traced back to a fertility festival. However, the distinction between the stage plays that entertain today's audiences and prehistoric religious celebrations rests on the ostensible fact that drama takes a fictional and idealized stance toward human experience whereas ritual purports to generate a sense of what is most awesomely real. Often, the common play is applauded because it provides avenues of escape from the monotony and desolation of an all-too-familiar landscape of life, but the objective of ritual is to bring to light the main contours of such a landscape. Ritual heightens experience for humanity, rather than giving new experiences. Unlike the theatergoers, the ritual celebrant is not a passive spectator. Through the ritual he clings to his appointed role in the real-life drama as though the lines he read were the actual plan of destiny.

The relationship of myth to ritual has been sketched in a similar vein by the noted historian and phenomenologist of religion, Mircea Eliade. "The foremost function of myth," Eliade writes, "is to reveal the exemplary models for all human rites and all significant human activities—diet or marriage, work or education, art or wisdom."[42] Man frames his myths, usually unconsciously, as "paradigms for all significant acts."[43] Such significant acts acquire ritual meaning, insofar as they are not merely arbitrary and idle pantomime, but integral attempts to align a person's bodily and social behavior with the very cadences of the cosmos. Moreover, these acts, according to Eliade, appear to the religious devotee as ongoing reenactments of the timeless stories of the gods encapsulated in the myth. The myth is an imaginative rendition of what certain deities or heroes performed "once upon a time" in an immemorial eternity. This eternity, however, is not tucked away forever prior to the creation of time, but is *here* and *now*. The eternal drama of the myth is constantly breaking through and becoming manifest in human time and space; the myth's timeless structure serves as the template of experience for religious man in his mundane activities. As Eliade says,

> Myth narrates a sacred history; it relates an event that took place in primordial Time, the fabled time of the "beginnings." In other words, myth tells how, through the deeds of Supernatural Beings, a reality came into existence, be it the whole of reality, the Cosmos, or only a fragment of reality—an island, a species of plant, a particular kind of human behavior, an institution. Myth, then, is always an account of a "creation"; it relates

how something was produced, began to *be*. Myth tells only of that which *really* happened, which manifested itself completely.[44]

The purpose of the ritual is to replicate the mythical *res gestae*—the great feats of the gods. According to Theodor Gaster, rituals "objectify, in terms of the present, situations which are intrinsically durative and sempiternal. Thus, they are, from the start, not only direct experience, but also . . . representations—not only rituals but also dramas."[45] Thus, in the East Asian ceremony of commemorating the Buddha's birthday, worshipers pour tea over the statue of their religion's founder. They thereby dramatize and emulate (as though he were making it real again) the event related in the myth whereby tea fell from the sky at Gautama's enlightenment. A comparable kind of simulative ritual is conducted at many places throughout the United States early each Easter morning when the passion of Christ is lived over in elaborate pageants requiring devout precision and consummate skill. Even our noisy and colorful Fourth of July fireworks displays may be said to compose a ritual that recaptures the glories and victories of the American War of Independence—a secular pageantry that provides the cornerstone to what Bellah has termed our "civil religion."

On the other hand, the models for cognition and action that myth and ritual provide cannot be regarded as self-explanatory, as though they were purely forms of expression and experience that bore no relation to the empirical circumstances in which man locates himself. Human beings work out myths and rituals as systems of rules for interpreting and behaving in concert with the laws of the unseen. Yet they fashion religious forms in order to make sense out of the perceptible environment and to arrange physical wants as well. Scholars generally agree, for instance, that the master myths of preliterate, agricultural societies invariably center on the vegetation cycle of growth, decay, and dissolution which marks the turning of the seasons. Often such societies depict the pattern of seasonal changes mythically as the life and death of a vegetation god or goddess. This mythical motif encompasses numerous cults including those of Tammuz in the ancient Near East, Osiris in Egypt, Adonis in Greece, and even Christ as conceived in the neo-pagan imaginations of certain rural peoples of the Mediterranean basin. By the same token, the transition from one phase of the cycle to the next is represented and lived out on fixed festive dates of the calendar. The most important type of such festivals, from the standpoint of religious historians and cultural anthropologists, is the sequence of rites that denotes the New Year, usually occurring around a change in the solar year or the growing season, such as the vernal equinox. The New Year's ceremonies become symbolic labors to renew or rebuild the cosmos, according to Eliade.[46] This intention is exhibited graphically in the Shawnee New Year's ritual in which the construction of the "cabin of new life" corresponds to the symbolic erection of the cosmos.[47]

But the incentive for symbolic renewal of the world arises primarily from anxiety about the coming of spring. The somber memory of a chill and desolate winter, the yearning for the return of light, warmth, and vitality, the inability of archaic humanity to fathom the ways of precarious and fickle nature combine to support the need for rituals of cosmic regeneration. In ancient Egypt the pharaoh was revered by his subjects as an embodiment of the savior god, and his coronation at each new year became a signal for the restoration of the universe, dispelling the reign of darkness and death. The monarch's newly established authority came to be seen as emblematic of the stability of nature and society together. Ancient Egyptians respected the pharaoh as being responsible through the ritual for ensuring the annual appearance of the life-giving spring floods of the Nile River and thereby for the continuance of the social order, which would disintegrate without its agrarian as well as authoritarian base. The cosmological images of rebirth and power henceforth mirror the deep dependence of a farming people on fertility and other natural factors. The ritual of the rebirth of the cosmos is not merely a dramatization of a primeval story, but an imaginative response to the ever present threats to human survival. A society's unconscious drive to stick together at all costs in the face of adversity is projected as myths of the gods' favor for their people as well as rituals that make the divine overlords personally present in the guise of earthly authorities such as kings or priests.

The renowned cultural historian Johan Huizinga has linked myth making and ritual action to the fundamental human habit of playing. Playing, according to Huizinga, is the creation of representations or images in which the player himself participates, images that allow him to step *"out of* common reality into a higher order."[48] Qualitatively, there is little difference between a child who "makes believe" that he is a great statesman and a religious supplicant who, through the motions of ritual, believes himself to have been invigorated with the spirit of the gods: the only possible exception, of course, is that the child most likely is dimly aware of the pretense he is fostering, while the religious votary draws no conscious distinction between imagination and reality. All forms of play consist chiefly in the *symbolic alteration* of immediate circumstances. "The participants in the rite are convinced that the action actualizes and effects a definite beatification, brings about an order of things higher than that in which they customarily live."[49]

The term "play," of course, as applied to religion, invites misconceptions; it may suggest caprice or whim rather than carefully crafted symbols and stereotyped traditional ritual. Nevertheless, Huizinga demonstrates how the use of imagination, as far as both children's make-believe and solemn worship are concerned, contributes to the construction of a vibrant world of meaning and salvation with intensely real significance. The reality of such a world to the religious participant allows him to endure and comprehend the pitfalls and suffering of practical life. Victor Turner, an anthropologist, has recounted in detail the *isoma* ritual of the African Ndembu, wherein an array of mundane objects from a simple hole in the ground to a white pullet are juxtaposed to make up a theater of ritual action, complete with protagonists and props, for performing a curative ceremony that the tribe views as a prototype of the journey of the human soul from birth to death.[50] Inevitably, *isoma* involves a sophisticated sort of play-acting; but it is play-acting with the intent of making human deeds congruent with the law of life.

Another illustration of ritual in this sense is the annual passion play, or drama about the life of Christ, held every year at the little south German town of Oberammergau. Preparation for the play entails more than simply rehearsing lines. Actors in the play have reported that they found themselves actually "becoming" in everyday life somebody very much like a Jesus, a Peter, or a Judas. Their feelings, thoughts, and behaviors tended to align with the legendary religious character whose role they assumed. The Greek novelist Nikos Kazantzakis wrote in his book *The Greek Passion* about a similar, but fictional, situation in which the experiences and destiny of simple village folk were modified in accordance with the part they played in such a yearly event.

MYSTICISM

Finally, we must consider a mode of religious experience that occurs in all religious traditions, but which is distinctly different from the common media of meaning found in myth and ritual. Like myth and ritual, mysticism supplies a matrix of learning in which man can relate to the ultimate conditions of his existence. Yet, unlike these previously discussed forms of symbolic representation, the mystical consciousness refuses to circumscribe or delimit the divine with any particular image or metaphor. Most mystics contend that God is *ineffable*; in other words, he cannot be named, conceived, depicted, or even spoken about meaningfully. Buddhism, whose central tenets are mystical in compass, declares that the bliss of nirvana is utterly beyond "name and form." Thus, it is hard to compare the human image with any analogous religious image contained within the mystical world-view. It would perhaps not be going too far to say that the mystical image is actually a kind of *anti-image*, a symbol of irrationality and negation, like $\sqrt{-1}$ in mathematics. Illustrations of the character of mystical language and symbolism include the *via negativa* of medieval Christian theology which held that God can only be described by stating what he is *not*, as well as the maxim of the ancient Hindu sages that God, or Brahman, is *neti neti* ("not this, not that").

One of the paramount distinctions between the myth-ritual complex and mysticism is that the former usually appears within a group context (through the transmission of sacred stories by teachers or elders and through the enactment of such stories in a corporate ritual), whereas the latter manifests itself as private meditation or devotion. Functionally, mysticism may be taken as the effort to penetrate beyond the human image, to renounce the artificial and relative character of one's symbols to the human condition, to enter into an awareness of a reality that is not inextricably bound up with the structure of self, society, and cosmos. Significantly, the keynote of the mystical experience is the annihilation of all linguistic and conceptual discriminations between subject and object, persons and world. Many mystical traditions, particularly Hinayana Buddhism, speak of the negation of the self, which from the standpoint of authentic knowledge is regarded as an error, in order to discover one's *not-selfness* (Buddhism: *anatta*). For the Hindu *vedantin*, to exist in a state of not-selfness is to be at the same time "one with the cosmos," yet no longer a mere part of the cosmos; for all distinctions such as part and whole fall away. A quotation from the *Upanishads*, the ancient Hindu wisdom texts, is a good illustration of such a theme. Speaking of the relationship between the finite self (*atman*) and the universal self, the ground and form of all things that exist, the anonymous author of this passage from the *Upanishads*, declares:

> "Now, when one is sound asleep, composed, serene, and knows no dream—
> that is the Self (*Atman*)," said he. "That is the immortal, the fearless. That
> is *Brahman*."[51]

Likewise, mysticism has no need for symbols that maintain the social order as such, because society melts like all transient elements of human life into the vast "void" or "unity," depending on the symbols one employs to indicate the mystical goal of man. It is thus not at all surprising that critics of mysticism frequently condemn it for nurturing antisocial attitudes. Arend van Leeuwen describes how mysticism historically has tended to provide avenues of flight for the individual from the obligations and statutes of a community. "Religiousness of a mystical kind is really a way of avoiding strict acceptance of the Law, because it regards the outward precepts as only the first step on the mystical path which eventually leads the religious seeker on the lonely heights of ineffable communion with God."[52] Western Gnosticism, a current of ecstatic experience and devotion that both runs through and conflicts with the traditions of Christianity, discussed in Chapter 3, stresses the freedom of the mystical consciousness from mere social convention. The Gnostic commonly believed that the attainment of mystical illumination liberated him at the same time from the evil and corrupt world, and thus he no longer was constrained to act as a responsible citizen of that world. Needless to say, many Gnostics have been condemned for immoral excesses, frequently for sufficient reasons. On the other hand, there is a great body of mystical literature that serves to justify the religious agent's contribution to a stable social order. The notion of *karma-yoga* in the *Bhagavad-Gita*, namely, that by acting out perfectly one's social role and discharging one's prescribed duties without interest in their fruits, the person reaches freedom from rebirth and redeath, is a case in point. The loyalty and service to the Roman Catholic Church exemplified by the Franciscan mystics of the Middle Ages gives further credence to the prosocial function of mysticism in particular situations.

Nevertheless, the psychological, philosophical, and sociological explanations for the mystical frame of mind are too elaborate to be raised here. Nor can we justly deal with the issue of whether mystics actually attain, as they often claim, identity with the godhead. Mysticism, however, as is the case with other religious practices, springs from the uniform human quest to reach the upper limits of experience and to secure a beacon of meaning in the light of which to pilot one's comings and goings. Historically, mysticism seems to arise when the other forms of religious meaning have lost their savor and persuasion. Mysticism is the endeavor to plumb the secret and hidden significance of outworn myths, rituals, or creeds. Thus Saint Bernard, having lost touch as a medieval European with the authentic Hebraic context of the Bible, interpreted the Song of Songs not as a tribal love song, which it may very well have been originally, but as an arcane account of the mystical conjunction of the spiritual pilgrim with God.

Interestingly, recent research into drug-induced mysticism has furnished some empirical evidence for the continuity between mythical symbolization and mystical discernment. Masters and Houston have documented from studies of patients under the influence of psychedelic chemicals how mythic images, suppressed or lost to the conscious recognition of their contemporary subjects, unfailingly emerge in the "mind-blown" field of an LSD or mescaline experience and fuse with the mystical sense of the oneness of all feelings and perceptions. Masters and Houston write:

> Comparative studies in the history of religion demonstrate the tendency in the life of a given religion or culture for the myth and ritual complex to exist as a state prior to the development of the individuated religious or mystical quest. Indeed, it is a matter of cultural and psychological necessity that the myth and ritual pattern should dominate and precede the emergence of the mystic way for the one serves a more comprehensive role in the organic ordering and revitalizing of society and psyche, while the other involves a movement away from the social complex to a region of radical individuation.[53]

Mysticism consists of the attempt to grasp much deeper meanings than the everyday meanings expressed in religious images will allow. In the mystical vision, the religious individual peers into the looking glass of traditional images and symbols and catches a glimpse, not of a familiar face, but of his own mysterious *nothingness*. Mysticism may be a way in which man ultimately comes to grips with the emptiness of his own images, images of both himself and his gods.

DEATH, SUFFERING, AND EVIL

The emptiness of images, or the image of emptiness that reigns in mysticism, perhaps reveals a most striking source of religious insight—the awareness on the part of all men that ultimately they must die. Freudians have often tendered the claim that the unitary experience of mystical rapture signifies, at bottom, a vicarious return of the self to the maternal womb, to the chaotic state of pre-existence which is the same as death itself. Indeed, the passion of the mystic pilgrim to pierce all structures of social or personal identity gives a hint of such a goal. For this reason, it may not be too farfetched to say that mysticism brings religious man to a profound rendezvous with the primeval darkness upon which the religious construction of light and order is composed.

The view that religion arises as a response to the threat of death dates back to the beginnings of philosophical speculation. It is as old as the Latin poet Lucretius and as recent as the writings of Paul Tillich, who in *The Courage to Be* discusses the origin of faith in the all too human anxiety about death.

> For existentially everybody is aware of the complete loss of self which biological extinction implies. The unsophisticated mind knows instinctively what sophisticated ontology formulates: that reality has the basic structure of self-world correlation and that with the disappearance of the one side the world, the other side, the self, also disappears.[54]

Anthropological discoveries support this kind of claim. The remains of Neanderthal man, exhumed from Shanidar Cave in Kurdistan, perhaps link the earliest known religious rites to concern about death and the afterlife. Evidently Neanderthal man, despite his stunted intellect, could visualize the onset of death and adorned the burial places of his deceased with flowers and utensils to make existence more congenial in the world to come. The universal occurrence of funeral rites and myths about immortality, from prehistoric to modern times, attests even more extensively to the centrality of concern with death in the making of man's faiths. Indeed, it may be the seeming finality and necessity of death, what Horace Smith has poetically called "the sleeping partner of life," that establishes this event in all human careers as the spore of all religious experience. If piety is properly understood as the suspension in imagination and hope at the ultimate boundaries of his existence, then it is possible to concur with Bowker that

> religions should be conceived as route-finding activities, mapping the general paths along which human beings can trace their way from birth to death and through death, and that the peculiarly "religious" quality is evoked by a focus on limitations which circumscribe the continuity of all human life-ways, of a particularly intransigent kind.[55]

Death, of course, is the most "intransigent" of "life-ways." It is, in truth, the insuperable limit of all life. The human image in all religious symbols surrounding death becomes a veritable form of cartography that aids in guiding mortal selves across this limit. Religious man seeks through his images a picture of deathlessness. The same quest shows itself in the Sioux Indian's belief in the return of the departed relative to the grandfather spirits, in the ancient Egyptian myth of the dead pharaoh who becomes the god Osiris, in the Christian expectation of the resurrection of the body, in the Tibetan Buddhist's posthumous journey through the stages of hell and rebirth to the "Clear Light of the Void" in which the frailties and pains of life are at last dissolved forever. Moreover, the word "eternity," which signifies in many religions the realm of divine transcendence of the earthly, man-inhabited order, derives from the Latin *eternitas*, connoting specifically the conquest of death.

Through death not only personal extinction but also the erosion of human community becomes a melancholy prospect. Thus religion undertakes to secure the integrity of social groupings before the onslaught of death as well. As Berger notes, "insofar as the knowledge of death cannot be avoided in any society, legitimations of the social world *in the face of death* are decisive requirements in any society."[56] Rituals tailored to assuage the sting of death and to make plausible the images of an ongoing viability for personal roles and the institutions of a culture become traditional among all peoples, even in highly secular periods. W. Lloyd Warner, for example, has analyzed the fashion in which the rhetoric and ceremonies involved in the observance of America's Memorial Day take on the atmosphere of a "cult of the dead" whereby members of our society express "in the organized form of concepts those sentiments about death which are common to everyone in the community" as well as "social reassurances that our culture provides us to combat . . . anxieties [about death]."[57] As a matter of fact, the ceremonial statement, "the king is dead, long live the king," points up the yearning in former feudal societies for the survival, if not the everlastingness, of the monarchial head who incarnates the strength and prosperity of the subjects themselves against the menace of disease, famine, plague, or social disorder. Self and society are secured through an interwoven complex of religious meanings inspired by the ever present possibility of their obliteration.

While, however, the images of death and deathlessness bulk large as cosmic seals of human fate, there remain also the lesser woes of workaday experience that require religion as a source of enlightenment and consolation. Death is the utmost indignity inflicted on humanity, but it is not the only one. Religions, therefore, minister to humanity's awareness of the countless little frustrations of its aims and values. Buddhism talks of the unavoidable and aggravating condition of the human species as the goad to seeking salvation. The Buddhist term is *dukkha*, usually translated as "suffering," but implying not simply excruciating pain or distress, but also a host of petty, everyday annoyances. The sufferings or discontents of humanity emerge as a powerful incentive for religious understanding. Thomas O'Dea has characterized religion as a distinctly human reaction to suffering, to what he calls the "breaking points" of man's comings and goings. These include primarily man's uncertainty about his own security and survival, the sense of powerlessness, as well as physical deprivations.[58]

The varieties of religious prescriptions for handling suffering, of course, cannot be enumerated briefly. In Judaism, suffering becomes the badge and responsibility for the people of Israel's having been "chosen" by God to achieve his will in creation: those who undergo tribulation are marked out either for their infidelity to God's laws or for having their righteousness put to the test, as in the case of Job. Christians look to the passion and crucifixion of Jesus, an archetype of redemptive suffering, as the royal road for all devout to follow in reaching reconciliation with their Lord. Hindus and Buddhists, while acutely sensitive to the burden of suffering on all individuals, regard the distresses of life as the fruits of a false consciousness, as the toils of *maya* or self-delusion from which they must disengage themselves through a new perspective on the universe. Suffering, like physical death, ultimately becomes for them a phenomenon perceived in ignorance.

The keen counterpoint between death and suffering on the one hand and the task of acting decisively to deal with them on the other is articulated masterfully in Hamlet's famous soliloquy:

> To be, or not to be, that is the question:
> Whether 'tis nobler in the mind to suffer
> The slings and arrows of outrageous fortune,
> Or to take arms against a sea of troubles,
> And by opposing end them?
>
> [Act III, Scene 1]

However, the religious personality does not necessarily make a bare choice between shrinking beneath "outrageous fortune" or taking his own life, as the gloomy Dane contemplated. The symbolism of religion supplies a meaning, and perhaps a purpose, to suffering which allows the tormented person to bear it courageously, to appreciate the hardness of his lot as somehow explicable in the scheme of God's providence or in the ways of the world. At the heart of the religious image of human beings wrestling with the destructive energies of their environment resides a certain discernment of how man should conduct himself and his own accountability in terms of the deserts he receives. In other words, the religious solution to the brute fact of suffering rests on a vision of good and evil, and it is religious man's conviction that a portion of the universe affects him in a manner adverse to the success of his best efforts, that impels him to seek refuge in a supreme reality where all contradictions between the world as it *ought* to be and the world as it *is*, in fact, are surpassed.

In the process of making sense out of suffering, religion sometimes attempts to interpret what befalls man as the consequence of certain moral or immoral deeds. The strict definition of what constitutes "morality" naturally shifts from tradition to tradition. But in all cases the complete inventory of moral acts is classified under a wider taxonomy of cosmic law. The order of value then coincides with the order of being. Man's endeavor to comprehend his fortunes in light of a higher model of good and evil comprises what has come to be called "theodicy." Literally, theodicy means an assessment of God's justice and it implies the assignment of a righteousness to the Creator that takes precedence over man's narrower criteria of right and wrong. The ways of God are not necessarily man's ways. Max Weber, in his study of theodicy in Western religion, discusses how first the ancient Hebrews and later Christian theologians overcame the conflict between a deep commitment to humane values and the cruelty and misery of life as witnessed from day to day by positing the existence of a sovereign deity who was directing history toward the eventual realization of the kingdom of God on earth. This "distinctively ethical view was that there would be a concrete retribution of justices and injustices on the basis of a trial of the dead, generally conceived in the eschatological process of a universal day of judgment."[59] The Christian myth of the Second Coming of Christ, who would carry the faithful to Paradise and cast the wicked into Hell is an obvious example of such a theodicy, which projects the reality of good victorious over evil into the future. In the religions of India the doctrine of *karma* forms the framework for popular answers to the riddle of evil. A person's *karma* consists of his ledger of moral debts that must be paid off either in this life or in some other form at a later phase of the cycle of reincarnation. The mishaps that may afflict him here and now are similarly construed as necessary effects of past behavior according to the universal rules of retribution. Theodicy works to clarify the significance of one's present predicament with respect to what has gone before, rather than in the hereafter, as with the myth of God's coming wrath and the dispensing of rewards for his elect.

In sum, religion achieves its most vital expression perhaps as a coalescence of sacred signs and gestures that relieves the trauma of living in what is otherwise experienced as an unsteady, contingent, and morally neutral universe. Death and suffering constantly threaten to disrupt the development of man's inborn talents and the soundness of his social organizations. The devastating hardships brought on by wars, natural calamities, and pestilence more often than not will turn individual against individual in a "war of all against all," as historical chronicles and newspaper reports have repeatedly recorded. On the other hand, when death and suffering make sense, when they are placed within a system of ideal values that ascribes them to either good or evil, they become bearable to a certain extent and at the same time do not necessarily induce a person to behave like a wolf to his fellows. Albert Camus, in his novel *The Plague*, has his leading character, the doctor Rieux, deny the religious claim of a transcendent God who has visited a fatal epidemic on the city of Oran as punishment for past sins. Apparently Rieux is an irreligious man who has no use for ultimate questions and answers. Yet, Rieux, in his heroic struggle as a physician against the plague, does at least affirm an ultimate commitment to withstand evil which has religious overtones.

> Nonetheless, he knew that the tale he had to tell could not be one of a final victory. It could be only the record of what had had to be done, and what assuredly would have to be done again in the never ending fight against terror and its relentless onslaughts, despite their personal afflictions, by all who, while unable to be saints but refusing to bow down to pestilences, strive their utmost to be healers.[60]

It is the healing of evil, in truth, that encapsulates the meaning of the religious image.

36   *Religion as a Mirror of Humanity: Self, Society, and Cosmos*

NOTES

1. See Thomas Luckmann, *The Invisible Religion* (New York: The Macmillan Company, 1967).

2. See Peter Berger, *A Rumor of Angels* (Garden City, N.Y.: Doubleday & Company, 1970).

3. John Bowker, *The Sense of God* (Oxford, Eng.: Clarendon Press, 1973).

4. Robert Bellah, "Religious Evolution," in *Beyond Belief: Essays on Religion in a Post-Traditional World* (New York: Harper & Row, 1970), p. 21.

5. See Frederick Streng, Charles Lloyd, Jr., and Jay Allen, *Ways of Being Religious* (Englewood Cliffs, N.J.: Prentice-Hall, Inc., 1973), p. 6.

6. See Clifford Geertz, "Religion as a Cultural System," in *Anthropological Approaches to the Study of Religion*, ed. Michael Banton (New York: Frederick Praeger, 1966), pp. 34 and *passim*.

7. Ibid., p. 4.

8. Ludwig Feuerbach, *The Essence of Christianity* (New York: Harper & Row, 1957), p. 5.

9. Ibid., p. 14.

10. Ibid., p. 26.

11. See Peter Berger and Thomas Luckmann, *The Social Construction of Reality* (Garden City, N.Y.: Doubleday & Company, 1967).

12. Ibid.

13. Peter Berger, *The Sacred Canopy* (Garden City, N.Y.: Doubleday & Company, 1967), p. 32.

14. Karl Marx and Friedrich Engels, *On Religion* (New York: Schocken Books, 1964), p. 41.

15. Ibid., p. 42.

16. Ibid.

17. Sigmund Freud, *The Future of an Illusion* (Garden City, N.Y.: Doubleday & Company, 1961), pp. 70–71. Reprinted by permission of W. W. Norton & Co.

18. Ibid., p. 81.

19. Ibid., p. 34.

20. Ibid., p. 25.

21. R. D. Laing, *The Politics of Experience* (New York: Ballantine Books, 1967), pp. 23–24.

22. Ibid., p. 116.

23. Ibid., pp. 112–13.

24. See Herbert Marcuse, *Eros and Civilization* (Boston: Beacon Press, 1955), p. 127.

25. Vittorio Lanternari, *Religions of the Oppressed* (New York: Alfred A. Knopf, 1963).

26. See Robert K. Merton, *Social Theory and Social Structure*, 2nd ed. (Glencoe, Ill.: Free Press of Glencoe, 1957), pp. 19–22.

27. Paul Tillich, *Theology of Culture* (Oxford, England: Oxford University Press, 1959), p. 42.

28. Ralph Waldo Emerson, *Selected Writings* (New York: New American Library, 1965), p. 314.

29. Berger, *Rumor of Angels*, p. 53.

30. Emile Durkheim, *The Elementary Forms of Religious Life* (New York: Collier Books, 1961), p. 43.

31. Ibid., p. 243.

32. Ibid., p. 245.

33. Berger, *The Sacred Canopy*, p. 9.

34. Ibid., pp. 9–10.

35. Ibid., p. 28.

36. Max Weber, *The Sociology of Religion*, trans. Ephraim Fischoff (Boston: Beacon Press, 1963), p. 1.

37. Ibid., p. 13.

38. Ibid., p. 1.

39. Carl Jung, *The Undiscovered Self* (New York: New American Library, 1957), p. 29.

40. Ibid., p. 77.

41. Carl Jung, ed., *Man and His Symbols* (London: Aldus Books, 1964), p. 95.

42. Mircea Eliade, *Myth and Reality* (New York: Harper & Row, 1963), p. 8.

43. Ibid., p. 18.

44. Ibid., p. 5.

45. Theodor Gaster, *Thespis: Ritual, Myth and Drama in the Ancient Near East* (Garden City, N.Y.: Doubleday & Company, Inc., 1961), p. 24.

46. Eliade, *Myth and Reality*, pp. 39–41.

47. Ibid., p. 46.

48. Johan Huizinga, *Homo Ludens* (Boston: Beacon Press, 1950), p. 13.

49. Ibid., p. 14.

50. Victor Turner, *The Ritual Process* (Chicago: Aldine Publishing Company, 1969).

51. S. Radhakrishnan and Charles A. Moore, eds., *A Source Book in Indian Philosophy* (Princeton, N.J.: Princeton University Press, 1957), p. 68.

52. Arend Th. van Leeuwen, *Christianity in World History*, trans. H. H. Hoskins (New York: Charles Scribner's Sons, 1964), p. 383.

53. R. E. L. Masters and Jean Houston, *The Varieties of Psychedelic Experience* (New York: Dell Publishing Company, 1966), p. 267.

54. Paul Tillich, *The Courage to Be* (New Haven, Conn.: Yale University Press, 1952), p. 42.

55. Bowker, *Sense of God*, p. 82.

56. Berger, *Sacred Canopy*, pp. 43–44.

57. W. Lloyd Warner, *American Life Dream and Reality* (Chicago: The University of Chicago Press, 1962), pp. 31–32.

58. See Thomas O'Dea, *The Sociology of Religion* (Englewood Cliffs, N.J.: Prentice-Hall, Inc., 1966), chap. 1.

59. Weber, *Sociology of Religion*, p. 147.

60. Albert Camus, *The Plague*, trans. Stuart Gilbert (London: Penguin Books, 1968), pp. 200–201.

FOR FURTHER READING

BELLAH, ROBERT, "Religious Evolution," in *Beyond Belief: Essays on Religion in a Post-Traditional World*. New York: Harper & Row, 1970. A landmark synthesis of data concerning religious life and experience with respect to the study of human history and society; develops a typology of "stages" in the evolution of human religious consciousness and its relationship to changing cultural forms.

BERGER, PETER, *A Rumor of Angels*. Garden City, N.Y.: Doubleday & Company, 1970. A controversial attempt on the part of a sociologist to go beyond cultural relativism and find a basis for accrediting the reality of religious belief and experience.

———, *The Sacred Canopy*. Garden City, N.Y.: Doubleday & Company, 1969. An important and influential analysis of religion as way by which society "constructs" its own reality and provides symbols of order.

BERGER, PETER, and THOMAS LUCKMANN, *The Social Construction of Reality*. Garden City, N.Y.: Doubleday & Company, 1967.

BOWKER, JOHN, *The Sense of God*. Oxford, Eng.: Clarendon Press, 1973. A profound but difficult book that explores the "sense of God" as the genesis of religious experience; deals with the problem of cultural relativism, scientific explanation of religious behavior, and man's attitude toward death as well as other themes.

CAMUS, ALBERT, *The Plague*, trans. Stuart Gilbert. London: Penguin Books, 1968. A famous novel by one of France's literary geniuses which wrestles with the fact of evil and the drama of human heroism.

DURKHEIM, EMILE, *The Elementary Forms of Religious Life*. New York: Collier Books, 1961. One of the great classics in the sociology of religion; examines the manner in which religious thinking is rooted in the structures of primitive society.

ELIADE, MIRCEA, *Myth and Reality*. New York: Harper & Row, 1963. Develops from the standpoint of the history of religions the relationship between myth and ritual; introduces the concept of myth as "archetype" and ritual as dramatic action.

FREUD, SIGMUND, *The Future of an Illusion*. Garden City, N.Y.: Doubleday & Company, 1961. A classic statement on the nature of religion by the father of psychoanalysis; views religion essentially as an "illusion" fostered by humanity's primordial psychological conflicts.

FEUERBACH, LUDWIG, *The Essence of Christianity*. New York: Harper & Row, 1957. The pioneering study of religious images as "projections" by a nineteenth-century German philosopher.

GASTER, THEODOR, *Thespis: Ritual, Myth and Drama in the Ancient Near East*. Garden City, N.Y.: Doubleday and Company, 1961. An investigation of the link between ritual, myth, and dramatic form in the context of the religions and societies of the ancient Near East.

GEERTZ, CLIFFORD, "Religion as a Cultural System," in Michael Banton, ed., *Anthropological Approaches to the Study of Religion*. New York: Frederick Praeger, 1966. An anthropologist's understanding of religion in light of copious field data; explores the relationship between symbolism and the perception of the "real."

40   *Religion as a Mirror of Humanity: Self, Society, and Cosmos*

HUIZINGA, JOHAN, *Homo Ludens*. Boston: Beacon Press, 1950. The definitive study of the "play" element in human culture; traces the affinity between play, creativity, art, sports, social custom, and mythology.

JUNG, CARL, ed., *Man and His Symbols*. New York: Aldus Books, 1964. A collection of essays, including one by Jung, that distills the orientation and method of analytical psychology.

———, *The Undiscovered Self*. New York: New American Library, 1957. Jung's short work which diagnoses the "spiritual" ills of modern civilization; pleads for a renewed appreciation of the irrational in life and of religion as a bulwark against the illegitimate claims of society on the individual.

LAING, R. D. *The Politics of Experience*. New York: Ballantine Books, 1967. Lays out the elements of the famous Scottish psychiatrist's discussion of religious experience and madness; sees "insanity" not so much as a loathsome illness as an invitation to experience the divine.

LUCKMANN, THOMAS, *The Invisible Religion*. New York: The Macmillan Company, 1967. A short but difficult book that seeks to uncover the "hidden" forms of religious commitment and expression in modern secular culture.

MARX, KARL, and FRIEDRICH ENGELS, *On Religion*. New York: Schocken Books, 1964. A collection of essays, articles, and book excerpts from the writings of Marx and Engels dealing with religion; contains all of Marx's important pronouncements about religion as an "opiate" of the people and as a symptom of social oppression.

MASTERS, R. E. L., and JEAN HOUSTON, *The Varieties of Psychedelic Experience*. New York: Dell Publishing Company, 1966. A review of the author's work in experimental psychology on the use of hallucinogenic drugs in generating "mystical" experiences.

TILLICH, PAUL, *Theology of Culture*. Oxford, Eng.: Oxford University Press, 1959. A famous theologian's commentary on the intimate bond between religion and culture; sees religion as the "form" of culture.

TURNER, VICTOR, *The Ritual Process*. Chicago: Aldine Publishing Company, 1969. A study by an anthropologist of African ritual in the context of social experience; introduces the concept of ritual as leading man through the state of "liminality."

TH. VAN LEEUWEN, AREND, *Christianity in World History*, trans. H. H. Hoskins. New York: Charles Scribner's Sons, 1964. A lengthy but rich treatment by a Dutch cultural anthropologist of the origins of the modern technological spirit in past civilizations.

WEBER, MAX, *The Sociology of Religion*, trans. Ephraim Fischoff. Boston: Beacon Press, 1963. The heart of the great sociologist's writings on the study of religion; discusses such "types" of religious personality and behavior as the prophet, the priest, and the mystic; introduces the notions of "charismatic" and "exemplary" religious leadership.

The Hebraic Image

2

Many contemporary Westerners probably no longer appreciate how deeply their everyday world-view and moral values are rooted in the religious universe of the ancient Hebrews. Hebraic civilization has provided us with that document which is far and away the most familiar and frequently quoted piece of literature today—the Bible. However, the long-standing influence of a distant people and their culture does not necessarily ensure that the human image which they enshrined in their thinking and writing has been construed uniformly over the centuries. Precisely because it has served as a source of personal inspiration and devotion for people of many cultures in the West for close to two thousand years, the message of the Bible has suffered repeated distortions and misinterpretations, all too often to promote the narrow interests of certain individuals or groups. Despite the major changes that have taken place with the passage of years, it is possible to discover the essential view of man in the universe to which the biblical tradition, rooted in Hebraic soil, long ago gave birth. Even in the twentieth century, when ancestral creeds and once powerful religious institutions have lost their authority for a large number of people, the visible reminders of the biblical world-view have not completely vanished. Even those critics, prophets, and social reformers of the modern age who have disparaged Judaism and Christianity, the two major religions that esteem the Bible as a whole or in part as sacred, for their historical failures still share many of the moral and cultural presuppositions of these faiths. The culture of the Hebrews, who have been called the "people of the Book," thus continues to be a rich lode of insight for persons who wish to grapple with the ambiguities of existence today.

THOSE WHO ARE CALLED

It has become something of a cliché among modern scholars that the ancient Hebrews were primarily a "hearing" people. In every cliché, nonetheless, there lingers an element of truth. The Hebrews, unlike other societies in the ancient Near East or elsewhere around the globe, tended to be preoccupied with the verbal and auditory dimensions of human experience, to elevate the ear over the eyes. In one crucial respect, this trait helps to explain why the Hebrews condemned pictorial representations of their God, Yahweh, as idolatry and, characteristically, why they passed on a magnificent literary heritage to the detriment of the plastic arts. Yet their distaste for visual symbols rested more on a fundamental religious sensibility than on simple aesthetic considerations. For the Hebrews, God is the "Other" who *speaks* to man. It is God's *Word*, manifest as *Law* or *Torah*, which determines who man is, why he has come into the world, and what he is to do with his life. God *calls* upon man to hearken to his word (*dābhār*), to carry out the divine plan that he has announced in the call, and to enter into an enduring relationship with him sustained through the mutual activity of addressing and being addressed, a relationship that the famous Jewish theologian Martin Buber has termed "the life of dialogue."[1]

The image of man as having a divine vocation (literally, a "calling") is laid down in the first book of the Bible, which bears the Greek title of Genesis. Abraham, the first biblical patriarch as well as the legendary father of later generations of Hebrews, is called by God at his home in Ur of the Chaldees to take his family and embark on a venture that traditionally marks the beginning of Hebraic history.

> Now [Yahweh] said to Abram, "Go from your country and your kindred and your father's house to the land that I will show you. And I will make of you a great nation, and I will bless you, and make your name great, so that you will be a blessing. I will bless those who bless you, and him who curses you I will curse; and by you all the families of the earth shall bless themselves." (Gen. 12:1–3)

Yahweh's call to Abraham includes not only a command but a *promise*. God promises Abraham that he will found a great nation and through it will bless all other nations. The divine word holds forth the promise of salvation on the strict condition that man also keep his part of the bargain. In ancient Hebrew thought this agreement between man and God was termed a *covenant*. The covenant was a guarantee, confirmed by God in a face-to-face encounter with his human subjects. The covenant stipulated that, should his people remain intimately loyal to him and attend to him for guidance, he will preserve and protect them throughout their days. As Yahweh declared to Abraham:

> And I will establish my covenant between me and you and your descen-

dants after you throughout their generations for an everlasting covenant, to be God to you and to your descendants after you. And I will give to you, and to your descendants after you, the land of your sojournings, all the land of Canaan, for an everlasting possession; and I will be their God. (Gen. 17:7–8)

The Bible describes the covenantal relationship between God and man as one of faith. Faith, the English equivalent of the Hebrew word *emūnāh* meaning not so much "belief" as "trust" or "steadfastness," involves an attitude of devotion, openness, and responsiveness on the part of man to the supreme power who has bestowed on him existence and who oversees his every move. In short, all the qualities of the divine/human relationship are conceived in *personal* terms. Only a personal God can converse with man and demand his confidence. Only a God who speaks can be approached in the guise of a constant friend and patron. The God who calls upon man to carry out his will is, from the ancient Hebrew perspective, the only object deserving of worship, rather than the heathen idols of wood and stone for which the requirements of service and sacrifice are at best ambiguous and which cannot be tested, for only through personal dialogue can the perils and puzzles of human destiny be clarified in light of new experiences.

Moreover, the ancient Hebrew did not limit the relationship of call and response, of promise and obligation, of covenant and faith merely to a few illustrative holy men. Man's engagement with God's Word is initiated at the beginning of time with the creation of the world. The first chapter of the book of Genesis points up this theme.

In the beginning God created the heavens and the earth. The earth was without form and void, and darkness was upon the face of the deep; and the Spirit of God was moving over the face of the waters.

And God said, "Let there be light"; and there was light. And God saw that the light was good; and God separated the light from the darkness. (Gen. 1:1–4)

In other creation myths of the ancient world, particularly the Babylonian story of which the Hebrew version contains traces, the gods are *not* the primary agents of creation, inasmuch as they emerge, as embodiments of the numerous powers of nature, out of the primeval chaos that stretches far beyond the frontiers of human memory. The gods themselves are subordinate to a vaster, impersonal system of order (which, for example, in ancient Greece was called *moira* or "fate") that governs the careers of mortals and immortals alike. Thus man, the handiwork or in some cases the afterthought of the gods, enjoys no special relationship with the ultimate cause of his existence. He survives in an uncertain and precarious balance with the unseen forces of life, which must be periodically appeased in an attitude of subservience and anxiety, lest he upset the accord and be destroyed. The sacrificial rituals of priests and kings constituted fumbling attempts to keep their people from violating the complex rules of conduct decreed by the heavenly regents. In the language of the ancient Sumerians, the predecessors of the Babylonians, the word for "human being" is equivalent to the word "slave," suggesting the fearful distance between the despotic rulers of the universe and their subjects. For the Hebrews, however, it is God and God alone who is prior to the appearance of the world, and it is God who overcomes the chaos (the "form and void") in a mighty creative *fiat* ("let there be ... "). God fashions cosmic order by dint of the spoken word. The separation of light from darkness, which in most religions represents the triumph of order over disorder, the process of redemption from evil and threatening influences, is accomplished through the creative act of *saying* what shall be for evermore. Furthermore, in the Hebrew mind the chief end of creation is itself the promise of a long, prosperous, and rewarding life for man. The Genesis narrative tells how God took six days to complete his creation, and how on the sixth day he created the human species as the finishing touch of his labors.

> Then God said, "Let us make man in our image, after our likeness; and let them have dominion over the fish of the sea, and over the birds of the air, and over the cattle, and over all the earth, and over every creeping thing that creeps upon the earth." So God created man in his own image, in the image of God he created him; male and female he created them. And God blessed them, and God said to them, "Be fruitful and multiply, and fill the earth and subdue it; and have dominion over the fish of the sea and over the birds of the air and over every living thing that moves upon the earth." (Gen. 1:26–28)

God forms humanity "in his image" at the beginning of creation. In essence, this feature of the myth illustrates the nub of the Hebrew's understanding of man's involvement with God. Man comes into existence so that he may be a *co-creator* with his divine author. Man is bidden to look upon himself as bearing the image of the Creator, as having "dominion" over the world in much the same way as God had from the beginning. Thus he must, in effect, give over his life to doing the work of God on earth. By realizing through his actions God's creative Word, man establishes a durable bond of trust and companionship with the sovereign of the universe. This bond is cemented by the verbal promise of continued well-being, as well as by man's faithful response to the divine call.

Yet the call does not go out to solitary individuals in themselves. The image of the call in the Hebraic tradition is bound up with the notion of *peoplehood*, a community made accountable to God as a body. The personal relationship between God and man, therefore, is defined in terms of a covenant with a people. Modern thought, in contrast, tends to interpret the meaning of the term "person" in the sense of "individual." But the ancient Hebrews knew nothing of singular individuals per se as a social category. A person's identity is totally integrated with the community into which he is born and to whose laws he is obligated. Therefore, God's chosen ones consist of, as H. Wheeler Robinson has shown, a "corporate personality" with a unified mind, will, conscience, and moral responsibility.[2] The community of God's people is like an organism with multiple parts and functions that must be injured or destroyed if even one part of the body does not execute its purpose.

Later, especially when the political and social order was disrupted by foreign invasions toward the middle of the first millennium B.C. the sense of corporate personality began to wane, and the notion of individual personalities with discrete duties and destinies filtered into Hebraic thinking. The image of an immortal soul that is judged and accorded its moral deserts does not appear in early Hebrew literature. Rather, personal immortality is neither conceived nor regarded as a problem, since the continuity of the Hebrew people through time, irrespective of the loss of single members, is the chief issue. Thus the covenant signifies God's compact with a community, and the weal or woe of that community depends on its steadfast adherence to that covenant. The Hebrew writers deduced from historical experience, though, that God's people, as an exemplar of "man himself," exhibit a dogged tendency to violate the covenant with God, to respond improperly to the divine vocation. It is this tendency to rupture the ordained partnership between Creator and creature that gives rise to the conception of what in English is called "sin" and in Hebrew *ḥēṭ'*. A person becomes a sinner when he disobeys or rebels against God and His Law.

MAN AS DISOBEDIENT SINNER

For good or for ill, the Hebrew experience has bequeathed to us the basic notion of man as the creature who repeatedly breaks his covenant with God and asserts his own will separately from that of his Maker. Nowadays the word "sin" has fallen into disrepute, possibly because of the narrowly moralistic overtones such a concept has acquired. However, in the biblical sense, "sin" does not connote so much the infringement of specific moral precepts as a breach of the compact between God and humanity. There are two principal kinds of infidelity or sin: a sin against God and a sin against one's fellow human beings. Nevertheless, the latter is integrally associated with the former type, since to cause harm to or break trust with another person is tantamount to dissolving the fundamental relationship of trust God demands with Himself and with all living things, and which is especially befitting of man made in the divine image.

The higher purpose that God has set before man and of which man unhappily, yet frequently, falls short is inscribed in the Law or *Torah*. It is man's willful rejection of the *Torah* that causes sin. *Torah*, nonetheless, is something much more meaningful and profound than an arbitrary list of "do's and don't's"; it is not merely a cold, abstract system of moral prescriptions and prohibitions which man must follow grudgingly and without question. As James Muilenburg puts it,

> Juristic categories do not exhaust the meaning of the bond. We must
> often think, rather, of the relationship within the family with its obliga-

tions and bonds of compassion, understanding, and love. The God of Israel does not simply meet his people with an unequivocal *do ut des*. On the contrary, the commands are frequently expanded by subordinate clauses of various forms supplying the motivations for the conduct that is required.[3]

Torah is not merely "law," but the very "law of life." That is, it comprises a body of general guidelines for humane conduct and for existing in harmony with nature and with human society. The so-called Ten Commandments that Moses gave to the people of Israel from Mount Sinai constitute the heart of *Torah*. But *Torah* is greater than mere injunctions graven in stone. Ultimately, *Torah* must become internalized in the mind of man; it must become a natural incentive to do what is right and appropriate in all situations.

> The law of his God is in his heart;
> his steps do not slip.
>
> (Ps. 37:31)

To live the life of *Torah* is to satisfy the conditions of faith, to sustain the ongoing ethical and spiritual covenant with Yahweh. Nevertheless, man is granted the choice of accepting or rejecting the Law, of pursuing or turning aside from discipline of what the Hebrews termed "righteousness" (*zedākāh*). Moses announces to the people of Israel just before his death as recorded in Deuteronomy:

> See, I have set before you this day life and good, death and evil. If you obey the commandments of the Lord your God which I command you this day, by loving [Yahweh] your God, by walking in his ways, and by keeping his commandments and his statutes and his ordinances, then you shall live and multiply, and [Yahweh] your God will bless you in the land which you are entering to take possession of it. (Deut. 30:15–16)

A faithful response to God's Word, manifest in *Torah*, brings assurance of "life"; it confirms God's promise of a meaningful place and continuity within the scheme of creation.

> I call heaven and earth to witness against you this day, that I have set before you life and death, blessing and curse; therefore choose life, that you and your descendants may live, loving the Lord your God, obeying his voice, and cleaving to him for that means life to you and length of days. (Deut. 30:19–20a)

On the other hand, refusal of the righteousness of *Torah* eventuates in "death," in an estrangement from the true source of human vitality. "Sin" and "death" (which connotes not so much the cessation of biological functions as a psychic or spiritual death that makes physical existence seem empty and purposeless) are virtually synonymous in Hebrew thinking.[4] It is in this connection that we can more easily grasp the key meaning of one of the central myths of the Bible— the saga of Adam and Eve in the Garden of Eden, their temptation, and fall.

The English name Adam is a transliteration of the Hebrew word '*ādām* which is the generic term for "mankind." To the anonymous author of this portion of Genesis, therefore, the tale of the first man and first woman becomes a prototype for all human behavior. It is characteristic of myth to represent in the form of a personal life story certain universal truths about the human condition. The Genesis narrative is no exception. The human image drawn in this account contains the idea of the human creature as God's trustworthy steward of a peaceful and harmonious world, symbolized by the Garden of Eden.

> [Yahweh] God took the man and put him in the garden of Eden to till it and keep it. And [Yahweh] God commanded the man, saying, "You may freely eat of every tree in the garden; but of the tree of the knowledge of good and evil you shall not eat, for in the day that you eat of it you shall die. (Gen. 2:15-17)

Although this passage has prompted various theological and textual interpretations throughout history, the drift of it seems to parallel the emphasis on covenant, faith, and law which we have already discussed. With the creation of man, an unwritten compact is established guaranteeing "life" for man, if he cooperates with the will of God. Should the compact be forsaken, "death" will ensue. The "tree of knowledge of good and evil" signifies the temptation to live apart from a personal relationship to one's Creator, which the Bible unmasks as a delusion. The serpent, representing defiance of God's Word, beguiles the woman into asserting the spontaneous drive for personal power over and above the reciprocal attitude of love and trust between deity and humanity intended from the beginning.

> Now the serpent was more subtle than any other wild creature that [Yahweh] God had made. He said to the woman, "Did God say, 'You shall not eat of any tree of the garden'?" And the woman said to the serpent, "We may eat of the fruit of the trees of the garden; but God said, 'You shall not eat of the fruit of the tree which is in the midst of the garden, neither shall you touch it, lest you die.'" But the serpent said to the woman, "You will not die. For God knows that when you eat of it your eyes will be opened, and you will be like God, knowing good and evil." (Gen. 3:1-5)

The cutting edge of the temptation to sin is expressed in the "promise" of the serpent that "you will be like God, knowing good and evil." For humanity's usurpation of God's position, similar to the Greek idea of *hubris* or trying to mount to the gods' stature, dissolves the bond of fidelity. The serpent's promise, however, turns out to be a false one, his "word" a mischievous lie; since when both the man and the woman have partaken of the forbidden fruit, their eyes are opened, not to their own divinity, but to the realization of their frailty, helplessness, and guilt. "They knew that they were naked," the Genesis writer tells us, implying that the man and woman became aware of their alienation from a world with which they were formerly at one. God's subsequent judgment and punishment of the first human pair (which involves banishment from the garden and the condemnation of their posterity to work hard for a living and to suffer the pains of hunger, injury, and childbirth [Genesis 3:8-24]) points not only to man's disenchantment with nature, but also to the continuing misery and anxiety that man experiences once cut adrift from his Creator.

Disobedience therefore becomes an image of the common situation in which man finds himself. Sin, according to the Hebrews, is the disposition to break trust with God, to ignore his Word, and to attempt to affirm his existence in isolation from the law of life.

On the other hand, God does not abandon his creatures altogether to the devastations of sin. The Hebrews laid heavy stress on the mercy of God with the metaphor of his "outstretched hand," always extended to be grasped by man when he has repented of his evil ways. For even though man proves unfaithful, God persists in holding forth the promise of new life and fellowship with him.

> [Yahweh] passed before him, and proclaimed, "[Yahweh, Yahweh,] a God merciful and gracious, slow to anger, and abounding in steadfast love and faithfulness, keeping steadfast love for thousands, forgiving iniquity and transgression and sin." (Exod. 34:6-7a)

In effect, the Hebrews clung to the notion that humanity, despite its lack of faithfulness and its repeated rebelliousness, might yet, upon God's own initiative return to fellowship in the covenant. Humanity is regarded, therefore, as divided against itself, torn between its own selfish desires and the call of allegiance to the divine purpose. Humanity can never "be as God"; it can never achieve by its own efforts the unqualified perfection of a holy life. Yet humanity is still able to share in that life through a personal relationship with the transcendent source of all reality. Repentance for disobedience to *Torah* opens the channel of God's mercy and restores man to fulfillment, meaning, and happiness. Though incomplete and iniquitous in his own right, he can yet have his failings alleviated by surrendering himself in the power of God. The most solemn ritual for Hebraic tradition wherein this surrender takes place is called *Yom Kippur* or Day of Atonement. In fasting and prayer the Hebrew devotee enumerates and repents all his sins, not merely his own private missteps but the transgressions of the entire community with which he is intimately identified and for which he is unreservedly responsible. It is such a tension in man's experience of both himself and the overshadowing presence of a divine person who is wholly "Other" that colors the Hebrew perception of the direction in which human affairs are headed. The portrayal of human beings as embroiled in an incessant struggle for a life of integrity, which mysteriously eludes them, yet is made possible through God's activity, points to a third dominant image within the Hebrew universe of symbols—the image of the chosen people caught up in history and bearing within themselves the meaning of past and future.

THE CHOSEN

Jews today typically refer to themselves, and in turn are often so designated by Gentiles, as the "chosen people." The theme of having been chosen or "elected" has its origins far back in the blur of the Hebrews' early historical memory. The symbols of faith and covenant, together with the image of the call and sin, coalesce around the pivotal conception that a certain group or a few select individuals have been singled out from the shapeless mass of humanity to actualize God's plan of salvation. In this respect it may be advisable to define more clearly the Hebrew image. The Hebrew did not entertain an abstract idea of a dialogue between God and man. Just as God possesses a personal name, Yahweh, which indicates a special relationship to those who speak to and are spoken to by him, so the human beings whom he protects and who in turn are summoned to confide in him have a peculiar identity that makes them luminous examples to the rest of mankind. The privileged relationship between God and his chosen ones is compared throughout the Bible to the intimate and loving tie between a father and his children.

The poignancy of God's love for his children, even when they have deserted him, is evoked in the "lamentation" of Yahweh spoken through the mouth of the prophet Hosea.

> When Israel was a child, I loved him,
>   and out of Egypt I called my son.
> The more I called them,
>   the more they went from me;
> they kept sacrificing to the Ba'als,
>   and burning incense to idols.
>
> Yet it was I who taught E'phraim to walk,
>   I took them up in my arms;
>   but they did not know that I healed them.
> I led them with cords of compassion,
>   with the bands of love,
> and I became to them as one
>   who eases the yoke on their jaws,
>   and I bent down to them and fed them.
>
> (Hos. 11:1–4)

In the biblical literature the image of the chosen is first intimated in the story of God's appointment of Abraham, as we have seen, to be the father of a future great nation and in the account of the making of the covenant. It also becomes evident in the rather odd episode involving Abraham's grandson Jacob. Jacob was sleeping alone one night in the wilderness, according to the narrative.

and a man wrestled with him until the breaking of the day. When the man saw that he did not prevail against Jacob, he touched the hollow of his thigh; and Jacob's thigh was put out of joint as he wrestled with him. Then he said, "Let me go, for the day is breaking." But Jacob said, "I will not let you go, unless you bless me." And he said to him, "What is your name?" And he said, "Jacob." Then he said, "Your name shall no more be called Jacob, but *Israel*, for you have striven with God and with men, and have prevailed." (Gen. 32:24b–28)

The name "Israel" for God's chosen people, of whom Jacob is a legendary ancestor, highlights the special nature of their role as executors of an historical design. Though the popular etymology of "Israel" given in the text ("He who strives with God") is probably forced and inaccurate, like so many explanations of the meanings of terms by the biblical authors, it underscores the way in which the ancient Hebrews interpreted the meaning of their own experiences in light of subsequent history. The paradigm of a wrestling match between the divine (in this case personified in the mysterious stranger, who may be either an angel or Yahweh himself) and human serves as a traditional mode of understanding the struggle that constitutes Israel's historical experience. Throughout their trials and tragedies brought about often enough by their resistance to God's intentions or by their failure to bear witness before men to a righteous life, the chosen ones, perhaps unwittingly, serve to compass and illustrate the divine will. To be chosen carries with it the awesome responsibility for man to choose, in return, the way God has chartered for him.

The paramount event that secures the setting in which the burden of the Hebrew people's choice of God is laid upon them is, of course, the Exodus or the liberation from Egypt. The Exodus story comprises the principal reference point for the ancient Hebrew's self-understanding of his own part in the play of historical forces. There is an unresolved and intricate controversy concerning what actually transpired in ancient Egypt over a thousand years before Christ, and neither historians nor archaeologists have been able to ascertain positively to what extent the account provided in the book of Exodus sufficiently describes, if at all, the real conflict between the people of Israel and the Egyptian pharaoh. Those Egyptian records that have been unearthed make no mention of this episode assigned such monumental importance in biblical eyes. However, the absence of hard, corroborative evidence for certain critical happenings recounted in the Bible is not exceptional. The problem of finding extrabiblical sources that might warrant or disprove the remarkable occurrences that the Bible reports indicates less the plain unreliability of historical chronicles than the fact that the meaning of Hebrew history was usually couched in terms of singular experiences that might hold only minimal interest for outsiders. Indeed, the Hebrews themselves were considered a foreign outgroup by the larger nations of the ancient world. The term "Hebrew" derives from the Semitic word *habiru* which means "outlaw" or "outcast." Thus their chosen status would have not necessarily been intelligible to an Egyptian or Babylonian who valued participation in dominant and orderly civilization.

The Exodus image shows how ultimate religious meaning can be attached to events that seem from the conventional vantage point to disrupt the integrity and continuity of civilization. Yahweh, whether challenging pharaoh to "let my people go" or rebuking the kings and princes of Israelite society itself, always calls on man to choose higher ethical and spiritual goals than the self-chosen interests of man, to forsake obedience to mere social ordinances if they conflict with God's will. A supreme and compelling truth is divulged to the chosen and faithful ones, and such a truth tends to remain at variance with the mere claims of self or with the need for order at any price in society. The idea, which we discern in many other religious systems (such as Hinduism) of self, society, and cosmos forming an eternal and unshakable unity is punctured in the Hebrew context. For the Law of God (*Torah*) transcends the finite laws and customs of all human societies as well as the rules of conduct that individuals write for themselves. We can contrast the view of humanity in the Egyptian mentality with that of the Hebrew. To the ancient Egyptians the pharaoh was the incarnation of the supreme god Osiris, and the law or system of justice that he enforced, called *ma'at*, appeared to peasant and noble alike as a transparent reflection of cosmic order. For any pharaoh to take seriously the fulminations of Moses, who claimed to speak in the name of a god mightier and holier than his own imperial majesty, would have been inconceivable. Thus it is possible to understand from a cultural standpoint why Pharaoh at first scoffed at Moses' demands to free the Hebrews from their bondage.

But the legend of the Exodus is precisely the story of such an emancipation. It was an event celebrated in the holiday rituals of Passover each spring. Through the Passover *seder* God's liberation of his people from bondage was remembered and recreated, then as well as today in modern Judaism. Passover symbolizes the constant concern of God for his suffering captives. But Exodus and the Passover ceremony represent liberation not only from physical captivity, but also from the traditional insistence of human society on unquestioned obedience and conformity. The chosen ones are those who sense that a greater destiny awaits them, and they are willing to defy social precedent to accomplish their aims. The irony is that what society may assume is a correct and expedient defense of the status quo with all the sanctity of orthodox religion behind it turns out, from the perspective of the chosen ones, to be apostasy. For it is not man's relationship to institutions and social mores that count in the final summation, but his righteousness "in the sight of God," the assimilation of man's moral rules to divine *Torah*.

THE PROPHETIC REBEL

Moses, the leader of an uprising of slaves against their Egyptian overlords which may be historical basis for the Exodus, generally wears in Hebrew lore the mantle of the first prophet. Moses' social origins are relatively obscure. It may well be that he was born of Hebrew parents, as the Bible tells us; but the name

Moses is Egyptian, and thus it is highly likely that he was raised in the house of pharaoh's family in keeping with the legend. At all events, Moses displays a conscious sympathy with the wretched, oppressed *habiru*, who were coerced into doing brutal manual labor by pharaoh's regime. His sympathy impels him one day to slay an Egyptian taskmaster who was beating a Hebrew worker, and in order to escape punishment for the crime Moses flees Egypt to the land of Midian (Exodus 2:11-16).

While in exile in Midian Moses has an encounter with God, which is characteristic of the prophetic experience.

Now Moses was keeping the flock of his father-in-law, Jethro, the priest of Midian; and he led his flock to the west side of the wilderness, and came to Horeb, the mountain of God. And the angel of [Yahweh] appeared to him in a flame of fire out of the midst of a bush; and he looked, and lo, the bush was burning, yet it was not consumed. And Moses said, "I will turn aside and see this great sight, why the bush is not burnt." When [Yahweh] saw that he turned aside to see, God called to him out of the bush, "Moses, Moses!" And he said, "Here I am." Then he said, "Do not come near; put off your shoes from your feet, for the place on which you are standing is holy ground." And he said, "I am the God of your father, the God of Abraham, the God of Isaac, and the God of Jacob." And Moses hid his face, for he was afraid to look at God.

Then [Yahweh] said, "I have seen the affliction of my people who are in Egypt, and have heard their cry because of their taskmasters; I know their sufferings, and I have come down to deliver them out of the hand of the Egyptians, and to bring them up out of that land to a good and broad land, a land flowing with milk and honey, to the place of the Canaanites, the Hittites, the Amorites, the Perizzites, the Hivites, and the Jebusites. And now, behold, the cry of the people of Israel has come to me, and I have seen the oppression with which the Egyptians oppress them. Come, I will send you to Pharaoh that you may bring forth my people, the sons of Israel, out of Egypt." But Moses said to God, "Who am I that I should go to Pharaoh, and bring the sons of Israel out of Egypt?" He said, "But I will be with you; and this shall be the sign for you, that I have sent you: when you have brought forth the people out of Egypt, you shall serve God upon this mountain."

Then Moses said to God, "If I come to the people of Israel and say to them, 'The God of your fathers has sent me to you,' and they ask me, 'What is his name?' what shall I say to them?" God said to Moses, "I AM WHO I AM." And he said, "Say this to the people of Israel, 'I AM has sent me to you.'" God also said to Moses, "Say this to the people of Israel, '[Yahweh], the God of your fathers, the God of Abraham, the God of Isaac, and the God of Jacob, has sent me to you': this is my name for ever, and thus I am to be remembered throughout all generations. Go and gather the elders of Israel together, and say to them, '[Yahweh], the God of your fathers, the God of Abraham, of Isaac, and of Jacob, has appeared to me, saying, "I have observed you and what has been done to you in

Egypt; and I promise that I will bring you up out of the affliction of Egypt, to the land of the Canaanites, the Hittites, the Amorites, the Perizzites, the Hivites, and the Jebusites, a land flowing with milk and honey.'" And they will hearken to your voice; and you and the elders of Israel shall go to the king of Egypt and say to him, '[Yahweh], the God of the Hebrews, has met with us; and now, we pray you, let us go a three days' journey into the wilderness, that we may sacrifice to [Yahweh] our god.' I know that the king of Egypt will not let you go unless compelled by a mighty hand. So I will stretch out my hand and smite Egypt with all the wonders which I will do in it; after that he will let you go. And I will give this people favor in the sight of the Egyptians; and when you go, you shall not go empty, but each woman shall ask of her neighbor, and of her who sojourns in her house, jewelry of silver and of gold, and clothing, and you shall put them on your sons and on your daughters; thus you shall despoil the Egyptians."

Then Moses answered, "But behold, they will not believe me or listen to my voice, for they will say, '[Yahweh] did not appear to you.'" [Yahweh] said to him, "What is that in your hand?" He said, "A rod." And he said, "Cast it on the ground." So he cast it on the ground and it became a serpent; and Moses fled from it. But [Yahweh] said to Moses, "Put out your hand, and take it by the tail"—so he put out his hand and caught it, and it became a rod in his hand—"that they may believe that [Yahweh], the God of their fathers, the God of Abraham, the God of Isaac, and the God of Jacob, has appeared to you." Again, [Yahweh] said to him, "Put your hand into your bosom." And he put his hand into his bosom; and when he took it out, behold, his hand was leprous, as white as snow. Then God said, "Put your hand back into your bosom." So he put his hand back into his bosom; and when he took it out, behold, it was restored like the rest of his flesh. "If they will not believe you," God said, "or heed the first sign, they may believe the latter sign. If they will not believe even these two signs or heed your voice, you shall take some water from the Nile and pour it upon the dry ground; and the water which you shall take from the Nile will become blood upon the dry ground."

But Moses said to [Yahweh], "Oh, [Yahweh], I am not eloquent, either heretofore or since thou hast spoken to thy servant; but I am slow of speech and of tongue." Then [Yahweh] said to him, "Who has made man's mouth? Who makes him dumb, or deaf, or seeing, or blind? Is it not I, [Yahweh]? Now therefore go, and I will be with your mouth and teach you what you shall speak." But he said, "Oh, [Yahweh], send, I pray, some other person." Then the anger of [Yahweh] was kindled against Moses and he said, "Is there not Aaron, your brother, the Levite? I know that he can speak well; and behold, he is coming out to meet you, and when he sees you he will be glad in his heart. And you shall speak to him and put the words in his mouth; and I will be with your mouth and with his mouth, and will teach you what you shall do. He shall speak for you to the people; and he shall be a mouth for you, and you shall be to him as God. And you shall take in your hand this rod, with which you shall do the signs." (Exod. 3:1–4:17)

The prophet was thus called suddenly and dramatically by God to proclaim the divine purpose. The prophet is distinguished not only by his outsider's status, but also by his humility and readiness to subordinate his will to that of his divine master. Moses' protest that he does not measure up to the task is similar, for example, to the complaint of the prophet Jeremiah that he is unfit for such a grandiose assignment.

> Then I said, "Ah, [Yahweh] God! Behold, I do not know how to speak, for I am only a youth." (Jer. 1:6)

Or to that of the prophet Isaiah:

> And I said: "Woe is me! For I am lost; for I am a man of unclean lips, and I dwell in the midst of a people of unclean lips; for my eyes have seen the King, [Yahweh] of hosts!" (Isa. 6:5)

Nonetheless, the prophet yields to the divine bidding and allows himself to become an instrument of Yahweh. In effect, the prophet acts as the "mouthpiece" of Yahweh, declaring God's Word and exhorting his contemporaries to heed it.

The prophet, though, is not merely some windy orator. He speaks God's Word in anticipation of His mighty actions in history. He pronounces not only what God has sternly demanded of those who hear his Word, but asserts also what is about to take place, if and when his audience does not take the message to heart. Moses' confrontation with Pharaoh gives us a typical illustration of the prophetic stance.

> Then [Yahweh] said to Moses, "Go in to Pharaoh and say to him, 'Thus says [Yahweh], "Let my people go, that they may serve me."'" (Exod. 8:1)

When Pharaoh balks, Yahweh informs Moses that he will visit numerous plagues upon the land of Egypt, and it is through Moses' mediation that the scourges come and are finally lifted (Exodus 7-12). However, Moses is not himself the author of these wondrous feats. The actions he takes and words he utters are only the earthly tokens of Yahweh's deeds, and Yahweh's Word is the driving force behind all events. The ancient Hebrews sensed, perhaps more than any other culture, that words have power, both in speaking and hearing. "Word" (*dābhār*) means much the same in Hebrew as "event." Words have the capacity for causing change, especially in the lives of those who listen to them and find their situation transformed thereby. The Hebraic prophet who, according to the origin of the Greek term *prophetes*, is one who "speaks for" or "on behalf of" and thus turns out to be substantially different from a simple soothsayer or forecaster of the future. The prophet through his declarations and denunciations releases into the stream of human history the powerful Word of Yahweh. He utters the divine judgment of what has gone wrong in the affairs of human beings along with the affirmation of what Yahweh is planning to do or will require in order to make amends.

From the social point of view the prophet may appear a bothersome malcontent or an unsavory social deviant. For instance, King Ahab denounced the prophet Elijah of the ninth century B.C. as a "troubler of Israel" (1 Kings 18:17), just as governing officials have perennially sought to quiet those who speak out defiantly against what they perceive as a corrupt and inequitable social system. The prophets, who exhibit a passion for social justice as fierce as their desire for religious and moral purity, have been called "God's revolutionaries." The prophetic rebel, however, does not exalt his own individual prerogatives against the prevailing norms and principles of social order. He is not a rebel by instinct so much as by calling. He speaks not on behalf of his own idiosyncratic vision of what life should be like, but with respect to the ideal of human existence enshrined in the tradition of his Hebrew ancestors who have "walked with Yahweh." In this regard he himself calls his wayward contemporaries to the life of righteousness and fidelity to the covenant that Yahweh has given to them as the gift of life. And in that process he reinterprets and applies that divine law to specific events.

The prophetic outburst becomes especially conspicuous in Israel during the years of political decline after the death of King David, whose reign, spanning the eleventh and tenth centuries B.C., is remembered for the most part by Jews as the "golden age" of the Hebrew people's political fortunes. Unlike Moses, who faced an alien adversary, the prophets of Israel were increasingly entrusted with the job of attacking the enemies of Yahweh who worked from the inside, who in fact had committed sins and sacrileges (in the prophets' eyes) under the pretext of conserving traditional Hebrew piety.

The bone of contention between the prophets and the guardians of the cultural status quo had to do mainly with the use and abuse of social privilege and political power. For such prophets as Isaiah, Jeremiah, Amos, Hosea, Micah, and Habbakuk, the source of strength for the people of Israel lay without reservation in the keeping of God's covenant and in living by the *Torah*. But more and more the central issue for Israel's rulers, and for the dominant social classes, which includes the temple priesthood, concerned the maintenance of national security in the face of formidable military threats by such imperial foes as Assyria and Babylonia, even if it meant compromising certain ethical and religious precepts. The rise of a defensive military state supported by a new semi-feudal aristocracy led, for example, to the intrusion of alien religious practices, such as the worship of the nature god Baal, which was done as a matter of diplomatic protocol whenever Israel made alliances with her neighbors. The worship of Baal under various forms and guises also entailed the introduction of numerous rites and sacred objects (such as small metal images of a bull) characteristic of agricultural religions into what had once been a primarily nomadic culture. Agricultural societies tend to be hierarchical and dominated by religious experts or priests who rule in cooperation with the military castes. Not surprisingly, the appearance of this pattern in Israelite society was attended by class divisions between rich and poor, powerful and powerless. The prophets usually championed the antimilitary and antiaristocratic elements in society by authority of Yahweh who defends the lowly against the violence and depredations of the mighty.

> Thus says [Yahweh]:
> "For three transgressions of Israel,
>   and for four, I will not revoke the punishment;
> because they sell the righteous for silver,
>   and the needy for a pair of shoes—
> they that trample the head of the poor
>   into the dust of the earth,
> and turn aside the way of the afflicted."
>
> (Amos 2:6–7a)

In pursuit of power, wealth, and security at the expense of social justice, the nation of Israel had broken their covenant with Yahweh.

> Ah, sinful nation,
>   a people laden with iniquity,
> offspring of evildoers,
>   sons who deal corruptly!
> They have forsaken [Yahweh],
>   they have despised the Holy One of Israel,
>   they are utterly estranged.
>
> (Isa. 1:4)

Thus the prophets looked to the downfall of the Israelite state at the hands of its more powerful enemies as Yahweh's righteous judgment upon the wicked and unfaithful. Only if the people repented their former sins and gave themselves over to Yahweh's will, rather than seeking to rely upon their own devices, could the terrible fate awaiting them be averted. When Israel finally succumbed to conquest, the northern part in 722 B.C. and the southern in 597 B.C., the prophetic message seemed to have been borne out. The prophets assailed the popular ideology that being chosen by God involved no ethical or social responsibility. Rather, the righteous "remnant," as the prophets called those who remained true to the covenant in surviving historical calamity, would learn that a relationship with Yahweh does not automatically mean a life of ease and prosperity, but frequently suffering and hardship in quest of a higher moral and historical purpose. The meaning of existence does not reside in some fugitive security of the present moment, but in the constancy of God's plan for humanity manifesting itself throughout the vicissitudes of time and change. The image that emerges, therefore, in the writings of the prophets is one of man in relentless conflict both with God and with other men. Such conflict, however, discloses the genuine meaning of human destiny.

THE SUFFERING SERVANT OF HISTORY

The writers of the Book of Deuteronomy, who lived during the seventh century B.C., propounded a very simple theory of historical explanation which left a definite stamp on the self-understanding of the Jews. For the Deuteronomic authors the social and political turmoil that afflicted Israel after the death of David was justly deserved for having transgressed the covenant. These authors viewed the king of Israel as a trustee of the covenant, as the intermediary between God and his people, and they extolled the reign of David as the model of what righteous regal behavior should be. Thus if a king should carry out social and political policies in accord with *Torah*, Yahweh would deal favorably with his people; but if he and his people should go astray, Yahweh would bring distress, usually in the form of military setbacks or foreign invasion. The "Deuteronomic history," as it is called, is woven into the Books of Samuel and Kings. A brief comment on each king's moral stature is inserted at the beginning of the account of his term in office, indicating whether he "did what was evil" or "did what was right" in "the sight of Yahweh."

In essence, the Deuteronomic writers regarded Israel's apostasy from the old ways of worshipping and obeying Yahweh and the creeping inequities in society as signs of shameless ingratitude for God's having saved them from the Egyptians long ago. The covenant, they reckoned, was not a solemn burden placed upon Israel's forebears, but an indissolvable union based on God's love for his chosen people, as shown in his act of mercy in the Exodus and in the people's pledge of faithfulness to God in appreciation for this expression of compassion.

> You shall therefore love [Yahweh] your God, and keep his charge, his statutes, his ordinances, and his commandments always. And consider this day . . . consider the discipline of [Yahweh] your God, his greatness, his mighty hand and his outstretched arm, his signs and his deeds which he did in Egypt to Pharaoh the king of Egypt and to all his land; and what he did to the army of Egypt, to their horses and to their chariots; how he made the water of the Red Sea overflow them as they pursued after you, and how [Yahweh] has destroyed them to this day; and what he did to you in the wilderness, until you came to this place. (Deut. 11:1–5)

If the people repented and returned to obedience to the covenant by observing the Mosaic *Torah*, then Yahweh would continue to watch over them.

> For if you will be careful to do all this commandment which I command you to do, loving [Yahweh] your God, walking in all his ways, and cleaving to him, then [Yahweh] will drive out all these nations before you, and

you will dispossess nations greater and mightier than yourselves. (Deut. 11:22–23)

To a certain extent the prophets of Israel also adopted this formula in their tirades against religious innovation and the deterioration of society. On the other hand, the later prophets, particularly in the seventh century and after, gradually came to be convinced that Israel would never rehabilitate itself and return to the covenant. Thus, they believed, Yahweh was preparing to wipe the slate clean and start all over again. Such was, in particular, the stance of the prophet Jeremiah. Israel had ignored Yahweh's exhortations and admonitions for so long that he would have to wreak horrible destruction in order to bring the people to their senses.

> I spoke to you in your prosperity,
> but you said, "I will not listen."
> This has been your way from your youth,
> that you have not obeyed my voice.
> The wind shall shepherd all your shepherds
> and your lovers shall go into captivity;
> then you will be ashamed and confounded
> because of all your wickedness.
>
> (Jer. 22:21–22)

Jeremiah prophesied when the newly resurgent Babylonian empire under King Nebuchadnezzar assaulted and finally conquered the city of Jerusalem. Jeremiah was persuaded that Yahweh meant for Jerusalem to fall as a final act of judgment upon Israel's long-standing betrayal, and when the city was sacked and burned, its temple razed, and the inhabitants deported and sent into slavery in Babylon in the year 587 B.C., his prophecy seemed to have been fulfilled.

Despite Jeremiah's counsels, the destruction of Jerusalem and the subsequent period of captivity, known as the Babylonian Exile, severely shook the faith of the average Israelite in the justice of God, and such an event ranks only with the Holocaust of World War II, in which six million Jews were exterminated by the Nazis, as the darkest hours in the history of the posterity of Abraham. It was during this period and afterwards that the theology of the Deuteronomists came under suspicion and new images and the sects that gave birth to them were developed. It was evident to many Hebrew thinkers that actual historical experience made the notion of an earthly covenant in which Israel would be blessed with prosperity inadequate. The meaning of Israel's religious life had to be articulated more in terms of its ongoing history than with exclusive emphasis on an event that had taken place long ago. It was on this note that a modified human image that lies at the center of the world-view of both later Judaism and Christianity arose on the scene.

Before examining what is implied in this modified image more closely, however, we should say something about the Hebrew conception of history as a whole. Certainly we do not exaggerate in stating that the Hebrews among all the peoples of the ancient world "discovered" history. That is not to say other peoples did not have their own perspective on past, present, and future. But it was the Hebrews who imputed an overarching significance to historical change. The Hebrews discerned that man is preeminently an historical being. It is in the rise and fall of nations, in the clash of armies, and in the swing of the historical pendulum from good to bad fortune for society that the reality of life is revealed. Whereas other ancient cultures recognized the fact of social change, they tended to devalue its importance and to construe it as part of the cosmic rhythm of things. The ancient Greeks, for example, depicted the life of society as a cyclical process of growth and decay, like all organic species, with little sense that any lesson could be learned from change; the authentic meaning of existence was to be found in a glimpse of a truth that went beyond the mutable and perishable forms of this world. The same applies to the peoples of ancient India and the Far East (as we shall see in Chapters 4 and 5) who looked at time and history as an interminable flow of life without any discernible beginning or end. Thus time and history proved to be of scarcely any interest to them.

The Hebrews, however, were constrained by their own theological, social, and geographical circumstances to take history seriously. Their homeland of Palestine lay at the crossroads of the great civilizations of the ancient Near East, and therefore every war or drive for imperial grandeur had repercussions on their everyday affairs. Whenever the armies of the east would push west toward the rich prize of Egypt, or the Egyptians launch probes toward their enemies in the east, the nation of Israel invariably stood in their path. Second, the ancient Hebrew state had coalesced out of a loose federation of wandering nomadic tribes who had never developed the sedentary attitudes and orientation of the cultures of the larger civilizations. Historical change was the rule, rather than the exception, in their experience. Finally, it was an historical event, the Exodus, that constituted the reference point for making sense out of all successive occurrences. Man, for the Hebrews, is the being who, by virtue of his restless quest for something that he does not now possess in light of his failure to live the life intended for him, *cannot escape history*. It is man's condition to be uprooted from the primeval paradise of Eden and cast into history, spelling both liberation and frustration, happiness and suffering. Yet it is only through history that humanity can find its way back to the state of equilibrium that he has lost.

The Hebrew idea of history, of course, was always a concrete one. As Gerhard von Rad has observed:

> It . . . seems evident that Israel was not capable of thinking of time in the abstract, time divorced from specific events. She found the idea of a time without a particular event quite inconceivable; all that she knew was time as containing events.[5]

History is meaningful because specific events are fraught with meaning. The Exodus, the sealing of the covenant, the establishment of the kingdom of David, the fall of Jerusalem are all epochal happenings which disclose Yahweh's intervention in the routines of humanity. History emerges as the significant record of what befalls the chosen ones, and history has an inner meaning that can be read in terms of God's purpose for his people. The woes that beset Israel, therefore, are elucidated according to deeds which the people themseves have done and the manner in which Yahweh has reacted to them. Unlike many other religious traditions, such as the Hindu and Buddhist, the Hebrew way did not treat suffering as an illusion to be dispersed by right knowledge of the universe, but as the critical context in which man learns to descry the significance of his past actions and God's plan for his life becomes apparent.

After the collapse of the Deuteronomic interpretation of Israel's legacy, therefore, the theme of redemptive suffering gains prominence. A principal architect of this new vision is the anonymous prophet who dwelt with the exiles in Babylon and who, because his writings are combined with those of the historical Isaiah of Jerusalem, has come to be known as the "second Isaiah." In the text attributed to him we have the indelible image of the "suffering servant," meant to be Israel. The "suffering servant" image appears in the fifty-third chapter of Isaiah.

> Who has believed what we have heard?
>   And to whom has the arm of [Yahweh] been revealed?
> For he grew up before him like a young plant,
>   and like a root out of dry ground;
> he had no form or comeliness that we should look at him,
>   and no beauty that we should desire him.
> He was despised and rejected by men;
>   a man of sorrows, and acquainted with grief;
> and as one from whom men hide their faces
>   he was despised, and we esteemed him not.
>
> Surely he has borne our griefs
>   and carried our sorrows;
> yet we esteemed him stricken,
>   smitten by God, and afflicted.
> But he was wounded for our transgressions,
>   he was bruised for our iniquities;
> upon him was the chastisement that made us whole,
>   and with his stripes we are healed.
> All we like sheep have gone astray;
>   we have turned every one to his own way;
> and [Yahweh] has laid on him the iniquity of us all.
>
> He was oppressed, and he was afflicted,
>   yet he opened not his mouth;
> like a lamb that is led to the slaughter,
>   and like a sheep that before its shearers is dumb,
>   so he opened not his mouth.
> By oppression and judgment he was taken away;
>   and as for his generation, who considered

that he was cut off out of the land of the living,
  stricken for the transgression of my people?
And they made his grave with the wicked
  and with a rich man in his death,
although he had done no violence,
  and there was no deceit in his mouth.

Yet it was the will of [Yahweh] to bruise him;
  he has put him to grief;
when he makes himself an offering for sin,
  he shall see his offspring, he shall prolong his days;
the will of [Yahweh] shall prosper in his hand;
  he shall see the fruit of the travail of his soul and be
    satisfied;
by his knowledge shall the righteous one, my servant,
  make many to be accounted righteous;
  and he shall bear their iniquities.
Therefore I will divide him a portion with the great,
  and he shall divide the spoil with the strong;
because he poured out his soul to death
  and was numbered with the transgressors;
yet he bore the sin of many,
  and made intercession for the transgressors.

The second Isaiah, in a break with his prophetic predecessors, abandons the call to repentance and the forebodings of Yahweh's wrath and judgment. The stress in his oracles falls almost exclusively on the wondrous redemption that Yahweh has and is working through the people's anguish. Thus Yahweh speaks to his chosen ones again with a new song:

Behold, I have refined you, but not like silver;
  I have tried you in the furnace of affliction.
For my own sake, for my own sake, I do it,
  for how should my name be profaned?
My glory I will not give to another.
(Isaiah 48:10-11)

In a word, the prophet declares that Yahweh has forgiven his people for all their former trespasses, and that he will make a new covenant with Israel, superseding the old, that has been secured by their very blood and hardship.

Remember not the former things,
  nor consider the things of old.
Behold, I am doing a new thing;
  now it springs forth, do you not perceive it?
(Isaiah 43:18-19a)

Despite the people's chronic unfaithfulness, Yahweh himself remains faithful, and he is now using the trials of his chosen ones as a proclamation of good tidings to all the world.

> And he said to me, "You are my servant,
> Israel, in whom I will be glorified."
>
> (Isa. 49:3)

> Listen to me, my people,
>   and give ear to me, my nation;
> for a law will go forth from me,
>   and my justice for a light to the peoples.
> My deliverance draws near speedily,
>   my salvation has gone forth,
> and my arms will rule the peoples.
>
> (Isa. 51:4–5a)

The historical event that prompted the second Isaiah's gracious message of salvation was the arrival of the Persian conqueror Cyrus in Babylon. Cyrus freed the Jews from their captivity and allowed them to go back to their homeland, rebuild their temple, and practice their religion once more. The implication of the second Isaiah's declamations, however, is that Israel has and will outlast all historical crises, for it is in the muddied ruts and bumps of historical time that the footprints of Yahweh's glory are seen. Yahweh is the Lord of all creation, who keeps revealing himself again and again in world-shaking incidents.

> Thus says, [Yahweh] : "Heaven is my throne
>   and the earth is my footstool;
> what is the house which you would build for me,
>   and what is the place of my rest?
> All these things my hand has made,
>   and so all these things are mine,"
>   says [Yahweh] .
>
> (Isaiah 66:1–2a)

Israel as the suffering servant becomes the normative human image for all peoples caught in the riptide of history to understand. God as the Maker of history becomes the master image which reflects humanity's unswerving hope that even within the darkest hours of pain and tribulation there glimmers a deeper meaning soon to be comprehended.

THE PROMISED LAND

The ancient Hebrews' understanding of history rested on a twofold apprehension of time: the hallowed past in which God has accomplished stunning works of salvation and the imminent future in which he will bring to fruition his design for mankind. In spite of the bleakness of the present situation, humanity need only remember what God has done before in order to become joyously aware that God will do the same again. The compass needle of history, therefore, always points toward the culminating "end time" in which all evil will be banished and all things replenished in the world. The "end time" does not mean, except in certain kinds of later Jewish speculation, ascent to an ethereal heaven that lies outside of time and space; nor does it imply a purely spiritual condition of mankind that lies hidden within the mundane order of life. The end of time, when God will make manifest his intentions once and for all, will include the total transfiguration of the world and of the human race, of society as well as individual persons.

The biblical orientation to this grand finale in God's performance is called *eschatology* or the doctrine of "last things" (Greek *eschatos* means "end" or "last"). The eschatological undercurrent of Hebraic religion has its historical beginning in the call to Abraham, as we have seen. God promises Abraham the bounteous land of Palestine for him and his descendants. The "promised land" theme keeps materializing in various forms throughout the Bible. Once the Hebrews were established in Palestine and began to suffer the distress of a ravaged and occasionally vanquished people, the content of the promise came to be identified more with the strength and steadfastness of the kingdom of God as ruled by King David. "Zion," a fortified hill in Jerusalem that David captured from the city's indigenous inhabitants, evolved as the symbol of a solid and secure political state founded on justice and safeguarded by Yahweh. As the prophetic tradition unfolded, the image of being God's chosen people worthy of possessing the promised land was removed from the present setting and projected into the future. The people of Israel, the prophets felt, had broken the covenant and therefore become disinherited from the promise. They could no longer rest secure in Zion because of their sins. "Woe to those who are at ease in Zion" (Amos 6:1a). Yet Yahweh promises a return to Zion once the people had been chastised for their misdeeds and the storms of history grow quiet.

> For [Yahweh] has a day of vengeance,
> a year of recompense for the cause of Zion.
>
> (Isa. 34:8)

In the writings of the later prophets, and those of Isaiah in particular, the restoration of Zion is associated with the enthronement of a righteous king, a scion of David.

> For to us a child is born,
> to us a son is given;
> and the government will be upon his shoulder,
> and his name will be called
> "Wonderful Counselor, Mighty God,
> Everlasting Father, Prince of Peace."
> Of the increase of his government and of peace
> there will be no end,
> upon the throne of David, and over his kingdom,
> to establish it, and to uphold it

with justice and with righteousness
from this time forth and for evermore.
The zeal of [Yahweh] of hosts will do this.

(Isa. 9:6–7)

Such a king, who attained the substance of myth in many instances, has come to be known as the *Messiah* or "savior." The promised land image, therefore, comes to imply an ideal picture of man living under prosperous and harmonious social conditions, presided over by a just and compassionate sovereign and sanctified by God himself. The messiah motif, as we shall see, figures quite famously in the shaping of the Christian image.

In later Judaism the theme of national identity, involving both land and culture, tends to assume major importance alongside the notions of chosenness and *Torah*. To be a Jew, a grandchild of the ancient Hebraic covenant, involves more than merely the worship of God or the right ethical propensities. "Judaism," which is the name we give to the society of the Hebrew people after the return from Babylon because of the preponderant influence of the traditions of the tribe of Judah in this period, has been called a culture as much as a religion. Jews have for centuries regarded their chosen standing as requiring visible marks, an all-encompassing set of routines (*halakah*), particularly in manners of dress, observance of certain holidays like Yom Kippur and Passover, a preoccupation with eating and avoiding certain foods, and the rooting of their culture in a soil they can call their own. But it is the symbol of land that dominates much modern Jewish thinking. Thus we might say that the Jewish faith, perhaps more than any modern religion, composes the human image as peculiarly "enlanded." To share in authentic humanity is to dwell within or in relation to a land that is a unique gift of God.

The creation of the modern state of Israel and the intense willingness of Jews to rally for its defense are together only one further demonstration of the tenacity of the promised land concept in the aspirations of Abraham's posterity. The absence of the Jewish people from the land for almost 1,900 years between the banishment of the Jews from Palestine by the Romans in A.D. 70 and the return of settlers through the Zionist movement in the early twentieth century fostered a longing for a homeland encapsulated in the Medieval Jewish passover prayer, "next year in Jerusalem." When the modern Israeli army captured the Old City of Jerusalem during the Six Day War in 1967, and many Jews were allowed for the first time in their lives the freedom to walk atop the ground where their ancestors had walked, the hope expressed in the prayer seemed, for many of them, to have been fulfilled.

THE IMAGE RECONSIDERED

Throughout our discussion of the Hebraic image as it evolves in the Bible we have seen that the idea of man always remains secondary to the concept of God who has made him and sustained him. Man's efforts to assimilate himself to God are rebuked as sin and as a usurpation of the divine power and authority. How then might we be permitted to speak of Hebrew faith, according to criteria set forth in the first chapter, as a special case of religious images mirroring man's self-understanding? Does not this interpretation tend to contradict the historical experience of the Hebrews?

As noted at the outset of the book, the images of God and man within any religious system constitute acts of human self-reflection. The Hebrews' prohibition against "graven images" of God as well as their depreciation of the given human condition as subject to divine transformation can be regarded as a tacit warning against accepting any arbitrary definition of God. The Hebrews perceived the myriad snares and means of self-deception by which man tends to make divine what is inferior and often inhumane within his character. The prophets, for instance, railed against the worship of pagan idols that demanded the commission of acts of promiscuity, bestiality, and even murder. In other words, the Hebrew God embodied a code of higher moral strictures that tended to conflict with man's ordinary wants and impulses. The German philosopher Karl Jaspers has called the period in which the prophets lived the "axial" period of human history. The word "axial" derives from the Greek word for "value." The axial period, therefore, was one in which humanity discovered for the first time certain supreme human values, such as love, fidelity, and universal justice that transcended the rude and sometimes barbarous customs of tribe and city-state. In the Hebrew mind Yahweh was always a God who demanded in man a strict conscience that rose above petty or parochial norms and commitments. Yahweh was also a God who favored the unfortunate and dispossessed, while ridiculing the finite concerns of individuals whose only values are social conformity and the cultivation of material interests. The Hebrews respected the intrinsic worth of persons over institutions, whereas Christianity eventually looked to the good of all mankind over the constraints of religious tradition and ritual.

The human image is never static. Through religion man steadily learns more about himself and about his place within the universe. The image of God that he projects may turn out to be a bald justification of self-interested or immoral undertakings, as was certainly true at times in Hebrew history and has been notoriously common within Christianity. Yet the normative or "canonical" literature of the Bible consistently invites man to smash the idols made as an emblem of his own base conceits, to uncover a higher image of himself, the image of God, which is not so easy to emulate. The Hebrew image over and over again has failed to legitimate the existing structures of self and society. Instead it has prodded man into reforming both self and society for the majesty of God and for the well-being of the human race.

NOTES

1. Buber has written numerous books and articles on biblical interpretation. Of principal interest, among others, are *The Prophetic Faith* (New York: The Macmillan Company, 1949); *Moses: The Revelation and the Covenant* (Oxford, Eng.: East and West Publishers, 1946); and *Good and Evil* (New York: Charles Scribner's Sons, 1953).

2. See H. Wheeler Robinson, *Corporate Personality in Ancient Israel* (Philadelphia: Fortress Press, 1964).

3. James Muilenburg, *The Way of Israel* (New York: Harper & Row, 1961), p. 66.

4. This attitude is echoed in the statement of Paul, the New Testament writer: "the wages of sin is death" (Romans 6:23).

5. Gerhard von Rad, *Old Testament Theology*, Volume 2 (New York: Harper & Row, 1965), p. 100.

FOR FURTHER READING

ALBRIGHT, WILLIAM F., *From the Stone Age to Christianity.* Baltimore: Johns Hopkins University Press, 1940. A review of the history, sociology, and archaeology that lie behind the contemporary understanding of the Bible.

ANDERSON, BERNHARD, *Understanding the Old Testament.* Englewood Cliffs, N.J.: Prentice-Hall, 1957.

CROSS, FRANK W., *The Ancient Library of Qumran and Modern Biblical Studies.* Garden City, N.Y.: Doubleday & Company, 1958.

GRANT, ROBERT M., *A Short History of the Interpretation of the Bible.* New York: The Macmillan Company, 1963. Looks at ways the study of the Bible has been approached and understood by scholars.

KLEIN, RALPH, *Textual Criticism of the Old Testament.* Philadelphia: Fortress Press, 1973. A study of Biblical literary forms and the methods of interpreting the texts of the ancient Hebrews.

MUILENBURG, JAMES, *The Way of Israel.* New York: Harper & Row, 1961. A brief but highly readable account of the literature, history, and theology of ancient Israel.

NEUSNER, JACOB, *The Way of Torah: An Introduction to Judaism.* Encino, Calif.: Dickenson Publishing Company, 1974. A compact and faithful summary of Jewish beliefs, customs, and rituals through the ages.

NOTH, MARTIN, *The History of Israel.* London: A & C Black, 1958.

RAST, WALTER, *Tradition History and the Old Testament.* Philadelphia: Fortress Press, 1973.

VON RAD, GERHARD, *The Theology of the Old Testament.* 2 vols. New York: Harper & Row, 1965. The definitive two-volume account of the thought forms of ancient Israel from its prehistory to the coming of Christianity; a very challenging, yet rewarding, work for beginners.

WOLFF, H. W., *The Old Testament: A Guide to Its Writings.* Philadelphia. Fortress Press, 1973.

The Christian Image

3

THE CHRISTIAN REVISION

That Christianity originally was not a new religion but a sectarian development within first-century Judaism is fairly clear to scholars these days. Only after Christianity moved out of its Palestinian home during the first century A.D. did it start to accommodate its teachings to the ways and preconceptions of Graeco-Roman culture. Christianity, especially in its later stages, represents the fusion of the Greek and Roman images of man in a new and more powerful synthesis than the Hebraic notions. However, the Hebraic image still undergirds the wider structure of Christian symbol and myth.

The various lines of the Christian image, of course, converge upon the life and sayings of Jesus of Nazareth. In the human portrait of Jesus, as well as the more mythical characterizations, conveyed through the Christian Gospels, we find sharp traces of both the prophetic and the Messianic themes. Jesus' preaching as delineated in the oldest Gospel material betrays the traditional prophetic concern with faith, righteousness, and the need for repentance in expectation of God's judgment. The kernel of Jesus' utterances is the idea of the kingdom of God, which parallels to a certain extent the prophets' vision of the Messianic age. In a manner similar to the prophets, Jesus taught that man must make himself eligible for the coming kingdom by relinquishing self-concern and establishing a relationship of fidelity with God.

> Therefore I tell you, do not be anxious about your life, what you shall eat or what you shall drink, nor about your body, what you shall put on. Is not life more than food, and the body more than clothing? Look at the

68

birds of the air: they neither sow nor reap nor gather into barns, and yet your heavenly Father feeds them. Are you not of more value than they? And which of you by being anxious can add one cubit to his span of life? And why are you anxious about clothing? Consider the lilies of the field, how they grow; they neither toil nor spin; yet I tell you, even Solomon in all his glory was not arrayed like one of these. But if God so clothes the grass of the field, which today is alive and tomorrow is thrown into the oven, will he not much more clothe you, O men of little faith? Therefore do not be anxious, saying, "What shall we eat?" or "What shall we drink?" or "What shall we wear?" For the Gentiles seek all these things; and your heavenly Father knows that you need them all. But seek first his kingdom and his righteousness, and all these things shall be yours as well. (Matt. 6:25–33)

In step with Jesus' emphasis on faith goes his insistence on social justice. The prophetic plea for the weak, misfortunate, and downtrodden, along with the denunciation of privilege, echoes in Jesus' Sermon on the Mount.

And he lifted up his eyes on his disciples, and said:
"Blessed are you poor, for yours is the kingdom of God.
Blessed are you that hunger now, for you shall be satisfied.
Blessed are you that weep now, for you shall laugh.
Blessed are you when men hate you, and when they exclude you and revile you, and cast out your name as evil, on account of the Son of man! Rejoice in that day, and leap for joy, for behold, your reward is great in heaven; for so their fathers did to the prophets.
But woe to you that are rich, for you have received your consolation.
Woe to you that are full now, for you shall hunger.
Woe to you that laugh now, for you shall mourn and weep.
Woe to you, when all men speak well of you, for so their fathers did to the false prophets."

(Luke 6:20–26)

Jesus' invectives against the "scribes and pharisees" who flaunt their religious reputations, yet who do not practice the primary virtue of what the prophets called "loving-kindness" (*hesed*) bolsters his profile as one of the heirs of Isaiah, Micah, and Jeremiah.

Traditionally most Jews have accepted Jesus as belonging to the prophetic order. The key issue over which Christians and Jews have become estranged, though, has to do with the former's veneration of Jesus as the Messiah. The word "Christ" is the Greek rendition of the Hebrew term for messiah. And biblical scholars have gone to great length in ascertaining exactly in what degree the New Testament, which is the distinctly Christian addition to the Bible, does indeed allude to Jesus' messianic role. Nowhere in the Gospels does Jesus brashly proclaim, "I am the Messiah, and you better believe it." On the other hand, his Messianic stature is depicted as implicit in many of his sayings and particularly in his performance of miracles of healing. The Gospel of Matthew tells us that whenever Jesus spoke, "the crowds were astonished at his teaching, for he taught them as one who had authority, and not as their scribes" (Matthew 7:28). In other words, Jesus radiated a presence that set him apart from most intellectual and political figures of his day.

The clue to Jesus' own understanding of his messiahship is furnished in the phrase "Son of Man" and, less frequently, "Son of God," as appropriate titles ascribed either by the prophet from Nazareth himself or by his contemporaries. The expression "Son of God," which is the most familiar title in Christian liturgy, was rarely used by Jesus to describe himself in the Gospels. Moreover, in its Hebraic context the term was not a synonym for the divine-human unity so much as an allusion to the legendary political Messiah who would replicate the personality of David. The term "Son of Man," which Jesus seems to have preferred, suggests an archetypal religious savior, very much after the fashion of the "suffering servant" of Isaiah. Though any verdict about Jesus' perception of his own place in the scheme of Israel's salvation must remain at best tentative, the evidence seems to shore up the view that he looked upon himself as a visible embodiment of the divine activity manifest through human suffering, and that his work among men was necessary to attract them to the way of self-giving love and faith as preparation for God's final intervention in history. The Son of Man thus lights up the path that must be trod into the coming kingdom of God.

The image of the savior who dies for the sins of mankind and is raised to a new life by God takes on crucial importance here. Such is the tacit meaning behind the story of Jesus' resurrection. The symbol of a dying and rising messiah was not entirely unprecedented in Jewish lore at the time. However, the early Christians interpreted Jesus' death and resurrection as the climax of the tradition. The ritual remembrance of the Resurrection, conducted during the holiday of Easter and solemnized in the acclamation "He is risen," dramatizes the central myth of Christianity. The arguments for or against the actual physical resurrection of Jesus following his death on the cross cannot be discussed here. What counts, though, is that Jesus' disciples and many zealous devotees of his way in subsequent centuries shaped their lives around the symbol of resurrection. In this respect, such a symbol counts as the master image imprinted on Christian consciousness as well as the point of departure for Christianity's basic analysis of the human condition.

A more systematic exposition of the Christian version of the human image, stemming directly from a reading of the Gospels, unfurls in the writings of Saint Paul, a converted Pharisee who never knew Jesus in the flesh, but who claimed to have experienced a vision of the risen Christ on the road to Damascus not long after Jesus' death. Saint Paul can be credited with having supplied the conceptual equipment of much subsequent Western Christian theology. Saint Paul's thought centers on two fundamental points: first, human sin; and, second, a promise of exultant release from sin through participation in the life of Christ. It was Saint Paul, in fact, who was the first Christian author to refine the essentially Hebraic view of Jesus as the historical Messiah and to attach to the notion of "Christ" a significance intelligible to Jews and Gentiles alike.

Paul preserved the prophetic doctrine of man as lacking the ability to ensure righteousness through his own will. His censure of those who trust in their own abilities for salvation, rather than having faith in their Creator reiterates the ideas first presented by the prophets.

> For although they knew God they did not honor him as God or give thanks to him, but they became futile in their thinking and their senseless minds were darkened. Claiming to be wise, they became fools, and exchanged the glory of the immortal God for images resembling mortal man or birds or animals or reptiles. (Rom. 1:21–23)

Sin is shaping one's own mortal desires or aspirations in the form of the divine, a subtle and insidious way of separating oneself from God. Sin, Paul declared, leaves man to reenact continually and to share in the fallen state of Adam, the first human being. Yet, just as man by the very fact of his birth shares in Adam's misery, so through entering into a relationship with Christ, may he be reborn and live once again.

> For as in Adam all die, so also in Christ shall all be made alive. (1 Cor. 15:22)

To live "in Christ" restores the broken image of God that man reflected at the creation; for Christ is the living and spiritual manifestation of the "new Adam" who supplants fallen humanity.

> The first man was from the earth, a man of dust; the second man is from heaven. As was the man of dust, so are those who are of the dust; and as is the man of heaven, so are those who are of heaven. Just as we have borne the image of the man of dust, we shall also bear the image of the man of heaven. (1 Cor. 15:47–49)

The resurrection reveals not only Jesus' messiahship, Paul contended, but also God's great act of love and mercy in freeing man from sin. Jesus' resurrection is a "second Exodus," we might say. And just as the original Exodus led to the establishment of the covenant between God and his chosen people, so the life and suffering of Christ lead to a new bond of fellowship between the divine and the human. Paul called such a bond "life in the Spirit." The Spirit represents the constant presence and redeeming power of Christ in people's lives.

In this respect Paul developed anew the concept of a personal relationship, defined as faith, between God and man which highlights the Hebraic image. The covenant is now intimate and experiential, based on the sense of Christ's presence rather than the principles of the *Torah*. Paul, in fact, argued that Christ supersedes *Torah*. The reason is that *Torah*, in Paul's view, is an impersonal set of constraints on man that gets in the way of the personal relationship with God, and thus tends to undermine faith and to obscure God's promise of free grace and redemption.

> The promise to Abraham and his descendants, that they should inherit the world, did not come through the law but through the righteousness of

> faith. If it is the adherents of the law who are to be the heirs, faith is null and the promise is void. For the law brings wrath, but where there is no law there is no transgression. (Rom. 4:13-15)

> I was once alive apart from the law, but when the commandment came, sin revived and I died; the very commandment which promised life proved to be death to me. (Rom. 7:9-10)

We must remember that Paul's understanding of the *Torah* was conditioned by his training as a Pharisee. The Pharisees stressed the life of self-perfection by adherence to the precepts of the Law, and it is primarily through such a process of moral improvement that man becomes "justified" or is deemed righteous by God. The old Mosaic notion of *Torah* as the prime manifestation of God's love for man tended to drop away in Jewish thinking after the Babylonian Exile, making God seem less personal and more remote. For many Jews *Torah* could be construed less as a set of moral instructions that express man's obligation to God and his fellows by virtue of faith, and more as a complicated skein of precise regulations that must be satisfied to the letter, lest God be angered and punish the wrongdoer. Law evolved into legalism, and the effect on the religious aspirant was to encourage, according to Paul, a striving after selfish rewards, a religiously sanctioned egotism rather than an attitude of self-surrender, humility, and charity toward others.

Harking back to Jesus' teaching, Paul taught that the Law must be subordinate to love.

> For the whole law is fulfilled in one word, "You shall love your neighbor as yourself." (Gal. 5:14)

The ethical demands of *Torah* are not cancelled, but at the same time must not be considered ends in themselves. Rather, obedience to *Torah* will flow naturally from a pure heart once a person has experienced the love of Christ in faith. Christ sets man free from the onus of self-protection by calling on him to participate in the perfect life of the Spirit. Thus man is justified not through works of the law, but through faith alone. In faith man acquires a taste once again of that for which he was fashioned by God in the beginning, as the premier agent of God's creative purpose in the world.

> Therefore, if any one is in Christ, he is a new creation; the old has passed away, behold, the new has come. All this is from God, who through Christ reconciled us to himself and gave us the ministry of reconciliation; that is, God was in Christ reconciling the world to himself, not counting their trespasses against them, and entrusting to us the message of reconciliation. So we are ambassadors for Christ, God making his appeal through us. (2 Cor. 5:17-20a)

The disciples of Jesus, who were the mainstay of the early Church for the first twenty years or so after the crucifixion, had looked for the coming of the kingdom of God which Jesus had foretold. They also expected the Second Coming or *parousia* of Christ within their own lifetime, whereby the kingdom, unrealized during Jesus' lifetime, would finally appear in all its glory. Gradually, though, the hope for Jesus' imminent return faded, and Paul's ideas about the significance of Christ's appearance in the world began to hold sway. While Christ might not come, like the legendary Messiah, on the clouds of heaven flanked by an army of angels, his vital presence in the Christian community as the spirit of faith and love established the kingdom now and forevermore. It was Jesus' resurrection that made all the difference, and it was communion with the resurrected Christ that founded the "new Israel" or the Church. In this connection Paul's teachings contributed fundamentally to the revision of the Hebraic image. Paul's message of salvation was truly a world-embracing one. Not just the blood descendants of Abraham, but now all mankind could be considered God's chosen ones. All are called to a life of faith in the universal God who revealed himself in an historical figure representative of authentic humanity. The Church is the new "people of Israel" extending beyond the borders of Palestine to envelop the entire population of the earth. Early Christianity enlarged the vision of the ancient Hebrews to become a veritable "image of man" in the generic sense. The "new man," Christ, becomes the model of humanity that abolishes external differences among individuals.

> There is neither Jew nor Greek, there is neither slave nor free, there is neither male nor female; for you are all one in Christ Jesus. (Gal. 3:28)

The unity of humanity, in the last reckoning, becomes one of the leading images of Christianity. But it was the image of man as the very image of God that defines the basic Christian sense of why human beings are as they are.

MAN IN THE IMAGE OF GOD

> Nearly all the wisdom we possess, that is to say, true and sound wisdom, consists of two parts: the knowledge of God and of ourselves. But while joined by many bonds, which one precedes and brings forth the other is not easy to discern. . . . No one can look upon himself without immediately turning his thoughts to the contemplation of God, in whom he "lives and moves." For, quite clearly, the mighty gifts with which we are endowed are hardly from ourselves; indeed, our very being is nothing but subsistence in the one God.[1]

This observation by the Protestant theologian John Calvin resounds throughout the Christian tradition: knowledge of God and knowledge of self are, for the Christian, inseparable. As early as the fourth century, one of Christianity's most insightful students of the human personality, Saint Augustine, declared, "O God, always one and the same, if I know myself, I shall know Thee!"[2] We might translate this into a more modern idiom by saying that religious belief is one of the most important factors that informs an individual's self-image, or helps one to formulate a clear sense of personal identity. The late H. Richard

Niebuhr went so far as to suggest that to be a self and to have a god are one and the same.

Our exploration of biblical terrain indicates that the close interrelationship between knowledge of God and of self lies deep in the Christian grain. In the first chapter of Genesis we already read,

> Then God said, "Let us make man in our image, after our likeness; and let them have dominion over the fish of the sea, and over the birds of the air, and over the cattle, and over all the earth, and over every creeping thing that creeps upon the earth." So God created man in his own image, in the image of God he created him; male and female he created them. (Gen. 1:26–27)

Because the Christian believes himself to have been created in the image of God, he maintains that knowledge of God and self-knowledge are closely interrelated. Our opening chapter suggested that God is a mirror in which man beholds his own image. But note the inversion that takes place as we move from psychologists and sociologists to churchmen and theologians. From the perspective of the Christian faithful, God creates human beings in his own image. To assert the contrary (that man projects God in his image) is the height of blasphemy. A contemporary German theologian, Wolfhart Pannenberg, explains the significance of this reversal.

> Weighty evidence favors the idea of the personal having its origins in religious experience, in the encounter with divine reality. According to this view, the notion of the personal was later transferred to man because man was honored with a special relation to the gods. In this way the very possibility of anthropomorphic conceptions of the divine may be explained. Man's projecting of himself and his personality upon the gods presupposes a more basic idea of personality and is based upon man's encounter with the divine, while the particular characteristics of the divine personality are shaped by man's attributing his own particulars to the gods.[3]

Whether we believe with many theologians that God has made man in his image, or hold with recent students of religion that man has made God in his image, it seems clear that throughout Christian history, there remains a close relation between the notion of God and the human image. When we turn from these general considerations to the details of the Christian tradition, however, we discover not *one* Christian image of God and of man, but a range of images expressing variations of common themes. The Christian image comes into focus very slowly. It persistently reflects and refracts the psychological, social, and cultural conditions in which it takes form. By telling the tale of the gradual emergence and refinement of the Christian image of man, we gain a more thorough understanding of the intricate dynamics relating self, society, and cosmos in the construction of man's religious symbols.

CONFUSION AND CONTROVERSY
IN EARLY CHRISTIANITY

In his masterful study of Gnosticism, Hans Jonas notes that "at the beginning of the Christian era and progressively throughout the two following centuries, the eastern Mediterranean world was in profound spiritual ferment."[4] As so often in the course of history, spiritual turmoil is a reflex of social unrest. An uncertain world seems to fuel the fires of the religious imagination. We have seen that through religious symbols, people attempt to construct a sacred canopy under which they seek shelter in an unpredictable and at times terrifying world. By carefully stitching a web of symbolic meanings, man endeavors to confer upon his world a semblance of order and consequently to establish for himself a relatively stable sense of identity.

Our study of biblical materials has shown that for the early Christian community, this web of meanings was closely knit to an historical individual—Jesus of Nazareth. To many persons, Jesus appeared to be the Messiah who, as promised by the Old Testament prophets, would usher in the golden age. Through their faith in Jesus, his followers could understand themselves to be members of a community that was playing an essential role in a drama dating from creation and pointing toward the end of history. Self, society, and cosmos were carefully sewn together to form the fabric of the believer's self-understanding. But this web of meanings unraveled with the death of Jesus. Jesus, the person believed capable of delivering individuals from the ambiguities and afflictions of human existence, suffered the death of a common criminal. At a distance of nearly two millennia, it is hard for us to appreciate the extraordinary crisis this turn of events brought for the followers of the infant religion. The dissolution of the entire symbolic framework through which the early community had interpreted itself and its world brought in its wake a deep-going sense of anxiety and a profound feeling of homelessness. The cross cast a dark shadow over the lives of Jesus' disciples.

There seemed to be only two alternatives. Either one could deny that Jesus had actually been the long-awaited Messiah and admit to having been deluded by a religious visionary, or one could interpret Jesus' crucifixion not as a final defeat, but as a necessary stage in a previously concealed plan of redemption. To have followed the former course would have meant that Christianity died with its founder. To pursue the latter path would open the possibility of mending the believers' web of meanings by rewriting the plot of the story of God's activity through Jesus. Clearly those who continued to fashion themselves believers in Jesus followed the second course. Gradually the conviction arose that Jesus was not, in fact, dead and defeated but alive and active in the Christian community. The Book of Acts records the reformulation of the early community's faith during the period immediately following Jesus' death.

> Men of Israel, hear these words: Jesus of Nazareth, a man attested to you
> by God with mighty works and wonders and signs which God did through
> him in your midst, as you yourselves know—this Jesus, delivered up
> according to the definite plan and foreknowledge of God, you crucified
> and killed by the hands of lawless men. But God raised him up, having
> loosed the pangs of death, because it was not possible for him to be held
> by it. (Acts 2:22–24)

Having reformed rather than rejected their belief in Jesus, the community was
able to rekindle the expectation that had ignited its faith. Many became convinced that in the near future, Christ would return to inaugurate the new age
they once had thought his earthly life would initiate. Jesus' time on earth was
then viewed as the necessary prelude to a second coming in which Jesus' lord-
ship would be vindicated and the powers of darkness would be soundly defeated.
This hope is expressed in apocalyptic form in the Book of Revelation.

> Then I saw a new heaven and a new earth; for the first earth had passed
> away, and the sea was no more. And I saw the holy city, new Jerusalem,
> coming down out of heaven from God, prepared as a bride adorned for her
> husband; and I heard a great voice from the throne saying, "Behold, the
> dwelling of God is with men. He will dwell with them, and they shall be
> his people, and God himself will be with them; he will wipe away every
> tear from their eyes, and death shall be no more, neither shall there be
> mourning nor crying nor pain any more, for the former things have passed
> away." And he who sat upon the throne said, . . . "It is done! I am the
> Alpha and the Omega, the beginning and the end. To the thirsty I will give
> water without price from the fountain of the water of life. He who con-
> quers shall have this heritage, and I will be his God and he shall be my son.
> But as for the cowardly, the faithless, the polluted, as for murderers, for-
> nicators, sorcerers, idolaters, and all liars, their lot shall be in the lake that
> burns with fire and brimstone, which is the second death." (Rev. 21:1–8)

But expectations again were disappointed; as the years passed Jesus still
did not return. For a second time, dark clouds of despair and anguish loomed on
the spiritual horizon. The community's response to this crisis of meaning was to
shift the second coming of Christ from the near to the distant future. Christ
would return to overthrow the powers of evil in some unspecifiable future
epoch. But this solution created further problems. As long as Christians believed
that Christ would soon return to overturn the present age, there was little need
to seek accommodation with the surrounding world. Indeed to do so could be
interpreted as cooperation with the forces of evil. If, however, the messianic age
no longer were held to be at hand, but were believed to lie in the indefinite
future, the continued existence of the Christian religion required the establishment of a positive relationship with the ongoing life of the society. Biblical
scholar Hans Conzelmann points out that "as the life of the world continues,
there arise certain problems concerning the relation of the Church to its environ-

ment, which had remained hidden at the beginning because of the belief that the End was imminent."[5]

When Christians began to turn their attention from hope for the future to the realities of the present, they found themselves immersed in an extraordinarily complex social, cultural, and spiritual world. By exploring briefly some of the outstanding features of this rich environment, we begin to uncover important dimensions of the interplay between psychological, social, and cultural factors and the religious imagination of the early Christians.

Although the rule of Augustus (emperor from 27 B.C. to A.D. 14) brought the Roman Empire a period of peace and optimism between eras of decline and decay, the initial centuries of Christian history were, for the most part, times of social and political unrest. Augustus' success lay in his effort to reverse the movement away from the ideal of republican principles for which Rome had stood that had started with Julius Caesar's (100-44 B.C.) assumption of dictatorial power. He attempted to return significant power to the Roman Senate and to serve as a representative of the people. This political program was part of Augustus' overall aim of bringing peace and stability to an empire that had so long been at war. In many ways, Augustus' efforts were successful. A semblance of republican government again was achieved, and peace came to the empire. For many persons, the years of Augustus' rule brought great hope.

But it soon became apparent that beneath this veneer of harmony, deep unrest was brewing. Throughout the empire, rumblings of dissent threatened to destroy the new stability. In order to establish peace, Augustus stopped wars aimed at expanding the empire and attempted to consolidate the lands that had been won in battle. Two important consequences followed. First, the end of expansion had serious economic repercussions. No longer were new markets available for Roman goods. This economic burden combined with the loss of political power involved with the return to republicanism to cause the Roman aristocracy to oppose many of Augustus' programs. The resistance of one of the empire's most powerful classes led to internal instability. Second, the only way to retain the territory already conquered was by military occupation. This led to further financial hardship for the empire and created friction between Rome and the occupied provinces. Both at home and abroad, seeds of discontent had been sown.

Augustus' successors were less skillful in maintaining the shaky peace. Times of relative tranquility were punctuated with violence and repression. The inability of later rulers to retain the delicate balance established by Augustus was especially evident in the crisis of the third century. During this period, the very social and moral fabric of Roman society seemed to be on the verge of destruction. Under internal siege at the hands of Roman warlords and faced with external attack by raiding barbarians, the empire's fragile stability crumbled. The situation was worsened by the outbreak of plague and famine in many of the provinces. Conditions became so bad that numerous peasant revolts erupted.

Civilized life as it had been known seemed on the verge of destruction. A leader of the early Church, Cyprian, reflected the terror felt by many people when he wrote,

> Behold, the roads closed by brigands, the sea blocked by pirates, the bloodshed and horror of universal strife. The world drips with mutual slaughter, and homicide, considered a crime when perpetuated by individuals, is regarded virtuous when committed publicly.[6]

The constant struggle among contenders for domination of various portions of the empire combined with growing social and political anarchy to foster a far-ranging mood of anxiety and a sense of rootlessness and powerlessness.

Relations between the early Christian community and the surrounding world were, to say the least, strained. In part, such was the result of Christianity's relationship with Judaism. The Jews, a persistent problem for the rulers of the Roman Empire, staunchly resisted Roman occupation forces. In A.D. 66, an overt rebellion broke out that culminated in the destruction of the temple at Jerusalem (A.D. 70). The final breakdown of a centralized Jewish community did not come until Hadrian's expulsion of the Jews from their homeland in A.D. 135. At this time the Jewish population was dispersed throughout the Mediterranean area. Nevertheless, animosity toward the Jews continued to be expressed throughout the formative years of Christianity. Initially it was clear to neither the Christians themselves nor to non-Christians whether the new religion was an outgrowth and continuation of ancient Judaism, or was a genuinely novel religious departure. This resulted in a tendency on the part of many members of the empire to identify Christianity with Judaism and to transfer their ill will for the Jews to Christians.

Another important characteristic of the membership of the early Christian community tended to create tensions with the empire. As John Gager has ably demonstrated, "early believers came primarily from disadvantaged groups."[7] This feature of the social composition of the young Church is reflected in the numerous biblical texts addressed to the socially disinherited. For instance, in the Gospel according to Luke, we read:

> Blessed are you poor, for yours is the kingdom of God.
> Blessed are you that hunger now, for you shall be satisfied.
> Blessed are you that weep now, for you shall laugh.
> Blessed are you when men hate you, and when they exclude you and revile you, and cast out your name as evil, on account of the Son of man! Rejoice in that day, and leap for joy, for behold, your reward is great in heaven; for so their fathers did to the prophets. (Luke 6:20-23)

Our analysis of the place of religion in human experience suggests that through such beliefs persons and groups attempt to come to terms with oppression and suffering. This form of faith brings hope to an apparently hopeless situation. From the perspective of those in positions of political power, however, the proletarian character of the early Christian community seemed to pose a threat of social disruption. These suspicions were deepened by the widespread belief among Christians that with the reversal of their unfortunate lot, their oppressors would be cast down. The passage from Luke continues:

> Woe to you that are rich, for you have received your consolation.
> Woe to you that are full now, for you shall hunger.
> Woe to you that laugh now, for you shall mourn and weep.
> Woe to you, when all men speak well of you, for so their fathers did to the false prophets. (Luke 6:24–26)

The point is made even more graphically in the Letter of James.

> Come now, you rich, weep and howl for the miseries that are coming upon you. Your riches have rotted and your garments are moth-eaten. Your gold and silver have rusted, and their rust will be evidence against you and will eat your flesh like fire. (James 5:1–3)

To many persons, such statements seemed to support strongly, if not espouse overtly, social hostility and political resistance. This anxiety led to further repression of the early Church.

Other aspects of the Christian religion aggravated this already difficult situation. Most importantly, it was not uncommon for Christians to be accused of atheism. Today this might seem incredible to you. But we must remember that Romans were, for the most part, polytheists, worshipers of many gods. The radical monotheism that Christianity inherited from Judaism made it impossible for Christians to bow down to the many members of the Roman pantheon. The charge of atheism carried with it serious political consequences. Many persons believed Rome's greatness to be the result of the favor of its gods. Therefore when the empire met with crises, it was natural to assume that the gods had been angered. The refusal of Christians to worship pagan deities frequently was interpreted by citizens of the empire to be the reason for the gods' displeasure and thus the cause of social and political problems. A second political dimension of Christian atheism concerned emperor worship. As it became increasingly difficult to hold together the falling empire, it was more important for the emperor to exercise absolute authority. Indeed, the figure of the emperor in the popular imagination came to embody the unity of the whole empire. As the emperor assumed such a central place, Augustus' understanding of the emperor as a representative of the people gave way to a theory of the divinity of the emperor more in keeping with Oriental monarchies than with the republican ideals of Rome. In order to legitimize his increasing authority, the emperor came to be regarded as divine, and the populace was required to worship him through sacrifices. Again, the principles of the Christian religion prevented participation in this form of religious activity. To many Romans, the Christians' refusal to worship the emperor was not simply a religious matter, but was, in effect, regarded as treason. The rejection of emperor worship, coupled with the unwillingness of Christians to engage in military activity led to the opinion that Christians were traitors.

The hostility toward the Christians on the part of many Roman citizens made them an easy target for political persecution. It was often expedient for rulers to blame the woes of the empire on the Christians. The first instance of this was in A.D. 64. Nero, an unpopular emperor, unjustly blamed the Christians for starting the great fire of Rome. Actually Nero himself had been suspected of arson, and his accusation of the Christians was an effort to divert public anger away from himself. Persecution followed accusation, setting a precedent to be followed repeatedly in later years. At first the persecutions were local and sporadic. But as the problems of the empire worsened, the persecution of the Christians grew more severe. In 177, Marcus Aurelius proclaimed that Christians were a menace to the empire and should be tortured to death. By the middle of the third century, the political and social crisis of the empire resulted in Decius' (emperor, 249-251) systematic persecution of Christians. The beginning of the fourth century brought emperor Diocletian's (284-305) prohibition of practicing Christianity, under penalty of death.

The Christian response to such persecution was mixed. Some persons responded by developing a very positive view of martyrdom. They believed that following in the footsteps of the crucified Lord gave the martyr immediate access to heaven. In one of the most remarkable documents of the early Church, Ignatius, a Syrian bishop of the early second century on his way to martyrdom in Rome, wrote,

> Grant me no more than to be a sacrifice for God while there is an altar at hand. . . . Let me be fodder for wild beasts—that is how I can get to God. I am God's wheat and I am being ground by the teeth of wild beasts to make a pure loaf for Christ. I would rather that you fawn on the beasts so that they may be my tomb and no scrap of my body be left.[8]

For the most part, however, Christians recognized such a view to be self-defeating. By attempting to explain the Christian religion to Roman citizens, a series of second-century authors such as Athenagoras and Justin Martyr (who apparently was not very successful!) sought to put an end to what seemed to them to be cruel and unfair treatment of Christians. The opening lines of Athenagoras' "Plea" express the flavor of these early defenses of Christianity.

> Although we do no wrong, but, as we shall show, are of all men most religiously and rightly disposed toward God and your Empire, you allow us to be harassed, plundered, and persecuted, the mob making way on us only because of our name. We venture, therefore, to state our case before you. From what we have to say you will gather that we suffer unjustly and contrary to all law and reason. Hence we ask you to devise some measures to prevent our being the victims of false accusers.[9]

Despite such apologetic efforts, it was not until the conversion of the emperor Constantine in 313 that the Christians' lot significantly changed for the better.

With Constantine's rise to power, Christianity's status shifted from that of a persecuted sect to that of a religion sanctioned by the empire. By the latter part of the fourth century, the reversal was complete, and Christianity was declared the official religion of the empire. Now persecution and ostracism befell those *who failed or refused to become Christians.*

In light of the theoretical insights garnered from our opening chapter, it should not be surprising that this complex and volatile world was a cauldron in which intense spiritual ferment brewed. Social unrest, political intrigue, plague, famine, and persecution created a need for great personal courage and heroism. To cope with such problems, people turned to religious symbols. Peter Berger's remark throws light on the situation we have been exploring.

> The sacred cosmos emerges out of chaos and continues to confront the latter as its terrible contrary. This opposition of cosmos and chaos is frequently expressed in a variety of cosmogonic myths. The sacred cosmos, which transcends and includes man in its ordering of reality, thus provides man's ultimate shield against the terror of anomy. To be in a "right" relationship with the sacred cosmos is to be protected against the nightmare threats of chaos. To fall out of such a "right" relationship is to be abandoned on the edge of the abyss of meaninglessness.[10]

By participating in old cults, or constructing new religious symbols, people of this era attempted to build a cosmic domicile that would help them overcome the anxious agony of homelessness.

"THE EXILED SOUL"

In many ways the world we have been describing bears a striking resemblance to our own time. The confusion that rapid social change, political flux, and warfare bring frequently leads to a reawakening of the religious impulse. Then, as now, an extraordinary flowering of religious fervor blossomed.[11] Christianity, Judaism, mystery cults, Babylonian astrology, Gnosticism, Neo-Platonism, Zoroastrianism, Mithraism, mysticism, and Manichaeism flourished to varying degrees. The formation of the early Christian image of man was not only influenced by the sociopolitical situation of the Roman Empire, but also was affected profoundly by the spiritual milieu of the day. In order to bring into sharp relief the distinctive contours of the early Christian view of self, society, and cosmos, we must consider briefly two of its primary competitors: Gnosticism and Hellenism, or the way of Greek culture. Christianity attempted to walk the precarious boundary between the extremes of these two spiritual visions.

Although Gnosticism was not a unified religious movement, central themes join its different strains. Most important for our purposes, the common image governing the Gnostic view of human being is "the exiled soul."[12] As will become apparent, this image is a perfectly understandable response to the uncertain times we have been examining. We might best begin with Hans Jonas's insight

insight that the Gnostic believed the universe "is like a vast prison whose innermost dungeon is the earth, the scene of man's life. Around and above it the cosmic spheres are ranged like concentric enclosing shells."[13] At each of the imprisoning spheres stands a guardian to prevent man's escape. Life on earth is pervaded by "darkness, utterly full of evil, full of devouring fire, . . . full of falsehood and deceit." Ours is a "world of turbulence without steadfastness, a world of darkness without light . . . a world of death without eternal life, a world in which good things perish."[14] For many persons, this seemed an accurate description of life in imperial Rome.

Beyond the domain of darkness, evil, and suffering, however, the Gnostic saw "a world of splendor and light without darkness, a world of mildness without rebellion, a world of righteousness without turbulence, a world of eternal life without decay and death, a world of goodness without evil. . . . A pure world unmixed with ill."[15] The fundamental tenet of Gnosticism, therefore, is a radical dualism between the evil and corruption of this world and the goodness and perfection of the divine realm. In such a dark world, a person's only hope lies in the utterly transcendent world of light.

Gnostic texts do not simply assert this duality. They attempt to render the human situation intelligible by presenting elaborately constructed myths to explain how man has fallen to such depths and how he might ascend the heights of perfection. The world, Gnostics maintained, is the result of a divine error. Between the transcendent God and the created order, there is a hierarchy of spiritual beings. Taken together, these beings form the divine Pleroma, which initially was a harmonious totality. But ages ago disorder was introduced to the Pleroma when one of the celestial beings sought to know the unknowable origin of all (that is, the most radically transcendent deity). To restore harmony to the Pleroma, the highest god expelled the perverse desire of the lower deity. This desire was hypostatized and eventually became the world. Thus the world cannot be regarded as good and actually never was intended by God. Rather it is the consequence of the disruptive and evil desire of a member of the divine Pleroma. The world continues to bear the impress of its corrupt origin. The poetry of one of the most famous Christian Gnostics, Valentinus, makes this point graphically:

> Ignorance of the Father
> Produced Anguish and Terror
> And Anguish thickened into mist
> Till none could see a way through
> And the Forces of Confusion grew
> Spinning its matter in emptiness,
> Not knowing the Truth, and began
> To form a creation.[16]

This cosmological dualism, the separation of God and the world, is paralleled by an anthropological dualism. As an exiled soul, man's position in the world is ambiguous. So far as he is a member of the created order, he is subject to the powers of darkness. But man also is joined with the heavenly realm of light. This interpretation of man and of his relationship to his surrounding world is developed in the Gnostic division of man into three distinct parts: body, soul, and spirit (or *pneuma*). While the body and the soul chain man to this world, the spiritual element in the personality is, in the final analysis, a part of the heavenly domain of light. By virtue of the spirit, man transcends his worldly existence. But the simple possession of such a spiritual dimension of the personality does not resolve the human dilemma. The powers of the world conspire to maintain control over humankind by keeping persons ignorant of their spirituality. Man becomes intoxicated with the world and forgets his heavenly origin and destiny. One text reads:

> They [that is, worldly powers] mixed me drink with their cunning and gave me to taste of their meat. I forgot that I was a king's son, and served their king. I forgot the Pearl for which my parents had sent me. Through the heaviness of their nourishment I sank into deep slumber.[17]

How, then, can man be freed from the suffering and travail that life in this world imposes upon him? For Gnostics, this could occur only if man awakes from his slumber by becoming aware of his divine spirit. In order to effect this liberation, a messenger is sent from the transworldly Pleroma. Gnosticism portrayed this messenger in various ways. Christian Gnostic sects interpreted Jesus Christ as the alien messenger sent to liberate man. For all forms of Gnosticism, however, the representative of the transcendent realm brings people the knowledge or *gnosis* (hence the name "Gnostic") of mankind's inherent identity with the sphere of light that allows the self's recognition of its fundamental alienation from the domain of darkness. Jaroslav Pelikan goes so far as to suggest that Gnosticism may be defined as a system that taught "the cosmic redemption of the spirit through knowledge."[18] An early Manichaean myth explains,

> They created the messenger and sent him to the head of the generations. He called with heavenly voice into the turmoil of the worlds. At the messenger's call Adam [i.e., man], who lay there, awoke . . . and went to meet the messenger: "Come in peace, thou messenger, envoy of the Life who hast come from the house of the Father. How firmly planted in its place is the dear Fair Life! And how sits here my dark form in lamentation!" Then replied the messenger: ". . . All remembered thee with love and . . . sent me to thee. I have come and will instruct thee, Adam, and release thee out of this world. Hearken and hear and be instructed, and rise up victorious to the place of light."[19]

Valentinus' *The Gospel of Truth* makes a similar point. This passage is particularly instructive, for it illustrates a common effort to present Gnostic ideas through Christian symbols.

> As Oblivion
> Arose because none knew
> The Father, so when, He

Is known, Oblivion will disappear.
This is the Gospel of Him
Who is sought, and which He has revealed
To those perfected, through the mercy of the Father, as
The Hidden Mystery,
He, Jesus the Christ.
He brought light to those in Darkness
Owing to Oblivion.
He illuminated them
Showing them a way.
That way is the Truth He taught . . .
Entering Terror's empty spaces
He reached those stripped of Oblivion,
Became Knowledge and Fulfillment,
Proclaiming what lies at the heart of the Father . . .
They who have been in Confusion
Find that (phantasmagoria)
To be nothing whatsoever
And cast off ignorance
Like sleep, which they think to be nothing
Like everything else (pertaining to sleep)
But leave it behind like a dream of the night,
Holding for the Light
Knowledge of the Father.[20]

As these texts suggest, the myths in which the basic principles of Gnosticism were expressed are numerous and complex. For our purposes, it is the general Gnostic image of man and of his place in the world that is of concern. According to the Gnostic, during his life on earth, man is homeless—he is an exiled soul, trapped in a thoroughly evil world and longing to return to his proper home, the transcendent realm of light. God, who is completely good, has no contact at all with the corrupt world. The world, in fact, never was intended by the highest god, but arose as a consequence of the error of a lower deity. Because the world is evil, people bear no responsibility toward this world and should seek to flee it in a heavenward ascent. This liberation comes with the knowledge or *gnosis* communicated by a divine messenger sent from the domain of light. Armed with this knowledge one finally can gain release from the pain and suffering of the world.

When we place these insights in the context of our conclusions of the foregoing section, it becomes apparent that Gnosticism offers vivid support for the main features of the interpretation of the nature and function of religion developed in our opening chapter. We may recall Marx's comment that "man makes religion" and that "religion is the sigh of the oppressed culture, the heart of a heartless world, as it is the spirit of spiritless conditions."[21] When oppressive psychological, social, and cultural conditions induce in man a sense of homelessness, he tends to construct a sacred domicile. Imagined life in this transcendent cosmos is an ideal representation of the perfection for which man longs, but which he is denied in his actual existence. As we have suggested in our first chapter, religion can be viewed as a looking glass in which humanity beholds its idealized image.

THE COSMOS DIVINE

The attraction of Gnosticism for many persons lay in the fact that it offered a more adequate symbolic framework for interpreting their experience than did more classical Greek ideas. Gnosticism was a radical departure from what had become a traditional Hellenic way of envisioning man, God, the world, and their interrelationship. In many ways, Gnosticism can be seen as the polar opposite of central convictions of many Greek thinkers. As Jonas points out, the extent of these differences emerges most sharply if we look at the implications of classical philosophy as they are developed in the Stoicism of someone such as Cicero.[22] Though himself a Roman, Cicero drew heavily on Greek philosophy to enlarge his views of man and of his place in the universe.

For the Greek mind, the universe was not a "vast prison," a "world of darkness without light," but was a *cosmos*. The term "cosmos" carries with it the specific connotation of order. "Thus when applied to the universe and becoming assigned to it as to its eminent instance, the word does not merely signify the neutral fact of all-that-is, a quantitative sum (as the term 'the All' does), but expresses a specific and to the Greek mind ennobling quality of this whole: that it is order."[23] The source of this order differs from philosopher to philosopher and from mythology to mythology. In the *Timaeus*, for instance, Plato suggested that the demiurgic creator imposes order on pre-existing chaos.

> Desiring, then, that all things should be good, and so far as might be, nothing imperfect, the god took over all that is visible . . . and brought it from disorder into order, since he judged that order was in every way the better. . . . He found that . . . no work that is without intelligence will ever be better than one that has intelligence, . . . and moreover that intelligence cannot be present in anything apart from soul. In virtue of this reasoning, when he framed the universe, he fashioned reason within the soul and soul within body, to the end that the work he accomplished might be by nature as excellent and perfect as possible. This, then, is how we must say . . . that this world came to be, by God's providence, in very truth a living creature with soul and reason.[24]

Here we have the suggestion that the cosmos is "a living creature with soul and reason." Though Plato remained reluctant to make such a move, it is apparently one short step from the conviction that the universe is a rational organism most perfectly exemplifying order to the outright divinization of the cosmos. This step was taken by later Stoicism, a Graeco-Roman philosophy that viewed the universe as suffused with God or with the spirit of reason.

In *The Nature of the Gods*, Cicero, who was influenced by the Stoics, wrote:

> There is then a nature [heat] which holds together and sustains the universe, and it possesses both sensibility and reason. For everything which is not separate and simple but joined and connected with other things must have within it some governing principle. In man it is mind, in beasts something similar to mind [sense], from which the appetites arise. . . . In each class of things nothing can be or ought to be more excellent than this its governing principle. Hence that element wherein resides the governing principle of Nature as a whole must be the best of all things and most worthy of power and dominion over all things. Now we see that in certain parts of the cosmos—and there is nothing anywhere in the cosmos which is not *a part of the whole*—sensibility and reason abide. In that part, therefore, in which the governing principle of the cosmos resides, these same qualities must of necessity be present—only keener and on a grander scale. Therefore the cosmos must also be wise, for that substance which encompasses and holds all things must excel in the perfection of its reason; and this means that *the cosmos is God* [italics added] and all its particular powers are contained in the divine nature.[25]

In this text emerges the explicit identification of the cosmos and the divine. Such a position is called *pantheism* or *monism*. It is, of course, the opposite of the radical dualism of Gnosticism, according to which God utterly transcends and has absolutely no contact with the world.

Man's place in the cosmos is construed as quite different from the way in which the Gnostics represented man's relation to the world. We recall that, for the Gnostic, man is chained to the realm of darkness by his soul and body, but stands above the mundane domain by virtue of his possession of a divine spirit. From the Greek-Stoic perspective, man is a part of the divine whole. Again, we quote Cicero:

> Now since she is such that excels all other things and no thing can obstruct her, it is necessary that the cosmos is intelligent and even wise. What can be more foolish than to deny that Nature which comprehends all things is the most excellent, or, if this is granted, to deny that it is firstly animate, and secondly rational and reflective, and thirdly wise? How else could it be the most excellent? For if it were like plants or beasts, it would have to be considered the lowest rather than the highest of beings. Again, if it were rational but not from the beginning wise, the state of the cosmos would be inferior to that of man; for man can *become* wise, but if the cosmos during the infinite aeons of the past has been lacking in wisdom, it will certainly never attain it, and will thus be *inferior to man*. Since *this is absurd*, it must be held that from the beginning the cosmos has been both wise and God. And there is naught else except the cosmos which lacks nothing and which is in all particulars and parts fit and perfect and complete.[26]

Rather than imagining man superior to a corrupt world, this perspective suggests that the divine cosmos incorporates man.

When a person's relation to the cosmos is understood in this way, it is implausible for one to seek escape from a hostile and alien world. To the contrary, man "was born *to contemplate the cosmos* and *to imitate it*; he is far from being perfect, but he is a little part of the perfect."[27] Imitation of a divine cosmos instead of flight from a corrupt world becomes the proper end of human existence. The perfection of the divine cosmos requires the harmonious inter-relation of all of its parts. Jonas specifies the importance of this viewpoint for man's self-understanding when he writes,

> The recognition of and compliance with his position as a part is one aspect of man's proper relation to the universe in the conduct of his life. It is based on the interpretation of his existence in terms of the larger whole, whose very perfection consists in the integration of all its parts. In this sense man's cosmic piety *submits* his being to the requirements of what is better than himself and the source of all that is good. But at the same time man is not just a part like other parts making up the universe, but through the possession of a mind a part that enjoys *identity* with the *ruling principle* of the whole. Thus the other aspect of man's proper relation to the universe is that of *adequating* his own existence, confined as it is to a mere part, to the essence of the whole, of reproducing the latter in his own being through understanding and action.[28]

It should be clear that on most important issues, this particular variation of the Hellenic image of man and of his place in the universe contradicts the Gnostic image. Man no longer appears as a captive of the evil powers of this world, yearning to flee to a realm of divine perfection. God is not utterly transcendent of this world, but is actually the cosmos itself. As a member of the cosmos, man too must be divine—to divinize the cosmos is to make a god of man. From both the Gnostic and Hellenic viewpoints, man and god are, in some sense, identified. From the Gnostic perspective, beneath man's body and soul is a divine spark that is really a part of the highest deity. For a Stoic such as Cicero, membership in the divine cosmos renders human being divine. Of course we have noted that different estimates of the world in these competing symbol systems lead to opposite views of man's relation to the world. The Gnostic attempts to escape a corrupt world, while the Greek seeks to imitate a divine cosmos. But the actors in both dramas remain godlike human beings.

The Gnostic and Hellenic images of man and of his universe obviously grew out of and spoke to very different worlds. For the Gnostic, the uncertainties and anxieties of life in the Roman Empire made hope in a wholly other realm of perfection a virtual necessity. The Hellenic image that we have been exploring seems to have reflected life in the Greek *polis* or city-state of classical times, before the growth of empire. Hans Jonas's perceptive analysis helps us grasp the relationship we have come to expect between products of the religious imagination and the sociocultural soil in which they grow.

According to classical doctrine, the whole is prior to the parts, is better than the parts, and therefore that for the sake of which the parts are and wherein they have not only the cause but also the meaning of their existence. The living example of such a whole had been the classical *polis*, the city-state, whose citizens had a share in the whole and could affirm its superior status in the knowledge that they, the parts, however passing and exchangeable, not only were *dependent* on the whole *for* their being but also *maintained* that whole *with* their being: just as the condition of the whole made a difference to the being and possible perfection of the parts, so their conduct made a difference to the being and perfection of the whole.[29]

But, alas, the empire was not a Greek *polis*! A new symbolic framework was required through which persons could attempt to render their lives meaningful. Gnosticism was one of the most influential efforts to articulate a new set of religious symbols that emerged during the centuries immediately following the death of Christ. But to some, the Gnostic cure seemed worse than the disease. Certainly it no longer seemed possible to imagine the cosmos a harmoniously ordered divine organism. But neither did the opposite point of view of the universe as utterly chaotic and corrupt solve the problem of meaning. The attempt to render meaningful one's life in this world by offering the possibility of escape to another world only confirms the utter meaninglessness of the ongoing course of world history. We might ask if the Gnostic and Hellenic images err in opposite directions: on the one hand we have a dualism that suggests a totally corrupt world in which man is trapped and from which he must escape, and on the other hand a monism that deifies the cosmos and leaves man the task of merging with the divine order. Might a mean between these two extremes offer a symbolic matrix that would enable a person to affirm the meaningfulness of worldly existence without denying evident evil and suffering?[30]

CREATURES OF GOD

Early Christianity sought to supply just that mean; it undertook to formulate a viable image of man in relation to the universe. As we have observed, throughout the Christian tradition the knowledge of God and the image of self are closely intertwined. This notion stems from the persistent Christian belief that man is created in the image of God, posed in the first chapter of Genesis. To begin to understand early elaborations of the Christian image of man, we must return to the biblical picture of creation. If knowledge of God and self-understanding are as closely connected as Christian authors suggest, we might best begin by asking about the ruling Christian image of God. The very first verse of the Bible states, "In the beginning God created the heavens and the earth." (Genesis 1:1). For early Christians, as for their Hebrew ancestors, God is above all a creator God. God is eminently personal, which is not to imply that God is believed to be *a* person, but to suggest that God is, in some significant way, personlike. As personal creator, God creates freely. The world is called into being by the exercise of God's free and omnipotent will. For the Christian, the Old Testament image of God as an all-powerful creator is tempered by the New Testament insistence that God loves the world (e.g., John 3:16), although the tension between power and love is not as strong in the Hebrew mind as Christianity later presumed. The divine power is, in the final analysis, benevolent. For Christians and Jews alike, however, this creator God is the supreme and only God. Christianity, as Judaism, is a strictly monotheistic religion. Unlike the Platonic demiurge, the Christian God creates *ex nihilo* or "out of nothing." Both the singularity of the divine and the notion of creation *ex nihilo* underscore God's sovereign power.

The correlate of the image of God as the creator is the image of man as a creature of God. Contrary both to the Gnostic and to the later Stoic image of man, Christians from the outset deny the identity of man and God by affirming the creaturely status of humankind. Human beings are not on the same plane with God and are in no way self-sufficient. They depend upon God absolutely for their initial creation and for sustaining their lives. In this respect, the image of man as a creature of God involves a novel departure from other images of that age. The work of Irenaeus, a second-century Christian apologist, serves to illustrate this change. In his famous treatise, *Against Heresies*, Irenaeus addressed himself directly to the major differences between Christianity and Gnoticism.

Near the opening of his argument, Irenaeus composed an early version of the Christian rule of faith that by the seventh century was known as the Apostles' Creed. According to Irenaeus and other members of the young Christian community, this rule gives a concise summary of the central tenets of the faith. The rule originally was worked out to offer Christians a guide by which to separate heretical claims from accepted Christian beliefs. The first lines of the rule read,

> Now the Church, although scattered over the whole civilized world to the end of the earth, received from the apostles and their disciples its faith in one God, the Father Almighty, who made the heaven, and the earth, and the seas, and all that is in them.[31]

Irenaeus' statement of the rule immediately distinguishes the Christian position from both the Greek and the Gnostic images. There is Irenaeus' belief in "one God." Irenaeus evinced a monotheistic standpoint that is in self-conscious opposition to pagan polytheism. Again, the one God is the creator of the world. This affirmation was deemed important enough to be placed at the very beginning of the creedal statement. Its significance becomes apparent when we recognize how Irenaeus' ideas vary from those of later Stoics such as Cicero. Irenaeus made it perfectly clear that God is not identical with the world, but exists apart from the cosmos as its creative source and continuing ground. But in rejecting a pantheistic monism, Irenaeus did not develop a radical dualism like Gnosticism. God and world are not opposed to one another as good and evil or light and darkness. The world is not a sink of corruption. Irenaeus' rule of faith affirms that the world has been created by the one and only Almighty God, the Father. That Irenaeus understood this conviction to be directly at odds with one of the most fundamental principles of Gnosticism is apparent from his statement that

> It is not true, as they [the Gnostics] say, that the Fashioner is one and the Father of the Lord another, the Son of the Fashioner one being, the Christ from on high another, who remained free from suffering, descending on Jesus the Son of the Fashioner and returning again to his Pleroma; [they allege] that the Beginning was the Only-begotten, and Logos the Son of the Only-begotten, and that this world order in which we live was not made by the supreme God but by some power far inferior to him and cut off from contact with those things which are invisible and ineffable. The disciple of the Lord [John] wished to cut off all such ideas and to establish the rule of truth in the Church, that there is one God Almighty who made all things by His Word, both visible and invisible, and also to indicate that through the same Word through whom God made this world order He also bestowed salvation on the men who belong to this order.[32]

Two noteworthy consequences follow from the claim that God created the world. In the first place, the Christian can believe with the Greek that the world is orderly. Against the Gnostic who regards the world as raging chaos, the Christian sees the world as the product of a divine creative mind. There remains, however, a significant cleavage between the Greek and the Christian positions on this issue. Unlike the Greek, for whom the principle of order is inherent in the cosmos, the Christian believes worldly order to ensue from the exercise of the creative will of a personal God who transcends the cosmos. For the Christian, the world is good. As Genesis proclaims, "God saw all He had made, and indeed it was very good" (Genesis 1:31). Because God is holy, just, and good, it seems impossible that his creation would be evil and corrupt. Here is a striking instance of the effort of early Christian authors to navigate the narrow pass between Gnostic and Hellenic images of the world. In opposition to the Gnostic view of the world as a completely evil prison, Irenaeus avowed that as the creation of a good God, the world itself is good. In contrast with the Greek deification of the cosmos, Irenaeus' doctrine of the goodness of the world did not imply its divinity, but asserted that it issues from a divine creator who is greater than his creation.

Christianity was sorely troubled by the prevalence of evil and disorder so apparent in the world. How would this vision of an ordered and good universe possibly make sense to people struggling through the darkness of imperial Rome, often facing fires, lions, and crosses for their religious beliefs? The emergent Christian world-view could not overlook the harsh reality of evil and suffering. The construction of the Christian image of man had to include the affirmation of the goodness of God and of his creation, while at the same time accounting for the origin of evil. With characteristic perception, Paul Ricoeur goes to the heart of the issue in his monumental book, *The Symbolism of Evil*:

> *Because* "Yahweh reigns by His Word," *because* "God is Holy," evil must enter into the world by some sort of a catastrophe in the created, a catastrophe that the new myth [the myth of Adam's fall] will endeavor to gather up into one event and one story in which original badness is disassociated from primordial goodness.[33]

What is this catastrophe by which evil emerges? Surely it cannot be a Gnostic faux pas! To show the way in which early Christians attempted to answer this question, we must turn our attention more directly to their image of man.

Because man too is a creature of God, he is created good. But man, Irenaeus insisted, is unique among creatures, for God has endowed him with freedom. Because of this freedom, man has the active capacity to confirm his creaturely status in the worship of God, or to attempt to assert his self-sufficiency by turning from God. Of course, Irenaeus believed human history to be a tale of man's repeated rejection of God, which is the root of evil itself. The Christian vision as articulated by Irenaeus is not blind to evil, but does deny that evil has a trans-human source. Neither the highest God nor a lower deity is the wellspring of evil. Evil is the consequence of the human abuse of free will. Because people are free, Irenaeus said, they "can bring upon themselves serious illness and many sins."[34] Man is the author of his own affliction, while God is responsible for the good that appears in the universe.

By arguing that evil erupts through man's free action, Irenaeus and other early Christians denied that evil is primordial. Though evil is a possibility entailed in human freedom, it is not designed by God. It is an aberration of an otherwise good creation that is brought about by man's misuse of God's gift of freedom. In sum, the created order is good, though fallen. It is clear, therefore, that in the Christian perspective, creation and fall do not coincide as they do for Gnostics. Innocence precedes fall. As a monotheistic religion, Christianity does not posit an evil first principle with which God must constantly battle, as in many Near Eastern myths of the time. Irenaeus maintained that the goodness of creation means it must be restored or redeemed rather than destroyed or renounced. A more complete rendering of his version of the rule of faith underscores this point.

> Now the Church, although scattered over the whole civilized world to the end of the earth, received from the apostles and their disciples its faith in one God, the Father Almightly, who made the heaven, and the earth, and the seas, and all that is in them, and in one Christ Jesus, the Son of God, who was made flesh for our salvation, and in the Holy Spirit, who through the prophets proclaimed the dispensations of God—the comings, the birth of a virgin, the suffering, the resurrection from the dead, and the bodily

reception into the heavens of the beloved, Christ Jesus our Lord, and His coming from the heavens in the glory of the Father to restore all things and to raise up all flesh, that is, the whole human race, so that every knee may bow, of things in heaven and on earth and under the earth, to Christ Jesus our Lord and God and Savior and King, according to the pleasure of the invisible Father, and every tongue may confess Him, and that He may execute righteous judgment on all.[35]

As the rule suggests, the only way in which the restoration of creation can take place is if the Son of God himself enters the world to undo the damage wrought by human rebellion. The doctrine of the incarnation of Christ points up the essential goodness of creation. Christ actually became flesh and suffered "for this created order to be restored to its pristine state."[36] The Gnostics, in comparison, wanted to disavow the full humanity of Jesus and thus the incarnation itself, for the idea that God could mingle with a corrupt world and depraved human flesh was abhorrent to them. For Irenaeus, such a view did not permit the redemption of the created order and ultimately denied the goodness of creation. Consequently he reiterated over and over that Christ was born of flesh, suffered, and died to make amends for what man had done.

Irenaeus' understanding of the results of Christ's redemptive work and of man's final end put the finishing touches on his rendition of the human image. He held that Christ's life and death "restored freedom to men and gave them the heritage of incorruption."[37] In brief, the freedom man had lost is returned to him by Christ's redemptive act. This does not mean, of course, that man immediately attains perfection. Invigorated with a new freedom, man is able to strive to realize the order God originally had intended. To the extent that man succeeds in fulfilling his role in the created domain, the suffering and the evil that follow his fall might gradually be surmounted. History, therefore, becomes a slow realization of God's intentions. Man's world is no longer completely chaotic, but is a process directed by God's creative purpose. Beyond this historical progress man can look forward to a time of full perfection which comes only after death. But even here, Irenaeus remained concerned to assert the goodness of creation. Unlike the Gnostic who seeks perfection through release from the flesh and ascent to a purely spiritual sphere, the Christian anticipates fulfillment in the form of a *bodily* resurrection. Irenaeus concluded,

Since men are real, they must have a real existence, not passing away into things which are not, but advancing [to a new stage] among things that are. Neither the substance nor the essence of the created order vanishes away, for he is true and faithful who established it, but the pattern of this world passes away, that is, the things in which the transgression took place since in them man has grown old. Therefore God, foreknowing all things, made this pattern of things temporary. . . . But then this pattern has passed away, and man is made new, and flourishes in incorruption, so that he can no longer grow old, then there will be new heavens and a new earth.[38]

Most of the important features of the Christian image of man appear in nascent form in Irenaeus' refutation of Gnosticism. Since man is made in the image of God, he can see himself reflected in the divine. Man, in God's likeness is free, which is at once man's glory and the source of his woe. Through the action of man's free will, evil enters the world. But this evil does not destroy the more primordial goodness of creation. Restoration of the impaired creation becomes the goal of history. To this end, Christ becomes flesh and suffers to rescue men, to vanquish the evil brought by man's rebellion against God, and to reinstate man's freedom to obey his creator. The possibility of a proper relationship between creator and creature having been reestablished, man can look forward to the gradual outworking of God's purposes and to the eternal life that comes at the end of time.

Neither the Hellenic nor the Gnostic image of man, as we have shown, could provide people with an adequate symbolic framework for discerning the meaning of life in imperial Rome. The darkness and suffering brought by social and political unrest made the vision of the world as a harmoniously ordered divine organism seem incongruous. Gnosticism proved acutely sensitive to the mystery of evil and suffering, but failed to offer counsel that could render life in this world significant. Early Christianity sought to redress the balance between the goodness of creation and the evil brought by man's free rebellion by proclaiming the meaningfulness of worldly existence without ignoring evil and suffering. Within the symbolic framework sketched by Irenaeus, early Christians attempted to come to terms with their violent and often baffling environment. The Christian vision engendered a hope for the realization of a more orderly, peaceful, and humane life, which embraced all the contradictions of their experience and provided a pattern that could guide believers' daily conduct.

FREEDOM AS DESTINY

In their book *Creation: The Impact of an Idea* Daniel O'Connor and Francis Oakley observe that "the idea of creation brings in its wake a whole chain of implications. Not that they were all perceived at once. Centuries were required before some of them . . . were clearly understood."[39] Irenaeus' formulation of the Christian image was a direct response to what he perceived as an imminent threat to the young religion. But the very specific situation to which Irenaeus addressed himself made the more general applicability of his insight somewhat problematic. It seemed necessary to give a broader and more systematic statement of the Christian world-view. This task was taken up by Origen (184–254), the head of the catechetical school in Alexandria.

Origen's *On First Principles* is the first systematic theological essay in Christian history. Since Origen, the genre of systematic theology has become endemic to Christian thought. From the medieval Catholic Thomas Aquinas and the Protestant reformer John Calvin to the twentieth-century titan Karl Barth, Christians have been incurable systematizers. Through systematic theology, Christians attempt to stitch their symbols into a coherent, all-embracing web of meaning. Such an enterprise presupposes, but does not create, religious symbols. The completed theological system functions as a lens through which the believer clarifies his place in the world. The quest for consistency and comprehensiveness is the constant guide of the systematic theologian's imaginative construction.

Origen was particularly well suited to attempt the demanding task of spinning the various threads of the emerging Christian vision into a tightly knit symbolic web. In addition to having a profound grasp of his Christian heritage, Origen was thoroughly schooled in Greek philosophy and was conversant with the thought and practices of contemporary religious sects. By trying both to integrate dominant themes of the Christian perspective and to address intellectual and religious currents of the day, Origen's work focuses many of the issues we have been exploring.

To appreciate the full scope of Origen's thought, we must recognize that his reflection grew out of and attempted to address his own experience and the experience of his fellow Christians. Origen was no stranger to the darkness and suffering that we have elaborated at some length. His father was martyred by Serverus in 202, and Origen himself died a martyr as the result of the Decian persecutions. Life in such a hostile world left a deep imprint upon his work.

One theme dominates Origen's image of man—human freedom. We have already noticed the importance of the affirmation of man's freedom in Irenaeus' encounter with the Gnostics. In Origen's work this issue assumes a pivotal position and becomes the fixed point around which all other questions revolve. Origen's ruminations on human freedom, however, are triggered by and are a response to the more basic puzzle of evil. As contemporary anthropologist Clifford Geertz writes, "the problem of evil, or perhaps one should say the problem *about* evil, is in essence the same sort of problem of or about bafflement and the problem of or about suffering. This strange opacity of certain empirical events, the dumb senselessness of intense or inexorable pain, and the enigmatic unaccountability of gross iniquity all raise the uncomfortable suspicion that perhaps the world, and hence man's life in the world, has no genuine order at all—no empirical regularity, no emotional form, no moral coherence." Origen's systematic development of his version of the Christian perspective should be read as a "formulation, by means of symbols, of an image of such a genuine order of the world which will account for, and even celebrate, the perceived ambiguities, puzzles, and paradoxes in human experience. The effort is not to deny the undeniable . . . but to deny that there are inexplicable events, that life is unendurable, and that justice is a mirage."[40]

Origen's deep concern about the problem of evil might seem to make him a probable candidate for a perspective such as Gnosticism. But Origen detected two of the fundamental problems with the Gnostic viewpoint to which we have alluded. In trying to explain evil, Gnosticism seems to undercut the significance of life in this world. The historical process is totally in vain and, in the final analysis, is unredeemable. For Gnostics, evil has a cosmic origin. Though the highest God does not will evil, evil nevertheless emerges through the agency of a transcendent, though lower, deity. For Origen, as for Irenaeus before him, "God is one, who created and set in order all things, and who, when nothing existed, caused the universe to be."[41] Moreover, this one creator God is "just and good." This notion of God made it impossible for Origen to accept the Gnostic view of the source of evil. To Origen, belief in an indifferent, ignorant, impotent, or malicious God offered little consolation. But if one denies the divine source of evil, how does evil arise?

Origen's answer to this crucial query again followed the course charted by Irenaeus: man is the author of evil. His statement of the Christian vision expanded the implications of the shift of the origin of evil from the cosmic to the human plane. Starting with the notion of human freedom, Origen combined this belief with Plato's doctrine of the preexistence of the soul. According to Origen, our lives on earth are preceded by a spiritual existence that is untarnished by corruption. In other words, Origen distinguished creation from the emergence of the material world. For Origen, God's "first creation of rational creatures was an incorporeal one, which was not meant to be in bondage to corruption."[42] Though this spiritual creation was intended to glorify God, rational creatures were created free, and therefore had the capacity to worship God or to turn from him. Man, of course, persistently exercises his freedom to rebel against God.

> All this shows that no one is stainless by essence or by nature, nor is anyone polluted essentially. Consequently, it lies with us and with our own actions whether we are to be blessed and holy, or whether through sloth and negligence we are to turn away from blessedness into wickedness and loss; the final result of which is, that when too much progress, if I may use the word, has been made in wickedness, a man may descend to such a state . . . as to be changed into what is called an opposing power.[43]

Origen related the important consequences of the abuse of human freedom. By virtue of man's turn from God, the material universe comes into being. Human beings fall from purely spiritual existence into bodily life. The turn from God, however, is not a simple either/or, but can be more or less serious. The degree of the rebellion against God determines one's station in the world.

> By some inclination towards evil these souls lose their wings and come into bodies, first of men; then through their association with the irrational passions, after the allotted span of human life, they are changed into beasts; from which they sink to the level of insensate nature. Thus that which is by nature fine and mobile, namely, the soul, first becomes heavy and weighed down, and because of its wickedness comes to dwell in a

human body; after that, when the faculty of reason is extinguished, it lives the life of an irrational animal; and finally even the gracious gift of sensation is withdrawn and it changes into the insensate life of a plant.[44]

In another context, Origen probed the ramifications of this idea.

So far as I can see, the foregoing discussion has sufficiently proved that it is not from any random or chance circumstances that the principalities hold their princedoms or the other orders are assigned their respective offices, but that each has obtained his degree of dignity in proportion to his own merits, though it is not our business to know or to inquire what the actual deeds were through which they earned their entrance into a particular order.[45]

According to Origen, one's situation in this life can be ascribed to our free actions during prior existence. If we suffer, we deserve it; if we succeed, we merit it. While this is Origen's way of exonerating God from responsibility for evil, it is also an important comment on his view of the human image. Man's free actions have unavoidable consequences. The self is, in large measure, what it becomes through its free decisions. The notion of the pre-existence of the soul, of course, was peculiar to Origen and wanes as the Christian tradition develops. But the conviction that man's free actions constitute his personality remains important for many versions of the Christian image of man. Nevertheless, if we consider Origen's argument carefully, we see that his view of the world is highly ambivalent. While he surely regarded the initial spiritual creation as good, Origen's evaluation of the present world is less clear. This world is the result of a mistake, but it is a human error and not a divine one, as with Gnosticism. Origen did not seem to voice the strong affirmation of the world's goodness that we have come to expect from Christians.

Origen sprang himself from this snare by resisting the idea that the fall of the spiritual creation into a material world entails a loss of freedom. Even in the fallen state, man retains the freedom to turn from evil ways and to return to God. To man is extended the possibility of progress to a more perfect spiritual state. Of this progress Origen wrote,

In these ages that are "seen" and "temporal" and in those that are "not seen" and "eternal," all those beings are arranged in a definite order proportionate to the degree and excellence of their merits. And so it happens that some in the first, others in the second, and others even in the last times, through their endurance of greater and more severe punishments of long duration, extending, if I may say so, over many ages, are by these very stern methods of correction renewed and restored, first by the instruction of angels and afterwards by that of powers yet higher in rank, so that they advance through each grade to a higher one, until at length they reach the things that are "invisible" and "eternal," having traversed in turn, by some form of instruction every single office of the heavenly powers. It appears to follow from this, in my opinion, that every rational nature can, in the process of passing from one order to another, travel through each order to all the rest, and from all to each, while undergoing the various movements of progress or the reverse in accordance with its own actions and endeavors and with the use of its power of free will.[46]

Since spiritual advance hinges on man's exercise of his free will and not divine fiat, redemption must be a long and arduous process. Origen thus postulated a succession of worlds through which man passes on his way back to God. As with the Indian belief in reincarnation, discussed in the next chapter, life in this world is seen as one stage in a long spiritual voyage. This world is a training ground where we acquire the capacity to worship God aright and therefore resume our intended place in the spiritual creation.

From this perspective, evil and suffering are always remedial—God does not allow man to suffer for no purpose. The final end toward which God directs this cosmic educational process is the restoration of the *entire* creation to the perfection that marked its beginning. When this occurs, the material world will fall away. The end, as the beginning, will be spiritual.

> Let us now see what is meant by the "freedom of the creation" and its "deliverance from bondage." When at the end and consummation of the world souls and rational creatures have been released as it were from their bars and prisons by the Lord, some of them by reason of indolence will move but slowly, while others by earnest effort will speed along in brisk flight. . . . When Christ "shall have delivered up the kingdom of God, even the Father," then those living beings, because they have before this been made part of Christ's kingdom, shall also be delivered up along with the whole of that kingdom to the rule of the Father; so that, when "God shall be in all," they also, since they are a part of all, may have God even in themselves, as he is in all things.[47]

Yet even at the final consummation, there is no lack of human freedom. The risk of another fall remains. In this event, a material world would reemerge and the educational process would begin anew.

Origen's detailed account of the Christian perspective emphasizes several important features of the Christian image of man and of man's relation to the world. Origen sought to establish human responsibility for free actions and to uncover the wide-ranging consequences of our deeds for ourselves and for others. Origen's position suggests that man's present situation is the outgrowth of past free actions. In this way Origen attempted to develop a framework within which evil, suffering, and injustice become meaningful, and thus the anxiety that Geertz sees arising from "the uncomfortable suspicion that perhaps the world, and hence man's life in the world, has no genuine order at all—no empirical regularity, no moral coherence" can be overcome. But Origen did not believe that the past totally determines the present. He held out the prospect of man's free progress toward more complete self-realization. We might summarize Origen's theology by saying that freedom becomes our destiny—we are what we become through the free exercise of our will. For the faithful, life in the world is a trial and testing that yields progress toward fulfillment. Origen, however, was less inclined than many other Christian thinkers to affirm wholeheartedly the goodness of the world. This is plain in his insistence that when all creation returns to God, the material world will fall away. A story about Origen's personal life underscores his ambivalence about the material world. Legend has it that Origen took literally the biblical assertion that a man should become a eunuch for the Kingdom of God (Matthew 19:12) by castrating himself.

Origen's analysis of human freedom and patient exploration of the significance of the historical process for human development greatly clarify important aspects of the Christian image of man. As free and responsible individuals, human beings are engaged in a life-long journey 'from a less to a more complete and authentic life. By living under the "sacred canopy" that Origen constructs, a person "is made capable of suffering 'correctly,' and, if all goes well, he may eventually have a 'correct death.' . . . In other words, he may 'lose himself' in the meaning-giving nomos of his society. In consequence, the pain becomes more tolerable, the terror less overwhelming, as the sheltering canopy of the nomos extends to cover even those experiences that may reduce the individual to howling animality."[48]

"PILGRIM'S PROGRESS"

In the life and work of Augustine (354–430) we see the culmination of both the social and the intellectual tendencies we have traced throughout the early centuries of Christian history. Undoubtedly, Augustine was the greatest theologian of the first five hundred years of Christianity. His work has remained enormously influential ever since his time.

The gradual dissolution of the Roman Empire reached a climax during Augustine's lifetime. In 410, Rome was pillaged by a barbarian tribe, the Goths. It is hard to imagine the psychological shock of the fall of Rome for the people of the day. Despite persistent problems, Rome remained, for many of her citizens, the highest achievement of civilized man. The fall of Rome seemed to many to spell the end of the world. In the face of this crisis, the old tactic of blaming the Christians for the collapse of the empire was revived. As Bishop of Hippo (in North Africa), Augustine was deeply involved in the social and political events of the era. In one of his most famous books, *The City of God*, he took up the task of defending the Christians against the renewed charge of causing the woes of the empire. In the course of this undertaking, he developed a theology of history that has remained a model for all later Christian thinkers.

But it is as a student of the human personality that Augustine is most remembered. Renowned historian Charles Norris Cochrane goes so far as to call Augustine "the discoverer of personality."[49] William James labels him "the first modern man." Many of Augustine's most penetrating insights about the self are developed in his autobiography, *The Confessions*. Augustine's use of the autobiographical form represents a novel departure in the history of thought. By recording the results of his introspective probings, Augustine defined a new literary genre. Augustine's self-analysis was driven by the conviction that he could reach knowledge of God through knowledge of himself. "O God, always one and the same, if I know myself I shall know thee!" Of course the reverse also holds—proper knowledge of self comes through true knowledge of God.

> I was admonished by all this to return to my own self, and, with you to guide me, I entered into the innermost part of myself, and I was able to do this because you were my helper. I entered and I saw with my soul's eye . . . an unchangeable light shining above this eye of my soul and above my mind. . . . It was higher than I, because it made me, and I was lower because I was made by it. He who knows truth knows that light, and he who knows that light knows eternity. Love knows it. O eternal truth and true love and beloved eternity! You are my God.[50]

In short, knowledge of self and of God are inseparable.

When Augustine turned from the tumultuous events of the time to his inner self, he found no less confusion and no fewer ambiguities. "What then am I, my God? What is my nature? A life various, manifold, and quite immeasurable."[51] For Augustine, the self seemed a boundless, mysterious abyss. This awareness by and large resulted from his recognition of the vast scope of man's memory.

> How great, my God, is this force of memory, how exceedingly great! It is like a vast and boundless subterranean shrine. Who has ever reached the bottom of it? Yet this is a faculty of my mind and belongs to my nature; nor can I myself grasp all that I am. Therefore, the mind is not large enough to contain itself. But where can that uncontained part of it be? Is it outside itself and not inside? In that case, how can it fail to contain itself? At this thought great wonder comes over me; I am struck dumb with astonishment.[52]

Long before psychoanalysis, Augustine realized that there are secrets hidden in the caverns of the mind.

Augustine's meditation on memory opened other equally important facets of the personality.

> From the same store too I can take out pictures of things which have either happened to me or are believed on the basis of experience; I can myself weave them in the context of the past, and from them I can infer future actions, events, hopes and then I can contemplate all these as though they were in the present.[53]

Augustine's introspection led him to the conviction that the self is undeniably temporal. In one of his best-known texts, he attempted to define time.

It is now, however, perfectly clear that neither the future nor the past is in existence, and that it is incorrect to say that there are three times—past, present, and future. Though one might perhaps say: "There are three times—a present of things past, a present of things present, and a present of things future." For these three do exist in the mind, and I do not see them anywhere else: the present time of things past is memory; the present time of things present is sight; the present time of things future is expectation.[54]

People live in memory, in sight, and in expectation. In other words, from Augustine's perspective, selfhood is temporal or historical. Selves always move from the past, through the present, and into the future. This is the constant rhythm of human existence.

When Augustine turned, more specifically, to his personal history, he glimpsed a story of restlessness and disintegration and a longing for peace and unity. He began his confession by declaring to God, "our hearts are restless until they find their peace in you."[55] As the plot of *The Confessions* unfolds, it becomes clear that Augustine's life is the story of his long pilgrimage from restlessness to final peace—a record of his journey to God.

The path, however, is treacherous and numerous obstacles must be overcome. Augustine described the inner turmoil that characterized his life in extraordinary detail and with remarkable psychological insight. Like Christian thinkers before him, Augustine maintained that man is created free, with the capacity to praise or to forsake God. He acknowledged,

My sin was in this—that I looked for pleasures, exaltations, truths not in God Himself but in His creatures (myself and the rest) and so I fell straight into sorrows, confusions, and mistakes.[56]

"Having turned from you, the One," Augustine continued, "I lost myself in the many."[57] It should be stressed that Augustine did not mean to imply creation itself is evil. In full agreement with other authors we have discussed, Augustine insisted that whatever God creates is good. The trouble arises when one views creation as independent from God. To turn from reliance on the Creator to creation alone breeds a restlessness and inner distress, that plagued Augustine through much of his life. But Augustine was perceptive and honest enough to realize his ambivalence about his condition. While he longed for the peace of God, he also found his sin sweet. His soul, he believed, is a battleground for two warring wills.

So it is not an absurdity partly to will and partly not to will; it is rather a sickness of the soul which is weighed down with habit so that it cannot rise up in its entirety, lifted aloft by truth. So the reason why there are two wills in us is because one of them is not entire, and one has what the other lacks.[58]

Moreover, Augustine admitted that he was unable to put an end to this war by his own powers. Though man falls by his own free action, he cannot lift himself from depths to which he descends. God alone can do this, for it is tantamount to a fresh creative act. We should note that the necessity of God's grace comes out much more strongly in Augustine than in Origen. Augustine would disagree with Origen's suggestion that man overcomes the dilemma of his sinfulness by his own free action. Having fallen, Augustine believed, human integrity can be restored only by God's creative power. Here, as elsewhere, Augustine was speaking out of the depths of his personal experience. Driven to a state of despair by his inner division, he could not overcome his plight by himself. He recounted his state immediately prior to receiving God's grace.

> I flung myself down on the ground somehow under a fig tree and gave free rein to my tears; they streamed and flooded from my eyes, an acceptable sacrifice to Thee. And I kept saying to you, not perhaps in these words, but with this sense: *"And Thou, O Lord, how long? How long, Lord; wilt Thou be angry forever? Remember not our former iniquities."* For I felt that it was these which were holding me fast. And in my misery I would exclaim: "How long, how long this 'tomorrow and tomorrow'? Why not now? Why not finish this very hour with my uncleanness?"[59]

At exactly this moment, God acted to give Augustine the peace he was seeking so desperately.

After his conversion from his selfish ways to the path of God, Augustine saw his entire life in a new light. He acknowledged that "God is the controller and creator of all things."[60] Though he had not previously realized it, Augustine now believed God's hand to have been guiding his whole life. Apparent evils and seemingly senseless experiences assumed intelligibility as phases in the process by which God was leading Augustine out of the bondage of his self-incurred sin. Augustine saw himself as a pilgrim who, under the watchful eye of divine providence, was gradually progressing to God. But Augustine, recognizing the action of God in his own life, knew that his personal pilgrimage could not be divorced from the pilgrimage of history as a whole. The story of his life then becomes but an episode in a much larger story.

The City of God is Augustine's effort to plot this overarching story. By building on principles discovered on his inward journey through personal history, Augustine attempted to construct a symbolic framework by which he could interpret the meaning of history as a whole. As his own life had been torn by two conflicting wills, so the entire course of history manifests the opposition of two "cities": the city of man and the city of God. He wrote,

> What we see, then, is that two societies have issued from two kinds of love. Worldly society has flowered from a selfish love which dared to despise even God, whereas the communion of saints is rooted in a love of God that is ready to trample on self. In a word, this latter relies on the Lord, whereas the other boasts that it can get along by itself. The city of man seeks the praise of men, whereas the height of glory for the other is to hear God in witness of conscience. The one lifts up its head in its own boasting; the other says to God: "Thou art my glory, thou liftest up my head." In

the city of the world both rulers themelves and the people dominate and are dominated by the lust for domination; whereas in the City of God all citizens serve one another in charity, whether they serve by the responsibilities of office or by the duties of obedience.[61]

Augustine maintained that Rome, though regarding itself as the "eternal city," actually epitomized the city of man that had been on the rise since Adam's rebellion. The fall of Rome is the first flush of victory by God's city over the city of man. It should not be viewed as a catastrophe, but as a watershed in world history that gives assurance of God's benevolent providence. God brings good out of apparent evil, for from the ruins of Rome, the heavenly city will rise. The dawn of the city of God is the end toward which history is moving. To the faithful eye, the historical process becomes the medium in which God realizes his kingdom. Life in this world becomes progress toward the city of God. Unlike Origen, however, Augustine did not believe the consummation of history to consist in universal redemption. God's last judgment will separate the citizens of the two cities.

In Augustine's two major treatises, we see a development of the Christian vision of the interrelationship of self, society, and cosmos. Man, for Augustine, is thoroughly historical—he lives on the frontiers of memory (past), attention (present), and expectation (future). Life is an odyssey through time. Personal history, however, must be understood as part of the history of one's society. Even this extension of the horizons of man's self-interpretation is insufficient. The individual self and its world are sewn into the tapestry of cosmic time. This all-inclusive cosmic process is not to be regarded as a random series of events, but should be appropriated as a purposive totality. Religious symbols integrate self, society, and world by constructing a meaningful pattern out of otherwise unrelated and unintelligible events. For Augustine, the cosmic process that envelops both man and his social-natural world is governed by God. From this perspective, historical and personal calamities no longer need to lead to the depreciation of and flight from the world process. To the contrary, Augustine saw the hand of God at work in even the most catastrophic events of personal and historical life. Augustine's attempt to come to terms with the history of his own self and of the times in which he was living led him to the conviction that the drama of human existence is a manifestation of divine providence. History is the story of pilgrims' progress—from sin to salvation, from the city of earth to the city of God. By accepting oneself and one's world as providentially ruled by God, one overcomes the disorientation and the anxiety that arise from the ambiguities, incongruities, and suffering of human existence. For Augustine, such self-integration, self-unification, and salvation were the "peace that passes all understanding." It is the goal of personal biography and cosmic duration.

While many of Augustine's most important ideas were developed in difficult theological treatises, his image of human life as a pilgrimage from and to God exercised great influence on the popular religious imagination for years to come. As early as the fourth century we see the beginning of the practice of ritual pilgrimage. This custom continued throughout the Middle Ages, and did not reach its height until well into the tenth and eleventh centuries. As Chaucer's *Canterbury Tales* so memorably record, these journeys often were undertaken out of a sense of adventure and a love of frolic. For those more devout, an eleventh-century abbot outlined the religious reasons for the symbolic journey by describing three types of pilgrims: "the first is of those who seek the holy places for the sake of piety; the second of penitents, on whom a pilgrimage has been imposed as a penance, or who undertake it of their own free will; the third of those near death, who desire sepulture in holy ground."[62] A pilgrim might travel within his own country or travel to distant lands. For instance, in France religious centers such as Mont St. Michel, Chartres, and Notre Dame were common destinations for pilgrims. But more significant were the long, difficult journeys to Rome and the Holy Land. In increasing numbers from the fourth century onward, Christians throughout Europe traveled as far as Rome and Jerusalem. A diary of a pilgrim from Bordeaux survives from the fourth century in which there is an account of the arduous trip through northern Italy, the Balkan peninsula, Constantinople, Asia Minor, and Syria.[63] For many persons the church Constantine had constructed at the supposed site of the Holy Sepulchre was the goal of their journey. Often the completion of the pilgrimage represented the culmination of a person's spiritual quest. R. W. Southern records a text from the eleventh century that captures the emotional significance of pilgrimage.

> At length he (the abbot) came to the venerable place towards which he had so long journeyed thirsting for the sight of it. It is not for me to describe the flow of tears with which he watered the places which were the object of his veneration: when he looked at the Pillar of Pilate in the Praetorium and went over in his mind the spitting, the smiting, the mocking, the crown of thorns; when, on the place of Calvary, he called to mind the Saviour crucified, pierced with the lance, given vinegar to drink, reviled by those that passed by, crying out with a loud voice and yielding up his spirit—when he reviewed these scenes, what pain of heart, what founts of tears do you imagine followed the pangs of pious reflection?[64]

Augustine's image of man as a pilgrim was not simply an abstract theological idea, but was concretely embodied in the lives of countless individuals. For many Christians, the ritual pilgrimage symbolically expressed the nature of human existence itself.[65] The profound influence of the human image that Augustine so skillfully carved on both sophisticated theological reflection and popular religious thought and practice testifies to its enduring importance for human self-understanding.

NATURE AND SUPERNATURE

To arrive at the next significant variation on the Christian image of man, we have to leap forward nearly eight hundred years. In large measure, this prolonged dormancy of creative Christian reflection was the result of events following the collapse of the Roman empire. The fall of Rome plunged Western Europe into a period known as the Dark Ages, from which it was not to emerge for some six centuries. With the destruction of the empire, Europe's entire social fabric unraveled. As late as the eighth and ninth centuries, barbarians continued to raid and pillage what once had been an all-powerful empire. As Francis Oakley points out, for most of Europe, "peace had long since ceased to be even a distant memory" and "prosperity had become an impossible dream."[66] Mere survival became a challenge. Moreover, the breakdown of trade that followed in the wake of the collapse of the empire contributed to social disintegration and encouraged a quest for economic and social self-sufficiency. Through the tenth century, medieval manors were, for the most part, operating independently of one another at a simple subsistence level.

The ensuing social chaos left a stamp on the intellectual life of the era. With few notable exceptions, original thought died out. Retention of the old, rather than discovery of the new, was the most for which one could hope. Christian monasteries that had come into being in the fourth century emerged as centers for the preservation of such knowledge.

The Christian Church was often able to fill much of the social and cultural vacuum left by the disappearance of the empire. During the years following the events of 410, the secular as well as the religious power and influence of the Church grew considerably. "As a result, by the time of the emperor Charlemagne in the early ninth century, there had emerged in the West a single public society—church, empire, Christian commonwealth, call it what you will—a universal commonwealth that was neither voluntary nor private. To that commonwealth all Europeans, even after the collapse of the Carolingian Empire, felt they belonged. And the idea of a universal Christian commonwealth coterminous with Christendom, sustained in theory by the memories of ancient Rome and guaranteed in practice by the universal and international character of the ecclesiastical structure itself, lingered on long after the appearance of the national monarchies until, with the advent of the Protestant Reformation, the unity of that ecclesiastical structure was itself finally destroyed."[67]

Between the eleventh and the fourteenth centuries Europe gradually recovered from the economic and social damage visited by the fall of Rome. In part this revival seems to have been spurred by advances in agricultural technology. During this period, the productivity of medieval farming increased substantially, and manors moved from subsistence agriculture to the production of a surplus that could be marketed. This at once freed part of the population from farming and made possible the support of an urban population. A revitalization of industry and commerce followed. As trade routes again opened, rural life and parochialism began to give way to city dwelling and cosmopolitanism.

During the same period, learning underwent a remarkable reawakening. Around A.D. 1000 Europe suddenly burst out of the Dark Ages with a flowering of genuinely creative scholarship. The social events of the time again had an impact on letters and learning. Increasing travel associated with growing trade combined with repeated Christian crusades to recover the Holy Land that had fallen into the hands of Islamic "infidels" brought Europeans in contact with alien cultures and novel intellectual traditions. The most important aspect of this development was the rediscovery of Aristotle's works by Western thinkers. Largely because of Augustine, Christian theological reflection had drawn its philosophical inspiration almost completely from Plato and Neo-Platonism. In the East, however, Arabic philosophy took Aristotle as its guide. The recovery of Aristotle sent shock waves through the European academic community. In Aristotle could be found a sophisticated and highly attractive vision of man, society, and cosmos that differed significantly from traditional Christian wisdom. Generally speaking, there were two Christian responses to Aristotle: either there was hostile rejection and a staunch reaffirmation of Augustinian and Platonic thought, or a deep appreciation of Aristotle's insight along with an effort to synthesize it with the Christian viewpoint. Thomas Aquinas (1225-1274) pursued the latter course.

Aquinas is the epitome of the medieval systematic theologian. To employ an often used metaphor, Aquinas constructed a theological edifice comparable to a high Gothic cathedral. Reason was his guide, Aristotelian logic his method. Aquinas worked his way relentlessly through every detail of religious import until he was satisfied that he had stitched Aristotelian philosophy and Christian doctrine into a seamless fabric.

In order to effect this synthesis, Aquinas made a fundamental distinction between the natural and the supernatural domains. Though expressed in various terms such as reason and faith, nature and grace, natural and theological virtues, state and Church, the relation between the natural and the supernatural is always the same. The supernatural completes and fulfills, but does not destroy the natural. Thus Thomas did not fall into the Gnostic trap of setting the natural and supernatural in a sharp dualism, but constantly saw one completing and perfecting the other. Aquinas' distinction between nature and the supernatural had repercussions far beyond the bounds of theological discussion. This distinction joined Aquinas' emphasis on the validity of reason to give a new autonomy and significance to the realm of nature. In hindsight, we may conclude that modern science would hardly have been possible apart from his theology. As we shall see in Chapter 6, however, it was the method of rational analysis in the study of nature that ultimately aided in the dissolution of the Christian universe. But that pass had not yet been reached. Instead of undermining the Christian universe, Aquinas explored and mapped it so that it became the durable frame of meaning in what is known as the "medieval synthesis."

By comparison with the turmoil of the Dark Ages, Aquinas' time was an era of revival. Confusion and anxiety gradually were replaced by a sense of order and of confidence. Above all else, Aquinas viewed his world as rationally coherent. The order of the world derives from God's creative power and intelligent government. Aquinas' God is always reasonable and never arbitrary. For God to act in an irrational way is, for Aquinas, unthinkable. As he put it, "There is will in God, just as there is intellect: since will follows upon intellect."[68] Because God's will is informed by his reason (or intellect), the world is always rational. Aquinas explained, "Now God is the cause of things by His intellect, and therefore it is necessary that the exemplar of every effect should pre-exist in Him, as is clear from what has gone before. Hence, the exemplar of the order of things toward their end must necessarily pre-exist in the divine mind: and the exemplar of things ordered towards an end is, properly speaking, providence."[69] In brief, *"Providence is the divine reason itself which, seated in the Supreme Ruler, disposes all things."*[70] Having created the world, God establishes rational laws by the means of which he then manages his creation.

Within this divinely created and rationally governed universe, there are different levels of being. Man's position in the hierarchy of creation is unique. Above him are purely spiritual beings known as angels. Below him is the domain of nature, comprised of animals, plants, and inorganic matter. Man, like the angels, is spiritual, but unlike angels, the human spirit has a material body. Aquinas stressed the duality of human nature by arguing that man is a synthesis of body and soul. In his view of both man and God, priority is given to reason. Aquinas maintained that "the difference which constitutes man is *rational*, which is said of man because of his intellectual principle. Therefore the intellectual principle is the form of man."[71] We have seen that figures such as Origen and Augustine focused primarily on man's will. Aquinas certainly did not overlook human volition, but he consistently favored reason as defining man. For man, as for God, the will must follow reason.

Aquinas argued that the proper end of human existence is *knowledge* of God, or Truth, for "it remains for us to conclude that man's ultimate happiness consists in the contemplation of truth."[72] But how can finite man know an infinite God? The expected answer, of course, is through reason. Aquinas, however, believed man to be an embodied soul. While rationality is man's distinctive characteristic, his physical existence cannot be slighted. This idea has important consequences for Aquinas' interpretation of how man knows. Knowledge, in the strict sense of the word, must be grounded in sense experience. Having received sense data through experience, man's active reasoning powers can abstract general notions that qualify as knowledge. Knowledge not rooted in experience is idle fantasy.

It might seem that this view of how man knows makes knowledge of God impossible, and hence implies that the proper end of humanity is unattainable. After all, how can a person sensibly intuit God? Aquinas insisted, however, that by the exercise of the natural ability to reason, individuals *can* arrive at certain knowledge of God's existence. Again, existing selves must begin with sense experience. By proceeding with care, a person can reason from given features of experience in the world to God. For instance, starting from the contingency of the world, one can argue to God as the world's necessary cause or creative ground. Or departing from the undeniable fact of the experience of motion, one can arrive at God as the Unmoved Mover who originates motion. In every case, the course of the argument is the same: from effect known through sense experience to a cause that is the necessary presupposition of the possibility of such experience.

This form of reasoning brings man considerably closer to his proper end of knowing God. In developing such arguments, philosophy, especially the Aristotelian variety, proves an invaluable guide. But reason alone falls short of total knowledge of God.

> Our natural knowledge begins from sense. Hence our natural knowledge can go as far as it can be led by sensible things. But our intellect cannot be led by sense so far as to see the essence of God; because sensible creatures are effects of God which do not equal the power of God, their cause. Hence from the knowledge of sensible things the whole power of God cannot be known; nor therefore can His essence be seen. But because they are His effects and depend upon their cause, we can be led from them so far as to know of God *whether He exists*, and to know of Him what must necessarily belong to Him, as the first cause of all things, exceeding all things caused by Him.[73]

To advance beyond natural knowledge of the divine, "the intellect's natural light is strengthened by the infusion of gratuitous light, and sometimes also the images in the imagination are divinely formed, so as to express divine things better than do those which we receive naturally from sensible things, as appears in prophetic visions."[74] Revelation completes and perfects the knowledge of God one has by virtue of reason, and must be appropriated through faith. Aquinas put it succinctly: "The existence of God and other like truths about God, which can be known by natural reason, are not articles of faith, but are preambles to the articles; for faith presupposes natural knowledge, even as grace presupposes nature and perfection the perfectible."[75] Though the articles of faith are not irrational, neither are they open to demonstration by man's unaided reason.

As a theologian writing when the Church's power was enormous, Aquinas maintained that the revealed knowledge which must supplement natural knowledge of God is available only through participation in the Catholic Church. In sum, the Church is the mediator of revelation and redemption. To the extent that grace must be added to nature for renewal to be complete, human salvation depends upon membership in the Christian community. More specifically, grace is mediated to individuals through the channels of the sacraments administered by the Church. Consequently medieval piety and worship focused on the sacraments. According to Peter Lombard's *Sentences*, an influential book throughout the Middle Ages, there are seven sacraments: baptism, confirmation, penance, extreme unction, the Lord's Supper, ordination, and matrimony. For most Christians of the time, the Lord's Supper assumed a position of primary importance in regular religious practice. Aquinas explained the central role of the Eucharist in the life of believers.

> Baptism is the beginning of the spiritual life and opens the door into the sacramental world; the Eucharist is the summit of the spiritual life and all the sacraments are ordered to it. ... They sanctify us and prepare us to receive the Eucharist or to consecrate it. Baptism is required in order to begin this spiritual life; the Eucharist is necessary in order to bring it to its culmination.[76]

The extraordinary significance of the Lord's Supper becomes more understandable when we recognize that it was believed that while the eucharistic elements appear to remain bread and wine, they are actually transformed by the words of the priest into the body and blood of Christ. This belief is expressed in the doctrine of transubstantiation. From this perspective, the celebration of the Eucharist is a continuation of Christ's incarnation and a repetition of his passion. By participating in the Lord's Supper, a person comes into communion with God through relationship with Christ. As Paul Tillich points out, this ritual "is the foundation of the presence of the divine and of the sacramental and hierarchical power of the church."[77]

Despite the importance that Aquinas attached to ecclesiastical ceremony for establishing a relation to God, he looked forward to a more perfect knowledge of the divine in the life to come.

> Seeing, then, that man's ultimate happiness does not consist in that knowledge of God whereby He is known by all or many in a vague kind of opinion, nor again in that knowledge of God whereby He is known in the speculative sciences through demonstration, nor in that knowledge whereby He is known through faith, as we have proved above; and seeing that it is not possible in this life to arrive at a higher knowledge of God in His essence, or at least so that we understand other separate substances, and thus know God through what is nearest to Him, so to say, as we have proved; and since we must place our ultimate happiness in some kind of knowledge of God, as we have shown: it is impossible for man's happiness to be in this life.[78]

Aquinas described this final happiness:

> *We see now through a glass in a dark manner; but then face to face.* It would be impious to understand this in a material way, and imagine a material face in the Godhead: for we have proved that God is not a body.

Nor is it possible for us to see God with a bodily face, since the eyes of the body, which are situated in the face, can see only bodily things. Thus then shall we see God face to face, because we shall see Him immediately, even as a man whom we see face to face.[79]

Knowledge of God leads to human fulfillment.

Aquinas' thought reflects a world more orderly than that of Augustine or of the early Christians. Plagued neither by the constant threat of persecution nor the anxiety of social and political upheaval, Aquinas remained free to view the universe as rationally designed. His image of both man and God is based on logical considerations. Man's proper end is the knowledge of God. Through the careful exercise of the natural ability to reason, man can advance toward this end. But reason alone can take him only so far. Having reached the limits of his natural capacities, man must rely on grace or submit to revelation mediated by the Church. For man cannot expect more complete knowledge during earthly life. Nevertheless, he may look forward to a final vision of God to be enjoyed after death.

Aquinas' image of man and of the world was suitable to his time. Compared to the chaos and darkness brought by the fall of Rome, the medieval picture of things as providentially ordered must have seemed quite plausible. Moreover, the extraordinary confidence in reason so common throughout the high Middle Ages is understandable against the backdrop of the virtual absence of creative thought during the preceding six centuries. But one has to wonder if such an image of man could survive in more uncertain times. The social and economic recovery of the high Middle Ages proved relatively short-lived. By the fourteenth century Europe once more had tumbled into anarchy and chaos. Christians soon found the vision Aquinas had constructed inadequate for making sense of their experience. A reformation of the Christian image was in the offing.

CHRISTIAN MYSTICISM

In recent years there has been a surge in interest in religious mysticism among as unlikely partners as scholars of religion and members of the American youth culture. "The Psychedelic Revolution" and journeys to the East, both literal and figurative, manifest more than simply an academic interest. In Chapter 7 we will examine this latter-day mysticism. We would be remiss, however, if our exploration of the Christian image of man omitted mention of the very strong strain of mysticism that runs throughout the tradition. Therefore, before proceeding to the last major step in the formation of the Christian image of man, we must pause to consider Christian mysticism. We take as our example another medieval theologian—Bonaventure (1221-1274).

Bonaventure represents a pole of medieval Christian reflection opposite to Thomas Aquinas. Rather than attempting to integrate the newly discovered works of Aristotle with Christian belief, Bonaventure reaffirmed Augustinian and Neo-Platonic thought. With Augustine, Bonaventure could say, "I desire to have knowledge of God and the soul. Of nothing else? No, of nothing else whatsoever."[80] The title of his most famous work, *The Mind's Road to God*, reveals his dominant concern. For Bonaventure, man's entire life is a journey to God. His theology seeks to chart the road to God, leaving signposts along the way for travelers who follow. Preoccupied with inward experience of God rather than with conceptual argument, Bonaventure did not elaborate a complete theological system in the manner of Aquinas. In Bonaventure we see not the urge toward systematic comprehensiveness, but the longing for union with the divine.

Bonaventure summarized the stages on the road to God as follows:

> By praying thus one is enlightened about the knowledge of the stages in the ascension to God. For since, relative to our life on earth, the world itself is a ladder for ascending to God, we find here certain traces [of his hand], certain images, some corporeal, some spiritual, some temporal, some aeviternal; consequently some outside us, some inside. That we may arrive at an understanding of the First Principle, which is most spiritual and eternal and above us, we ought to proceed through the traces which are corporeal and *outside us*; and this is to be led into the way of God. We ought next to enter *into our minds*, which are the eternal image of God, spiritual and internal; and this is to walk in the truth of God. We ought finally to pass over into that which is eternal, most spiritual, and *above us*, looking to the First Principle; and this is to rejoice in the knowledge of God and in the reverence of His majesty.[81]

For Bonaventure the mystical ascent involves three stages. The journey starts with the contemplation of the outer world.

> Since, then, we must mount Jacob's ladder before descending it, let us place the first rung of the ascension in the depths, putting the whole sensible world before us as a mirror, by which ladder we shall mount up to God, the Supreme Creator, that we may be true Hebrews crossing from Egypt to the promised land of our fathers; let us be Christians crossing with Christ from this world to the Father; let us also be lovers of wisdom, which calls to us and says, "Come over to me, all that desire me, and be filled with my fruits." For by the greatness of the beauty and of the creature, the Creator of them may be seen.[82]

Bonaventure believed "that all creatures in this sensible world lead the mind of the one contemplating and attaining wisdom to the eternal God; for they are shadows, echoes, and pictures, the traces, simularca, and reflections of that First Principle most powerful, wisest, and best."[83] There is, of course, an important difference between Aquinas and Bonaventure even at the initial stage of the ascent. For Aquinas too, our knowledge of God begins with the experience of the physical world. But Aquinas began with sense experience and argued to God as its necessary cause. Thus God is not directly experienced through the world, but is inferred from it. Bonaventure maintained that such an inferential process is unecessary, for through contemplation we come to immediate awareness of God. Direct intuition rather than discursive reason leads us to God.

But Bonaventure pointed out that we do not simply observe the world; we also delight in it and make judgments about it. How, Bonaventure mused, can we judge the truth, beauty, and goodness of our experience and of our world? With this question in mind, Bonaventure turned from the outer world inward. By reflection on the "mirror of his mind," he concluded that

> those laws by which we make certain judgments concerning all sensible things which come into our consideration—since they [the laws] are infallible and indubitable rules of the apprehending intellect—are indelibly stored up in the memory as if always present, are irrefragable and unquestionable rules of the judging intellect. And this is so because, as Augustine says, no one judges except by these rules. It must thus be true that they are incommutable and incorruptible since they are necessary, and boundless since they are illimitable, and endless since eternal.[84]

Bonaventure believed that our capacity to make judgments about the relative truth, beauty, and goodness of what we experience presupposes innate knowledge of truth, beauty, and goodness that is not a product of concrete experience. Thus he referred back to Plato and Augustine instead of Aristotle, insofar as he grounded what we know more in personal illumination than in common sense.

Here the question of the origin of this innate knowledge inevitably arises. Thus Bonaventure was led beyond his own mind to the transcendent source of his innate knowledge.

> Certain judgment of the objects of deliberation comes about through some law. But none can judge with certainty through law unless he be certain that the law is right and that he ought not to judge it. But the mind judges itself. Since, then, it cannot judge the law it employs in judging, that law is higher than our minds; and through this higher law one makes judgments according to the degree with which it is impressed upon it. But there is nothing higher than the human mind except Him Who made it. Therefore our deliberative faculty in judging reaches upward to divine laws if it solves its problems completely.[85]

The course of the mind's journey to God now is clear. Man progresses from the outward, through the inward, and finally upward. Starting with an immediate awareness of God in the outer world, one moves to the innate knowledge of truth, beauty, and goodness by virtue of which one realizes that such knowledge must be the result of the illumination of one's intellect by God, who is truth itself, beauty itself, and goodness itself. Consequently the last move is from the self to God.

> In this passage, if it is perfect, all intellectual operations should be abandoned, and the whole height of our affection should be transferred and

transformed into God. This, however, is mystical and most secret, which no man knoweth but he that hath received it, nor does he receive it unless he desire it; nor does he desire it unless the fire of the Holy Spirit, Whom Christ sent to earth, has inflamed his marrow. And therefore the Apostle says that this mystic wisdom is revealed through the Holy Spirit.[86]

The end of Bonaventure's journey is what medieval historian David Knowles calls "the unitive ecstasy of love"[87] between man and God. It is important to stress that in distinction from some Eastern forms of mysticism, Bonaventure does not believe this ecstatic mystical experience to involve the extinction of individual selfhood. The self remains, though joined to God in the most intimate bond of love.

Bonaventure's image of man as the self in transit to a mystical union with God is by no means unparalleled in the Christian tradition. Though often overshadowed by academic theology, for many, mysticism remains an important dimension of the Christian image. A clearer recognition of this fact opens avenues of communication between Western Christianity and Eastern religions. Moreover, it enables us to see that many forms of the contemporary "search for transcendence," discussed in Chapter 7, actually have profound roots in Western religious history.

THE FORGIVEN SINNER

"A theologian is born," writes Erik Erikson in his ground-breaking study of Martin Luther, "by living, nay by dying and being damned, not by thinking, reading, or speculating."[88] A more apt characterization of the gulf between Luther and Aquinas can hardly be imagined. With Martin Luther (1483-1546), we see the reawakening of the introspective consciousness that typified Augustine's work. But we cannot understand the significance of Luther's formulation of the Christian image of man apart from some familiarity with the world in which it took shape.

Luther's and Aquinas' worlds were significantly different from each other. By the sixteenth century, the certainty of the high Middle Ages about man's place in the cosmos had given way to searching doubt, confusion, and anxiety. As Paul Tillich writes,

> toward the end of the Middle Ages the anxiety of guilt and condemnation was decisive. If one period deserves the name of the "age of anxiety" it is the pre-Reformation and Reformation. The anxiety of condemnation symbolized as the "wrath of God" and intensified by the imagery of hell and purgatory drove people of the late Middle Ages to try various means of assuaging their anxiety. . . . In short they asked ceaselessly: How can I appease the wrath of God, how can I attain divine mercy, the forgiveness of sin?[89]

This decisive shift in mood grew, in part, out of changed social and economic circumstances. The revived prosperity of the high Middle Ages was not to last. A series of social calamities during the first half of the fourteenth century brought radical change throughout most of Western Europe. We have seen that many of the advances from the eleventh to the fourteenth centuries were made possible by the increasingly efficient farming methods employed on medieval manors. Such success, of course, depended on an ample labor supply. Under feudalism, a vassal would pledge his loyalty to a lord and would work the manor's land in return for the protection his lord could offer. This arrangement benefited both parties. In theory, a serf could earn his freedom, but in fact most serfs remained on the same manor throughout their lives, resulting in a stable work force. But all of this changed by the early fourteenth century. During this period, France suffered a succession of severe droughts that bred famine, economic instability, and social unrest. In the 1340s the Black Death swept through much of France, Britain, and Italy. In many areas from one-fourth to one-half of the population perished. This human tragedy severely weakened the structure of feudalism. Widespread death and illness prompted a labor shortage, and manor lords had to compete for surviving workers. Such bargaining gave common laborers both greater mobility and more power and wealth than they had enjoyed previously. The eventual result of these developments was the abolition of serfdom and with it the collapse of feudalism. Freed from lord and land, many sought a better life in the city only to have their hopes crushed by growing urban ills. Pervasive suffering and social dislocation brought anxiety for many persons. Gone was the stable social order they had come to expect, and to many it seemed that Europe might be on the threshold of another Dark Age.

In such a situation people ordinarily would have turned for consolation and assurance to the very Church that had dominated their lives in the Middle Ages. But fissures were opening in the ecclesiastical structure as well. The most damaging blow to the power and prestige of the Church came with the so-called Babylonian Captivity. From 1305 to 1376, the pope abdicated from Rome to the French town of Avignon under the watchful eye of that country's monarch. In the course of the Church's effort to regain control of the papacy, two, and for a time, three persons claimed the See of Saint Peter. As a result, the secular power and religious authority of the pope (and consequently of the Church as a whole) suffered irreparable damage. As if this were not enough, severe financial pressures forced the Church into practices that did not help its declining position. Religious offices were often sold to the highest bidder, and common folk were duped into believing that if they paid enough money to the Church, they could gain indulgence from eternal punishment. Long before Luther posted his "Ninety-five Theses" at Wittenberg in 1517, cries for reform rang loudly throughout the Church. Needless to say, a church in shambles offered no balm for the despair of the times.

It hardly needs to be pointed out that Aquinas' rationally ordered universe had vanished. It was an enigmatic, mysterious, and often cruel world. The individual was thrown back on his own resources, both in his daily economic concerns and in his quest for religious assurance. One of the most influential philosophical and theological movements of the era, nominalism, reflected these changes. Though nominalism is a fascinating and a complex movement, we can see its significance for our purposes by noting the way in which its founder, William of Ockham, viewed God's activity. We will recall that, for Aquinas, God always acts reasonably—God's intellect presides over his will—producing a rational world. Ockham, however, gave priority to God's omnipotent will, rather than to his reason. He maintained that God is altogether free and acts in ways that are apparently arbitrary. God is bound by nothing, not even his own reason. God's world exhibits neither evident order nor rationality. In such a theology we have a hint of the mysterious and threatening world of the late Middle Ages. The absence of discernible order in the world also means that there is no way to reason from the world to God. Against Aquinas, Ockham argued that faith and reason are opposed and are not complementary. One is not faithful because it is reasonable or because reason points to faith, but one believes *against* reason. Alone in a jumbled and confusing world ruled by an arbitrary God, man must cling fast to a faith that, by all rational standards, is absurd. Ockham's world left room for little other stance.

Like so many other people of this period, Luther was preoccupied with a search for certainty in an uncertain universe. The urgency of Luther's quest was heightened by his profound sense of personal sinfulness. In an effort to overcome his own self-doubt and guilt, Luther entered an Augustinian monastery. Through the conscientious observation of the rules of the religious order, Luther sought to cleanse himself of corruption. Yet the more he tried to be devout, the more aware he became of his unworthiness. At last he realized that his own efforts would never secure the certainty he sought. This insight plunged him into deeper despair. But in a manner similar to Augustine, salvation came for Luther only after passing through a "dark night of the soul." His despair lifted when he became convinced that God freely pardons man's sins. Luther's entire theology rests on the belief in the forgiveness of sins. Erikson phrases the matter well: "A theologian *is* born by living, nay by dying and being damned."[90]

Although the Reformation is an extraordinarily complex social, economic, political, and religious phenomenon, it was sparked by controversy over a relatively simple theological formula. The cornerstone of Reformation theology is Luther's doctrine of justification by faith alone, which he opposed to the medieval Catholic idea that man becomes acceptable to God by accumulating merit or by doing good works. The doctrine of justification by faith instead of works was not entirely novel with Luther. As we have seen, the teaching had its beginning in the writings of the Apostle Paul. However, it was the freshness and personal relevance of the idea that galvanized the work of Luther. Luther recounted his discovery:

At last, God being merciful, as I thought about it day and night, I noticed the context of the words, namely, "The justice of God is revealed in it; as it is written, the just shall live by faith." Then and there, I began to understand the justice of God as that by which the righteous man lives by the gift of God, namely, by faith, and this sentence "The justice of God is revealed in the Gospel" to be that passive justice with which the merciful God justifies us by faith, as it is written: "The just lives by faith."[91]

Luther discerned that his error had been to believe that sinful man can, by his own initiative, win salvation. However, it is not effort but the *character* of a person that determines his standing with God. A man whose heart is wicked cannot win favor with God merely by engaging in right conduct. Citing a biblical metaphor, Luther declared that evil trees bear evil fruit! If man is to overcome the sinfulness he has brought upon himself and gain righteousness, it must be by the sheer grace of God. Man has to receive righteousness "passively."

But this most excellent righteousness, of faith, I mean (which God through Christ, without works, imputeth unto us), is neither political nor ceremonial, nor the righteousness of God's law, nor consisteth in our works, but is clean contrary: that is to say, a mere passive righteousness, as the other above are active. For in this we work nothing, we render nothing unto God, but only we receive and suffer another to work in us, that is to say, God. Therefore it seemeth good unto me to call this righteousness of faith or Christian righteousness, the passive righteousness.[92]

Man can receive such righteousness because the forgiveness of his sins has been accomplished once and for all by the sufferings of Christ. Through Christ God establishes a *personal* relationship with each individual. Thus one's relation to God need not be mediated by the Church hierarchy of pope, bishops, and priests, but can be direct. In this personal relation God forgives man's sins by imputing to him Christ's righteousness. In a characteristic passage Luther explained,

Because of this faith in Christ, God seeth not my doubting of His goodwill towards me, my distrust, heaviness of spirit, and other sins which are yet in me. For as long as I live in the flesh, sin is truly in me. But because I am covered under the shadow of Christ's wings, as is the chicken under the wing of the hen, and dwell without all fear under that most ample and large heaven of the forgiveness of sins, which is spread over me, God covereth and pardoneth the remnant of sin in me: that is to say, because of that faith wherewith I began to lay hold upon Christ, he accepteth my imperfect righteousness even for perfect righteousness, and counteth my sin for no sin, which notwithstanding is sin indeed.[93]

The notion of imputing Christ's righteousness to the believer lies at the heart of Luther's thought. For Luther, a person never in himself actually becomes righteous. The most for which he can hope is to become a forgiven sinner. Since he is pardoned through faith, however, he need no longer be anxious about sin. As

Luther put it, man is at the same time justified and sinful, *simul iustus et pec-cator*. This belief is paradoxical and is utterly contrary to reason. It cannot be established by rational argument, but must be held against reason's protest.

Moreover, for Luther, man is absolutely dependent on God for his salvation. Luther's God, like Ockham's, possesses a sovereign will and can in no way be coerced—not even by good deeds or a devout life. If God chooses to extricate man from the dilemma of sinfulness, it is not because of any claim man has on God, but is simply the result of God's *free* grace. Luther's contention that man never really becomes righteous is another way of emphasizing man's constant dependence on God.

The lesson of absolute dependence on God and refusal to rely on oneself is not easily learned. From the time of Adam's fall, the human race has sought to stand on its own, to be dependent on no higher power. But Luther's experience in the monastery convinced him that self-reliance proves futile. The quest for personal power yields nothing but a forlorn sense of impotence. The certainty for which Luther longed comes when one arrives at the belief that one's guilt and sin are overcome only by God's action. Drawing together the central features of his image of the human condition, Luther wrote,

> This is a righteousness hidden in a mystery, which the world doth not know, yea, Christians themselves do not thoroughly understand it, and can hardly take hold of it in their temptations. Therefore it must be diligently taught and continually practiced. And whoso doth not understand or apprehend this righteousness in afflictions and terrors of conscience, must needs be overthrown. For there is no comfort of conscience so firm and so sure, as this passive righteousness is. But man's weakness and misery is so great, that in the terrors of conscience and danger of death, we behold nothing else but our works, our worthiness and the law: which when it sheweth unto us our sin, by and by our evil life past cometh to remembrance. Then the poor sinner with great anguish of spirit groaneth, and thus thinketh with himself: "Alas! how desperately have I lived! Would to God I might live longer: then would I amend my life." Thus man's reason cannot restrain itself from the sight of beholding of this active or working righteousness, that is to say, her own righteousness: nor lift up her eyes to the beholding of the passive or Christian righteousness, but resteth altogether in the active righteousness: so deeply is this evil rooted in us. . . . Wherefore the afflicted and troubled conscience hath no remedy against desperation and eternal death, unless it take hold of the promise of grace freely offered in Christ, that is to say, this passive righteousness. Which if it can be apprehended, then may it be at quiet and boldly say: I seek not the active working righteousness, although I know that I ought to have it, and also to fulfill it. . . . Thus I abandon myself from all active righteousness, both of mine own and of God's law, and embrace only that passive righteousness of grace, mercy and forgiveness of sins.[94]

In this belief lies the assurance and the peace for which Luther had been searching.

To Luther, the world seemed as volatile and as hostile as it did to Augustine. Confronted with uncertainty and confusion, Luther therefore turned inward. But the self Luther discovered mirrors the turmoil of its world. Faced with outer insecurity and inner anxiety, Luther asked how one can find assurance and peace. His response was radical: left to his own resources, man can never find the security for which he longs. God alone can provide what man most desires. Through his theology, Luther attempted to come to grips with the anxiety occasioned by the breakdown of the Middle Ages. But the lasting impact of his work makes it clear that the problems Luther addressed are not restricted to sixteenth-century Europe, but are part of human existence itself.

Luther's works, however, do not represent a comprehensive statement drawn from his own autobiography of religious experience. Neither his times nor his personality allowed Luther to become a systematic theologian like Aquinas. The very urgency of his quest for forgiveness precluded speculative undertakings. The task of systematically elaborating the consequences of the Reformation image of man was left to a second-generation reformer, John Calvin (1509-1564).

The key differences between the two main branches of Protestantism, Lutheranism and Calvinism, are, for our purposes, less interesting than their similarities. In his famous theological treatise, *Institutes of the Christian Religion*, Calvin voiced wholehearted support for Luther's image of man as a forgiven sinner, justified by the free grace of God. He maintained that

> he is justified who is reckoned in the condition not of a sinner, but of a righteous man; and for that reason, he stands firm before God's judgment seat while all sinners fall. . . . Justified by faith is he who, excluded from the righteousness of works, grasps the righteousness of Christ through faith, and clothed in it, appears in God's sight not as a sinner but as a righteous man. Therefore, we explain justification simply as the acceptance with which God receives us into his favor as righteous men. And we say that it consists in the remission of sins and the imputation of Christ's righteousness.[95]

Again, in agreement with Luther, Calvin was acutely aware of man's sinfulness. As a result of man's rebellion and fall, humankind is sunk in a mire of corruption. Adam, Calvin argued,

> was not the only one to suffer this punishment—that, in place of wisdom, virtue, holiness, truth, and justice, with which adornments he had been clad, there came forth the most filthy plagues, blindness, impotence, impurity, vanity, and injustice—but he also entangled and immersed his offspring in the same miseries.[96]

In passage after passage, Calvin summoned all his literary skill to describe the terror of the depths to which man has fallen.

We must recall, however, the passage from Calvin with which we began this chapter. "Nearly all the wisdom we possess, that is to say, true and sound wisdom, consists of two parts: knowledge of God and of ourselves."[97] The other side of man's depravity is God's glory. Developing what we have seen to be an essential aspect of the Christian notion of God from its earliest formulation, Calvin saw God primarily as the sovereign creator of the universe. For a systematic theologian such as Calvin, much followed from this basic image of God. As he explained,

> Moreover, to make God a momentary Creator, who once and for all finished His work, would be cold and barren, and we must differ from profane men especially in that we see the presence of divine power shining as much in the continuing state of the universe as in its inception. . . . For unless we pass on to his providence—however we may seem both to comprehend with the mind and to confess with the tongue—we do not yet properly grasp what it means to say: "God is Creator."[98]

In other words, if one actually believes God to be the creator of the world, he must also acknowledge that God governs or rules his creation. The doctrine of God as creator necessarily entails the doctrine of God's providence. Calvin saw his interpretation of God's providence as fully consistent with principles laid down by Christian thinkers from Augustine to Luther. He did not shy away from drawing the conclusion to which his argument led him: everything that happens in the world is the outworking of divine providence. He argued,

> We make God the ruler and governor of all things, who in accordance with His wisdom has from the farthest limit of eternity decreed what He was going to do, and now by His might carries out what He has decreed. From this we declare that not only heaven and earth and the inanimate creatures but also the plans and intentions of men, are so governed by His providence that they are borne by it straight to their appointed end.[99]

The two chief poles of Calvin's theology, the corruption of man and the sovereignty of God, are linked in his notion of predestination. Predestination, perhaps the most infamous of Calvin's doctrines, really has its roots in Augustine's thought. For Calvin, however, predestination is the outworking of the implications of Luther's notion of justification by faith and his own stress on the sovereignty of God. He maintained that "no one who wishes to be thought religious dares simply deny predestination, by which God adopts some to hope of life, and sentences others to eternal death. . . . We call predestination God's eternal decree, by which He compacted with Himself what He willed to become of each man. For all are not created in equal condition; rather, eternal life is foreordained for some, eternal damnation for others."[100] Thus Calvin outrightly affirmed "double predestination"—God elects some for salvation and allows others to fall to eternal damnation. But, he insisted, there is no injustice in such a prospect. Because all men are sinful, they all really deserve to be damned. God's election of some to be saved from such woe is an act of sheer benevolence that in no way violates justice.

Though Luther never talked about passive righteousness in precisely these terms, Calvin believed God's sovereignty, providence, and predestination are implicit in the fundamental Reformation image of man as a sinner forgiven through God's free grace. Calvin did not find this picture of man and of his place in the world disheartening, but saw it as a source of consolation. He maintained that "as Christ teaches, here is our only ground for firmness and confidence: in order to free us of all fear and render us victorious amid so many dangers, snares, and mortal struggles, He promises that whatever the Father has entrusted to His keeping will be safe. From this we infer that all those who do not know that they are God's own will be miserable through constant fear."[101] For those tortured by sin, nothing less than the conviction that the soul is under God's providential care suffices to overcome anxiety and bring peace.

The image of man constructed by the Protestant reformers depicts human beings as sinners seeking forgiveness. The righteousness for which people long, however, can come only as God's free dispensation. Calvin maintained that the recognition of man's dependence on God for the forgiveness of sins is simply further testimony to God's sovereign creative power. As God's creation, the entire world is constantly under his providential care. Nothing happens by mere chance. Whether it be in the face of the persecutions suffered by early Christians, the darkness following the fall of Rome, or the uncertainties of life in sixteenth-century Europe, the ability to believe that history is governed by God gives people a framework through which to make sense out of an otherwise senseless world. If, as Berger suggests, "Men are congenitally compelled to impose a meaningful order upon reality,"[102] we might suspect the absence of such a symbolic framework to make the agony, frustration, and ambiguity of life unbearable.

IMAGES AND IMAGE

This concludes our exploration of the Christian statement of the human image. We have charted the nuances and refinements of that image from the earliest days of Christianity through the height of medieval Catholicism to the two primary divisions of Protestantism. It might seem, however, that we have unearthed Christian images rather than the Christian image of man. As we close this chapter, we are compelled to ask: is there *a* Christian image of man among all these images? If we mean by this a single form of the human image upon whose details all the authors we have discussed could agree, our answer must be "no." Nevertheless, despite the differences, we can pick out common themes that converge in a fundamental Christian perspective on the human condition.

Most important, Christians imagine that man is a creature of God. Because Christians believe God is the creator of the universe, they regard the world as neither divine (as it was thought to be by some Greek philosophers), nor as totally evil (as the Gnostics believed). The world is good, though finite and corruptible. Man has a special place in the created order—he is made in the image of God. For early and medieval Christians, especially, this meant that man is rational and free. It is God's hope that human beings will exercise their reason and freedom to praise their creator. But man, who is also a rebellious child, turns from his heavenly father and seeks to live apart from his maker. By this action he incurs sin, from which he cannot, by his own efforts, extricate himself. Man's destiny is decided by the way in which he uses his freedom. God, however, is unwilling to allow his creation to fall short of its intended end. Therefore He providentially guides history toward its proper consummation. Thus God not only creates but also governs the world. From this point of view, history is the gradual realization of a divine plan. The historical process has a purpose, for it is moving toward the city or kingdom of God. The present era is an "in-between" time—between fall and redemption. Hence life is often ambiguous, sometimes cruel and wretched. Yet the misery of existence need not foster despair, for the human condition is always improving. Moreover, human life is a small thing, but it is a necessary act of a larger drama that can be judged only when the final curtain falls. Insofar as man believes he knows where the drama is taking him, he understands the role he must perform. If he rejects his role, he runs the risk of being annihilated and swallowed up in an everlasting darkness.

NOTES

1. John Calvin, *Institutes of the Christian Religion*, Vol. 1, trans. F. L. Battles (Philadelphia: Westminster Press, 1960), p. 35.

2. Augustine, *Soliloquies*, chap. 11.

3. Wolfhart Pannenberg, *Theology and the Kingdom of God*, ed. R. J. Neuhaus (Philadelphia: Westminster Press, 1969), p. 58.

4. Hans Jonas, *The Gnostic Religion* (Boston: Beacon Press, 1970), p. 31.

5. Hans Conzelmann, *The Theology of St. Luke*, trans. Geoffrey Bushwell (New York: Harper & Row, 1960), p. 137.

6. Quoted by Charles Norris Cochrane, *Christianity and Classical Culture* (New York: Oxford University Press, 1957), pp. 154–55. The discussion at this point draws on Cochrane's analysis of this period.

7. John Gager, *Kingdom and Community: The Social World of Early Christianity* (Englewood Cliffs, N.J.: Prentice-Hall, 1975), p. 24.

8. Ignatius, "Letter to the Romans," in *Early Christian Fathers*, ed. C. C. Richardson (Philadelphia: Westminster Press, 1968), pp. 103–4.

9. Athenagoras, "A Plea Regarding Christians," in *Early Christian Fathers*, ed. C. C. Richardson (Philadelphia: Westminster Press, 1968), p. 301.

10. Peter Berger, *The Sacred Canopy* (Garden City, N.Y.: Doubleday & Company, 1969), pp. 26–27.

11. We will have an opportunity to consider some contemporary expressions of religious spirit in the concluding chapter of our study.

12. This term is borrowed from Chapter 4 of Paul Ricoeur's brilliant book, *The Symbolism of Evil*, translated by Emerson Buchanan (New York: Harper & Row, 1967), included in *Religious Perspectives*, Vol. 17. Planned and edited by Ruth Nanda Anshen.

13. Jonas, *Gnostic Religion*, p. 43. Without doubt, Jonas's study is by far the best work on Gnosticism available in English. His penetrating insight has been an invaluable guide in developing this section of our discussion.

14. Quoted by Jonas, *Gnostic Religion*, p. 57.

15. Ibid.

16. Valentinus, "The Gospel of Truth," in *Gnosis: Character and Testimony*, trans. and ed. Robert Haardt (Leiden: E. J. Brill, 1971), pp. 206–12. The foregoing account is characteristic of Valentinian Gnosticism.

17. Jonas, *Gnostic Religion*, p. 69.

18. Jaroslav Pelikan, *The Christian Tradition: A History of the Development of Doctrine*, Vol. I (Chicago: University of Chicago Press, 1971), p. 82.

19. Ibid., p. 84.

20. Valentinus, "The Gospel of Truth," pp. 206–12.

21. See Chapter 1.

22. See Jonas, *Gnostic Religion*, pp. 239–89.

23. Ibid., p. 241.

24. Plato, *Timaeus*, 30B; 34A. Quoted by Jonas, *Gnostic Religion*, p. 242, note. While this particular text lends itself to interpretations consonant with later Stoicism, we should not overlook other aspects of Plato's thought that are more in keeping with elements of Gnosticism. Paul Ricoeur indirectly suggests some of these similarities in his discussion of the Orphic myth from which so much Greek speculative philosophy derived. (See: "The Myth of the Exiled Soul and Salvation Through Knowledge," in *The Symbolism of Evil*, pp. 279–346.) The most basic point to note is that the radical dualism underlying Gnostic mythology also plays a significant role in much of Plato's thought. Plato identified the cosmological duality of time and eternity that he believed to be mirrored in the anthropological distinction between body and soul. The self once lived in an eternal realm, but now has become involved in the flux of this world and longs to return to the peace of eternity. It is evident that this image of the human condition shares more with the Gnostic position than with the Stoic image we are about to consider. In order to appreciate the complexity of the formation of the Christian image, we must recognize that throughout the first 1000 years of Christian history Plato's thought exercised great influence on religious thinkers. Some early Christian theologians sought to integrate tenets of their religious heritage and the philosophical framework defined by Plato. Despite these efforts, however, fundamental differences separate the Platonic and the Christian versions of the human image. The nature of these distinctions becomes apparent as we trace the refinement of the Christian image.

25. Quoted by Jonas, *Gnostic Relgion*, p. 243.

26. Ibid., pp. 244–45.

27. Ibid., p. 245.

28. Ibid., pp. 246–47.

29. Ibid., p. 248.

30. As we have seen, the spiritual environment in which Christianity arose was especially diverse and complex. Many different religious movements contended with each other for followers. Our concentration on Gnosticism and late Stoicism does not imply the absence of interesting and important relations between Christianity and other religious tendencies of the day. For our purposes, however, the consideration of Gnosticism and Stoicism should enable us to see more clearly the distinctiveness of the Christian version of the human image.

31. Irenaeus, "Against Heresies," in *Early Christian Fathers*, ed. C. C. Richardson, p. 360.

32. Ibid., p. 378.

33. Paul Ricoeur, *Symbolism of Evil*, p. 240.

34. Irenaeus, "Against Heresies," p. 377.

35. Ibid., p. 360.

36. Ibid., pp. 391–92.

37. Ibid., p. 377.

38. Ibid., p. 396.

39. Daniel O'Connor and Francis Oakley, *Creation: The Impact of an Idea* (New York: Charles Scribner's Sons, 1969), p. 7.

40. Clifford Geertz, "Religion as a Cultural System," in *Anthropological Approaches to the Study of Religion*, ed. Michael Banton (New York: Frederick Praeger, 1966), pp. 23–24.

41. Origen, *On First Principles*, trans. G. W. Butterworth. First published by SPCK 1936, reprinted by Harper Torchbooks 1966, p. 2. Reproduced by permission of SPCK.

42. Ibid., pp. 246–47.

43. Ibid., p. 50.

44. Ibid., p. 73.

45. Ibid., p. 71.

46. Ibid., p. 57.

47. Ibid., p. 65.

48. Peter Berger, *Sacred Canopy* p. 55.

49. See Cochrane, *Christianity and Classical Culture*, chap. 11.

50. Augustine, *The Confessions*, trans. Rex Warner (New York: New American Library, 1963), p. 149.

51. Ibid., p. 227.

52. Ibid., p. 219.

53. Ibid., pp. 218–19.

54. Ibid., p. 277.

55. Ibid., p. 17.

56. Ibid., p. 39.

57. Ibid., p. 40.

58. Ibid., p. 177.

59. Ibid., p. 182.

60. Ibid., p. 27.

61. Augustine, *The City of God*, Vol. 14 from *Fathers of the Church* series, trans. G. G. Walsh and G. Monahan (Washington, D.C.: Catholic University of America Press, 1952), p. 410.

62. Quoted in Joan Evans, *Life in Medieval France* (London: Oxford University Press, 1925), p. 102.

63. Hans Lietzmann, *A History of the Early Christian Church*, Vol. 3, trans. B. L. Woolf (New York: Meridian Books, 1953), p. 302.

64. R. W. Southern, *The Making of the Middle Ages* (New Haven, Conn.: Yale University Press, 1972), p. 52.

65. Victor Turner recently has done some very suggestive work on the religious significance of pilgrimages. See "Pilgrimages as Social Process," *Dramas, Fields, and Metaphors: Symbolic Action in Human Society* (Ithaca: Cornell University Press, 1974), pp. 166–80.

66. Francis Oakley, *The Medieval Experience* (New York: Charles Scribner's Sons, 1974), p. 78.

67. Ibid., pp. 53–54.

68. Thomas Aquinas, *Introduction to St. Thomas Aquinas*, ed. A. C. Pegis (New York: Random House, 1948), p. 193.

69. Ibid., p. 215.

70. Ibid.

71. Ibid., p. 292.

72. Ibid., p. 453.

73. Ibid., pp. 93–94.

74. Ibid., p. 95.

75. Ibid., p. 24.

76. Thomas Aquinas, *Summa Theologica*, Vol. 58 (New York: McGraw-Hill Book Company, 1963), p. 11.

77. Paul Tillich, *A History of Christian Thought*, ed. Carl Braaten (New York: Harper & Row, 1968), p. 157.

78. Aquinas, *Introduction to St. Thomas Aquinas*, p. 463.

79. Ibid., p. 469.

80. Augustine, *Soliloquies*, chap. 11.

81. Bonaventure, *The Mind's Road to God*, trans. G. Boas (New York: Bobbs-Merrill Company, 1953), p. 8.

82. Ibid., pp. 10–11. Italics added.

83. Ibid., p. 20.

84. Ibid., pp. 18–19.

85. Ibid., p. 25.

86. Ibid., p. 44.

87. David Knowles, *The Evolution of Medieval Thought* (New York: Random House, 1962), p. 242.

88. Erik H. Erikson, *Young Man Luther* (New York: W. W. Norton and Company, 1962), p. 251.

89. Paul Tillich, *The Courage to Be* (New Haven, Conn.: Yale University Press, 1952), pp. 58–59.

90. Erikson, *Young Man Luther*, p. 251.

91. Quoted in "Introduction" to *Luther: Lectures on Romans*, trans. and ed. W. Pauck, (Philadelphia: Westminster Press, 1961), p. *xxxvii*.

92. Luther, "Commentary on Galatians," *Martin Luther: Selections from His Writings*, ed. J. Dillenberger, (Garden City, N.Y.: Doubleday & Company, 1961),

p. 101. Originally published by James Clarke & Co. Ltd., 1953.
93. Ibid., p. 129.
94. Ibid., pp. 101–2.
95. Calvin, *Institutes*, p. 726.
96. Ibid., p. 246.
97. Ibid., p. 35.
98. Ibid., p. 197.
99. Ibid., p. 207.
100. Ibid., p. 926.
101. Ibid., p. 922.
102. Berger, *Sacred Canopy*, p. 22.

FOR FURTHER READING

AQUINAS, ST. THOMAS, *Introduction to St. Thomas Aquinas*, ed. Anton C. Pegis. New York: The Modern Library, 1948. A collection of readings taken from Aquinas' two major works, *Summa Theologica* and *Summa Contra Gentiles*; includes topics on Aquinas' view of God, man, the law, and grace.

AUGUSTINE, *The Basic Writings of Saint Augustine*, 2 vols., ed. Whitney J. Oates. New York: Random House, 1948. Selections from Augustine's most important writings, such as *The Confessions*, *Soliloquies*, *On Nature and Grace*, *The Enchridion*, and *On Grace and Free Will*; lengthy sections of *The City of God* and *On the Trinity* reproduced.

BERNARD OF CLAIRVAUX, *The Steps of Humility*, trans. G. B. Burch. South Bend, Ind.: University of Notre Dame Press, 1963. A significant work by one of the leading medieval mystics; Burch's insightful introductory essay on Bernard's epistemology makes this a particularly useful edition.

BETTENSON, HENRY, ed., *Documents of the Christian Church*. New York: Oxford University Press, 1963. An extensive collection of ecclesiastical documents dating from the earliest years of the Church.

BONAVENTURE, *The Mind's Road to God*, trans. G. Boas. New York: Bobbs-Merrill Company, 1953. A classic statement of medieval mystical theology.

BROWN, PETER, *Augustine of Hippo: A Biography*. Berkeley: University of California Press, 1969. A masterful study of Augustine and his time; illuminates both intellectual and social currents characteristic of the fourth and fifth centuries.

CALVIN, JOHN, *The Institutes of the Christian Religion*, 2 vols., ed. J. T. McNeill, trans. F. L. Battles. Philadelphia: Westminster Press, 1976. The definitive systematic statement of Reformation theology; careful organization of this edition makes it easy to locate Calvin's thoughts on specific issues.

CANNON, WILLIAM R., *History of Christianity in the Middle Ages*. New York: Abingdon Press, 1960. Covers the period from the fall of Rome to the fall of Constantinople; attempts to place theological discussions in their social, political, and ecclesiastical contexts.

COCHRANE, CHARLES NORRIS, *Christianity and Classical Culture*. New York: Oxford University Press, 1957. An enormously learned study of social and intellectual developments during the first four centuries of Christian history; difficult, but one of the best books on this period.

ERIKSON, ERIK, *Young Man Luther*. New York: W. W. Norton and Company, 1962. A subtle study of the influence of psychological and social factors on the life and thought of Luther; not only valuable as a piece of historical analysis but raises many important methodological issues related to the study of religion.

GAGER, JOHN G., *Kingdom and Community: The Social World of Early Christianity*. Englewood Cliffs, N.J.: Prentice-Hall, 1975. An innovative study of social forces that exerted strong influence on early Christianity; skillfully draws together many of the most important recent advances in sociological analyses of religion to develop a novel and accessible argument.

GRANT, R. M., *Gnosticism: A Source Book of Heretical Writings from the Early Christian Period*. New York: Harper & Row, 1961. A useful collection of early writings not otherwise readily available.

125

JONAS, HANS, *The Gnostic Religion*. Boston: Beacon Press, 1963. Remains the best treatment of Gnosticism in English; integrates a large body of diverse literature by organizing study around central themes; generous quotations from Gnostic texts included.

KELLY, J. N. D., *Early Christian Doctrines*. New York: Harper & Row, 1960. A lucid summary of doctrinal debates from the apostolic period through the Council of Chalcedon.

KNOWLES, DAVID, *The Evolution of Medieval Thought*. New York: Random House, 1962. An excellent single-volume study of medieval thought; clear and concise summary of the importance of Plato and Aristotle for philosophy and theology during the Middle Ages covered in the introductory chapter.

MCNEILL, JOHN T., *The History and Character of Calvinism*. New York: Oxford University Press, 1970. Gives a detailed account of Calvin's life and thought; traces the development of Calvinism in Europe and America.

OAKLEY, FRANCIS, *The Medieval Experience: Foundations of Western Cultural Singularity*. New York: Charles Scribner's Sons, 1974. A very careful exploration of the texture of medieval experience and the character of medieval thought; thoughtful, lively account on themes as diverse as economic life, politics, reason and faith, and ecclesiastical history.

PETRY, RAY C., ed., *Late Medieval Mysticism*. Philadelphia: Westminster Press, 1967. A collection of readings from the works of mystics such as Bernard, the Victorines, Francis of Assisi, Bonaventure, Eckhart, Suso, and others; helpful commentary added to the readings.

TILLICH, PAUL, *A History of Christian Thought*, ed. Carl Braaten. New York: Harper & Row, 1968. Development of Christian thought from biblical times to the Englightenment by one of this century's most distinguished theologians; focuses sharply the significance of numerous theological and philosophical issues.

Religions and the Human Image
In India

4

The ancient roads to India wind through mountains of perpetual snow, crossing passes over 11,000 feet high, and in the shadow of peaks rising 5 miles above sea level. These strenuous trails disgorge upon vast high plains stretching, it would seem, to the edges of the earth. Those who came to India—the conquerors, traders, adventurers, ambassadors, and pilgrims—arrived by passing through an experience of immensity. They were dwarfed by mountains so high they must have wings, so dangerous that their auspicious powers must be placated. These mountains and high plains lifted them near the stars, to gaze upon the face of the moon, but also to be seared by the infernal heat of the summer sun. The hills and sky, the endless stretching plains, the billowing clouds that build for months, the drenching monsoon rains are all drawn in colossal scale. They reiterate and continually renew the experience of immensity.

THE IMAGE OF IMMENSITY

Having come through immensity to India, and having organized a new style of civilization for themselves and those they conquered, both in the valley of the Indus and across the great central plain into the valleys of the Jamnā and the Ganges Rivers, the ancient poet-priests sang a hymn of the Cosmic Person, *Puruṣa*. This hymn is one of the famous passages from Book X of the *Ṛg Veda*.

"Hymn to Puruṣa"

Thousand-headed was the Puruṣa,
thousand-eyed, thousand-footed.

He embraced the earth on all sides,
and still stood beyond by the breadth of ten fingers.

The Puruṣa is this all,
that which was, and which shall be.
He is the Lord of Immortality,
which he grows beyond through the food of sacrifice.

Such is his greatness,
and still greater than that
is the Puruṣa.

One fourth of him is all beings.
Three fourths of him is the immortal in Heaven.
Thence in all directions he spread abroad,
as that which eats,
and that which eats not.

From him Viraj[1] was born;
from Viraj the Puruṣa.
He, when born, reached beyond the earth
as well as before.

When the Gods spread out the sacrifice
with Puruṣa as oblation,
spring was its ghee,
summer the fuel,
autumn the oblation.

As the sacrifice on the strewn grass
they besprinkled the Puruṣa,
born in the beginning.
With him the Gods sacrificed,
and the *Sādhyas* and the sages.

From that sacrifice completely offered
was the sprinkled ghee collected.
He made it the beasts of the air,
of the forest, and those of the village.

From that sacrifice completely offered
were born the Verses (*Ṛg Veda*).
and the rhythmic melodies (*Sāma Veda*).
The meters were born from it.
From it were born the sacrificial formula (*Yajur Veda*).

From it were born horses,
and they that have two rows of teeth.
Cattle were born from it.
From it were born goats and sheep.

When they divided the Puruṣa,
 into how many parts did they arrange him?
 What was his mouth?
 What his two arms?
 What are his thighs and feet called?

The *brāhmin* was his mouth,
 his two arms were made the *rājanya* (warrior),
 his two things the *vaiśya* (trader and agriculturalist),
 from his feet the *sūdra* (servile class) was born.

The moon was born from his spirit (*manas*),
 from his eye was born the sun.
 From his mouth Indra and Agni,
 from his breath Vāyu (wind) was born.

From his navel arose the middle sky,
 from his head the heaven originated.
 From his feet the earth,
 the quarters from his ear.
 Thus did they fashion the worlds.

Seven were his sticks that enclose the fire,
 thrice seven were made the faggots.
 When the Gods spread out the sacrifice,
 they bound the Puruṣa as a victim.
 With the sacrifice, the Gods sacrificed the sacrifice.

These were the first ordinances.
 These great powers reached to the firmament,
 where are the ancient Sādhyas, the Gods.
                                    (*Ṛg Veda* X. 90)[2]

Among the hymns of the Veda the "Hymn to Puruṣa" is relatively late, though the inner structure of its imagery was probably already ancient before the hymns were edited. Several images of the greatest significance for Indian religious thought appear in this hymn. In the first place there is the image of the sacrifice as the act of creation, the sacrifice from which were born the eternal truth (*vedas*), the sacred and powerful sound (*Vāc, Om*) that is the essence of reality, the measures of prosperity, and all the objects of experience. From this sacrifice/creation came the order of society, the images of the gods and of the cosmos, and the prototype of the single, most important act man can perform to assure the preservation of the cosmic order, for man too must conduct the sacrifice. This hymn is filled with significant hints fundamental to the history of Indian reflection. There is the suggestion of immensity. All beings of the cosmos are but one-fourth of the cosmic spirit, who occupies the space of a soul, leaving three-fourths of his being to be revealed in ways beyond the powers of present imagination. *Puruṣa* embraces the earth on all sides, but goes beyond these dimensions, that is, beyond the powers of experience to disclose. "Such is his greatness, and still greater than that . . ." is the key to the comprehension of this mode of thought.

The creator-god *Brahmā*'s etymological identity is The Immense Being, and one possible translation of the principle of *Brahman*, the ultimate from which even gods derive, is simply "the immensity."[3] The image of immensity is a difficult one to project. Perhaps it derives by psychic transmutation from the experience of the topography of the Himalayan range and the vast high plains and broad valleys. Perhaps its sources lie elsewhere. Some Hindus understand that they lie in the direct experience of the ancient poet-seers (*Rṣis*), who lived in a more favorable intellectual and spiritual age. In the *Bhagavad-gita*, a much later text, Arjuna is given such a vision of the cosmic form of God (see Chapter XI of the *Bhagavad-gita*) and responds in fascinated dread. Perhaps a story from the traditional Puranic literature will illustrate the concept more graphically.

The Story of the Wonder-Boy

When Indra, the King of the Gods, slew Vritra, the great, grey dragon who had absorbed all the waters of the earth into himself, the world was refreshed and restored. Indra resolved to rebuild the ancient city of the gods on an unequaled scale. He set the cosmic architect, Vishyakarman, to work building his palace, but as the work progressed Indra's visions became ever more elaborate, vast and grand. Finally petitions were sent to Brahmā, and thence to Viṣṇu himself, to subdue Indra's pride and ambition.

The next day Viṣṇu appeared at Indra's palace, in the form of a young boy, a holy pilgrim. He was received graciously by the King of Gods, and after proper amenities Indra inquired of the purpose of the visit of the auspicious, holy boy.

The beautiful child replied with a voice that was as deep and soft as the slow thundering of auspicious rain clouds. "O King of Gods, I have heard of the mighty palace you are building, and have come to refer to you the questions in my mind. How many years will it require to complete this rich and extensive residence? What further feats of engineering will Vishvakarman be expected to accomplish? O Highest of the Gods,"—the boy's luminous features moved with a gentle, scarcely perceptible smile—"no Indra before you has ever succeeded in completing such a palace as yours is to be."

Full of the wine of triumph, the King of the Gods was entertained by this mere boy's pretension to a knowledge of Indras earlier than himself. With a fatherly smile he put the question: "Tell me, Child! Are they then so very many, the Indras and Vishvakarmans whom you have seen—or at least, whom you have heard of?"

The wonderful guest calmly nodded, "Yes, indeed, many have I seen." The voice was as warm and sweet as milk fresh from the cow, but the words sent a slow chill through Indra's veins. "My dear child," the boy continued, "I knew your father, Kashyapa, the Old Tortoise Man, lord and progenitor of all the creatures of the earth. And I knew your grandfather, Marīchi, Beam of Celestial Light, who was the son of Brahmā. Marichi was begotten of the god Brahmā's pure spirit; his only wealth and glory were his sanctity and devotion. Also I know Brahmā, brought forth by Vishnu from the lotus calix growing from Vishnu's navel. And Vishnu himself— the Supreme Being, supporting Brahmā in his creative endeavor—him too I know.

"O King of Gods, I have known the dreadful dissolution of the universe. I have seen all perish, again and again, at the end of every cycle. At that terrible time, every single atom dissolves into the primal, pure waters of eternity, whence originally all arose. Everything then goes back into the fathomless, wild infinity of the ocean, which is covered with utter darkness and is empty of every sign of animate being. Ah, who will count the universes that have passed away, or the creations that have arisen afresh, again and again, from the formless abyss of the vast waters? Who will number the passing ages of the world, as they follow each other endlessly? And who will search through the wide infinities of space to count the universes side by side, each containing its Brahmā, its Vishnu, its Shiva? Who will count the Indras in them all—those Indras side by side, who reign at once in all the innumerable worlds: those others who passed away before them; or even the Indras who succeed each other in any given line, ascending to godly kingship, one by one, and, one by one, passing away? O King of Gods, there are among your servants some who maintain that it may be possible to number the grains of sand on earth, and the drops of rain that fall from the sky, but no one will ever number all those Indras. This is what the Knowers know.[4]

Immensity—this is what the knowers know, according to Hindu imagination. From immensity come important philosophical consequences. The Hindu mind places relatively less emphasis on the world of immediate experience, which is only one of many worlds. The doctrine of specific creation of the earth has relatively little importance in such a system, and creation *ex nihilo* has none at all. Emergence and disappearance of world systems are continual and cyclical, so that it must be the eternal, abstract principles that provide the clues to understanding. Indian philosophy acknowledges a preference for the abstract over the concrete. The categorical image of immensity, however, endows the imagination with enormous cognitive power and responsibility. In an interpretation in which innumerable worlds exist simultaneously and in succession, any feature that can be imagined is capable of actually existing somewhere or at some time. While this principle does not really eliminate the relevance of the laws of thought and the principles of logic that may be based on them, it does raise the possibility that such laws do not apply to all worlds. In the far reaches of imagination a thing may be what it is not, or lie somewhere between or beyond an affirmation and a negation. Only imagination, working through mythology, can structure and reveal such a world, and even imagination can only illustrate, never completely describe it. The religious image of man and god and all their relationships is absolutely essential if there is to be any meaning whatsoever in the midst of such vastness as Hindu thought presupposes. This image of immensity is one of the most fundamental and fertile images emerging from the human experience in India and has much to do with the fashioning of Hindu religious reflections.

THE FLOW OF LIFE

Just as the mountain barrier and high plains compelled the immigrant leaders of Indian civilization to pass through the experience of immensity, so the flow of life in that civilization is the product of the great river systems. It is not accidental that every river of India is a goddess and that many of their names are chanted in the national anthem. In an important sense, Hinduism may be called a river religion.

The principal culture of pre-Aryan India was found within a group of cities along the ancient courses of the Indus and its tributaries. This Indus Valley civilization attained a high degree of urban culture, a sophisticated and complex social system, economic order, and religion, although we can only make conjectures about the details of life among its people. It was through this same area, probably a couple of centuries after the substantial decline of these cities, that the Aryans first established their Indian hegemony. Within a couple of centuries (ca. 1200–1000 B.C.E.) the predominant influence of the Aryan culture had also spread across the central plain and joined the river systems of the Jamnā and the Ganges. Down this broad valley the culture spread, forming the great centers and cities of the Gangetic valley. By 800 B.C.E. these people and their language (Sanskrit) were established everywhere along these great rivers.

The popular novel *Siddhartha* by Hermann Hesse evokes the image of the river to intertwine and coordinate significant religious attitudes and concepts. A great river is a remarkable thing. Its ceaseless and irresistible flow is the epitome of the constant change that is always the same, the becoming that is being. The river originates in some unknown upstream source and in the continual discharge of sidewaters into the main flow. Its destiny likewise is obscure, to join the ocean, perhaps to remain there for some time, amid the waters of all other rivers, yet with a current that remains its own. What we know of the river is its immediate flow, its power, its rise and fall. The comparison with human life in a cosmic frame is inescapable. We awaken to self-awareness already well along in the flow of life. Our ultimate origins remain obscure, and new forces and factors seem constantly to be joining us in the stream. Our destiny appears remote and ambiguous. It seems certain enough that we move on to join the ocean of departed ancestors and all their works, but whether that is the end of form or the emergence of new form for the current of life is uncertain. In any case we are thrown back upon the immediacy of the given life, its needs and possibilities, its power and potential, features to which we must attend. In this way the Hindus visualized life, in the image of the river, the stream, the flow, the "passing through" (*saṃsāra*). This image, along with that of immensity, may be regarded among the presuppositions of Hindu reflection, that is, among those basic ideas which may be taken for granted as true and need only to be properly interpreted, understood, or explained.

This image of the continual flow and "passing through" of life has proved fertile for philosophical reflection. It raises several important questions. Insofar as life is essentially a flow, what is it that flows? At least three different answers have been given to this question in the major traditions of India. The first answer has its origin in the most archaic layer of Vedic literature. These ancient Indo-Aryans personified natural forces and energies and believed that these forces were regulated by a pattern of order. In its earliest phase this was interpreted as the cosmic order (*ṛta*), which stands beyond all the deities. This order is in itself the most fundamental nature of things. On the one side *ṛta* expresses itself in what we would call the laws of nature, yet it implies no absolute distinction between natural and moral qualities, so that it is also a moral order, the law of *karma*, the connection between moral qualities and their necessary consequences. According to this view, then, what passes on are the karmic connections. Events are neither simply the repetition nor the maintenance of their antecedents, but are the consequences of the conditions of the past in a continually moving present. Causes are found in their effects, and moral causes may have effects in other life forms. *Karma* puts morality into an absolute cosmic context.

In a somewhat later stage of Hindu thinking, as reflected particularly in the *Upaniṣads*, this concept of universal order was linked to that of the personal self by means of a series of basic concepts. In the *Kaṭha Upaniṣad* a famous interview between Yama, God of Death, and Naciketas, a brahman pupil, develops the following interpretation.

> Death asks:
> Apart from the right (*dharma*) and apart from
>   the unright (*adharma*),
> Apart from both what has been done and what
>   has not been done here,
> Apart from what has been and what is to be—
> What thou seest as that, speak that!

Naciketas being unable to mention that absolutely unqualified object, Death continues to explain:

> The word[5] which all the Vedas rehearse,
> And which all austerities proclaim,
> Desiring which men live the life of religious
>   studentship (*brahmacarya*)—
> That word to thee I briefly declare.
>
> That is *OM*!
>
> That syllable,[6] truly, indeed, is Brahma!
> That syllable indeed is the supreme!

Knowing that syllable, truly, indeed,
Whatever one desires is his!

That is the best support.
That is the supreme support
Knowing that support,
One becomes happy in the Brahma-world.

The wise one [*ātman*] is not born, nor dies.
This one has not come from anywhere,
    Has not become anyone.
Unborn, constant, eternal, primeval,
This one is not slain when the body is slain.

More minute than the minute,
    Greater than the great,
Is the Soul (*Ātman*) that is set in the heart
    of a creature here.

One who is without the active will (*a-kratu*)
Beholds Him, and becomes freed from sorrow—
When through the grace (*prasāda*) of the Creator (*dhātṛ*),
He beholds the greatness of the Soul (*Ātman*).[7]

Similarly, in the *Muṇḍaka Upaniṣad* a simile is developed that picks up and reinterprets the imagery of the poem of *Puruṣa* which we have already quoted from the Veda.

1. This is the truth:
    As from a blazing fire,
    Sparks by the thousand issue forth of like form,
    So from the imperishable, my friend,
    Beings manifold are produced, and thither also go.

2. Heavenly (*divya*), formless (*a-mūrtta*) is the Person (*Puruṣa*).
    He is without and within,
    Unborn, breathless (*a-prāṇa*), mindless (*a-manas*), pure,
    Higher than the high, imperishable.

3. From Him is produced breath (*prāṇa*),
    Mind (*manas*), and all the senses (*indriya*),
    Space (*kha*), wind, light, water,
    And earth, the supporter of all.

4. Fire is His head; His eyes, the moon and sun;
    The regions of space, His ears; His voice, the
        revealed Vedas;
    Wind, His breath; His heart, the whole world.
    Out of His feet, the earth.
    Truly, He is the Inner Soul (*Ātman*) of all.

10. The Person (*Puruṣa*) himself is everything here;
    Work (*karman*) and austerity (*tapas*) and Brahma,
    beyond Death.
    He who knows That, set in the secret place of the heart—
    He here on earth, my friend, rends asunder
    the knot of ignorance.[8]

These passages embody the fundamental Hindu concepts of the essential Self (*Ātman*), its eternal, uncreated, immeasurable reality, and its identity with the principle of the immensity itself, *Brahman*. This Self, in turn, is also known more concretely as *Puruṣa*, the Cosmic Self, and the knowledge or realization of these identities of Self, Cosmic Self, and *Brahman*, opens the way to release. Such an interpretation came to prevail in normative Hinduism and teaches that what flows from embodiment to embodiment is *Ātman*—the eternal, uncreated Self, that is in fact to be identified with the Universal Self (*Brahman-Ātman*).

The third answer concerning the nature of the flow of life emerged in later Buddhism. It would seem that primitive Buddhism accepted what may be interpreted as a much more sophisticated version of the first view; that is, the Buddha is widely reported to have denied the existence of *Ātman*, to have taught that the "self" is a misleading verbal symbol that has no object of reference. The self is merely the flow of its constituent elements; the physical body, sensations, perceptions, feelings, and states of consciousness, and to think otherwise is to plant the seed that will ultimately flower in suffering. Later, however, the philosophical obscurity that surrounds the "no-self" (*anātta*) doctrine was challenged by other Buddhists, and a theory that attributed the "passing through" to a deeper type of consciousness became important. This development brought Hindu and Buddhist philosophers into closer relationship with each other on this point. The concept of a "storehouse consciousness," of which our personal conscious awareness is one aspect, suggested the possibility that a sequence of manifestations of the ultimate cosmic consciousness is what appears from life to life. What is particularly interesting is the fact that these traditions could more readily deny the real existence of the self than they could the continuity of the flow. Indian man observed the flow of life from generation to generation, from obscurity to manifestation to obscurity, like the rivers along which he lived. Every obscurity for one village is the manifestation of another, and every manifestation is also an obscurity. Somewhere must lie that point of view—or state of consciousness—from which one sees and knows the whole flow of things, but it would be a supreme vision to see. Attaining that perspective becomes a goal in life. To so envision the flow of everything and thus to be apart from its daily, continual movement is the image of liberation in Indian religion. By these two images—immensity and flow—we are brought into two basic realms of Indian religious reflection. Immensity ushers our thoughts into the understanding of God, and flow depicts the life of man. Therefore it is the relations of these two presuppositions that form the strategies and goals of Indian religious life and thought in its various forms.

HINDUISM I: THE PATH OF THE ANCESTORS

The dominant social structure of classical Indian culture with important religious sanction is *caste*, and caste is a complex social notion. It is important to see how it is that caste functions both within the structures of the society and daily life and, more importantly for our purposes, within the system of images and visions of what life is for and about. Caste must be understood as both a theoretical construct of more or less ideal types of personality and social structures and also, in a somewhat different form, as a network of actual social relationships. The *theory* of caste has origins and sanctions in the ancient Veda, particularly in the "Hymn to Puruṣa" quoted earlier, elaborated in the *Laws of Manu* and elsewhere. The social structure has its origins and sanctions in a complex web of interpersonal transactions, status, and local tradition, which governs the daily relations in persons in an hierarchical society. These two meanings have never been fully harmonized. The theory of caste portrays primarily the division of society into four great categories (*varna*)—the Brahman intellectual and priestly leadership, the *Kṣatriya* warriors and administrators, the *Vaiśya* agriculturalists and merchants, and the *Śudra* servants and menial laborers. Although this obviously is both a division of labor and a theory of personality types, its basic intent is rooted in an interpretation of the cosmic structure. *Varna* is a kind of species designation. One's *varna* is inescapable and inevitably fixed by birth, though it can be misinterpreted or misapplied. One is born into caste. It is not really possible to be human and casteless, any more than it is possible to be human and boneless. Just as the doctrine of *samsāra* predicates a series of births for the eternal *ātman*, so also Hindus visualize a series of births through which one will pass in the normal course of any one lifetime. Each birth inducts one into new possibilities and responsibilities (*dharma*). Some of the major religious/ social ceremonies of home and family (*samskāras*) mark these major intervening births and the stages of life which they represent.

The imagery of three of these intervening births may especially be noted. The first is *upanāyana*, the investiture with the sacred thread, marking the birth of an upper-caste boy into his religious inheritance. This ceremony concludes the gestation of infancy and childhood and expels the person into the serious world of truth and adult experience. By it one becomes *brahmacārin*, a student of the Vedic lore and tradition, becomes the ward of a preceptor, and is morally accountable for his own personality. Another of the ceremonies marking the basic stages of life is marriage. Marriages usually are arranged by the families so as to take full account of the necessities of caste, astrological readings, and inter-family relations. This *samskāra* inducts one into the stage of life of the house-holder. In this stage one is obliged to the ancestors to provide a son and heir, and to the gods to worship properly, honoring the ancestors, to greet the sun ritually, to tend the household fires, and to conduct *pūja*, worship, before the household images. One is expected to cultivate, for the sake of oneself and one's family, the seeds of prosperity and joy. These needs for security (*artha*) and pleasure (*kāma*) must be nurtured with a sense of personal and social responsibility that will make true prosperity and happiness possible. Householder and wife have been born together, through their marriage, into a responsibility and hope that they will share, to respond to the gifts of the gods by worship, by careful rearing of their children, by the full expression of the talents and opportunities that their particular place in the whole scheme of things has given them. The third birth is death. For the vast majority it is marked by the *piṅda* rites, the funerary observances whereby the corpse is destroyed by cremation fires and the soul is conducted, with all due respect and devotion of the living, to the world of the ancestors. For some few, however, the funeral precedes the physical death and is conducted by a man already dead to a world that life normally represents. This is the initiation of the *sannyāsī*, the holy man, the one who enters into the stage beyond.

In an autobiographical account, *The Ochre Robe*, Agehānanda Bhāratī, a contemporary monk-professor, described his experience of this ceremony. Though a European he was accepted for initiation into *sannyāsa* by a distinguished Swami from South India. The Swami spent the afternoon instructing him concerning the life and needs of a *sādhū* (holy man). Then he rested. Just before midnight, he joined the Swami at the Maṇikarṇikā ghat of Benares, at the edge of the Ganges, the largest and most sacred cremation grounds in India. Three cremation fires burned brightly in the Indian night.

A *maṇḍala* had been drawn near the centre of the platform in red and white of the prescribed form. I sat down and now I noticed that I was sitting in the geometrical centre of an almost equilateral triangle formed by the three pyres. Swami Visvānanda sat in front of me and did *ācamana* with his left hand: the left hand rules over rituals connected with *sannyāsa*, whereas the right hand functions on all other occasions. He lit another fire from sandlewood, placing it between himself and the *maṇḍala* wherein I was sitting. He handed me two handfuls of sesamum seed and kept about the same amount. The chant began: (. . . I am now beyond life and death, hunger and grief, satisfaction and dissatisfaction.) With twenty-three *svāhās*, the sesamum and the rest of the oblational ingredients are thrown into the *virajā-homa*, the fire of final renunciation. Lastly the *ācārya* cut off the *śikhā* (hair tuft) from my head, the well-trained, well-oiled, stately *śikhā*, and threw it into the fire as the last gift.

The swami asked me to stand up. I followed him to another, much smaller platform which I had not seen before. Here was a small pyre of wood, not yet alight. I was asked to lie on it. He touched my body in seven places. Symbolically the pyre was set on fire. Symbolically, I was now being cremated. As I stood up, I made my own obsequial rite, with the *mantras* which are chanted by the living for the dead. I was now dead, though the body lived. It signifies: when the *sannyāsī* says "I," he does not mean his body, not his senses, not his mind, not his intellect. "I" means the cosmic spirit, the Brahman, and it is with This that he henceforth identifies himself. This is the only important difference between the monk and the layman. The layman too is Brahman, and so is all that lives. The monk is Brahman, too, but the monk is aware of it; the *sannyāsi* is aware of nothing else. Or at least, he should be aware of nothing else. I now threw off my white novice's robe and all the other items of the neophyte wardrobe—they are not many—and walked down the few steps into the Ganges, with the four directions as my garments. . . . As I emerged from Gaṅga's womb, Swami Visvānanda, who had followed me, gave me the ochre robe, which I donned immediately. "Victory to you, HOMELESS BLISS, Victory, Master Agehānanda Bhāratī, be thou a light to the three worlds."—he spoke loudly and distinctly. This then, was the name he had chosen for me—and he must have known why. Bliss through homelessness, bliss that is homelessness, bliss when there is no home—the Sanskrit compound covers all of these meanings.[9]

Such a ceremony visibly and ritually converts death to birth and establishes the one who experiences it into a new order of life with its own objectives and style. The point is clear. Every birth has its specific conditions to be respected and its responsibilities to be fulfilled. This applies to the physical birth and to the important subsequent " births" as well. Each birth inducts one into a *dharma*, a cluster of specific responsibilities, acceptable procedures, and correct associations. These "procedures" and "associations" governed by firm but not unchanging traditions coordinate the theoretical system of caste as species with the actual social experience of interlocking transactions and status roles.

The rules that govern these responsibilities and obligations are determined by one's role in the system of givers and receivers. In such an hierarchical system, givers are always superior to receivers, and givers of superior gifts have higher status than those whose gifts are more mundane. The articulation of this elaborate traditional network of mutual giving and receiving is the social side of the caste system. Like *varna* the social caste system (*jati*) must be seen as a cosmic as well as a cultural system. *Brahman*—the ultimate itself—gives reality and existence to all that is. The high gods give birth and power to the lower deities, who in turn create the material, evolving world. No one can give anything to *Brahman*. Therefore it remains supreme and absolute. To Viṣṇu or Śiva men can and do give their devotion and commitment. Devotion, in Hinduism, is the "food of the gods." In turn, the gods give men the conditions of life—rain, fertility, the order of the seasons, a dependable structure of nature. Brahmans, priests, and holy men give persons access to the gods through performance of the sacrifices, the *samskāras*, and *pūja* (worship) in the home and temple, so that their devotion may reach the gods and thereby support the world. These exalted individuals, of course, receive gifts of food, clothing, and necessary support from the individuals and families whom they serve. The *kṣatriyas* by tradition give order, peace, and justice to the world, food to brahmans, and devotion to the gods. They receive respect and support (taxes, military conscription, and so on) from the people. The *vaiśyas* give the produce of farm, mine, and market and receive the profit of their labor and intelligence. The *śudras* give service and receive security. Since they must receive from nearly everybody virtually everything that matters and can offer only humble service in return, they are outranked by almost everyone—except those outside of the whole system of truly human births. It is important to see that the caste system is intended to reflect the ultimate order of nature and the interrelated dependencies of complex personal, social, and cosmic orders. At the heart of this view lies the fundamental notion of the harmony of the sociocosmic whole. This harmony is more important than the freedom or even fulfillment of the particular individual. The *dharma* requires a social structure that justifies and rewards the subordination of purely personal interests to the larger pattern. In a perfectly modulated system (as often envisioned in Brahmanic literature) all classes will be happy and fulfilled by the *dharma* of their castes, but whether this is so or not in an imperfect, but authentically human society, the harmony of the whole justifies the imperfect happiness of the part. The ideal of the harmonious social, cosmic order, divine/human relation remains fundamental to Hindu thought at every level. The image can be illustrated by a great tapestry or a handknotted rug in which each thread plays its required part in the pattern of the whole, although its meaning could not possibly be discerned in isolation. This quest for harmony with the needs of a cosmic pattern is another of the basic presuppositions of Indian reflection.

The fourth presupposition we encounter in India is a special interpretation and understanding of peace. Peace is sometimes defined as an *absence of* hostilities, *freedom from* quarrels, or more positively as public security and inner contentment, serenity, and tranquility. The latter of these definitions approximates the Indian meaning. Peace is Being in its purest state. Therefore it cannot be found in any impure state; and once Being has been attained, becoming ceases. Of such peace there may be varying modes and avenues of approach, but there are in the final analysis no degrees. Ecstatic moments of experience, transcendental modes of consciousness may give hints and passing glimpses, but they are only suggestive of the real thing. The world of experience is always muddied with its own imperfection and can never provide an adequate model for the peace beyond all worlds. *Sat-chit-ananda*—infinite being, consciousness, bliss—point the direction, but cannot define the reality. Man, caught in the flow of life, learns so to harmonize with its inner essence through *dharma*, which must be determined by his caste, his temperament, and his stage or progress in life, and the inexorable consequences of his choices, leading to a gradual recognition of this authentic character as *Ātman*, until at last he achieves the full realization that the *Ātman* (Self) is the *immensity* (*Brahman*), and in that realization finds total peace.

The path of the ancestors—doing things properly and in good order—discloses the images of man for classical Hinduism as practiced in India. This path enables each person to find a place in an evolving cosmic system, to acknowledge dependence upon the ultimate divine powers by regular ritual in the home and special observance at the temple and in the streets, to mark and celebrate the movement of life from conception to death and beyond by observance of the *saṁskāras*, and to govern personal and social relationships by reference to a specific *dharma* appropriate to caste and stage of life. Alienation, sin, and moral perfection are strange and unnecessary notions for the Hindu. He follows a well-worn path in confidence that, though the way is long, it is an evoluation toward perfection in which he is engaged, and he will never be expected to do more than he can. He can in no way divide his life between the sacred and the secular. The unique and strenuous disciplines of holiness are for other persons. His religion is to find his place and fill it daily, to have confidence in the gods, to fulfill his *dharma* and not that of any other person. It is a path that does justice to his sense of immensity, makes use of the continual flow of the life stream, always urges harmony, and promises absolute peace. He venerates his ancestors and tries to live as they lived. In turn he expects to be remembered by the living and ultimately to evolve to the utter realization of the true self.

Religious reflection in India frames a vast, comprehensive system of interrelated images. The ultimate and absolute principle of reality—the immensity as such—is beginning, source, and original energy as well as ultimate fulfillment, resting place, and realization of all that is. Within the totality, two basic orders of reality interact. This first one, the path of the ancestors, derives from the image of social harmony and mutual relatedness articulated in the system of caste. Within this general order of personality types, vocational orientation, and traditional responsibilities and status are the subsystems of the stages of life and another subsystem of values and achievements in security, pleasure, and responsibility. By these interpretations the normal course of life is traced from student, through householder, to the reflective "forest dweller" stage. These births induct those who enjoy them into a special way of being, that is, the *dharma* of that birth. The worship of the gods in temple and home, veneration for tradition, gifts to holy men, pilgrimage to holy places, all find significance as part of the way the ancestors taught, practiced, and respected for the fulfillment of the objective of existence, the evolution of soul back to its point of origin in *Brahman*. This path is a great wheel, a wheel of karma, caste, dharma, worship, and rebirth, rotating in incalculable cycles of evolving and devolving forms. The heart of this image is the finding of one's place and filling it.

HINDUISM II: THE PATH OF THE YOGI

Over against the path of the ancestors, in curious tension with and yet completing it, is the way of the *yogi*, a more direct but strenuous path through the labyrinth of life. To develop this image we need to turn back briefly to the history of Indian religion and trace the origins and elaboration of certain fundamental attitudes. The Aryan infiltration of the Indian river valleys and the development of

a major composite culture there continued to about 1000 B.C.E. By this time
the religious cult and social order, which we call Brahmanism, had emerged and
developed its distinctive institutional forms which centered in the performance
of the sacrifice, the use of the sacred *mantra* to achieve supernormal power, and
the social development of caste. The major sacrificial occasions became more
and more elaborate and their perfect recitation more important, so that the
claims of the priests who managed them became more extensive also. Gradually,
however, especially in the regions along the central and upper Gangetic valley,
new interpretations of the significance and power of the *sacrifice*, along with a
new method of internalizing and individualizing the sacrifice were developed.

The individuals who led this ancient reformation are mostly unknown, but
apparently represented both *brahman* and other, especially *ksatriya* (noble),
castes, a number of different geographical locations, and, most important, several different versions of the new teachings, leading to different sects, although
the life style that produced all of them is remarkably similar. Four of these views
will come to our attention. The first attitude we shall call simply Upanisadic
Hinduism, that is, the orthodox form of the reformation, which reinterpreted
without denying the Vedas. By this interpretation the *sacrifice*, which had previously been a public, sponsored, religious event, was to be internalized. The
rediscovery, realization, and reunion of the soul with its source was regarded as
the true sacrifice, that is, the divorce of self from ego and its identification with
the ultimate. The true sacrifice would not be performed externally for external
values, but would transpire internally for the values of absolute freedom and
peace. No direct challenge to the power of the traditional sacrifice to accomplish
its purpose had to be made, because there had been a shift in purposes considered primary. From the *Chāndogya Upanisad*, for example, we read:

> Verily, for him who sees this, who thinks this, who understands this,
> Vital Breath (*prāna*) arises from the Soul (*Ātman*); Hope, from the Soul;
> Memory from the Soul, Space (*ākāsa*) from the Soul; Heat, from the Soul;
> Water from the Soul; Appearance and Disappearance from the Soul; Food
> from the Soul; Strength from the Soul; Understanding from the Soul;
> Meditation from the Soul; Thought from the Soul; Conception from the
> Soul; Mind from the Soul; Speech from the Soul; Name from the Soul;
> sacred sayings (*mantra*) from the Soul; sacred works (*karman*) from the
> Soul; indeed this whole world from the Soul. As to this there is the verse:—
>> The Seer sees not death,
>> Nor sickness, nor any distress.
>> The seer sees only the All,
>> Obtains the All entirely.[10]
>
> (26th *Khanda*)

The meditative, philosophical enterprise of "knowing the *Ātman*" replaced
the task of serving the gods with outward sacrifice. Meditative discipline (*yoga*),
utilizing traditional postures, breath control, and developing ecstatic states of
consciousness characterized this approach. Some practitioners became boldly

experimental with these techniques, while others emphasized a more philosophical style and used meditation and the Vedic traditions as means of achieving special knowledge. Still others (in the later stages of the development of Upanisadic Hinduism) emphasized the performance of one's normal *dharma, without concern for the fruits of one's action*, as the proper sacrifice leading to *moksha* (peace, freedom from rebirth). It is that italicized phrase that separates this teaching of "Karma yoga," as in the *Bhagavad-gita*, from the traditional way of the ancestors described earlier. To do one's *dharma*, with indifference as to the results, by devoting the outcome to God, is a true *discipline*, a *yoga*, and not merely the observance of tradition.

THE HETERODOX FORMS
OF THE HINDU REFORMATION

In the sixth century B.C.E. three very important figures emerged in this Upanisadic tradition. They were Vardhāmana Nataputta, Gosāla Maskarīputra, and Siddhārtha Gautama, principal figures of the Jain, Ājīvaka, and Buddhist sects, respectively. In the ancient Vedic tradition, austerities (*tapas*), that is, energetic or rigorous religious disciplines, were used primarily as *purification rites* for those who would participate in or lead the great sacrifices. In the Upanisadic reformation these austerities became a form of the sacrifice itself. No longer functioning merely to warm up or prepare the ritual performer, they became the central means whereby the freedom of the soul from its weight of karmic debt might be achieved. In the practice and thought of Vardhāmana Mahāvīra (Great Victor), founder of the Jain religion, these rigors became the key to salvation. Abandoning the Vedas themselves as unable to release souls, and the gods as well, since they too are caught in the cycles of rebirth, he emphasized the *vows* which, if lived scrupulously, would not only fail to produce additional misfortunate existence due to *karma*, but could gradually compensate for and remove the karmic burden already accumulated. Chief among these vows is that of *ahimsa*, noninjury to all soul-life. The rigorous asceticism of the Jain monk follows from this vow and its absolute centrality as the only true path to peace.

A very similar view was apparently held by the Ājīvakas under the leadership of Gosāla Maskarīputra, a contemporary of Mahāvīra and the Buddha. These teachings elaborated the theory of karma into a strict and inexorable determinism with materialistic atheism as a corollary. The rigorous discipline of the sect is rigidly welded with their sense of purposeless inevitability.

THE HUMAN IMAGE IN THE MYTH OF THE BUDDHA

It was, however, the Prince Gautama, whose life and ministry as the Buddha caught the imagination of so many, who serves as a pivotal figure among the Upanisadic reformers. For all subsequent history his life has served as a powerful image or model of the human situation. It is not merely an account of the career of a North Indian Prince and religious teacher, but a true myth, a two-sided story, which is also the story of our lives. We should find ourselves in the story of the Buddha.

Like Mahāvīra, Siddhārtha Gautama, of the Sakya clan, belonged to the *kṣatriya* (princely) caste. The traditional accounts of his life, as shared among all Buddhists, can be divided into three phases. The first phase deals with his many previous lives, in which he formed the vow to become a Buddha and gradually developed all the noble qualities of character which that role would demand of him. All of those thousands of lifetimes of preparation were gathered together into the conception of the holy son by Queen Maya. For the last time, in her womb, he was immersed into the darkness of forgetfulness of previous existences in which all are born. Intimations of his character showed through, however. At his birth (beginning of Phase II) in the garden of Limbini, learned brahmans and sages read the omens of his birth and prophesied his greatness. His youth was confined within the gentle prison of luxury, as his father, King Suddodhana, sought to prevent fulfillment of the prophesy that he might leave home and undertake the holy hermit's life. He was protected as far as possible from experience of the sufferings of life, but all the texts agree that in one way or another the realities of life broke through to his consciousness in the form of profound awareness of illness, aging, and death in their personal and universal character. His melancholy deepened. Finally he became aware of a paradox—a monk, standing in the midst of an ordinary village, that is, a village populated by feverish, sick people, exhausted people, a city of the dead and the dying, but the monk glowed with the radiance of an incredible tranquility. The possibility of peace in the midst of full awareness of the suffering of existence was most perplexing of all. But the time was not yet. Prince Gautama married the lovely Princess Yasodhara, who bore his son, Rahula, heir-apparent to the rulership of Kapilavatsu. But despite these ties of kingdom, wife, and child, the personal tension of the paradox of peace and suffering became too great. The Prince departed from the palace in the dead of the night. He undertook an ancient and honorable way, that of the wandering beggar and student, but he gave up a kingdom and all the luxuries of royal life, as well as all the affections of a householder's life to do so. Siddhārtha, the wandering beggar, studied first with Brahmanically oriented Upanisadic philosophers and learned mastery of their meditative techniques, but he found their teachings unable to bring peace, at least to him. He then followed the path chartered by the Jains, that is, strenuous self-discipline and asceticism. This Jain approach gave him courage for and mastery over suffering, but not understanding or appreciation of its cause. Finally he abandoned all, except meditation itself, and through a final siege of temptations won enlightened understanding. Out of this enlightenment came his *dharma*, that is, his teaching or doctrine. His enlightenment made him the *Buddha*, the enlightened one, and initiated the third phase of his existence. For the remaining forty-five years of his life, he continued to wander across India, begging food, practicing meditation, and teaching the truths by which enlightenment may be won. The general principles of his life story are widely shared among humankind. Almost all people are overprotected and reared in the false assumption that the appropriate way of dealing with a need is to satisfy it. Most awaken to the distress of their situation in disquiet at the signs of aging, uneasiness at the possibility of illness, terror at the thought of death. Many engage in fruitless quests to find solutions to this distress, but almost all settle for the available orthodoxies of sensate fulfillment, philosophical dogmatism, or sectarian self-justification. The Buddha breaks through to the true source of the difficulty, the false self that creates and maintains itself and yet is unaware of itself as the very root of all suffering. According to the Buddha's teaching (The Four Noble Truths), to live is to suffer. This suffering is the result of the kind of craving based on the false concept of the self, which we create in our own minds. But it is possible to overcome this ignorance and the desire which it fosters by means of the disciplines of the eightfold path. If one will follow this prescription or path of disciplined morality, knowledge, and meditative wisdom (right beliefs, right aspirations, right speech, right conduct, right means of livelihood, right endeavor, right mindfulness, right concentration) a person will no longer manufacture the false self with its desires and its sufferings. It is the task of the monastic order (the *Saṅgha*) to live and teach this pattern of discipline.

Although this Buddhist interpretation of existence is built upon many of the same images that inform the Hindu tradition, images such as an immense and essentially aimless physical universe, a flowing river of lives and their consequences, a disciplined path that leads through truth to freedom and peace, it is all organized by the radiant image of the *man who awakened to the truth*, the Buddha. His presence was the teacher, his life the message, his fellowship the order of monks and nuns. Together these are called the "Threefold Refuge" or the "Three Jewels" of the Buddhist. They constitute the three primary vows of the layman and of the monk. "I take refuge in the Buddha (the principle of enlightenment). I take refuge in the Dharma (the teachings by which enlightenment may be attained). I take refuge in the Saṅgha (the fellowship and discipline of the followers of the Buddha-way)." In each of these vows, the full meaning is to be found primarily in the career of the Buddha. He was the man in whom his followers can have confidence. He had found and taught the way. He had established the order, its rules, and its purposes by precept, but more importantly by example. For the layman these are expressed as ideals which he supports by charity, study, and devout hope. For the monk the triple refuge is his way of life. One of the most remarkable features of the ministry of the Buddha and therefore of Buddhism is the way in which he combined enlightenment with compassion, the realization of freedom from suffering, which is the achievement of the holy man, with the altruistic devotion to the interests of others, which is the character of the teacher and friend. It is this combination of compassion with insight, made available to humanity by means of a discipline of life, and symbolized by the monastic order, that constitutes the refuge of the Buddhist.

There were, then, several different religious responses to the Brahmanical image of the sacrifice, ranging from an atheistic determinism (*Ājīvaka*), through an ascetic internalization of the sacrifice (*Jain*), and the extinction of individuality in the mode of the universal awakening (*Buddhist*), to the Upanisadic reformers with their *Orthodox Hindu* reinterpretation of the quest for the identity of self-hood and god-hood. In India all of these alternative religious images flourished through the classical age of the Imperial Guptas (third to seventh centuries C.E.). Gradually, however, out of these interacting images emerged another, the way of the devotee, the *bhakta*.

HINDUISM III: THE PATH OF THE DEVOTED SOUL

In one way or another all the native religions of India are daughters of the sacrifice. Its purification rites became ascetic religion. Its inner essence in the sacred *mantra* became the object of vedantic "self"-realization. Its divine powers and presences, mingled with local deities of many cults, became the many gods and goddesses of the Indian pantheon, expressions of the *deva*-power, the power for good, of the ultimate itself. Its traditions of birth and *dharma* became the rites of passage, and its fires, the fires of home and family rituals in ancestral religion. The sacrifice of the Self became the *dharma* of the Buddha and the objective of ascetics. Preeminently it was in the emergence of the vast mythological corpus, first of the *Mahābhārata* and then the more sectarian books, the *Purāṇas*, that the ground was laid for the understanding of the sacrifice by means of Indian devotionalism. It seems reasonable to assume that the power of the image of the person of the Buddha also helped to inspire this Hindu tradition. When Kṛṣṇa was identified with Viṣṇu and the various accounts of his career were blended together, the fulfillment of the emotional power of true devotionalism was possible.

The basic ingredient in devotionalism is a sense of the *grace of god*. The struggle to reach the divine is too difficult for man alone. Save for a few ascetic heroes (like the Jain monks), humanity is caught again and again in the cycles of rebirth and suffering. The slowly evolving spiritual life offers a hope too remote, a self-mastery too difficult, an ideal too austere. But this has been known also to god. He has Himself already prepared a way for us. Even within the archaic traditions of the sacrifice, it had been understood that the primal sacrifice was that of god to Himself, that there was a certain divine initiative to which man could respond by imitation. From ancient times the gods had shared the sacrifice with man through *prasāda*, the food of the gods, returned to man as god's gift and symbol of the richer prosperity available through devotion to him. In the Puranic literature the god Viṣṇu determines that his gift of food is not enough. He will himself be born among men whenever and in whatever form is needed to restore balance to the good. This concept became a complex theory of the manifestations of god, in numerous forms and ways, by which he has redeemed the world, or at least his devotees, from the powers of evil. When this image of the grace of god encompassed the culture hero of the great epic, the *Rāmāyana*, and finally, the whole cycle of mythological imagery associated with Kṛṣṇa, it reached full flower. In the *Bhagavad-gita*, Kṛṣṇa, an incarnate form of god (Viṣṇu), defines this theory to account for his presence at the climactic battle of *Kurukṣetra*, at the outset of the Kali (dark) Age.

> For whenever of the right
> A languishing appears, son of Bharata,
> A rising up of unright,
> Then I send Myself forth.

> For protection of the good,
> And for destruction of evil-doers,
> To make a firm footing for the right,
> I come into being in age after age.[11]

The *Purāṇas* are a class of literature that generally contains collections of material such as mythological accounts of the creation of the world, of its first civilizations and rulers, legendary stories and accounts of the gods as preserved orally by traditional bards for many centuries. As the sects of *Śiva and Viṣṇu* worshippers developed, these accounts were brought up to date to extol the claims of one or the other of these deities. This process covered an enormous historical period from before the Christian era to the ninth or tenth century of this era. Among the Vaisnava texts, biographies of Kṛṣṇa began very early and culminate in the extremely popular *Bhāgavata Purāṇa*, perhaps A.D. 500–950. These biographies interweave material concerning a West Indian warrior prince who appears in the *Mahābhārata* epic, the incarnate deity who drives Arjuna's chariot and delivers the lessons of the *Bhagavad-gita*, a rustic cow-herd boy, of the hills of Vṛndāvan, and the beloved dancer who plays his enchanting flute and sports with his entranced companions in the moonlight glen. The *Bhāgavata* contains this account in its richest and most developed form. This image of the biography of Kṛṣṇa, along with different but comparable developments in the Śaivite tradition, became the paradigm and parable of the path of devotionalism.

It is important to note that the Kṛṣṇa image provides a connection with the authoritative tradition of the *Gīta*, *Mahābhārata*, and *Upaniṣads*, giving a kind of orthodoxy to the devotional tradition, but it is not the Kṛṣṇa of the *Gīta* or *Mahābhārata* who is primary to the devotee. We may trace three basic segments in the developed Kṛṣṇa tradition. One segment has to do with his birth, in which he is conceived by Devaki as an incarnation destined for the destruction of evil, personified as the wicked King Kamsa, but then transferred at birth to Yaśoda in the Vṛndāvan village. This segment includes infancy and childhood stories in which his divine power is disclosed but never fully understood. The baby Kṛṣṇa evokes all the imagery that infancy entails, and this child is the delight, as well as the protector, of the village. The second segment of his life introduces his dancing, by which he rids the river, Yamunā, of the venomous snake Kaliya, but culminates in his enticement of the *gopis*, the wives and daughters of the herdsmen, to dance with him under the autumnal moon. Here the image is of love and of love's play. It is tacitly erotic, richly emotional, and distinctly antinomian. In a fascinating study of "The Social Teaching of the Bhāgavata Purāṇa," Thomas J. Hopkins has shown its emphasis upon devotionalism, its difference from traditional Vedic religion, its independence as a means of salvation in its own right, and its association with the poor, the religious nonprofessional, the humble, and the intensely devoted.[12]

In the image of Kṛṣṇa the full range of devotional response may be felt—delighted affection for a child, profound friendship and comaraderie with the divine friend, love of lover for beloved, as well as awe before the supreme power of reality. By these images god comes to man as pure, as grace, as holy gift and giver. He awakens our response as an infant draws forth the delight and pride of the mother. He arouses our passionate desire to be one with him as the lover activates the passion of love and satisfies it in an uncalculating ecstasy of joy.

Inevitably this imagery pours forth in poetry and exploits the range of erotic symbols that carry grace beyond the limits of formal modesty, decorum, or reasonableness. The poet Vidyāpati speaks for Kṛṣṇa's beloved when he sings:

> O Friend, I cannot tell you
> Whether he was near or far, real or dream,
> Like a vine of lightning,
> As I chained the dark one (Kṛṣṇa),
> I felt a river flooding in my heart.
> Like a shining moon,
> I devoured that liquid face.
> I felt stars shooting around me.
> The sky fell with my dress,
> Leaving my ravished breasts.
> I was rocking like the earth.
> In my storming breath
> I could hear my ankle-bells,
> Sounding like bees.
> Drowned in the last waters of dissolution,
> I knew that this was not the end.
>
> Says Vidyāpati:
> How can I possibly believe such nonsense?[13]

Even in the signature line of the poet, he sees the grace of god passing beyond the world of "proper" sense. The devotees of the god Śiva likewise speak of the rapture and entrancement that their dancing god evokes. Such exuberant faith flaunts, inverts, and violates all purely formal rules: its form is the end of form.

In practice this style of the religious tradition expresses itself in song and dance, in the pouring forth of devotional hymns—both in ancient and in modern times. It would be a fruitless quest to decide whether devotional song produced these traditions or whether they produced the songs. The two belong most intimately together. At the singing of such devotional hymns the following may be recited by the group.

> Bhagavān says: [God of the devotee]
> I do not live in Vaikuṇtha [the world and heaven of Viṣṇu].
> Nor do I live in the heart of the *yogī* [performing penance]
>   or in the sun.
> Where my devotees [are gathered] and sing [My Name]
> There do I stand, O Nārada!

> By meditation in the Kṛta Age,
> By sacrifices [*yājna*] in the Tretā Age,
> By worshipping [through the help of an image having
>   God's presence] in the Dvāpara Age
> What one attains thus, that he reaches in the Kali Age
>   by having sung about Krishna [*Kesava*].

> O king Praikṣit: in the Kali Age
> There is a great and unique quality:
> By the mere devout singing of Krishna,
> One released from the bondage [of samsara] can reach the
>   highest.[14]

To sing of Kṛṣṇa is to love Him, to come into relation with him. In respect to this relation, it is both necessary and possible for the human spirit to assume new forms. For men to identify themselves with the feminine (*gopis*) to see the world in the gentler mode is one such shift. To relate to god as baby, as mischievous child, and to love him with a mother's love is another. To share him as a friendship shares the whole personhood of friends. These modes and moods of the religious life do much to bring god closer, to make him most emotionally real. But it is especially in the *rasa*, the dance of the *gopis* with Kṛṣṇa, and the love of Rādha, that this experience is overwhelming. The remoteness of the great cosmic god is transcended by the closeness of a divine embrace, a symbolic, emotional ravishment beyond the power to satisfy, thus lifting the self by grace to that perfect freedom for which even total ecstasy is only a feeble hint. The flow of the river is the lover's heart. The immensity becomes the beloved lover. The duties of love have no calculated rules. This is the path of the devoted soul entranced by its divine source.

CONTINUITY AND CHANGE AMONG THE IMAGES

In Indian religion nothing once given is ever totally lost. The images of the archaic past—the immensity of universal systems, the flow of generations, the harmony of social orders, and of the personal Self with the deeper Self, and the peace that freedom gives informed the Brahmanical sacrifice, the Upanisadic quest for identity of *Brahman* and *Ātman*, the austerities of the Jain, and the perfect discipline of the Ājīvaka. When they were observed through the image of the cosmic personality of the Buddha, a new era of interpretation opened and came to flourish, not only in Buddhism, but also and even more dramatically in the devotional cults of Kṛṣṇa and Śiva.

Despite the fairly obvious differences among the various sects of the Indian religions there is an overall pattern to this tapestry of society and the imagination. If the native environment of India gives rise to the image of immensity, and the perpetual motion of great rivers from mountains of eternal snow to oceans of infinite capacity gives rise to the image of flow, these have served as presuppositions for any Indian interpretation of reality. For the Hindus, at least, a necessary corollary to these presuppositions is the idea that different kinds of persons have different natures, requiring the slow unfolding of their natural traits, and flourishing within a social order that draws upon and is sustained by a natural harmony of all types. For such a society, peace is inevitably the image of fulfillment. A composite society such as has developed in India seeks to reconcile varied interests. It dares not demand uniformity by refusing to permit variation. It achieves uniformity precisely by accepting variation, by interpreting all significant varieties as merely so many stages, manifestations, disciplines, phases, styles, or approaches to the same underlying reality. For at least three thousand years Indian culture has had to contend with the fact of its own composite character. There are and have virtually always been significant differences in race, tribal groups, languages, invading cultures, patterns of governmental order and structure, and local religious traditions. The totality of Indian culture is probably at least as complex as that of all of Europe, with traditions as diverse and powerful as those of Italians and the Irish. What has held this conglomerate culture together? One integrating factor has been a series of fundamental images of the human situation that have functioned as presuppositions and fundamental beliefs of the entire culture. In the ancient *Vedas* this unifying image was perhaps based on *ṛta*, the cosmic order, a force or energy manifest in everything, including gods and men, before which even the gods themselves were forced to yield their wills. Alignment with that energy made available an enormous power, to produce and sustain prosperity, to find a source of meaning and reality outside of the changing cycles of time and space. It is identification with this ultimate reality that all the techniques of yogic discipline, all observance of the ways of the ancestors, all devotion to the Buddha, all practices of austerity, all ecstasies of devotion are designed to accomplish. Harmony presupposes multiplicity. Everyone is invited to make his own music, controlled only by the central scale or mode of the cosmos. If all the parts are played well, the result will be harmony, flow, grandeur, and peace. Tensions may arise, of course, whenever one is out of sympathy with his own proper place. But these tensions will be resolved whenever one plays his proper part in tune. No sound in the whole orchestra of cosmic life is unimportant to the harmony of the whole. The way of the ancestors, the way of the *yogi*, the way of the Buddha, the way of the devotee are but different sections of the orchestra. Together they create the rhythms and resonances of the ultimate spheres. This is the image of tolerance and mutuality which is also fundamental to basic Indian religious attitudes. The human images in India are as complex and fascinating and delicately interwoven as her music.

NOTES

1. Viraj represents the feminine generative principle through which creative potentiality is enabled to act. She is the counterpart or creative activity of the Puruṣa.

2. Translated by Edward J. Thomas, *Vedic Hymns*, Wisdom of the East Series, (London: John Murray, 1923).

3. Alain Daniélou, *Hindu Polytheism* (New York: Bollingen Foundation, 1964), pp. 20–22 and 232–49.

4. Henrich Zimmer, *Myths and Symbols in Indian Art and Civilization*, ed. Joseph Campbell (New York: Pantheon Books, 1946), pp. 3–6.

5. "Word" has many possible meanings such as "way," "place," "goal," and "abode."

6. "Syllable" is also variable, meaning especially "imperishable." Try this meaning in each context also.

7. Robert E. Hume, trans., *The Thirteen Principal Upanishads*, 2nd ed., revised (London: Oxford University Press, 1931), pp. 348–50.

8. Ibid., pp. 370 and 371.

9. Agehānanda Bhāratī, *The Ochre Robe: An Autobiography* (Garden City, N.Y.: Doubleday & Company, 1970), pp. 153–54.

10. Hume, *Thirteen Principal Upanishads*, pp. 261–62.

11. Franklin Edgerton, trans., *The Bhagavad Gita* (Cambridge, Mass.: Harvard University Press, 1944), p. 43.

12. Thomas J. Hopkins, "The Social Teaching of the Bhāgavata Purāṇa," in *Krishna: Myths, Rites, and Attitudes*, ed. Milton Singer (Honolulu: East-West Center Press, 1966), pp. 3–22. The several essays of this book are extremely valuable for interpreting the devotionalism associated with Krishna.

13. Deben Bhattacharya, trans., and W. G. Archer, ed., *Love Songs of Vidyāpati* (New York: Grove Press, 1970), p. 44.

14. T. K. Venkateswaran, trans., "Rhādā-Krishna Bhajanas of South India," in *Krishna: Myths, Rites, and Attitudes*, pp. 143–44.

FOR FURTHER READING

The first two groups of texts are largely translations of scriptures or other important traditional religious writings of India. Some of them contain helpful introductory and interpretive material as well. The third group are more general studies of the religions of India:

Hindu Texts

EDGERTON, FRANKLIN, trans., *The Bhagavad Gita*. Cambridge, Mass.: Harvard University Press, 1944. A scholarly translation and interpretation of major themes of the classic religious poem of Hinduism.

EMBREE, AINSLEE T., ed., *The Hindu Tradition*. New York: Modern Library, 1966. A collection of translations of selections from original Hindu sources from the Vedas to Gandhi and Radhakrishnan.

HUME, ROBERT E., trans., *The Thirteen Principal Upanishads*, 2nd ed., revised. London: Oxford University Press, 1931. A readily available scholarly translation of the most important Upanishads.

KRAMER, SAMUEL N., ed., *Mythologies of the Ancient World*. Garden City, N.Y.: Doubleday & Company, 1961. Essays by notable scholars on the mythologies of most of the world's cultures; exceptionally clear and helpful one on the mythologies of India by W. Norman Brown.

THOMAS, EDWARD J., *Vedic Hymns*. Wisdom of the East Series. London: John Murray, 1973. One of the translations of selected Vedic literature.

Buddhist Texts

DE BARY, WM. THEODORE, ed., *The Buddhist Tradition in India, China and Japan*. New York: Modern Library, 1969. A collection of selections from original sources of Buddhist literature in translation; includes somewhat brief but useful samples of most of the types of Buddhist materials.

CONZE J. EDWARD, ed., *Buddhist Texts through the Ages*. New York: Harper & Row, 1964. Readings from Buddhist texts from Pali, Sanskrit, Tantric texts, and Chinese sources in translation; a companion volume to Conze's excellent general introduction, *Buddhism: Its Essence and Development*.

HAMILTON, CLARENCE H., ed., *Buddhism: A Religion of Infinite Compassion*. New York: Liberal Arts Press, 1952. The story of early Buddhism by readings from Buddhist literature with brief introductory comments to each selection.

WARREN, HENRY C., trans., *Buddhism in Translations*. New York: Atheneum, 1963. A relatively complete collection of translations of basic Buddhist literature from Indian sources in Pali.

General Texts

ASHBY, PHILIP H., *Modern Trends in Hinduism*. New York: Columbia University Press, 1974. A recent book focused on the changes emerging in Hinduism in the last century.

BURCH, GEORGE B., *Alternative Goals in Religion: Love, Freedom, Truth*. Montreal: McGill–Queen's University Press, 1972. A comparative study of Christianity, Hinduism, and Buddhism by analysis of their objectives.

CONZE, EDWARD J., *Buddhism: Its Essence and Development*. New York:

Harper & Row, 1959. A good introduction to Buddhism with special attention to the intellectual and spiritual presuppositions required for understanding the subject.

COOMARASWAMY, ANANDA K., *Buddha and the Gospel of Buddhism.* rev. Dona L. Coomaraswamy. New York: Harper, 1964. A popular presentation of the history and philosophy of traditional Buddhism.

DANIÉLOU, ALAIN, *Hindu Polytheism.* New York: The Bollingen Foundation, 1964. A comprehensive study of the symbols of the gods—both linguistic and literary in popular Hinduism.

DASGUPTA, S. N., *Hindu Mysticism.* New York: Ungar Press, 1927. A brief study of Upanishadic Hindu mysticism.

DIMOCK, EDWARD S., and DENISE LEVARTOV, trans., *In Praise of Krishna: Songs from the Bengali.* Garden City, N.Y.: Doubleday & Company, 1964. A collection of devotional poems concerning Krishna from the Bengali poets.

ELIOT, CHARLES, *Hinduism and Buddhism: An Historical Sketch.* London: Routledge and Kegan Paul, Ltd., 1949. A comprehensive historical study of the classical Hindu and Buddhist traditions.

HOPKINS, THOMAS J., *The Hindu Religious Tradition.* Encino, Calif.: Dickenson Publishing Company, 1971. A recent introductory text with special attention to practical Hindu life and worship.

KIRK, JAMES A., *Stories of the Hindus: An Introduction through Texts and Interpretations.* New York: The Macmillan Company, 1972. A collection of Hindu stories, mostly from the *Puranas*, with comments on the themes the stories contain.

MOORE, CHARLES A., ed., *The Indian Mind.* Honolulu: East-West Center Press, 1967. Essays presented at the East-West Philosophers' Conference in Hawaii by Hindu scholars.

MORGAN, KENNETH, ed., *The Path of the Buddha.* New York: Ronald Press, 1956. A well-edited, advanced introduction to Buddhist history, philosophy, and life written by Buddhist scholars.

——, *The Religion of the Hindus.* New York: Ronald Press, 1953. A well-edited, advanced introduction to Hindu history, philosophy, and life written by Hindu scholars.

RADHAKRISHNAN, SARVEPALLI, *The Hindu View of Life.* New York: The Macmillan Company, 1927. A brief statement on mature Hinduism by its most famous recent philosopher—an interpretation of *Dharma.*

——, *Indian Philosophy,* 2 vols. New York: The Macmillan Company, 1923, 1927. The standard presentation of the many traditions of Indian philosophy.

RENOU, LOUIS, *Hinduism.* New York: Brazillier, 1961. A brief but distinguished treatment of the early Hindu teachings by a famous French scholar.

——, *Religions of Ancient India.* London: Athlone Press, 1953.

ROBINSON, RICHARD H., *The Buddhist Religion.* Belmont, Calif.: Dickenson Publishing Company, 1970. A basic introduction to Buddhism by a distinguished American scholar; especially good on India and Japan.

ROSS, FLOYD H., *The Meaning of Life in Hinduism and Buddhism.* New York:

Harper & Row, 1972. A graceful comparative study of an important theme basic to understanding Hinduism.

SINGER, MILTON, ed., *Krishna: Myths, Rites, and Attitudes*. Honolulu: East-West Center Press, 1966. A collection of significant essays on Krishna and Hindu devotionalism, including new translations and important historical studies.

STROUP, HERBERT H., *Like a Great River: An Introduction to Hinduism*. New York: Harper & Row, 1972. One of the most recent of the general introductions to Hinduism.

THOMAS, EDWARD J., *The Life of Buddha as Legend and History*. London: Routledge and Kegan Paul, 1927. Traces the accounts of the life of the Buddha by translation and analysis of Buddhist sources.

WILLIAMS, ROBERT H. B., *Jain Yoga*. London: Oxford University Press, 1963. An examination of the Jain philosophy and discipline.

ZIMMER, HEINRICH, *Myths and Symbols in Indian Art and Civilization*, ed. Joseph Campbell. New York: Pantheon Books, 1946. A marvelous collection and discussion of Indian myths and symbols and their use.

The Human Image
In East Asia

5

The notion that a culture visualizes the human situation in a series of fertile images that are shaped by their intellectual tradition and by their historical circumstances is congenial indeed in the life and thought of ancient China and those other East Asian cultures dependent to some extent upon her wisdom. One of the most archaic and fundamental strands in the fabric of Chinese self-understanding envisions all reality on the model of interhuman relationships. Man, in his personal character and in his social relations, is himself a central image of reality within the Chinese perspective. The humanism of China is ancient, pervasive, complex, and sophisticated. It profoundly conditions the social and ethical relationships to which the thought of Confucius and his successors was primarily addressed. Humanism also influences the more distinctively religious and mystical traditions expressed in the classical heritage centering in ancestor veneration and in Taoist and Buddhist imagery as well.[1] This human image at the center interpenetrates even very diverse forms of Chinese thought and, in various ways, informs them all, so that distinctions that are completely natural in India or the Middle East or Western culture evaporate in China. The definition of religion, for example, cannot readily be discerned using Western categories and Chinese material. The vexing question of whether to treat Confucianism as a religion is an example of this perplexity. The same would hold for any general attempt to distinguish the sacred from the secular, to locate and identify the Chinese sense of ultimacy, to distinguish religion from magic, sorcery, divination, or even filial respect. The cultures of East Asia are incredibly complex and the images proliferate like blossoms in a greenhouse. The order and simplicity that we must introduce into the description of Chinese religion are arbitrarily imposed on the material, squelching to some extent the original vitality and richness of symbolic life that has always characterized the Orient. Though this procedure necessarily leaves much out, we will hope that it does not inject alien images.

China's religious life has been nourished from many sources, among which we discuss four: the classical religious heritage, Taoism, Buddhism, and some Confucian themes. Then we discuss the images in the independent Japanese heritage (Shinto) and in the Japanese forms of Buddhism. Neither the Korean contributions nor the use of foreign traditions other than Buddhism (for example, Christianity and Islam) will be considered in this chapter. Nor, of course, can we do full justice to the intricate variations on the images at the hands of individual scholars or schools.

FUNDAMENTAL IDEAS IN
THE BOOK OF CHANGES

There is a story that in very ancient times, when men still caught what they could catch and ate it raw, as beasts do, and found wild nuts, berries, grains, and eggs as best they could, a venerable, wise, and holy man, Fu Hsi, taught them how to cook their food and also left them a system for discerning the course of events by understanding the principles of change inherent in things.[2] The system is symbolized in a primitive set of trigrams composed of three lines, one above the other, in which each individual line is either positive or negative. These two related opposites are called the *yang* and the *yin,* the positive and negative, dominant and recessive, active and passive, but in their manifold combinations they are associated with a broad range of phenomena, so that they came to be regarded as encompassing all reality and disclosing its various tendencies. There is much dispute as to what we can make of this and the historical sequence of stages in the development of a comprehensive metaphysical doctrine on the basis of the principles enunciated in the *I Ching, The Book of Changes.* It seems probable that this development was cumulative and prolonged, but fortunately the details of its progress are not central to our interest. There can be no question that the underlying premises and images of *The Book of Changes* have exercised pervasive influence throughout the recorded history of Chinese thought.[3] The whole set of associations and relationships is much too complex and subtle for full discussion, but an examination of the eight primitive trigrams and their assumptions will indicate some of the possibilities. These eight exhaust all the possibilities of combination of three *yang* or *yin* lines. The trigrams and their associated interpretations are given in the chart on the following page.

There are two extremely fundamental elements that cannot be illustrated on such a chart. One is the dynamism, the movement, that the relationships among the trigrams presuppose. *The Book of Changes* offers a way of understanding the processes of reality and discerning their direction and probable

THE EIGHT SYMBOLS THAT FORM THE BASIS
OF *THE BOOK OF CHANGES*[4]

Trigram	Name	Attribute	Image	Family Relationship
yang ———				
yin — —				
☰	Ch'ien The Creative	strong	heaven	father
☷	K'un The Receptive	devoted yielding	earth	mother
☳	Chen The Arousing	inciting movement	thunder	first son
☵	K'an The Abysmal	dangerous	water	second son
☶	Ken Keeping Still	resting	mountain	third son
☴	Sun The Gentle	penetrating	wind wood	first daughter
☲	Li The Clinging	light-giving	fire	second daughter
☱	Tui The Joyous	joyful	lake	third daughter

outcome. There has been some dispute among authorities as to whether *The Book of Changes* is a book of divination or a book of wisdom. It is reasonably obvious now that it involves both. Its customary use in Chinese society (and increasingly, we are told, in the West as well) has been as a book of divination, a way of interpreting the signs in the presence of some serious question or quandary to determine the most appropriate course of action or attitude to take. In an "Introduction" to the English publication of Richard Wilhelm's translation, the prominent Swiss analytic psychotherapist, Carl Jung, took seriously the possibility that the book taps resources of unconscious awareness of fundamental psychic, social, and metaphysical forces and brings them to attention in relation to a question.[5] Such a procedure, of course, can degenerate into shallow fortunetelling. But insofar as it is to be taken seriously—as apparently it was by most of the prominent Chinese intellectuals, including Lao Tzu and Confucius—it will be because of its wisdom in discerning the inner laws of change and movement, exhibiting the factors that might otherwise be overlooked, avoided, suppressed, or denied.

In *The Book of Changes* the eight original trigrams are used in pairs (making six lines each) which, when combined in all possible arrangements, create sixty-four different hexagrams. Each *yang* or *yin* line of the six that form the hexagram is either a changing or a nonchanging line. The determination as to whether the line will be *yin* or *yang,* and also whether it will be changing or nonchanging, is determined by a kind of lottery. Originally it appears that this was done by heating a turtle shell or a piece of shoulder bone of an ox, and then cooling it sharply in order to read the cracks that formed across some of the predetermined areas of the surface. Later this complex system gave way to a procedure of letting a handful of yarrow sticks fall upon the table, dividing them arbitrarily so that, at the last selection, one ends with either an odd or an even number. The third method was that of casting three coins together and determining the reading of each line, both whether it is *yang* or *yin* and its character as changing or nonchanging, by the number of heads and tails. Both of these latter systems are still in common use. One performs a separate cast of the coins or sticks for each of the six lines of the hexagram, beginning at the bottom. There is a general reading in the *I Ching* for the hexagram as a whole and for each of its significant lines. The so-called change lines are the least probable casts of the lots, but are the most significant when they do occur. Their special relevance is based on the belief that some conditions are inherently instable. Objects or events may mysteriously but imperceptibly perch on the brink of change, their energies teetering on the threshold between two forms. A very slight shift in emphasis may, in the appropriate circumstances, realign the flow of energy and change the direction in events, releasing whole new trains of consequences and opportunities. It is these subtle interstices of change to which the *I Ching* draws attention, and this presupposes the image of movement, growth, and decay as fundamental.

The second primary assumption underlying both *The Book of Changes* and its many derivative or related philosophies is the use of a kinship model. No institution has been more important for traditional Chinese thought and life than the family. The significance of the family, in this case extended through all the living generations, for basic socialization and personal identification of each individual is fundamental for all cultures. In China, however, the hierarchical pattern of the family, with its differentiated roles, division of labor, and specific lines of authority, is not only a personal experience but also a philosophical principle. As one can see by the meanings given to the basic trigrams, each primary family role is associated with specific features and elements of the natural world, with the topography of the land, and with characteristic personal attributes. These particular associations are only the beginning. The basic idea of a family model has been used to interpret metaphysics, with a Sky-father and Earth-mother forming the elemental matrix, and also to organize statecraft with the Emperor as father of the people and the bureaucracy as the nurturing mediator. It is also used to conceive of nature in terms of its complex internal relations of growth and reciprocities of loyalty and responsibility. Many of the specific ways in which the family model has been applied seem to be connotations or mere suggestions with little logical support or factual evidence. Sometimes the basis of these associations can be explained as functions of language, in which characters or sounds have been associated with each other arbitrarily. Once such a connotation has developed the strength of tradition, however, it has continuity and force of its own. One of the most archaic of these traditional associations is to see reality in terms of three interacting worlds—the world of heaven, the world of earth, the world of man. Heaven is preeminent and sometimes ruled or personified by Old Shang-Ti. Earth is the more or less benevolent world of things for man's use and enjoyment. It has both hazards and delights. Man is the immediate world that matters, and it is his attitudes, his culture, and politics that must harmonize his world and that of nature with the Way of Heaven. The emperor, the gentry, and the peasants should exhibit the same relations of authority, dependence, and use which govern the cosmic family. Basic morality can thus be visualized in terms of the same kind of relationships which govern a well-ordered family. Reality as a whole is a society of interacting and interrelated *families*.

In the primitive trigrams the most basic pattern is that of the family, led by the father, the Creative, the symbol of Heaven, identified with the sun, with active power and strength, and complemented by the mother, who receives the creative impulse and gives it birth into the world through the gestation of her quiet, irresistible simplicity. The three sons [note that each is characterized by a single, more important *yang* line that dominates his feminine qualities] are considered exemplifications of the principles of movement—evocation, agitation, and rest—while the daughters enshrine the subtle powers—penetration, illumination, and joy. Though the second daughter, and more especially the second son, personify dangerous, sometimes uncontrollable, forces, there is no unit in the system that is purely evil or good without qualification, and no unit is complete. Reality is an integrated and indissoluble *family* with all the complex relationships of interdependence which that involves. This image of the human family as the pattern of reality has proved to be pregnant with possibilities for interpreting social, political, metaphysical, and religious situations and has a great endurance record in human thought. Whether it will survive the compulsive force of more mechanistic and materialist Communist thought in modern China is open to dispute, but it is at least one possibility to interpret the classless society as a final realization of the *human* family.[6]

Nowhere is the family image more apparent and fundamental than in the conglomerate of local, regional, and culturewide activities and attitudes that we shall call Chinese traditional religion. Any effort to define clearly the "theology," "ritual," or institutional forms of this indigenous Chinese religious heritage seems doomed to despair in a morass of data so rich and confused as to defy generalization. Yet sticking up out of the mass of facts are a few particular traditions of nearly universal Chinese occurrence. These would include the rites and attitudes associated with ancestor veneration, including mortuary rites and attitudes toward death; the establishment of the family, ancestral and imperial sacrifices; the calendar and agricultural rituals; and the Mandate of Heaven.

ANCESTOR VENERATION

The common people of China and many of the intelligensia as well understand themselves as inhabitants of a world order generally beneficial but unpredictable, populated by numerous spirits and divine beings both benevolent and dangerous. These spirits were recognized in nearly every home, in the altar to *T'u-ti,* the Earth God, the courtyard shrine of *T'ien-kuan,* the Heavenly Official, and, near the stove or hearth, *Tsao-shen,* the Kitchen God. These spirits and others protected the prosperity and health of the family and promoted their harmony. In addition to these more or less obviously divine personages and personifications, the family would also cherish especially its ancestor tablets on the ancestral altar in the main room of the house. With the tablets, containing the official designations of revered ancestors, standing in the glow of candle and fragrance of incense, addressed in regular ritual or on the special occasions of a birth, marriage, or some other momentous event, and invoked in the case of death to receive another family member into their company, the continuity of the family was visible and alive in the thought of all its members. The heart of the image of life in China is genealogical. One is born because of and into a family, finds meaning in its relationships, and continues forever under its care. The family would report the death of one of its members to some proper divine spirit depending on local tradition—perhaps the Earth God, or *Ch'eng-huang,* the City God, or *Wu-tao,* the God of Five Roads. They would also engage in ritual and social acts symbolizing their concern to usher the spirit speedily to a pleasant destiny. The immediate rituals would be followed by a series of less frequent and decreasingly intense services of remembrance and veneration. A number of gestures symbolic of the effort to neutralize or prevent any potential malevolence toward the living by the spirit would also be routine.[7] The aim of the ritual was to prepare for and send an illustrious family member on an auspicious and lengthy journey, at the completion of which he will surely wish still to be remembered and informed of his family's progress, but will also care for and remember them and welcome his successors into the land of the departed. Certainly the image of the family and its continuity through time is fundamental in ancient China.

SACRIFICES

To make an offering to the spirits is a sacrifice. Here we do not (at least originally) have the elaborate exchange that lay at the heart of the Vedic sacrifice in India. The lighting of candles, the burning of incense, bowing, the offering of food or drink, the recitation of a traditional account, remembrance of a name, title, and distinctions were styles of regular sacrifice. They honor and venerate the spirit, reinforce the cohesiveness of the family with its spiritual associates (ancestors, local heroes, divinities), and enliven the year with good times, good food, good fellowship, and, in the case of annual or ancestral sacrifices, with relaxation of many social restrictions and enjoyment of a holiday. The great ancestral and seasonal sacrifices were usually festive and joyous occasions at which special marketplaces might be established, elaborate foods served, and large clans and communities gathered together. In some of the surviving rituals we can see that the meaning of the decorations, the costumes, the music, and so forth, is to transform the place of meeting into a Hall of Heaven. In this transmundane realm the sacrifice can be shared appropriately with illustrious ancestors. The Chinese are often said to be a very practical people, so much so that they clearly realized the practical value—in economic exchange, social intercourse, and refreshed personal vitality and memory—which were incorporated in the ritualized worship of the spirits great and small and thus cherished and observed their traditional sacrifices regularly.[8]

THE IMPERIAL SACRIFICE

The case of the annual imperial sacrifice at the Altar of Heaven in Peking requires special attention. It is an image that drew together tradition and spiritual sanctions, the family model at its highest level of generality, and preeminently the power and authority of the state. By this event the Emperor reaffirmed his special filial relation with Heaven and Earth and renewed Heaven's mandate to be exercised by himself as "True Son of Heaven." In the mythology and folk tradition that supported the imperial institution this event gave rise to a curious blend of images. The Emperor bowed before Heaven and Earth, but he in turn was identified with the mythical dragon, symbol of clouds and rivers, power and prosperity, and all sorts of secret lore. Powerful emperors were, of course, careful to reserve to themselves exclusive authority to sanction and interpret national sacrifices, the calendar on which they were based, and the meanings of prominent omens, but they did not object if the people thought of them in the image of the dragon.

These attitudes and images we have discussed so far arose in the obscurity of prehistory and continued to evolve through cycles of popularity and decline up to and perhaps to some extent through the Communist revolution in 1949. They are not distinctively, or at least not exclusively, religious, but they have been pervasive assumptions of the culture. It is, however, in the mystical musings of Taoist sages and the Buddhist conceptions of reality and the way of human salvation that we encounter the religious images of man as such.

MYSTICAL TAOISM

In the *Book of the Lao-Tzu* one of the poems that tells about the sage speaks of his self-effacing nature.

Poem VII

Heaven is eternal, the Earth is everlasting.
How come they to be so?
It is because they do not foster their own lives;
That is why they live so long.

Therefore the Sage
Puts himself in the background; but is always to the fore.
Remains outside; but is always there.
Is it not just because he does not strive for any personal end
That all his personal ends are fulfilled?[9]

The cluster of attitudes and activities that go under the general name of Taoism have a special image of the recluse sage, the "Man of the Way (*Tao*)." In another poem (XVII) the suggestion is made that the work of the highest sage is so unobtrusive that the people will be uncertain as to whether he ever really existed, so that "When his task is accomplished, his work done, throughout the country everyone says, 'It happened of its own accord.'"[10]

The enigmas and delights of that most translated of all Chinese books are not likely to be resolved here, but some of its prominent images may disclose themselves to us. One is this image of the sage. For Taoists the sage has a very special meaning. He is an obscure, undemanding, nonjudgmental, open person, peculiarly free because he requires no praise or blame from others, no prominence in their thoughts or affections. He has an impenetrable depth of personal character perfectly able to maintain its own nature while superficially shaped by outward circumstances. In the poems of the *Tao-Te-Ching* this integrity is called the "Uncarved Block," using as an analogy the way in which a block of fine wood displays its superior quality whatever the object into which it is shaped. What enables the sage simultaneously to maintain both this firm inner character and an uninterrupted adaptability to the ebb and flow of circumstance is the harmony he has with *Tao*, the ultimate way of things. The most characteristic pattern that *Tao* displays, even though its whole nature is not revealed even to the sage, is the way of inaction (*wu-wei*), the way of noninterference, of letting things be, as suggested by water which seeks the lowest place yet carves deep valleys, or by the infant who knows no anxiety, cries without becoming hoarse, and simply adapts without connivance to the way things are. The poems of the *Tao-Te-Ching (Book of the Lao-Tzu)* do not teach true laissez-faire or full nonaction. Rather they call for so subtle a comprehension of the inner laws and nature of things and such sensitivity of timing that one's influence may be introduced so gently and effectively that the result comes as if it were the routine flow of nature. For this interpretation—which, then, also sees *The Lao-Tzu* as in part a kind of administrative handbook for the Taoist advisor—the following selection from Poem LXIII is a key to the basic teaching.

In the governance of empire everything difficult must be dealt with while it is still easy. Everything great must be dealt with while it is still small. Therefore the Sage never has to deal with the great; and so achieves greatness.[11]

This attitude was developed with even livelier grace, humor, and delight by the later Taoist philosopher, Chuang-Tzu, who continues to ponder the sage and asks his reader to listen in a special way.

> I'm going to try speaking some reckless words and I want you to listen to them recklessly. How will that be? The sage leans on the sun and moon, tucks the universe under his arm, merges himself with things, leaves the confusion and muddle as it is, and looks on slaves as exalted. Ordinary men strain and struggle; the sage is stupid and blockish. He takes part in ten thousand ages and achieves simplicity in oneness. For him, all the ten thousand things are what they are, and thus they enfold each other.[12]

And then he tells a story:

Nameless Man (of Tao)

T'ien Ken was wandering on the sunny side of Yin Mountain. When he reached the banks of the Liao River, he happened to meet a Nameless Man. He questioned the man, saying, "Please may I ask how to rule the world?"

The Nameless Man said, "Get away from me, you peasant! What kind of a dreary question is that! I'm just about to set off with the Creator. And if I get bored with that, then I'll ride on the Light-and-Lissome Bird out beyond the six directions, wandering in the village of Not-Even-Anything and living in the Broad-and-Borderless field. What business do you have coming with this talk of governing the world and disturbing my mind?"

But T'ien Ken repeated his question. The Nameless Man said, "Let your mind wander in simplicity, blend your spirit with the vastness, follow along with things the way they are, and make no room for personal views—then the world will be governed."[13]

In addition to the image of the mysterious sage as found in the philosophy of Lao and Chuang, the Taoists of the Han Dynasty (206 B.C.–A.D. 220) added the symbol of the fish and water. The image was by no means new, since it was presupposed by the *I Ching* and in some ways also by the *Lao-Tzu* and *Chuang-Tzu*. This image is the familiar diagram of the *yin/yang,* a dynamically divided circle of interacting movements. The circle as a whole is *Tao. Yang* is the fish,

and *yin* the water, each occupying its own place yet each always displacing the other. The curved diameter suggests this constant reciprocal motion. A special school of *yin/yang* thought, and an analysis of the substance of reality in terms of five elements (metal, wood, water, fire, and soil) emerged.[14] The philosophical examination and development of these images proved to be exceedingly sophisticated and complex, but for practical life perhaps one of the most significant features was the way in which this approach draws attention to what is subtle and otherwise unnoticed, the water that is not the fish, the space that generates the solid which defines it, the decline that sets in before the process of growth is yet complete, the process of growth that comes through decay and death. When one reads the interpretations of the *I Ching,* with all the later appendices and commentary, which include this *yin/yang* philosophy in fully developed form, one is struck by the way in which Chinese thought is sensitive to minute and subtle change, beginning before the apparent fulfillment of any action, but becoming obvious to everyone by the time an action is complete. Lao-Tzu says it this way, "Things age after reaching their prime."[15] The image of the seeds of decay that begin to germinate in the moment of success, and its converse, the seeds of success that lie dormant but alive in the midst of unpromising difficulties typify the Chinese manner of looking at the world.

CONFUCIUS AND THE HUMAN IMAGE

One of the most remarkable characters in the history of human thought has to be Confucius (551–479 B.C.). His importance is immeasurably enhanced by the continued development of his thought by generations of subsequent philosophers interpreting and reinterpreting its themes and assumptions. The humanism of Chinese thought which we have already mentioned clearly reaches its maturity in the Confucian and Neo-Confucian tradition.[16] Neither the technical nor the historical analysis of Confucian categories is essential to our purpose, since they are not understood by the Chinese to exemplify religious images, but rather came to be the presuppositions of the educational, political, and ethical institutions of traditional, pre-Communist China. However, three prominent Confucian themes have such fundamental relevance for human self-understanding that we must mention them because of the broader interpretation of religion which we have here employed. These are: the concept of *jên,* goodness; the concept of *Chün-tzu,* Superior Man; and the process of the *Rectification of Names.*

For Confucius one's noblest humanity is outwardly expressed in filial relations, the reciprocal (but not symmetrical) relations of responsibility and loyalty for which family is the paradigm: Emperor and people, father and son, husband and wife, older and younger, brothers and friends. But what ultimately must govern these external relations is the internal character of the person. This character is founded in *jên.* Arthur Waley endeavors to reconstruct the actual meaning of this term for Confucius. Originally the term meant "the common people," the members of one's group, though later it came to mean "human being" and the conduct worthy of a man. Confucius uses the term as an ideal, a symbol of a cluster of characteristics that together define the highest possible human character. He refuses to grant the title *jên* to any living contemporary. He presents *jên* as a *direction* toward which man should strive. It is a transcendental moral character, the source of one's private courtesy, public diligence, and personal loyalty [Analects 8:19]. Perhaps one of the most illustrative qualities of *jên* is found in *Analects,* Book VI, 28, where Confucius, while insisting that *jên* is a human rather than divine quality, put it in terms of helping others realize their desires, turn their merits to account, and finding one's own feelings a guide to the true feelings of others.[17] From a heart filled with such a spirit all actions will flow with natural grace and filial devotion. The image of *true man* is the man of human-heart moving always toward goodness. The epitome or fulfillment of that image is the Gentleman, Superior Man, *Chün-tzu.* Originally this term meant the "son of a ruler,"[18] but came to be separated from the idea of distinguished birth, without losing its meaning of superior character and nature. In Book X of Confucius' *Analects,* which is devoted to aphorisms concerning the Gentleman, Confucius notes the Superior Man's simple and unassuming ways at home and his graceful propriety and careful self-confidence at court or in the ancestral temple. Much of the book deals with *Chün-tzu's* distinctive sense of propriety and proportion, of his firm control of physical expression, of words, of appropriate dress and behavior. In another place Confucius said, "A gentleman takes as much trouble to discover what is right as lesser men take to discover what will pay."[19]

The tradition was unanimous that Confucius was himself just such a gentleman as he encouraged others to be. Therefore it may be especially significant that when he was asked what he would place as the matter of first importance in the administration of a state he said:

> "It would certainly be to correct language [rectify names]."
>
> Tzu-lu said, "Can I have heard you aright? Surely what you say has nothing to do with the matter. Why should language be corrected?"
>
> The Master said, "Yu! How boorish you are! A gentleman, when things he does not understand are mentioned, should maintain an attitude of reserve. If language is incorrect, then what is said does not concord with what was meant; and if what is said does not concord with what was meant, what is to be done cannot be effected. If what is to be done cannot be effected, then rites and music [the arts of peace] will not flourish, then mutilations and lesser punishments will go astray. And if mutilations and lesser punishments go astray, then the people have nowhere to put hand or foot.
>
> Therefore the gentleman uses only such language as is proper for speech, and only speaks of what it would be proper to carry into effect. The gentleman, in what he says, leaves nothing to mere chance."[20]

One can readily appreciate both the philosophical and ethical implications of this notion that the language of wise and thoughtful men must correspond in great detail to the experiences they discuss. Only then is appropriate control of behavior by law or tradition possible. Until the language is so corrected, stripped of its emotional improprieties, and made precisely reflective of the subject discussed, confusion reigns and the human image is distorted.

The chief component of this image as we find it in this influential tradition is a largely rational, eminently gentle, profoundly attractive, humane ideal founded in an inner character that is identified with the deepest and most broadly human interests, exemplified in the Superior Man, and carried into action with precise understanding of the way things really are. It was not at all inappropriate that Mencius (372-289 B.C.) should develop further this implication of an essential confidence in the innate goodness of such a human being. Ever since the Han Dynasty (206 B.C.) the literati and bureaucrats of China have found the image of the life of Confucius himself, as idealized and stereotyped, to be a model of significant human values. As scholars and students of China's past (which they made increasingly illustrious), as gentlemen-statesmen, as epitomes of protocol and culture, they lived toward the ideal of Confucius, the man of wisdom, character, and grace.

THE HUMAN IMAGE IN CHINESE BUDDHISM

For the Chinese, Buddhism was a very exotic foreign import. Repeatedly in Chinese history it has been attacked on grounds of its "barbarian" character and its incongruity with Chinese values. The reasons are not hard to find. Where the Chinese exalt the family and make it the archetypical symbol of reality, the Buddha had abandoned his family and established as the principal institution of Buddhism an order of homeless, celibate monks and nuns, who set themselves to break all ties of affection and remembrance. Where the Chinese center their philosophy in the human situation and display a relatively underdeveloped interest in speculation on the cosmos as a whole or on the supernatural, Buddhism, as it came to China, was especially richly endowed with such speculative philosophical material. Where the Chinese tried to bend every effort to give life all the immediate pleasure which propriety affords, from gourmet cooking, through education of bureaucrats, to imperial order and agricultural festivals, Buddhism held forth the notion that this life is suffering, rotten at the core, and empty of ultimate meaning. The Chinese had believed themselves to occupy the central kingdom of the world and to exhibit its most advanced intellectual and material culture. Buddhism was unquestionably foreign and in many matters of dress, diet, decorum, and doctrine seemed to betray an uncouth origin. Such charges occur repeatedly in Chinese history, and it is in many ways surprising that against such odds Buddhism made as much progress as it did in China. Of course there is also an inverse side to each of these arguments. The most popular forms of Buddhism in China ultimately were those that did not stress the monastic life for most people. In many ways China shaped Buddhism to her own image of life. On the other hand the family system in China exacted a great price from some people, the illegitimate or orphaned, the unmarried, the early widowed, the childless, those who for any reason were unable or unwilling to fulfill the family model. For such people the monastery or nunnery provided a place where they could devote themselves to goals higher than those of the householder. Partly because Chinese thought was relatively less rich in metaphysical and cosmological schemes, Buddhism had something to offer which filled a vacuum and did not offend local tradition. We must underscore the *"relatively less,"* however. It seems clear that it was because mystical Taoism found Buddhist metaphysics and meditation congenial that Buddhism was able to make such rapid inroads among certain segments of the population. Taoism provided most of the critical Chinese vocabulary into which Buddhist doctrines and texts were translated. Along this line there was another specific advantage for Buddhism. Chinese thought in the field of ethics was highly developed. While Buddhism requires ethical sensitivity both as prerequisite for and as part of its spiritual disciplines, it was not wedded to the specific ethical values (as, for example, the caste system) of India. Confucian ethical thought could readily be incorporated (with certain reservations concerning the relative position of filial responsibility) within Buddhist thought in China. Chinese ethics, of course, did not undervalue either truth or kindness, which are so important to Buddhists. This fact made possible what came to be a characteristic pattern in China, the mutual acceptance and veneration, a peaceful coexistence and interaction, of several traditions simultaneously—ancestor worship; Taoist mysticism; Confucian ethical, political, and educational philosophy; and Buddhist salvationism. The fact that there would appear to be a severe inconsistency between, say, ancestor worship and the Buddhist belief in reincarnation did not seriously impede their mutual functioning throughout the whole society. Finally, it is generally the case that where the Chinese imperial dynasties were strong and prosperous, popular Buddhism was relatively weak. Buddhism tended to flourish in China precisely in those times when disorder prevailed, suffering was a common experience, and the affairs of this world offered relatively little of permanent joy or hope. It was in the break-up of the powerful Han Dynasty that Buddhism successfully migrated to China in a substantial way. In the powerful T'ang Dynasty (A.D. 618–906) only the Ch'an, a highly individualistic, meditative Buddhism, flourished, and in the Sung Dynasty (960–1276) Buddhism went into permanent decline in China. By this time, of course, it had been transplanted to Japan where it continued to develop and flourish.

Buddhism in China took many forms, often named for the translation of a particular dominant sutra. Some sects resembled their Indian or Southeast Asian parents very closely. Probably the earliest serious interest in Buddhism concerned its mystical and magical techniques. One of the Buddhist traditions of China, derived primarily from Tibet, continued this emphasis. A second form of Chinese Buddhism was the *Hua-yen,* the teaching of Allness, the Round Doctrine, based on the *Avataṁsaka Sutra.* This was a profoundly philosophical approach of emptiness, of absolute wisdom, and the infinite compassionate powers of the *Bodhisattva* as discussed on page 168. There is, however, an interesting Chinese account of how one aspect of this doctrine was once explained. During the T'ang Dynasty the controversial Empress Wu Tse-T'ien was a great patroness of Buddhism. Under her sponsorship the eighty-volume version of the complete text of the *Hua Yen* Sutra was completed in A.D.699. She invited the celebrated Master Fa'Tsang to the capitol to explain the sutra. One day Empress Wu asked Fa'Tsang the following question:

> Reverend Master, I understand that man's knowledge is acquired through two approaches: one is by experience, the direct approach, and the other by inference, the indirect approach. I also understand that the first five consciousnesses and the *Ālaya* only take the direct approach; whereas, the mind, or the sixth consciousness, can take both. Therefore, the findings of the conscious mind are not always trustworthy. The superiority and reliability of direct experience over indirect inference is taught in many scriptures. You have explained the Hua Yen Doctrine to me with great clarity and ingenuity; sometimes I can almost see the vast *Dharmadhātu* in my mind's eye, and touch a few spots here and there in the great Totality. But all this, I realize, is merely indirect conjecture or guesswork. One cannot really understand Totality in an immediate sense before reaching Enlightenment. With your genius, however, I wonder whether you can give me a demonstration that will reveal the mystery of the *Dharmadhātu*—including such wonders as the "all in one" and the "one in all," the simultaneous arising of all realms, the interpenetration and containment of all *dharmas,* the Non-Obstruction of space and time, and the like?

After taking thought for a while, Fa'Tsang said, "I shall try, your Majesty. The demonstration will be prepared very soon."

A few days later Fa'Tsang came to the Empress and said, "Your Majesty, I am now ready. Please come with me to a place where the demonstration will be given." He then led the Empress into a room lined with mirrors. On the ceiling and floor, on all four walls, and even in the four corners of the room were fixed huge mirrors—all facing one another. Then Fa'Tsang produced an image of Buddha and placed it in the center of the room with a burning torch beside it. "Oh, how fantastic! How marvelous!" cried the Empress as she gazed at the awe-inspiring panorama of infinite interreflections. Slowly and calmly Fa'Tsang addressed her:

"Your Majesty, this is a demonstration of Totality in the *Dharmadhātu.* In each and every mirror within this room you will find the reflections of all the other mirrors with the Buddha's image in them. And in each and every reflection of any mirror you will find all the reflections of all the other mirrors, together with the specific Buddha image in each, without omission or misplacement. The principle of interpenetration and containment is clearly shown by this demonstration. Right here we see an example of one in all and all in one—the mystery of *realm embracing realm ad infinitum* is thus revealed. The principle of the *simultaneous arising of different realms* is so obvious here that no explanation is necessary. These infinite reflections of different realms now simultaneously arise without the slightest effort; they just naturally do so in a perfectly harmonious way . . . .

"As for the principle of the non-obstruction of space, it can be demonstrated in this manner . . . (saying which, he took a crystal ball from his sleeve and placed it in the palm of his hand). Your Majesty, now we see all the mirrors and their reflections within this small crystal ball. Here we have an example of the small containing the large as well as of the large containing the small. This is a demonstration of the non-obstruction of 'sizes,' of space.

"As for the non-obstruction of times, the past entering the future and the future entering the past cannot be shown in this demonstration, because this is, after all, a static one, lacking the dynamic quality of the temporal elements. A demonstration of the non-obstruction of times, and of time and space, is indeed difficult to arrange by ordinary means. One must reach a different level to be capable of witnessing a 'demonstration' such as that. But in any case, your Majesty, I hope this simple demonstration has served its purpose to your satisfaction."[21]

Part of the interest in this charming little story derives from its contrast with the Indian sources that it sets forth to explain. In the Indian account sugtillions of Buddhas preside over gerbillions of Buddha-worlds, driving the individual to the shattering awareness of his own insignificance and nothingness. In the Chinese illustration the totality of things becomes the infinite reflection of the Buddha image, and then is enclosed in the marble held in a man's palm. Both are, of course, metaphors but the difference in approach is telling. Indian thought annihilates man before the Totality; the Chinese approach enlarges man to represent the Totality.

The sects emphasizing the "pure and happy land" comprise a third basic type of Chinese Buddhism. Based usually upon the popular *Sukhāvati* and the *Lotus Sutras* these sects stress the career of the *Bodhisattva* as agent of salvation. This style of thought had developed first in the Mahayana Buddhism of North India, but it was in East Asia that it became the most popular and enduring form. The concept of the *Bodhisattva* emerged naturally from reflection about the nature of Buddha. Why did the Buddha teach? It must have been because of his gracious compassion, not because he was compelled to do so. Did this compassion then cease with his death? No! His career was understood as itself a parable, the incarnation of the Buddha principle, which has no boundaries or limits. His "skill in means" as a teacher led him to use, even the death of his apparent form, as a teaching device, luring others toward the *nirvana* he had in fact renounced for himself. His power and knowledge were infinite so that even in these later days when spirituality and discipline are at low ebb, his compassion ensures freedom from suffering. The Mahayana sutras speak of many such *Bodhisattvas,* who exist even now in a variety of forms, in various heavens, and exercise their benevolent compassion on behalf of all beings. Among these one of the most popular is *Amitabha* (Japanese, *Amida*), the Buddha of Boundless Light, who has made several vows to aid sentient beings who cannot by their own effort alone hope to attain *nirvana.* He has vowed to assist all those who call upon him in faith. Now of course *nirvana* itself can be achieved only by perfectly skilled and disciplined disciples. In this world, in this age, it is virtually impossible. But faith in the power of the

Bodhisattva to fulfill his vow will result in rebirth in a pure and happy land, a western paradise, in which one will readily learn the disciplines of *nirvana,* and enjoy the delights of heavenly reward while learning.

The image here is radically different from that of the homeless man of India, free from all desires. The Buddha has become a cosmic principle (called *Dharmakaya*—Body of the Law) and the cosmic principle has become a series of mythological manifestations (*Bodhisattvas*), divine personages in whom one can have faith and who can reward faith with the finest of all gifts, rebirth in the pure land. This great vehicle of compassion will carry all humankind across the sea of suffering to the indescribable peace beyond. No longer is the discipline of monk or nun generally required. The compassion of the *Bodhisattva* can compensate for these. Sincere faith, trust, and chanting of the holy name suffice for the religious life. Religion centers on the means of salvation from suffering and uncertain futures, to rebirth in the happy land and what is even higher than such happiness. The image is that of a compassionate cosmic ruler who can and will give a place in a happy kingdom to those who please and honor him. It is not surprising that this became the popular form of middle- and lower-class religion in China, and its promises were integrated with the traditional interest in a prosperous future for departed ancestors. Man, as the devotee of the Cosmic Savior, reveres, honors, and trusts His power and keeps his spiritual accounts in order.

A fourth type of Chinese Buddhism is *Ch'an.* Ch'an is substantially different from the forms of Buddhism which we have just described. The word *Ch'an* (pronounced Zen in Japanese) is the Chinese transliteration of the Sanskrit word for meditation (*Dhyāna*), indicating a dominant feature of this approach. Ch'an goes back to the way in which the Buddha himself attained enlightenment, that is, by seated meditation. A second characteristic is a general distrust of discourse, philosophical argument, or any other indirect mode of dealing with experience. Third, Ch'an emphasizes the specific, usually sudden, realization of an experience of enlightenment in which life is made free and spontaneous, and which provides some kind of total unity in the individual's experience. Within these principles there are rather wide variations. On its arrival from India the Buddhism which developed into Ch'an was heavily imbued with the metaphysics of emptiness. It was this Buddhism (even more than the Taoist Church) that utilized the mystical philosophy of Lao Tzu and Chuang Tzu, including its enigmatic spirit and love of nature. Finally, like the Pure Land cults, Ch'an increasingly came to focus on the problem of salvation, the specific experience of enlightenment. But unlike the Chinese Pure Land sects it saw this salvation (*nirvana*) as here and now, a way of perceiving the life you have—without suffering—rather than rebirth into a different, heavenly life. The ideal of human achievement was neither the *beggar monk* (though Ch'an did encourage monasteries) nor the *recluse sage* of the Taoists, nor the *gentleman-bureaucrat* of the Confucianists, nor the *Cosmic Companion* of the Pure Land Sectarians, but the *Master.* The Master is an artist of the spirit, a man free from concern with any opinions that may be held about him or that he might otherwise have about himself. He is one with everything; he merges with life's flow, its composition, and its disintegration. He is characterized by perfectly spontaneous responses to any situation, by a colossal sense of humor, total unpretentiousness, and yet also by a disciplined passion to assist others to awaken this experience in themselves. He is the kind of master whose action makes the rule rather than following it. All four of these forms of Buddhism gradually spread from China to the rest of East Asia and will be traced again mingling in the experience of the Japanese.

THE HUMAN IMAGE IN JAPAN

The buildings of the Grand Shrine of Ise, in central Japan, are simultaneously examples of the most ancient architecture and of the most recent important religious structures. This apparent paradox occurs because these Shinto buildings are completely rebuilt every twenty years, following an extremely archaic and specific process, and using the original plans of the simple buildings. Most of the ancient Buddhist temples have been destroyed or heavily damaged by fire, and those that have been rebuilt have usually adopted the evolving styles of architecture then in current use. This gentle anomaly suggests something relevant to interpretation of Japanese images. Like all cultures they build upon the past, but they treat it in their own special ways. Sometimes the distant past is directly visible in current images, and sometimes there are layers of different reflections, one on top of the other in gay profusion and confusion. It is generally agreed that the indigenous traditions of Japan attained their characteristic pattern at about the seventh century of our era. At this time the Yamato clan had secured its hegemony among the gentry families and authorized the publication of the mythological accounts that both established the normative genealogies of the noble clans and accounted for the physical and spiritual existence of the Japanese people and homeland. These accounts relate the imperial family to *Amaterasu,* the sun goddess and leading *kami* of the land. They also relate many specific places and processes as well as families to this sense of numinous power and mysterious presence which the concept of *kami* enshrines.[22] It is impossible to give an exact translation or meaning to the word *kami. Kami* refers to the presence of a mysterious power or potency; the acknowledgment of a unique superiority; a semianthropomorphic vision of the relations of heaven, earth, and underworld; and a sacralizing of every essential task from smelting and weapon making through fishing and agriculture to the centralization of ultimate political sanction in the Imperial house. Respect for *kami* gives warrant for these primary traditions which came to be enshrined in what we call Shinto, or *kami-no-michi,* the "way of the *kami.*"[23]

 There are three elements in these basic Shinto traditions: the genealogical, the domestic, and the cultural. In the genealogical heritage lie all the traditions associated with the Emperor and the Imperial clan. A rich cycle of ceremonies, traditionally celebrated in the Shrine of the Imperial Palace or in the Grand Shrine of Ise, revere the status and authority of the Emperor and mystically protect the security and prosperity of the nation. In the inaugural ceremony, and in the agricultural rites of planting and first fruits, the Emperor, serving as national priest, celebrates the special relation of the people and the *kami* of the sun and of the rice by which they live. Another cycle, celebrated mainly At Ise, elaborate with dance and drama, traditionally led by an Imperial princess, follows the whole annual cycle of the year. And a third set of formal ceremonies by the Imperial court acknowledges and rewards the highest achievements in the arts and sciences on behalf of the nation. The distortions of Shinto in the period of World War II led to much misunderstanding of the role of the Emperor, both in Japan and in the West. Throughout literate Japanese history the unity of the nation, its close association with various divine powers, and the protection of the vital interests of the people have been ritualized in the role of the Emperor and the *kami* he worships. The Emperor personally observes a complex cycle of worship activities from which others are generally excluded. He is responsible for maintaining harmonious relations with the *kami* of the land.[24] Thus the genealogical heritage, both for the islands themselves and for the noble clans, which are specified in the *Kojiki,* is fundamental to the continuity and prosperity of the nation and character of its people. The "Civil Religion of Japan" has been fundamental to Shinto even through long periods in which the Emperor himself had little or no significant political authority.

The second major strand of Shinto consists of the domestic rites that unite the people of a household with the powers of life, fertility, and health on which they are dependent. Its symbol is the *kami-dana,* the "god-shelf" in the home, which recognizes the presence of the protective *kami* of the household by means of a small shrine and place for food and drink offerings on a shelf, usually above a door. Here the family acknowledges its ancestors and the benevolent *kami* who have always protected them from misfortune. Mingling of traditional Shinto and Buddhist notions has long been characteristic of domestic Shinto. In this category we would also include much of the traditional practice of exorcism, sometimes associated with rigorous personal disciplines, for recovery of health. Domestic Shinto also comes to expression in the architecture which makes a spot of beauty, the *tokonoma* or alcove, central in a home, delights in a garden in the courtyard, and provides for art and flowers as graces of life. These Shinto/Buddhist traditions have put a unique stamp on the aesthetic element in Japanese culture. In modern times this heritage of beauty and purity seems often to have lost its meaning as a show of respect for *kami,* but sometimes continues as a cultural habit.

The wider cultural pattern of Shinto is even more diverse than the imperial and the domestic. Every strangely beautiful spot—a mountain, shoreline, rock, tree, grotto—and Japan has many, and the places or times of mythical or historical events are also residence of *kami*. These come to function mainly in seasonal, annual, or occasional festivals associated with each of the principal shrines. The most pervasive element in this elaborate ceremonial life is that of purification. By many explicit symbols, including the gateway (*torii*) of the shrine, the purification basin where sips of water purify the lips and fingers, the waving of *sakaki* branches by priests, the tying of white strips of paper called *shimenawa*, on ropes, a stylized ritual dance, food and drink offerings, and finally a sacred eating or drinking of the consecrated material, the need to purify one's self and place is acknowledged and the means provided. There is no deep-rooted sense of sin or alienation or absolute suffering, only a recognition of the misfortune of pollution due to blood, death, decay, or misbehavior, which must be washed away and purged. Most festival occasions require that the priests who officiate engage in various acts of ritual cleansing, such as bathing, fasting, abstinence, concentration, special costumes, and sometimes trance, in preparation for their observance.

It is impossible to locate any single image that can convey the multiform character of Japanese self-understanding. From a functional perspective Shinto is an unsystematic but sophisticated psychology. The *kami* have no visible form, but are located in shrines and symbolic objects, may express an awareness of internal relations among the symbols of natural beauty or eccentricity, the inner sources of human intentions and purposes, and the dominant social structure of the country. This correlation comes to fulfillment in the primary ethical and spiritual categories of Shinto. The inner essence of reality is classified in terms of four spirits, *ara-mi-tama,* rough or violent soul; *nigi-mi-tama,* quiet, tranquil, mature soul; *saki-mi-tama,* luck spirit; and *kushi-mi-tama,* mysterious, awesome, or wondrous spirit.[25] The purpose of the effort to purify, pacify, and harmonize one's self is to recognize these psychic dispositions and to allow appropriate expression of each. The rites of Shinto for pacifying the soul are undertaken to assure that a natural, harmonious flow of action will issue from the properly disposed heart. This image, which resonates with insight of depth psychology, accounts for the adoption of *sincerity* as the primary Japanese virtue. The harmony of the people, their devoted loyalty to their Emperor, and their pride in their islands rise from sincerity. The power of this "pacification of soul" and "absolute sincerity," was made obvious, even if in distorted form, in World War II in the devotion of the Japanese people to their national interests, and in their acceptance of the dramatic reversal of attitudes that was required by surrender. Their absolute loyalty was founded on an underlying consistency of the inner hearts of men and women whose souls were tough and soft, responsive to fortune and misfortune, and prepared for mysterious shifts of their destiny. These indigenous traditions of Japan, of course, had long since been melded with other influences, Buddhist and Confucian, Chinese and Western, some of which we discuss in a moment, but the root, which is exceptionally Japanese, is the image of the person of perfect sincerity and ever renewed purity and harmony with the *kami* of the land and people.

THE HUMAN IMAGE IN JAPANESE BUDDHISM

Buddhism was already thoroughly East Asian before it arrived in Japan. We need not repeat what has already been said about the primary images of Chinese Buddhism, but only trace their new variations and forms of emphasis in Japanese culture. The Buddhism that first came to Japan was derived directly from Korea, though indirectly from China. It was established in the city of Nara and was almost exclusively associated with the Imperial and gentry families there. This form of Buddhism centered its devotion in the *Vairochana Buddha*, a solar-related *Bodhisattva*, who was identified in Japan, of course, with the presiding Imperial *kami, Amaterasu*, the Sun-goddess. This aristocratic Buddhism made no effort to appeal to the lower classes but remained associated with the upper classes, Chinese language, and the cultured few. In the ninth century, however, Japanese Buddhists began the process of going to the source, that is, to China, to study and returned from their experiences with the flourishing Buddhist cultures of the T'ang and Sung dynasties with new attitudes, images, and approaches. Two of the most distinguished and influential of the early traveling monks were Saichō and Kūkai.

Saichō (posthumously called Dengyo Daishi) was particularly influenced by the *T'ien-tai Buddhism* of China and its use of the broad teachings of the Lotus Sutra. On his return to Japan (in 805) he succeeded in expanding his new center for Buddhism on Mount Hiei, northeast of Kyoto, where the new imperial capital was being established. The Tendai sect which he founded was characterized by demand for devotional purity and Buddhist fervor and by a syncretic approach which found place for many tendencies, appealing to the "mountain hermit" tradition of ascetic discipline, the Zen tradition of meditation, and the classical heritage of *sutra* recitation and Buddha veneration.[26] It was from this center of Buddhism on Mount Hiei that most of the specific Japanese forms of Buddhism emerged in later centuries.

Kūkai (774–835), like Saichō, moved away from the courtly atmosphere of Nara when he returned from China in 806. His Buddhism, centering in the *Vairochana Buddha* maintained special continuity with Tibetan Buddhism, then important in China. In particular this Shingon Buddhism developed both an outer (exoteric) form and an inner (esoteric) tradition. It brings all of the mechanisms of awareness and expression to play together in the awakening of the universal Buddha nature. Dynamic *mudra* or gestures, visual representations of the elements of existence (*mandāla*), prominent use of fragrance and of the sonorous elements of the chant were emphasized as well as more customary forms such as meditation and devotional expressions. Articulately and persuasively Kūkai (Kōbō Daishi) tried to show how all the Buddhist variations are but intimations of, pointers toward, or ingredients in the Shingon (True Word) school. Though Zen usually takes credit for developing the familiar emphasis upon and use of art, calligraphy, and flower arrangement in Japanese religion, that credit should certainly be shared with Kūkai and Shingon.[27]

The Tendai Buddhism of Mount Hiei was syncretic and tolerant. Naturally it developed in several forms—one leading to secularism itself, another developing the ascetic disciplines still characteristic at Mount Hiei, a third building exclusively on the Pure Land themes of the Lotus and other similar sutras, and a fourth influencing Zen. Of secularism and mountain priests we shall not speak just now, but some of the events that led to them led also to a Japanese renaissance of Pure Land thought and to several innovations in its expression. Just as the Shingon of Kūkai understands itself as ancient truth kept alive in secret doctrines, so Pure Land is ancient Buddhism given specific form in Japan. A beautiful story tells of Kuya, the dancing saint of the streets, who left the monastery of Mount Hiei, sang his own ditties of praise to Amida Buddha, and danced in Kyoto's streets with a jingling bell about his neck. He called upon the common folk to receive and join him in his simple faith in Amida's vow to save them all. Here we have the characteristic pattern: identification with the common folk, true piety and devotion, emphasis upon the recital of Amida's name and trust in His grace and a certain irrepressible flair.[28] However, it was Hōnen and his still more famous disciple, Shinran, who gave fully developed form to this image of man in the Pure Land.

Hōnen (1133–1212) drew a distinction between his own approach and what he called the "Path of Personal Sanctity." In his view the path of personal sanctity, which involved the practice of all traditional Buddhist disciplines, was unnecessary and, in fact, even harmful because it implied some lack of trust in Amida's power or mercy. For his heresy he and Shinran were both exiled from Kyoto to remote provinces. Just before he died, in response to inquiry from a friend, Hōnen wrote his famous "One Page Testament" in which he summarized his faith in these words:

> The method of final salvation that I have propounded is neither a sort of meditation, such as has been practiced by many scholars in China and Japan, nor is it a repetition of the Buddha's name by those who have studied and understood the deep meaning of it. It is nothing but the mere repetition of the *"Namu Amida Butsu,"* without a doubt of His mercy, whereby one may be born into the Land of Perfect Bliss. The mere repetition with firm faith includes all the practical details, such as the three-fold preparation of the mind and the four practical rules. If I as an individual had any doctrine more profound than this, I should miss the mercy of the two Honorable Ones, Amida and Shāka, and be left out of the Vow of the Amida Buddha. Those who believe this, though they clearly understand all the teachings Shāka taught throughout his whole life, should behave themselves like simple-minded folk, who know not a single letter, or like ignorant nuns or monks whose faith is implicitly simple. Thus without pedantic airs, they should fervently practice the repetition of the name of Amida, and that alone.[29]

The *Namu Amida Butsu* (*nembutsu*) is a chant reciting and honoring the name of Amida Buddha, the Buddha of Boundless Light. Shinran (1173-1262), fulfilling Hōnen's teaching, took a wife, although he was still a priest and was likewise exiled by the government authorities. In his exile he came to identify himself ever more closely with all the life situations of common folk, for whom Amida's compassion was exerted. His reliance upon Amida was complete and absolute. He was himself a scholar, a learned and pious man, but he gave himself no credit for that. It was the invocation of Amida's name alone, with the absolute sincerity of a pacified heart, that was useful for salvation. He became a village worker, husband and father, teacher and writer, but no individual virtue or merit was relevant to his Buddhist salvation, which, he held, flowed from Amida's grace alone. A collection of his sayings reports Shinran to say:

"If even a good man can be reborn in the Pure Land, how much more so a wicked man!"

People generally think, however, that if even a wicked man can be reborn in the Pure Land, how much more so a good man! This latter view may at first sight seem reasonable, but it is not in accord with the purpose of the Original Vow, with faith in the Power of Another. The reason for this is that he who, relying on his own power, undertakes to perform meritorious deeds, has no intention of relying on the Power of Another and is not the object of the Original Vow of Amida. Should he, however, abandon his reliance on his own power and put his trust in the Power of Another, he can be born in the True Land of Recompense. We who are caught in the net of our own passions cannot free ourselves from bondage to birth and death, no matter what kind of austerities or good deeds we try to perform. Seeing this and pitying our condition, Amida made his Vow with the intention of bringing wicked men to Buddhahood. Therefore the wicked man who depends on the Power of Another is the prime object of salvation. This is the reason why Shinran said, "If even a good man can be reborn in the Pure Land, how much more so a wicked man!"[30]

This was Pure Land Buddhism at flood tide. It emerged in Japan in a time of disorder and rapid change. Actual governmental authority had already shifted from the Emperor to the military, and then away from the imperial center at Kyoto altogether. Contending feudal lords threatened stability and order and defined justice to suit themselves. The piety and restraint of the monasteries seemed weak and ineffectual. In such a desperate time Buddhism was made available to common folk without impossible demands of discipline or scholarship. They need but recite the Holy Name of the Compassionate Amida with true sincerity to receive a gift of blessedness beyond the power of any earthly authority to grant. Shinran lived in the twelfth and thirteenth centuries, but the comparison with a similar period of social upheaval and the life and thought of Martin Luther some 400 years later is remarkable. Both Shinran and Luther were pious clergymen whose religious fervor was intense. Both abandoned the celibate life but not the priesthood. Both stressed the absolute need of man for a power outside of himself to make possible his salvation. Both stressed the access to this power directly through faith by common folk, and both devoted themselves to work with the common people and to the energetic promotion of their respective views. There are, of course, important differences, but the similarities are striking. Shinran's school of Pure Land Buddhism, called Jodo Shinshu, develops the image of pious common folk, lifted by their trust in a Cosmic Grace out of a troubled and uncertain world to a pure and happy, transcendent existence and whatever still better may lie beyond even that happy land. In several specific sects this became one of the most popular and widespread versions of Japanese Buddhism.

The other main form of Buddhism to illustrate the special consciousness of Japan is Zen. Japan inherited the distinctive pattern of Zen from China. It had already incorporated Taoist mystical sensitivity to unity and emptiness and love of nature. Zen had already accepted the ideal of the master and his artful use of strange and powerful devices such as koan meditation, shouting and beating, seated meditation, and discipline of the monasteries in which monks engaged in labor as well as contemplation. For the most part we should say that the Japanese Zennists perfected—or in some cases perhaps overrefined—these procedures. One more or less unique Japanese element, however, was the historical accident that Zen came in a special, though not exclusive, way to be identified with the warrior class, the *samurai,* in Japan. The enigmatic story of The Teaman and the Ruffian, as told by D. T. Suzuki, will illustrate several points.

The Teaman and the Ruffian

What follows is the story of a teaman who had to assume the role of a swordsman and fight with a ruffian. The teaman generally does not know anything about swordplay and cannot be a match in any sense of the word for anybody who carries a sword. His is a peaceful profession. The story gives us an idea of what a man can do with a sword even when he had never had any technical training, if only his mind is made up to go through the business at the risk of his life. Here is another illustration demonstrating the value of resolute-mindedness leading up to the transcendence of life and death.

Toward the end of the seventeenth century, Lord Yama-no-uchi, of the province of Tosa, wanted to take his teamaster along with him on his official trip to Yedo, the seat of the Tokugawa Shogunate. The teamaster was not inclined to accompany him, for in the first place he was not of the *samurai* rank and knew that Yedo was not a quiet and congenial place like Tosa, where he was well known and had many good friends. In Yedo he would most likely get into trouble with ruffians, resulting not only in his own disgrace but in his lord's. The trip would be a most risky adventure, and he had no desire to undertake it.

The lord, however, was insistent and would not listen to the remonstrance of the teamaster; for this man was really great in his profession, and it was probable that the lord harbored the secret desire to show him off among his friends and colleagues. Not able to resist further the lord's earnest request which was in fact a command, the master put off his teaman's garment and dressed himself as one of the *samurai,* carrying two swords.

While staying in Yedo, the teamaster was mostly confined in his lord's house. One day the lord gave him permission to go out and do some sight-seeing. Attired as a *samurai,* he visited Uyeno by the Shinobazu pond, where he espied an evil-looking *samurai* resting on a stone. He did not like the looks of this man. But finding no way to avoid him, the tea-man went on. The man politely addressed him: "As I observe, you are a *samurai* of Tosa, and I should consider it a great honor if you permit me to try my skill in swordplay with you."

The teaman from Tosa from the beginning of his trip had been apprehensive of such an encounter. Now, standing face to face with a *rōnin* of the worst kind, he did not know what to do. But he answered honestly: "I am not a regular *samurai,* though so dressed; I am a teamaster, and as to the art of swordplay I am not at all prepared to be your opponent." But as the real motive of the *rōnin* was to extort money from the victim, of whose weakness he was now fully convinced, he pressed the idea even more strongly on the teaman from Tosa.

Finding it impossible to escape the evil-designing *rōnin,* the teaman made up his mind to fall under the enemy's sword. But he did not wish to die an ignominious death that would surely reflect on the honor of his lord of Tosa. Suddenly he remembered that a few minutes before he had passed by a swordsman's training school near Uyeno park, and he thought he would go and ask the master about the proper use of the sword on such occasions and also as to how he should honorably meet an inevitable death. He said to the *rōnin,* "If you insist so much, we will try our skill in swordsmanship. But as I am now on my master's errand, I must make my report first. It will take some time before I come back to meet you here. You must give me that much time."

The *rōnin* agreed. So the teaman hastened to the training school referred to before and made a most urgent request to see the master. The gate-keeper was somewhat reluctant to acquiesce because the visitor carried no introductory letter. But when he noticed the seriousness of the man's desire, which was betrayed in his every word and in his every movement, he decided to take him to the master.

The master quietly listened to the teaman, who told him the whole story and most earnestly expressed his wish to die as befitted a *samurai.* The swordsman said, "The pupils who come to me invariably want to know how to use the sword, and not how to die. You are really a unique example. But before I teach you the art of dying, kindly serve me a cup of tea, as you say you are a teaman." The teaman of Tosa was only too glad to make tea for him, because this was in all likelihood the last chance for him to practice his art of tea to his heart's content. The swordsman closely watched the teaman as the latter was engaged in the performance of the art. Forgetting all about his approaching tragedy, the teaman serenely proceded to prepare tea. He went through all the stages of the art as if this were the only business that concerned him most seriously under the sun at that very moment. The swordsman was deeply impressed with the teaman's concentrated state of mind, from which all the superficial stirrings of ordinary consciousness were swept away. He struck his own knee, a sign of hearty approval, and exclaimed, "There you are! No need for you to learn the art of death! The state of mind in which you are now is enough for you to cope with any swordsman. When you see your *rōnin* outcast, go this way: First, think you are going to serve tea for a guest. Courteously salute him, apologizing for the delay, and tell him that you are now ready for the contest. Take off your *haori* (outer coat), fold it up carefully, and then put your fan on it just as you do when you are at work. Now bind your head with the *tenugui* (corresponding to a towel), tie your sleeves up with string, and gather up your *hakama* (skirt). You are now prepared for the business that is to start immediately. Draw your sword, lift it high up over your head, in full readiness to strike down the opponent, and, closing your eyes, collect your thoughts for combat. When you hear him give a yell, strike him with your sword. It will probably end in a mutual slaying." The teaman thanked the master for his instructions and went back to the place where he had promised to meet the combatant.

He scrupulously followed the advice given by the swordmaster with the same attitude of mind as when he was serving tea for his friends. When, boldly standing before the *rōnin,* he raised his sword, the *rōnin* saw an altogether different personality before him. He had no chance to give a yell, for he did not know where and how to attack the teaman, who now appeared to him as an embodiment of fearlessness, that is, of the Unconscious. Instead of advancing toward the opponent, the *rōnin* retreated step by step, finally crying, "I'm done, I'm done!" And throwing up his sword he prostrated himself on the ground and pitifully asked the teaman's pardon for his rude request, and then he hurriedly left the field.

As to the historicity of the story I am in no position to state anything definite. What I attempt here to establish is the popular belief underlying the story cited here and others of similar character; this is that, underneath all the practical technique or the methodological details necessary for the mastery of an art, there are certain intuitions directly reaching what I call the Cosmic Unconscious, and all these intuitions belonging to various arts are not to be regarded as individually unconnected or mutually individually unrelated, but as growing out of one fundamental intuition. It is indeed firmly believed by Japanese generally that the various specific intuitions acquired by the swordsman, the teamaster and masters of other branches of art and culture are no more than particularized applications of one great experience.[31]

The loyalty and character of the *samurai* were founded on a powerful blend of the archaic Japanese tradition of the pure heart, with an elaborate honor code derived from Confucianism, and complete equanimity before death as taught by Buddhism. As the story suggests, the preoccupation with death with honor results in a state of consciousness that brings together the most tranquil and inward form of Buddhism and the life-or-death violence of the *samurai*. This state of consciousness separates the mind from all intrusion of particular thoughts, from all calculation or ordinary reasoning, and permits the mind to experience its unity with the Buddha nature. This state of perfect concentration and awareness, called in Zen "no-mindedness," makes possible uncalculated spontaneity remarkably effective for hand-to-hand combat. Both traditions stress discipline. Because the Zen emphasis was primarily upon the individual experience of enlightenment, visualized as a life-and-death contest, it was possible for Zen to minister to the warriors and for the warriors to nourish the discipline and character of Zen without ever fully resolving the contradiction between the Buddhist ethic of noninjury and warrior duties. In general monks were not warriors, and warriors used Zen training for merit building rather than to attain enlightenment, *satori,* religious salvation itself. Through traditional Shinto teachings and values, however, these two sometimes were more closely related than we can easily imagine.

A final implication from the story of the Teaman and the Ruffian would see Zen itself as a fulfillment of the ancient Buddhist understanding of the identity of *samsara* and *nirvana.* To serve and sip tea in total awareness and undistracted immediacy is to be free from all suffering right now. It is the image of the fully realized person, the man of enlightenment beyond all desires.

The human image underlying these various forms of mature Mahayana Buddhism reflects the whole structure of that style of Buddhist life and thought. No one pattern of description has ever been adequate for Buddhist self-expression, but through the plurality of specific sects, doctrines, and traditions we may glimpse the shadows of a larger form. The underlying unity of the Mahayana tradition is traceable in the conception of the Bodhisattva, which includes the concept of the Buddha-body/Buddha-nature. The world of experience is the product of certain qualities of consciousness. "All that we are is the result of what we have thought," says the *Dhamapada.* The ultimate quality of consciousness is symbolized by the *Dharma kaya,* the Buddha-body of truth, in which all forms of consciousness participate. From this standpoint all beings share the Buddha-nature. The human problem lies in the obstructions we create to the free functioning of this Buddha-nature, obstructions that take the forms of egoism, discriminations that separate us from the depths of our own experience and possibility, forms that are expressed in desire and result in suffering. The solution of the human dilemma lies in a refusal to create these obstructing conditions, a refusal to superintend the world. Put as positively as possible, Buddha-consciousness is to see the true emptiness of all the fabrications of experience with respect to their power to create significant suffering. The paths to this consciousness are varied. Shingon Buddhism stresses the attitude that all the mechanisms of human consciousness, fragrance, movement, sound, contemplation, and visualization have equal access to the open awareness. Pure Land Buddhism concentrates the energies into the recitation of the vow of faith.

Zen Buddhism seeks dramatically to break the hold of the discriminating consciousness in order to release the original *satori,* the original freedom. When this happens, by whatever means, *samsara* is *nirvana,* the perspective has been changed, consciousness will produce only awareness of the flow, without suffering, sorrow, or discontent. Outwardly life is not so different. People will still eat, drink, sleep, serve each other, laugh, contend, and contemplate, but they will do these things in this pure and happy land in which no sorrow is created by their minds. It makes all the difference in the world. It is a human image that combines a complete sense of Oneness with the unobstructed flow of all existence. Almost everyone has had intimations of this kind of exhilarating unity and peace. It is the objective of Buddhism to produce the conditions that make it the ordinary experience, to awaken the Buddha-nature in all sentient beings.

The conditions that created modern Japan and fractured or distorted so many of these images will be discussed briefly in Chapter 6. There are considerable differences among the models of life offered by Shinto and by the mystical, the popular, and the meditative types of Buddhism that we have discussed, but there is also a curious coherence among them. In one way or another all these different symbols suggest that there is an original unity amid the real plurality of things—that when one's consciousness is open to that unity the heart is pure and pacified, art, sound, and gestures resonate with the power of the Dainichi, Great Illuminator, and man acts and meditates in spontaneous freedom and appropriateness. The Japanese religions seek in their various ways to induce this state of consciousness and to make it the habitual frame of orientation of all life's acts.

SUMMARY: THE HUMAN IMAGE IN EAST ASIA

There are many images of the highest life in East Asia: the genealogical and mythical tradition of the venerable ancestors, the mystical hermit-sage, the circumspect scholar-sage, the grateful devotee, the pure-hearted observer of the *kami-way,* the fearless concentration of the teaman, *samurai,* and all the other artists of life, the free and disciplined *master* of life and death. Although there are in these various traditions several concepts, such as the Will of Heaven, the Tao, the Dharma-body of the Buddha, the Great Kami of the Sun, and so on, that might have been used to give complete unity to the pattern, there seems to have been no strong impulse to use them in this way. Monotheism or even monism seems to be foreign in spirit to the East Asian sense of immediacy, of tolerance for and appreciation of variety, the full recognition of the divinity present in many things. This deep-rooted pluralism brings all forms of "this-worldly" and "other-worldly" thought into close and continuous relation. The most practical and immediate forms of Chinese Confucianism rise out of the harmony between the inner character of the individual person (*jên*) and the ultimate Tao; the most other-wordly forms of Pure Land promises relate to an immediately practical gift of freedom and hope to common folk. East Asia is a world of many images and the mutual flourishing of all of them. In contrast with India where harmony is built on monism in which all differences are reduced to the one, *Brahman,* the images of East Asia find harmony in un-redeemed pluralism.

In *The Chuang-Tzu*[32], the mystic philosopher formulates a suggestive analogy in which the world and all its people and their sectarian viewpoints are compared to many pipes or hollows (as in the apertures of a great mouth-organ). The breath of Tao blows across the ten-thousand things, causing each to sound its characteristic pitch. Both *each* and *all* are produced by the inter-action of Tao and individuality. The whole truth is not contained in any one configuration of sounds, but only in the transcendental and inexplicable unity of all of them. Man's access to unity can never rise above his experience of multiplicity. Beyond this the wise have nothing more to say.

NOTES

1. Charles A. Moore, ed., *The Chinese Mind: Essentials of Chinese Philosophy and Culture* (Honolulu: East-West Center Press, 1967), especially chaps. 1 and 2 by Professors Moore and Wing-Tsit Chan concerning Chinese humanism.

2. Richard Wilhelm, *The I Ching,* trans. Cary R. Baynes (Princeton, N.J.: Princeton University Press, 1967), "Introduction," pp. *xxi* and *xxii,* and Diagram of the Eight Trigrams.

3. Ibid., pp. *lviii–lxi.*

4. Ibid., pp. 1–11.

5. Ibid., "Foreword," by Carl Jung, pp. *xxi–xxxix.*

6. C. K. Yang, *Religion in Chinese Society* (Berkeley: University of California Press, 1961), chap. 2.

7. Ibid., pp. 33–35.

8. Ibid., chap. 4.

9. Arthur Waley, trans. *The Way and Its Power* (New York: Grove Press, 1958), p. 150.

10. Ibid., p. 164.

11. Ibid., p. 219.

12. Burton Watson, trans., *Chuang Tzu: Basic Writings* (New York: Columbia University Press, 1964), p. 42.

13. Ibid., pp. 90.

14. Fung Yu-Lan, *The Spirit of Chinese Philosophy,* trans. E. R. Hughes (Boston: Beacon Press, 1962), especially chap. 5.

15. Lin Yutang, trans., "Laotse, the Book of Tao," in *The Wisdom of China and India,* ed. Lin Yutang (New York: The Modern Library, 1942), p. 600.

16. Moore, *The Chinese Mind,* chaps. 1 and 2.

17. Arthur Waley, *The Analects of Confucius,* trans. and annotated by Arthur Waley (London: Allen and Unwin, 1938), p. 122.

18. Ibid., pp. 34–41.

19. Ibid., p. 105.

20. Ibid., p. 171. Waley expresses the reservation, based on style of the chain argument, that this passage is comparatively late. It does, however, represent what the compiler of the Analects believed to be Confucius' mature view.

21. Garma C. C. Chang, *The Buddhist Teaching of Totality* (University Park: Pennsylvania State University Press, 1971), pp. 22–24.

22. Donald L. Philippi, trans., *Kojiki* (Princeton, N.J.: Princeton University Press, 1969), pp. 4–15.

23. Floyd H. Ross, *Shinto: The Way of Japan* (Boston: Beacon Press, 1965), chap. 3.

24. Ibid., especially chap. 5.

25. Ibid., pp. 39 and 112.

26. *Sources of Japanese Tradition,* Vol. 1, compiled by Ryusaku Tsunoda, Wm. Theodore de Bary, and Donald Keene (New York: Columbia University Press, 1958), chap. 6.

27. Ibid., chap. 7.

28. Ibid., pp. 187–88.

29. Ibid., pp. 202–3.

30. Ibid., p. 211.

31. Daisetz T. Suzuki, *Zen and Japanese Culture* (Princeton, N.J.: Princeton University Press, 1959), pp. 189–93.

32. Watson, *Chuang Tzu,* pp. 31–45.

FOR FURTHER READING

ANESAKI, MASAHARU, *History of Japanese Religion*. Rutland, Vt.: C. E. Tuttle, 1963. The basic text on Japanese religions; good capsule biographies of Buddhist leaders and description of sects.

ASTON, WILLIAM G., *Shinto: The Ancient Religion of Japan*. London: Constable and Company, 1910. Old book with special emphasis on the classical and early heritage of Shinto.

CHANG, GARMA C. C., *The Buddhist Teaching of Totality*. University Park: Pennsylvania State University Press, 1971. The only translation of major sections of the Hua Yen sutra with comprehensive explanations of the teaching of totality in Buddhism.

CH'EN, KENNETH, *Buddhism in China*. Princeton, N.J.: Princeton University Press, 1964. An overview of the history and divisions of Chinese Buddhism.

———, *Buddhism: The Light of Asia*. New York: Barron, 1968. A survey of all Buddhism primarily from historical and doctrinal perspectives.

ELIOT, CHARLES, *Japanese Buddhism*. New York: Barnes & Noble, 1959. A careful, scholarly study of Japanese Buddhist traditions.

KITAGAWA, JOSEPH, *Religion in Japanese History*. New York: Columbia University Press, 1968. A modern study by an Asian-American scholar, develops more of the social, cultural side than most.

MOORE, CHARLES A., ed., *The Chinese Mind: Essentials of Chinese Philosophy and Culture*. Honolulu: East-West Center Press, 1967. Collections of essays by the scholars attending the East-West Philosophers conferences at Hawaii.

———, *The Japanese Mind: Essentials of Japanese Philosophy and Culture*. Honolulu: East-West Center Press, 1967. Collections of essays by the scholars attending the East-West Philosophers conferences at Hawaii.

NAKAMURA, HAJIME, *Ways of Thinking of Eastern Peoples: India, China, Tibet, Japan*. Honolulu: East-West Center Press, 1964. A comparative study based on differences in Buddhism as interpreted in these four Asian cultures.

ONO, SOKYO, *The Kami Way: An Introduction to Shrine Shinto*. Rutland, Vt.: Bridgeway Press, 1961. Provides descriptions of Shrine Shinto traditions and practices.

PHILIPPI, DONALD L., trans., *Kojiki: Translated with an Introduction and Notes*. Princeton, N.J.: Princeton University Press, 1969. The definitive translation of the Kojiki with very helpful introduction and index to the names of *kami* and clans.

ROSS, FLOYD H., *Shinto: The Way of Japan*. Boston: Beacon Press, 1965. A sympathetic and eminently readable account of Shinto which gives interesting examples of Shinto as a cultural form.

SAUNDERS, E. DALE, *Buddhism in Japan*. Philadelphia: University of Pennsylvania Press, 1964. A fairly recent and detailed study of the Buddhist sects in Japan.

SPAE, JOSEPH J., *Shinto Man*. Tokyo: Orlens Institute for Religious Research, 1972. Monograph on Shinto anthropology meant for advanced readers.

SUZUKI, DAISETZ T., *An Introduction to Zen Buddhism*. New York: Philosophical Library, 1949. Essays by Zen's most well-known interpreter in English; stresses the centrality of *satori* experience in Zen.

———, *Zen and Japanese Culture*. Princeton, N.J.: Princeton University Press, 1959. A collection of essays on the Zen contributions to Japanese life and thought.

WALEY, ARTHUR, *The Analects of Confucius*. New York: Vintage Books, 1938. One of the best translations of the aphorisms of Confucius, with a very helpful introduction and analysis.

———, *The Way and Its Power*. New York: Grove Press, 1958. A fine translation of and introduction to the *Tao-Te-Ching*. Other good translations by Lin Yutang, Wing-Tsit Chan, D. C. Lau, or James Legge may be consulted for interesting variations.

WATSON, BURTON, trans., *Chuang Tzu: Basic Writings*. New York: Columbia University Press, 1964. A felicitous translation of a fabulous Chinese book.

WELCH, HOLMES, *The Practice of Chinese Buddhism*. Cambridge, Mass.: Harvard University Press, 1967. Major study of Chinese Buddhist life.

———, *Taoism: The Parting of the Way*. Boston: Beacon Press, 1965. A beautiful, brief, and useful description of Taoist philosophical and religious teachings.

WILHEIM, RICHARD, *The I Ching*, trans. Cary F. Baynes. Princeton, N.J.: Princeton University Press, 1950. The English translation of the German translation of the Chinese text; well-organized for consultation but requires supplementary explanations.

WRIGHT, ARTHUR E., *Buddhism in Chinese History*. Palo Alto, Calif.: Stanford University Press, 1959. A brief book that traces clearly major stages in the development of Chinese Buddhism.

YANG, C. K., *Religion in Chinese Society*. Berkeley: University of California Press, 1961. A sociological approach to Chinese religion—a valuable alternative approach.

YU-LAN, FUNG, *The Spirit of Chinese Philosophy*, trans. E. R. Hughes. Boston: Beacon Press, 1962. A brief reflection on the history of Chinese thought by a leading philosopher.

The Broken Image

6

FROM LIGHT TO DARKNESS

In his penetrating philosophical essay, *The Myth of Sisyphus,* Albert Camus mused, "In this unintelligible and limited universe, man's fate henceforth assumes its meaning. A horde of irrationals has sprung up and surrounds him until his ultimate end. In his recovered and now studied lucidity, the feeling of the absurd becomes clear and definite."[1] As much as any other recent author, Camus has captured and probed twentieth-century man's profound anxiety and deep despair. To generations that have endured Auschwitz, Dachau, Hiroshima, and My Lai, the world often seems alien, hostile, and absurd. Human intentions and ideals are frequently frustrated by seemingly senseless suffering. Surely unexplained suffering is nothing new—Job gave eloquent testimony to the abiding nature of this problem. But modern man no longer hears a voice from the whirlwind. He has lost an overarching perspective from which to view his world and with which to grasp his experience. While old modes of explanation have died, new forms of interpretation are yet to be born. The poet W. H. Auden labeled our time "The Age of Anxiety." Contemporary theologian Paul Tillich elaborated Auden's insight when he pointed out that ours is an era in which "the anxiety of emptiness and meaninglessness is dominant." According to Tillich, "Twentieth-century man has lost a meaningful world and a self which lives in meanings out of a spiritual center."[2] Plagued by meaninglessness and suffering despair, modern man's spiritual landscape has become a "Waste Land," from which there seems to be, in the words of Jean-Paul Sartre's well-known play, "No Exit."

How, we might ask, has this pervasive malaise arisen? This question cannot be answered simply, for the sources of the contemporary spiritual climate are many and complex. Within the context of our study, we are concerned to explore the way in which changing attitudes toward religious belief have contributed to modern man's dilemma. More particularly, by considering the breakdown of the dominant religious image of man, particularly in the West, we seek to unearth the roots of our confusion and despair. One of the dominant features of the modern world is the waning of religious belief. Standing at the threshold of the twentieth century, the German prophet-philosopher Friedrich Nietzsche declared, "God is dead!" By mid-century, a group of influential theologians appeared to be attempting to make virtue out of necessity by voicing support of Nietzsche's proclamation through the development of an apparently self-contradictory "death of God theology." For many persons, the word of God's death came as welcome news. Scientific, technological, secular man no longer seems to need a providential God. As a matter of fact, for many forward-looking intellectuals, the price of man's coming of age was nothing less than the death of God.

Our consideration of the function of religion in human life and society, however, leads us to suspect that the death of God is at best a mixed blessing. We have seen that "The sacred cosmos is confronted by man as an immensely powerful reality other than himself. Yet this reality addresses itself to him and locates his life in an ultimately meaningful order."[3] By dwelling within the framework provided by religious symbols, a person is able to understand the meaning of his life, to feel at home in the world, and to know who he is. This implies that when religious symbols lose their power over the human imagination, meaning gives way to meaninglessness, sense is overcome by absurdity. Berger's insight again is valuable:

> The sacred cosmos, which transcends and includes man in its ordering of reality, thus provides man's ultimate shield against the terror of anomy. To be in a "right" relationship with the sacred cosmos is to be protected against the nightmare threats of chaos. To fall out of such a "right" relationship is to be abandoned on the edge of the abyss of meaninglessness.[4]

The eclipse of God often casts a dark shadow over man's world. Paradoxically, to discover the sources of contemporary darkness, we must turn the clock back over 200 years to a period of Western history known as the Enlightenment.

ENLIGHTENED MAN
AND THE ECLIPSE OF GOD

Writing toward the end of the eighteenth century, Prussian philosopher Immanuel Kant defined what he regarded as the outstanding features of enlightenment.

Enlightenment is man's release from his self-incurred tutelage. Tutelage is man's inability to make use of his understanding without direction from another. Self-incurred is this tutelage when its cause lies not in lack of reason but in lack of resolution and courage to use it without direction from another. Dare to know! Have courage to use your own reason!—that is the motto of enlightenment.[5]

Kant's remark suggests why the eighteenth century often is called "The Age of Reason." The human image during the Enlightenment emphasizes almost exclusively the capacity to reason. Above all else, man is rational. The implications of this image reach far beyond the philosopher's study. For enlightened man, reason is *critical;* it is the instrument of intellectual and social criticism. Paul Tillich points out that "in the name of critical reason the way was prepared for the French Revolution, which transformed the world. Before that the American Revolution occurred, uniting religious and rational dimensions in the Constitution."[6] In brief, during the Enlightenment, reason was *revolutionary.* To the label "The Age of Reason" we might add "The Era of Revolutions." Bounded on one end by Britain's Glorious Revolution of 1689 and on the other by the American and French Revolutions, the Enlightenment was a time of extraordinary social and political change.

Kant noted the revolutionary potential of reason when he identified enlightenment with "man's release from his self-incurred tutelage." This was Kant's way of talking about man's coming of age—his emergence from the immaturity of childhood to the maturity of adulthood. The essence of immaturity is dependence on external authority. This authority might be that of another person, a social group, or an institution such as church or state. By contrast, maturity amounts to self-reliance, a declaration of personal independence. Kant aptly described the mature person as "autonomous." He has become a law (*nomos*) to himself (*autos*). Reliance on external authority is unnecessary, for one is his own authority. The source of the independent individual's authority is his reason. Moreover, human reason remains untainted by corruption. In addition to viewing man as rational, the Enlightenment upheld his inherent goodness. Gone was the Reformation picture of man as a fallen, corrupt sinner. Philosopher Ernst Cassirer concludes that "The concept of original sin is the common opponent against which all the different trends of the philosophy of the Enlightenment join forces."[7] Free from sin, man can distinguish right from wrong and truth from falsehood by the unaided exercise of reason. In opposition to the prevailing opinion of the Middle Ages, many of the thinkers of the eighteenth century maintained that reason does not need to be supplemented by divine revelation. Man can discover truth and goodness through rational reflection and can express them in his actions if he so chooses. Ignorance rather than sinfulness is his problem. And ignorance, unlike sinfulness, can be overcome by man's own efforts.

For an enlightened person, dependence on divine revelation, priestly guidance, and absolute political authority is at best superfluous and at worst enslaving. During the eighteenth century, the free use of reason led to ecclesiastical, intellectual, and social revolution. As confidence in the human capacity to reason increased, the willingness to submit to alien authority decreased. All things had to be brought before the bar of reason for careful review and rigorous evaluation. If venerated beliefs or long-established institutions failed the test of reason, they had to be rejected or overthrown. Only what could be rationally demonstrated or justified remained acceptable. Whether in the effort to replace political despotism with democratic forms of government or to overcome theological irrationalism with reasonable argument, criticism was the Enlightenment's ideal, reason its weapon.

Nowhere are the fruits of increased confidence in human reason more apparent than in the rise of modern science. The discoveries of pioneers such as Galileo (1564–1642), Robert Boyle (1627–1691), and Sir Isaac Newton (1642–1727) mark the birth of the modern world. Newton's work in particular left an indelible mark upon the intellectual history of the eighteenth century. For many persons, the monumental scientific advances achieved by Newton served as examples of what human reason could accomplish. Alexander Pope captured the attitude of many of his contemporaries toward Newton when he wrote:

> Nature and Nature's laws lay hid in night,
> God said: "Let Newton be," and all was light.[8]

A more careful examination of major aspects of Newton's work reveals significant features of the emerging eighteenth-century world-view. Newton's scientific investigations set the future course of both scientific inquiry and philosophical reflection.

One of Newton's most enduring contributions to intellectual history was his effort to redefine the proper domain of reason and to articulate the appropriate method by which reason should operate. Cassirer points out that throughout much of the history of Western philosophy, "truly 'philosophical' knowledge had seemed attainable only when thought, starting from a highest being and from a highest, intuitively grasped certainty, succeeded in spreading the light of this certainty over all derived being and all derived knowledge."[9] Beginning with metaphysical first principles that are immediately known, one seeks to arrive at the concrete particulars of everyday experience by means of careful deduction. For Newton, the proper course of reason is precisely the reverse. Drawing on a uniquely British tradition dating back to the late medieval nominalism of William of Ockham[10] and more recently elaborated in the scientific work of Francis Bacon (1561–1626) and Robert Boyle, Newton maintained that reason must always begin with an analysis of concrete experience, rather than with a priori principles, that is, general notions arrived at prior to or independent of experience. Having carefully observed and precisely recorded data of experience, the scientist attempts to formulate general principles or laws to account for his observations. Where possible, controlled experiments should be carried out to lend weight to scientific conclusions. By means of reason one can discern the logic of the facts of experience. Repeated observation enables the scientist to establish mathematical principles that describe observed data. Newton's thought progresses from the particular to the general or universal, and not from the universal to the particular. His method is inductive, establishing general principles from specific experience, instead of deductive, determining particularities from abstract notions. This revision of the proper method of reason exerted considerable influence throughout the Enlightenment, and that influence continues down to our own day. A person as different from Newton in interest and in character as Voltaire could agree that inquiry should never "begin by inventing principles according to which we attempt to explain everything. We should say rather: Let us make an exact analysis of things. . . . When we cannot utilize the compass of mathematics or the torch of experience and physics, it is certain that we cannot take a single step forward."[11]

Newton's formulation of the universal law of gravitation offers a graphic illustration of the scientific use of reason. Building on principles developed by Kepler to describe the form of planetary orbits, Newton established a law to explain the mutual attraction of all masses. Through this single law, he described the relationship of all bodies in the universe—be that body the most distant star or the nearest apple. Newton did not postulate this law a priori, but arrived at it a posteriori, or from observation of the world around him. Having established the universal law of gravitation, Newton theorized that all natural phenomena might be explained by mathematical principles extrapolated from direct observation. The universe, according to Newton, is controlled by a vast network of reciprocal laws. The implication of this suggestion is that the world is a finely tuned machine that runs according to universal laws that can be discovered by rational inquiry.

Three interrelated themes identified by Newton continued to be important throughout the eighteenth century. The first was the *principle of universality*. Later thinkers found Newton's ability to define one law under which all phenomena could be subsumed to be one of the most compelling features of his work. Newton showed that though the motions of distant planets and the falling of an apple seem to be qualitatively different, they are actually instances of a single law. In short, the laws of nature are universal or valid under all circumstances. For many during this era, the principle of universality was not only descriptive of the outer, objective sphere of nature. It also applied to the realm of man's intellectual, ethical, and religious life. The universality of the laws of nature is mirrored in human reason. "The eighteenth century is imbued with a belief in the unity and immutability of reason. Reason is the same for all thinking subjects, all nations, all epochs, and all cultures."[12] Through the employment of the universal laws of reason, a person can discover the universal laws by which nature operates. The principle of universality appeared again in the era's veneration of political and religious toleration, in its effort to define universal principles of morality, and in the quest for a natural religion proper to all humankind. We shall have occasion to consider the moral and the religious expressions of the principle of universality in what follows.

Closely related to the principle of universality is the *principle of unity* or of *harmony.* Cassirer points out that "the rationalistic postulate of unity dominates the minds of this age."[13] The discovery of universal laws enables one to see unity where previously only differences were visible. Contradiction is only apparent and dissolves when underlying universal principles are uncovered. The constant operation of universal laws creates a *uni*-verse in which ostensible oppositions are finally harmonized. From Adam Smith's *laissez-faire* economics and Jean-Jacques Rousseau's "general will" to Leibniz's monads, the ideals of unity and harmony pervade the Enlightenment world-view. Pope summarized this point in his poem, "An Essay on Man."

> The general ORDER, since the whole began,
> Is kept in Nature, and is kept in man.

The final theme related to Newton's scientific theories that needs to be highlighted is the idea of *mechanism,* or the use of the mechanical metaphor for envisioning the world. As a result of the advances of science during the late seventeenth and early eighteenth centuries, many intellectuals felt constrained to conclude that the world is a giant machine regulated by universal laws. Some people continued to believe that God created the world and established the laws by which it operates. But the very perfection of God's product leaves him little to do. The world can run by itself, and God is free to retire in leisure to his heavenly abode. By the end of the century, there seemed little need of the notion of God at all to account for the data of experience. With God removed from the scene, the world was viewed as a self-perpetuating and self-regulating apparatus, a finely crafted clock that never needed to be wound or set.

The modern scientific view of the world that developed during the Enlightenment was rooted in the Christian image of man and of his place in the universe. Newton insisted on the close connection between belief in a providential creator God and scientific investigation. As if to underscore his point, Newton supplemented his scientific works with theological treatises. The belief that the world and its laws are created by God is a basic presupposition of Newton's inquiry. For Newton, the order of the world that science attempts to discover depends on God's ordering activity. Historian Francis Oakley notes that Roger Cotes prefaced the second edition of Newton's *Principia* with the following words:

> The true business of natural philosophy [i.e., science] is ... to inquire after those laws on which the Great Creator actually chose to found this most beautiful Frame of the World, not those by which he might have done the same, had he pleased. ... Without all doubt this world ... could arise from nothing but the perfectly free Will of God directing and pre-

siding over all. From this Fountain it is that those laws, which we call the laws of Nature, have flowed, in which there appear many traces indeed of the most wise contrivance but not the least shadow of necessity.[14]

Newton believed that natural laws are not inherent in the cosmos, but are imposed by a creative God who transcends the world. Because natural laws are a function of divine volition, they cannot be established by deductive reasoning, but must be ascertained through empirical analysis and rational extrapolation. For Newton as for many other early scientists, scientific investigation was the faithful exploration of God's creation. Newton's aim remained the enhancement and not the destruction of the Christian image of man. In spite of this, forces released by Newton's work were a major factor in the breakdown of the Christian image.

Though an amateur theologian, Newton's work was essentially scientific. It is evident, however, that his ideas have implications that reach far beyond the bounds of scientific inquiry. Enlightenment philosophers seized Newton's insights as the basis upon which to construct a new image of humanity. The British philosopher John Locke (1632-1704) played a crucial role in the elaboration of Newton's vision for human self-understanding. Locke agreed wholeheartedly with the empirical orientation of reason defined by Newton. Offering an illustration of Pope's contention that "The proper study of mankind is Man," Locke devoted his major philosophical work, *An Essay Concerning Human Understanding* (1690), to an investigation of how we know. By so doing, he placed the problem of epistemology or the theory of knowledge at the center of philosophical debate for succeeding generations and established the course that British philosophy has followed down to the present day.

To understand the significance of Locke's essay, we should recognize that he consciously opposed what had become the mainstream of modern philosophical thought. From the time of Descartes (1596-1650), philosophers had argued that the mind possesses innate ideas. Innate ideas are notions that man has independent of experience, or in more precise philosophical terms, a priori forms of reflection. Descartes maintained that the mind has a given structure that determines the way in which experience is ordered. Innate ideas are the forms of thought or patterns of perception through which knowledge is acquired. For Descartes, general principles are not abstracted from the particulars of sense experience, as Newton would have us believe. Rather the a priori principles of the mind organize sense data. Sense experience is merely an occasion for the expression of innate ideas. "In our ideas there is nothing which is not innate in the mind or faculty of thinking, except only those circumstances which point to experience."[15] The mind's possession of innate ideas establishes the possibility of defining truth deductively with all the precision and rigor of a mathematical proof and frees one from reliance on induction from concrete experience.

Locke rejected the entire tradition of innate ideas that Descartes represented. In keeping with principles laid down by Newton, Locke contended that "all ideas come from sensation or reflection." Furthermore,

> Let us suppose the mind to be, as we say, white paper, void of all characters, without any ideas: How comes it to be furnished? Whence comes it by the vast store which the busy and boundless fancy of man has painted on it with an almost endless variety? Whence has it all the *materials* of reason and knowledge? To this I answer, in one word, from EXPERIENCE. In that all our knowledge is found; and from that it ultimately derives itself. Our observation employed either, about external sensible objects, or about the internal operations of our minds perceived and reflected on by ourselves, is that which supplies our understandings with all the *materials* of thinking. These two are the fountains of knowledge, from whence all the ideas we have, or can naturally have, do spring.[16]

By asserting that the mind is "white paper, void of all characters, without any ideas," or a *tabula rasa* as it often is called, Locke went against Descartes and his followers. According to Locke, man has no innate ideas that determine the form of his experience. To the contrary, all knowledge is rooted in or grows out of experience—either sense experience of the outer world or the experience of observing our own minds. The mind begins as a blank slate and gradually accumulates knowledge through sense experience. Agreeing with Newton, Locke held that concrete experience can form the basis of justifiable extrapolation. For instance, we might intuit simple ideas. But these particular notions can become building blocks for more complex ideas. Through association or by combination, we pass from simple to complex ideas. Of course such elaboration can never divorce itself from the fundamental experiences of sensation and reflection. Locke insisted that the mind does not have

> the least glimmering of any ideas which it doth not receive from one of these two. *External objects* furnish the mind with the ideas of sensible qualities, which are all those different perceptions they produce in us; and *the mind* furnishes the understanding with ideas of its own operations. These, when we have taken a full survey of them, and their several modes, we shall find to contain all our whole stock of ideas; and that we have nothing in our minds which did not come in one of these two ways.[17]

Locke's analysis of the way in which we know might seem to sever the connection between reason and faith. If knowledge proper must rest upon concrete experience, how can we know an infinite God? Locke's problem was similar to the one faced by Thomas Aquinas centuries earlier.[18] In a manner reminiscent of Aquinas, Locke argued that his epistemological investigation does not undercut the relation between faith and reason, but forms a foundation upon which the reasonableness of faith can be established. For instance, Locke held that, given the principles of knowledge as he defined them, it is possible to prove rationally the existence of God. As always we must start with concrete experience. In this instance, we begin with the undeniable fact of our own existence. With this as our point of departure, we can argue that God is the necessary cause of our being. In Locke's words,

> If, therefore, we know there is some real being, and that nonentity cannot produce any real being, it is an evident demonstration, that *from eternity there has been something;* since what was not from eternity had a beginning; and what had a beginning must be produced by something else.[19]

This line of argument led Locke to conclude that "from the consideration of ourselves, and what we infallibly find in our own constitutions, our reason leads us to the knowledge of this certain and evident truth,—*That there is an eternal, most powerful, and most knowing Being.*"[20]

The argument for God's existence that Locke proposed is usually called the cosmological argument. In substance it repeats views expressed by Aquinas. The cosmological argument starts from a given feature of the cosmos (in this case the contingency of our existence) and proceeds to God as the necessary cause of this observed effect. What made this line of argument especially attractive to Locke was its agreement with the empirical principles of his epistemology. The cosmological argument for God's existence was repeated throughout the Enlightenment. Often this general approach to God was combined with scientific insights to formulate what is known as the teleological argument for God's existence. In this form of the argument, one moves from the design or order of the world to a divine designer or orderer. We see a striking illustration of the way in which the mechanical metaphor for comprehending the world can be used as the basis for the teleological argument for God's existence in the work of William Paley (1743-1805). Paley proposed that we conceive the world after the model of a watch whose "several parts are framed and put together for a purpose."[21] Having suggested this analogy, he argued that "this mechanism being observed . . . the inference, we think, is inevitable, that the watch must have had a maker; that there must have existed, at some time, and at some place or other, an artificer or artificers, who formed it for the purpose which we find it actually to answer; who comprehended its construction, and designed its use."[22] Such an artificer, Paley maintained, is God. Whether in the form of the cosmological or the teleological argument, much eighteenth-century defense of belief in God's existence rested on the principle of causality.

From Locke's point of view, however, such rational argumentation did not exhaust the domain of faith. In the fourth book of his *Essay Concerning Human Understanding,* he made a distinction that proved fateful for later philosophical and theological reflection.

> By what has been before said of reason, we may be able to make some guess at the distinction of things, into those that are according to, above, and contrary to reason. 1. *According to reason* are such propositions whose truth we can discover by examining and tracing those ideas we have from sensation and reflection; and by natural deduction find to be true or probable. 2. *Above reason* are such propositions whose truth or probabil-

ity we cannot by reason derive from those principles. 3. *Contrary to reason* are such propositions as are inconsistent with or irreconcilable to our clear and distinct ideas.[23]

Locke maintained that religious belief does not deny truths defined "according to reason." Indeed we have seen that certain truths of religion (such as the existence of God) actually can be established *through* reason. Neither does religious belief assert anything "contrary to reason," for "faith is nothing but a firm assent of the mind: which, if it be regulated, as is our duty, cannot be afforded to anything but upon good reason; and so cannot be opposite to it."[24] Nevertheless, revelation does disclose truths that, while not contrary to reason, are "above reason." This in-between sphere is the proper realm of faith. Locke summarized his position on this issue when he wrote, "Faith . . . is the assent to any proposition, not thus made out by the deductions of reason, but upon the credit of the proposer, as coming from God, in some extra ordinary way of communication. This way of discovering truths to me, we call *revelation.*"[25] Reason and faith (or revelation) form an alliance: reason can establish certain truths of faith, and revelation can disclose truths above, but not contrary to, reason. It soon became apparent, however, that this was not an alliance between equals. Reason had the upper hand. At the conclusion of his argument, Locke indicated that *"reason must be our last judge and guide in everything."*[26] In an effort to develop the implications of his position, Locke devoted one of his most influential books to the attempt to demonstrate *The Reasonableness of Christianity* (1695). This work tried to show that though Christianity reveals truths that are above reason, "as soon as they are heard and considered, they are found to be agreeable to reason, and such as can by no means be contradicted."[27] Through careful reflection, Locke insisted, the reasonableness of the entire Christian faith can be affirmed.

Locke, like Newton, believed his philosophical reflection to be in agreement with the main features of the Christian image of man and his place in the universe. In many of his works, he attempted to present a rational defense of Christianity. But also like Newton, Locke's works contained the seeds of the breakdown of the Christian image. Throughout the remainder of the eighteenth century, these seeds sprouted and eventually bore fruit.

In the years following the publication of Locke's major works, the confidence in human reason increased and the dependence on divine revelation waned. Gradually revealed religion was replaced by a completely rational, natural religion. In England this development took place in a movement known as *Deism.* We see the beginning of the dissolution of Locke's alliance between reason and revelation in John Toland's *Christianity Not Mysterious,* published only one year after Locke's *The Reasonableness of Christianity.* In many ways Toland's influential work seems to support Locke's arguments. Toland admitted that revelation might serve a useful function, but insisted that "what is once reveal'd we must as well understand as any other Matter in the World, *Revelation* being only of use to enform us, whilst the Evidence of its Subject perswades us."[28] Despite apparent similarities between the viewpoints of Toland and Locke, it became clear that Toland was more suspicious of revelation than Locke. Advancing beyond Locke's position, Toland denied that revelation can disclose any truths above or beyond reason.

> From all the Observations, and what went before, it evidently follows that *Faith* is so far from being an implicate of Assent to any thing above Reason, that this Notion directly contradicts the Ends of Religion, the Nature of Man, and the Goodness and Wisdom of God.[29]

The implications of the growing doubts about divine revelation became explicit in a book that represents the culmination of British Deism—Matthew Tindal's *Christianity As Old As Creation* (1730). Tindal argued that there is "an exact Agreement between Natural and Reveal'd Religion; and that the Excellency of the Latter consists in being a Republication of the Former."[30] Christianity can teach us nothing that we cannot discover by the free use of our reason. Here we see that by 1730 in England, reason and natural religion have supplanted revelation and Christianity. Christianity had no distinctive contribution to make to human self-understanding, but simply confirmed what people already knew about themselves and their world. Deism's search for a rational, natural religion was an important aspect of the Enlightenment's quest for autonomy. Because each person possesses universal reason or has an implicit knowledge of the principles of natural religion, reliance on external authority (for instance, divine revelation, the Church, or the Bible) is unnecessary. If people have courage to use their own reason, external authority becomes superfluous. Despite reason's increasing infringement on the territory of revelation, British Deists remained reluctant to take the final step of completely overthrowing religion.

But things were different in eighteenth-century France. Although profoundly influenced by the work of Locke and Newton, thinkers of the French Enlightenment tended to radicalize what they had inherited from England. In part this tendency was due to France's religious and political situation. Unlike the British, the French had yet to pass through their revolution. The *ancien régime* or old monarchy retained considerable power and managed to thwart social and political change. In religious matters, the Catholic Church retained extensive power and continued to exercise considerable control over the lives of many people. There was a strong bond between the Church and wealthy families of the French aristocracy, whose sons and daughters often assumed positions of responsibility within the ecclesiastical hierarchy. The combination of the Church's own wealth and its alliance with upper social classes made it appear to be an institution of privilege that opposed social change. This impression was deepened by the Church's persistent effort to suppress disturbing intellectual inquiry. Most French Catholics of the eighteenth century still believed the Church to be the final arbiter of truth. This truth, moreover, was believed to be supernaturally ordained and guarded by an unbroken apostolic succession dating back to Jesus' original followers. To doubt the authoritative proclamations of the Church was heresy and could not be tolerated. Extensive censorship and at times violent repression resulted. As late as 1757 a law was passed that condemned to death any person who expressed irreligious opinions. Less extreme, though no less significant, was the fact that those persons who were not members of the Catholic Church had no recognized religious or civil status. Needless to say, such policies created deep opposition between the Church and many of Europe's most creative and thoughtful citizens. More often than not, the Church appeared to be the enemy of intellectual progress and social change.

To the careful eye, however, significant cracks in the Church's façade of power become apparent. Historian Robert Palmer points out that by the eighteenth century, "the Catholic religion was no longer as vital to many people as it once had been. It no longer seemed as essential to public order or to a satisfactory understanding of the world."[31] Though the reasons for this change were many and complex, Palmer points out that:

> Probably the most important of these causes was the growth of the state. There had been a time in Europe when the state, for practical purposes, did not exist. A man at that time, say in the twelfth century and earlier, had had little government and no country; his loyalties, rights, and obligations were local, personal, and concrete, running from himself to some other particular men. So far as he belonged to anything else he belonged to the universal Catholic Church. So far as he was more than a villager, he was a Christian. Only by the church was he joined to men outside his own nexus of rights and duties; only the church gave him a public status, an abstract existence, an impersonal system of law, a body of administrative superiors whose powers inhered in their offices. By the eighteenth century this situation was radically altered. It was the state now, more effectively than the church, which made a man more than a villager, and regarded law as more than a body of personal relationships. This triumph of the state was not to be assured until the French Revolution, but nowhere in Europe in the eighteenth century had the progress gone farther than in France.[32]

In other words, the larger framework within which many individuals understood themselves was no longer primarily the universal Church, but was the state. Religious concerns gradually gave way to secular preoccupations. In such a setting, criticism of religion and the effort to gain greater political and economic independence joined forces in a battle to overthrow old forms of authority and to win new autonomy. The climax of this strife, of course, was the French Revolution.

This radical turn of events came about only slowly. For much of the eighteenth century, French intellectuals found themselves in hearty agreement with the main outlines of British Deism. An illustration is the work of one of the most outstanding figures of the French Enlightenment—Voltaire (1694-1778). There can be little doubt about Voltaire's vehement opposition to many of the practices into which Christianity had fallen. In *Les Idées républicaines, par un membre d'un corps,* he wrote:

> The most absurd of despotisms, the most humiliating of human nature, the most contradictory, the most deadly, is that of priests. Of all priestly dominations, that of the priests of Christianity is beyond question the most criminal. (V)
> When our bishop, who is there to serve and not to be served, to comfort the poor and not to devour their substance, to teach the catechism and not to dominate, dared, in a time of disorder, to call himself the prince of a town of which he should be the shepherd, he was clearly guilty of rebellion and tyranny. (VI)[33]

Voltaire's misgivings about Christianity, however, did not lead him to oppose religion per se. By drawing freely on the work of Newton and Locke, he argued that essential religious truth is best expressed in the form of universal natural religion that is untainted by particular claims of historical religions. In his own words, "The whole philosophy of Newton leads necessarily to the knowledge of a Supreme Being who has created everything and arranged everything freely."[34] Although his trenchant criticism of the Catholic Church made him less inclined to insist on the congruence between natural religion and Christianity than someone like Tindal, Voltaire never relinquished his Deistic belief in God.

At the hands of Baron Paul d'Holbach (1723-1789), however, Voltaire's criticism of Christianity in particular turned against religion in general. In d'Holbach's celebrated essay, *The System of Nature* (1770), French atheism reached its most militant expression. D'Holbach saw nothing either natural or rational about religion. Religion, he argued, is the product of an ignorant and fearful imagination. To support this contention, d'Holbach developed a theory of projection to account for the origin of the idea of God. He suggested that "it is after ourselves, that we assign to God, intelligence, wisdom, and perfection, in abstracting from him that which we call defects in ourselves."[35] D'Holbach maintained that historically it was priests, anxious to retain power over the people, who perpetuated the fiction of an almighty and jealous God. He called upon his readers to recognize that continued religious belief keeps man in servitude to the Church and is an enemy of intellectual and moral progress. Religion is contrary to human nature and stands in the way of human happiness. The following passage gives the flavor of d'Holbach's attack on religion.

> Nature invites man to love himself, to preserve himself, to incessantly augment the sum of his happiness: religion orders him to love only a formidable God, that deserves to be hated; to detest himself, to sacrifice to his frightful idol the most pleasing and legitimate pleasures of his heart.[36]

Man can come of age only when he divests himself of the self-incurred tutelage his religion imposes. Man creates religion, and man can destroy it. If human fulfillment is to be reached, the Christian image of man as a creature of God

198 The Broken Image

who, by his own free action has fallen into sin, must be replaced by the image of an independent, rational being who has freed himself from domination by an other-worldly, irrational God. Enlightened man must rebel against God.

As his analysis unfolds, it becomes apparent that d'Holbach understood his position to be the logical extension of Newton's insights.

> It is true, we adore God like ignorant slaves, who tremble under a master whom they know not; we foolishly pray to him, although he is represented to us as immutable; although, in truth, this God is nothing more than nature acting by necessary laws necessarily personified, or destiny, to which the name of God is given.[37]

There is no need of a transcendent Creator to account for our world. Nature is a self-perpetuating system governed by inherent natural laws. We do not even need to postulate God to start the world going, for matter is not inert. Motion flows necessarily from matter. Two important consequences for our study of the breakdown of the Christian image of man grow out of d'Holbach's argument: *determinism* and *materialism.*

D'Holbach did not hesitate to extend the laws of nature to man. He believed that if we take seriously what modern science tells us, no part of the universe can be excluded from the rule of law. The conclusion seemed inevitable: all of man's thoughts and actions are determined by universal, natural laws; freedom is a chimera. The deterministic picture of man was given popular expression in a book written by a French doctor, Julien Offray de La Mettrie (1709–1751), which bears the revealing title, *Man a Machine* (1747). La Mettrie was a devout disciple of Newton's scientific method. But whereas Newton's primary concern had been the discovery of the laws governing the world, La Mettrie attempted to use scientific method to study man. Man, La Mettrie held, is a machine. All human thought, feeling, and action can be reduced to physiological states. In words fitting for a country renowned for its gastronomic excellence, he argued,

> The human body is a machine which winds itself up, the living image of perpetual motion. Food nourishes the movements which fever excites. Without food, the soul pines away, goes mad, and dies exhausted. It is a candle whose light flares up the moment before it goes out. But nourish the body, pour into its veins invigorating juices and strong liquors; then the soul, taking on their strength, arms itself with a proud courage, and the soldier whom water would have made flee, now made bold, runs joyously to death to the sound of drums.[38]

La Mettrie's vision of man leaves no room for human freedom. Thought and action are viewed as reflexes of bodily functions.

Our discussion of the determinism growing out of the application of natural law to man directs our attention to another important development of the French Enlightenment—materialism. Here too French thought was a radical version of British philosophy. In this case, Locke was the point of departure.

We have seen that the basis of Locke's philosophy was his empiricism, that is, his conviction that all of our ideas are rooted in concrete experience. But for some of his French followers, Locke's empiricism was incomplete. Locke's critics had a double target. First, they took aim at his general definition of experience. We recall that Locke identified two forms of experience that give rise to true ideas: sense intuition of the external world and observation of our own minds. Many mid-eighteenth-century philosophers objected to Locke's second form of experience. They argued that a consistent empiricism must accept direct experience of the outer world as the only source of accurate ideas. Reflection on the inner workings of the mind leads one into an imaginary realm unrelated to the "real world." Second, they took issue with Locke's contention that while thought must begin with concrete experience, more abstract notions can be derived from it, and that the mind can extrapolate accurately from sense information. The closer we stay to immediate sense data, the critics argued, the less likely we are to be led astray. From this viewpoint, an undertaking as speculative as the proof of God's existence is particularly susceptible to error.

The two French philosophers who most clearly illustrate the progression from empiricism to materialism are Étienne Bonnot de Condillac (1715-1780) and Claude Adrien Helvétius (1715-1771). In his *Treatise on Sensations* (1754), Condillac held that all ideas arise from sense experience. To prove his point, he attempted to demonstrate that each sense taken separately can generate man's entire mental life. The effort to ground all ideas in sensation continued in Helvétius' *On the Mind* (1758). Helvétius' work was a formidable statement of the materialist perspective. Neither Condillac nor Helvétius believed that his materialism undermined religious faith. Nevertheless, there is no doubt that the implications of their positions dealt a serious blow to what had become the traditional Enlightenment defense of natural religion. If we can properly assent only to what arises directly from sensation, it seems impossible to acknowledge God's existence.

It was not only in France, however, that Locke's ideas developed in directions that proved a problem for religious belief. Locke's countryman David Hume (1711-1776) elaborated a philosophical position that raised serious questions about the prevailing Enlightenment image of man and view of religion. We have observed one of the primary characteristics of the Enlightenment to be an extraordinary confidence in human reason. During the early years of the eighteenth century, reason and faith formed a partnership in which one complemented without contradicting the other. But gradually enlightened man grew headstrong. Through reason he attempted to overthrow religious faith. By the latter part of the century, the revolutionary potential of reason was realized not only in connection with religion, but also in relation to political institutions. In the work of Hume, reason extended the scope of its criticism to itself. As his French counterparts, Hume understood his philosophical inquiry to be an extension of work initiated by Locke and Newton. Yet Hume's effort to establish a science of man in his monumental book, *A Treatise of Human Na-*

ture (1738–1740), resulted in a skepticism differing substantially from Locke, Newton, and most other influential thinkers of the period. Hume shook the Enlightenment's confidence in reason and in so doing opened a path for the next major era in Western thought.

Hume began his analysis of human knowledge on a note that by now has become familiar: the primacy of "experience."

> All the perceptions of the human mind resolve themselves into two distinct kinds, which I shall call IMPRESSIONS and IDEAS. The difference betwixt these consists in the degrees of force and liveliness, with which they strike upon the mind, and make their way into our thought or consciousness. Those perceptions which enter with most force and violence we may name *impressions;* and under this name I comprehend all our sensations, passions and emotions, as they make their first appearance in the soul. By *ideas* I mean the faint images of these in thinking and reasoning.[39]

It is important to notice that Hume made a quantitative rather than a qualitative distinction between sense impressions and ideas. Ideas are simply faint copies of sense impressions. On this basis Hume tried to establish the origin of the entire content of the mind in perception.

Hume's empiricism had implications neither Newton nor Locke had anticipated. Most important, Hume argued that a strictly empirical epistemology calls into question the principle of causality. He began his consideration of causality by pointing out that "the idea . . . of causation must be deriv'd from some relation among objects."[40] Objects or events that stand in a causal relation, he suggested, must be close together in space and time, with the cause always appearing before the effect. Moreover, the same cause must always produce the same effect. Hume next asked how the notion of cause arises and concluded that the idea of causality must be the product of perception.

> The only connexion or relation of objects, which can lead us beyond the immediate impressions of our memory and senses, is that of cause and effect; and that because 'tis the only one, on which we can found a just inference from one object to another. The idea of cause and effect is deriv'd from experience, which informs us, that such particular objects, in all past instances, have been constantly conjoin'd with each other: And as an object similar to one of these is suppos'd to be immediately present in its impression, we thence presume on the existence of one similar to its usual attendant.[41]

The point made in this passage is extremely important. Causality, Hume insisted, is not a necessary and universal law of nature, but is a subjective habit of mind. Ever since we can remember, we have always perceived certain events or objects together. For example, a given event, B, always follows another event, A. As a result of the repeated experience of this conjunction, we tend to assume that there is a necessary connection between A and B. In another text, Hume made his point more concisely:

> When two *species* of objects have always been observed to be conjoined together, I can *infer,* by custom, the existence of one wherever I *see* the existence of the other; and this I call an argument from experience.[42]

To express this relation, we postulate a universal law, and expect B *always* to follow A. But in fact, Hume argued, there is no warrant for the movement from particular past experiences to a universal level that holds these given events always to occur together. All we can reasonably claim is that past experience leads us to believe that it is probable that B will follow A.

Hume's view of causality was important for two of the primary issues to which we have devoted considerable attention in this chapter: the principle of universality and the reasonableness of religious belief. Our discussion has disclosed that belief in the principle of universality was one of the pillars upon which Enlightenment thought rested. For most Enlightenment thinkers, the laws of nature, reason, and morality were universal. But Hume suggested that the notion of universality is only an idea, that it has its reality in the mind alone. What seem universal natural laws are only arbitrary habits of reasoning. In addition, knowledge and morality do not have an objective basis, but are the outgrowth of individuals' unique and contingent experiences. Past experience is no guarantee of what to expect in the future. Hume's argument logically led to skepticism, to uncertainty about the lawful character of the outer world as well as the relation of one's private experience to the experiences of others. Hume's world resembled Ockham's late medieval world, discussed in Chapter 3, more than the ordered universe of the eighteenth century.

The implications of Hume's reconstruction of the principle of causality were no less far-reaching for religious matters. We have seen that the effort to prove God's existence by reason alone was a mainstay of the Enlightenment search for a natural religion. However, Hume turned such an effort at proof inside out. Eighteenth-century proofs for the existence of God almost invariably argued from observed effects in the world to God as the necessary cause of these effects. But for Hume, such arguments from effect to cause were not justified. He believed that the idea of causality results from the repeated experience of the conjunction of two things in a regular temporal sequence. As such, causality is a subjective habit of mind that cannot establish certain knowledge of objective reality. On this basis alone Hume made it impossible to use the notion of causality to demonstrate that God created the world. The only way we can be led to suspect a causal relation between objects or events is to intuit them together. But we never intuit either God or the world as a whole. Therefore no causal relation between them can be established. Finally, the postulation of a causal connection presupposes *repeated* observation of the conjunction of events or objects. Hume contended that in order to be persuaded that God creates or causes the world, one would have to observe the creative act repeatedly. But, he pointed out, religious tradition leads us to believe that God's creation of the world was a unique, once-and-for-all event. On all counts, therefore, it seems we have no basis upon which to establish a causal relation between God and the world, or to argue from the world to a creative God.

Hume showed the consequences of his analysis of causality for the proofs of God's existence in his book entitled *Dialogues Concerning Natural Religion.* The statement of the argument he intended to criticize offers a convenient summary of the viewpoints of many Enlightenment authors we have discussed.

> Look round the world, contemplate the whole and every part of it: you will find it to be nothing but one great machine, subdivided into an infinite number of lesser machines, which again admit of subdivisions to a degree beyond what human senses and faculties can trace and explain. All these various machines, and even their most minute parts, are adjusted to each other with an accuracy which ravishes into admiration all men who have ever contemplated them. The curious adapting of means to ends, throughout all nature, resembles exactly, though it much exceeds, the productions of human contrivance—of human design, thought, wisdom, and intelligence. Since therefore the effects resemble each other, we are led to infer by all rules of analogy, that the causes also resemble, and that the Author of nature is somewhat similar to the mind of man, though possessed of much larger faculties, proportioned to the grandeur of the work which he has executed. By this argument *a posteriori,* and by this argument alone, do we prove at once the existence of a Deity and his similarity to human mind and intelligence.[43]

To this argument Hume, through the mouth of the central character in the dialogue, Philo, replied,

> Have you ever seen nature in any such situation as resembles the first arrangement of the elements? Have worlds ever been formed under your eye, and have you had leisure to observe the whole progress of the phenomenon, from the first appearance of order to its final consummation? If you have, then cite your experience and deliver your theory.[44]

In the absence of any direct experience of God's creative activity, Hume denied the validity of the supposedly rational proofs of God's existence.

In Hume's work "the Age of Reason" turned skeptical, and the confidence of enlightened man faltered. The influence of Hume's ideas continued long after his death. The eighteenth-century witnessed the first major cracks in the traditional Christian image of man. The Enlightenment opened with the effort to express the essence of Christianity in universal terms and ended with the outright rejection of religious faith as an obstacle to human progress. The Enlightenment believed that for people to come of age, they must divest themselves of religious faith. The price of human self-affirmation was the denial of God. But fissures in the Christian image came from other quarters in the course of the century. Locke's empiricism became French materialism, and Newton's scientific method applied to man yielded determinism and skepticism. Whether as the result of defiant self-affirmation or of growing self-doubt, the Christian image of man as a free creature of a creative and benevolent God was in eclipse by the end of the Enlightenment. But the eclipse of God was not God's death altogether. Several chapters remain to be written before our story of "the broken image" is complete.

THE MORAL ACTOR

Immanuel Kant (1724–1804) is one of those rare geniuses in the history of philosophy whose work both brings to an end one major period of thought and begins another era of intellectual history. Kant's work draws together major Enlightenment themes and sets the course that most important nineteenth-century philosophical and theological thought followed. We might best begin our study of Kant's influential work by considering his response to philosophical and religious developments of the Enlightenment that we have examined.

Kant's relation to the Enlightenment was ambivalent. We have already noted his definition of enlightenment as man's "release from his self-incurred tutelage" through the autonomous use of reason. Kant applauded the effort to overcome reliance on alien authority and to extend the domain of reason. But he was deeply troubled by some of the intellectual, moral, and religious implications of the radical extension of important Enlightenment insights. In the realm of knowledge, Kant recognized the significance of Hume's skepticism. In moral matters, Hume's ideas were equally disquieting, especially his doctrine that ethical values can be reduced to mere custom, habit, or disposition and are not universally binding principles. Kant worried that the denial of human freedom through the application of natural laws of causality to all aspects of human life would make any talk of morality meaningless. And he was bothered by the effort to sever the bond between reason and religion. Whether it be the result of the French atheists' overconfidence in reason or the British empiricists' lack of confidence in reason, Kant rejected the contention that the main tenets of religious belief cannot be demonstrated rationally. He preferred instead an image of man as a moral actor who relies on the disciplined use of reason and the inspiration of religious belief in carrying out his ethical obligation. To construct and to defend this image of man, Kant had to respond to the criticisms of knowledge, morality, and religion generated by the Enlightenment.

Kant's first major work, *The Critique of Pure Reason* (1781), is a prime example of his ability to integrate major trends of eighteenth-century philosophical thought. In addition to man's moral activity, Kant stressed the human capacity to know the world through rational reflection. Reason, for Kant, is involved in our knowing and our acting. Kant labeled man's capacity for knowledge "theoretical" or "speculative" reason and our ability to act "practical" reason. In the *Critique of Pure Reason,* Kant was concerned with how we know. His analysis of knowledge sets the stage for his consideration of moral activity.

To appreciate Kant's contribution, we must set his discussion in its historical context. We have seen that Enlightenment philosophers devoted considerable attention to the problem of knowledge. Two major positions dominated late seventeenth- and eighteenth-century epistemological discussions. According to the first, our most certain knowledge is independent of or prior to sense experience. For Descartes and his followers, the mind possesses innate ideas that are the first principles of all knowing. Sense experience does not really increase our knowledge, but serves as an occasion to actualize the mind's latent notions. According to the second point of view, certain knowledge arises only through sense perception. Locke and his followers viewed the mind as a blank slate with neither innate ideas nor an a priori structure. Our knowledge is a posteriori; it always emerges from concrete experience. Ideas not grounded in sensation are idle fantasies.

Kant believed there is an element of truth in both of these positions, even though previously they had been regarded as mutually exclusive. Kant maintained that we can formulate an adequate understanding of how we know by combining the most important features of the rationalism growing out of Descartes with the empiricism initiated by Locke. In agreement with the empiricists, Kant argued that all bona fide knowledge is rooted in sense experience. Our minds receive sense data from the world around us. But in opposition to the empiricists and in agreement with the rationalists, Kant contended that our minds are not *tabulae rasae,* but have a definite structure that orders our experience. This structure consists of universal, a priori forms of intuition (space and time) and categories of understanding (such as causality, substance, quantity, quality, and so forth). The minds of all persons share a common structure, despite the different experiences individuals encounter. Our knowledge consists of an ordering of the a posteriori data of sensation by means of the a priori categories of understanding. If either aspect of this process is lacking, there can be no knowledge.

According to Kant, this analysis of how we know overcomes the difficulties of the dominant epistemological positions of the Enlightenment. The contention that knowledge must be grounded in sense experience safeguards against wild speculation. More important, however, the universality of the a priori forms of intuition and categories of understanding allowed Kant to avoid Hume's skepticism. Notions such as causality are not arbitrary subjective habits, but are universal forms of the mind. To the extent that we know anything at all, we must employ these categories.

Kant explained that the purpose of his philosophy was to "limit" knowledge "to make room for faith." He saw a very close relationship between his theory of knowledge and the consideration of morality and religion. While Kant sought to restore confidence in reason in the face of Hume's skepticism, his confidence was not as naïve as that of many eighteenth-century philosophers. Kant was acutely aware of the limitations of reason, and there is a strong strain of agnosticism in his position. The very nature of the complex activity by which we come to know the world around us makes it impossible to be sure that the world as it appears to us corresponds to the world as it is independent of us. For example, we know that the human mind always orders experience according to the category of causality. Yet we cannot be certain that this law actually applies to events that transpire in the world.

Kant's limitation of knowledge had two important consequences for his view of religious matters. In the first place, he concurred with Hume's rejection of arguments for the existence of God based on the principle of causality. Since we cannot be sure that our notion of causality really is descriptive of the world, we are unable to argue from effects observed in the world to God as a necessary causal agency. When we combine this insight with the restriction of knowledge to awareness arising from sense experience, it becomes clear that Kant believed man is unable to gain any positive *knowledge* of God. Kant's image of man restored a sense of human finitude that much of the eighteenth century had lost.

Kant, of course, did not believe that the impossibility of attaining knowledge of God snaps the bond between reason and faith. Religious belief is inherently rational and derives from the experience of moral obligation. Although man's knowledge is limited in countless ways, he is able to recognize and to respond to the unconditional command of the "moral law." The moral law that Kant had in mind is not a particular ethical rule that we learn to obey. It is the general principle that we must "do unto others" as we would have them "do unto us," or, more technically, that we must act as if what we do were valid for all human beings beside ourselves. In his *Critique of Practical Reason*, Kant attempted to define the presuppositions and the consequences of man's moral activity. The cornerstone of Kant's moral philosophy was his image of man as a free being. He maintained that if human beings are machines, mindless robots, as La Mettrie had suggested, it simply makes no sense to talk of morality. A machine cannot be responsible for its actions. If moral awareness is more than an illusion, we must assume that people have the ability to choose among competing alternatives. In short, we must presume that man is free. Kant believed his study of knowledge established the possibility of human freedom. Since causality is a category of the mind that does not necessarily apply to the entire world, man is not fully enmeshed in a causal network. Awareness of the moral imperative compels man to affirm the actuality of his freedom, to believe that he is free; for without such a belief, the idea that one is accountable for his deeds becomes a cruel jest.

Freedom, however, is not the only presupposition of the moral life. Kant maintained that "a clear exposition of morality of itself leads to the belief in God."[45] In the abstruse language of the second *Critique:*

> The concept of freedom, in so far as its reality is proved by an apodictic law of practical reason, is the keystone of the whole architecture of the system of pure reason and even of speculative reason. All other concepts (those of God and immortality) which, as mere ideas, are unsupported by

anything in speculative reason now attach themselves to the concept of freedom and gain, with it and through it, stability and objective reality.[46]

Kant held that every action always has an objective or an aim, though one might not be clearly conscious of this objective at the time he acts, and the action might not be motivated by the intended object. The object of a *moral* will is "the highest good," which Kant defined as the proportionality of happiness and moral virtue. According to Kant, whenever we act morally, we implicitly will a world in which each person's happiness is a just reward for his virtue. Kant, of course, did not suggest that we act morally in order to become happy. Any action motivated purely by a desire for happiness cannot be considered moral. A moral act must be done out of pure respect for the moral imperative, with no concern for personal gain. Virtue is its own reward. Paradoxically speaking, we can hope for happiness only when we act without regard for our own happiness. Such a happiness in our lives must be conferred by God and not by ourselves. Thus, Kant insisted, it is necessary for man to believe in the existence of a God who apportions happiness to virtue, if not in this life, then in the next. The image of man as a moral agent necessarily implies the idea of a benevolent deity who ensures that the highest good for which humanity strives—the conjunction of the moral life and general well-being—will become a reality. In this respect, the image of God and the understanding of man as free and morally responsible cannot be separated.

In short, Kant concluded that religious faith is a corollary of moral activity. Human freedom, the immortality of the soul, and the existence of God are postulates or necessary presuppositions of his image of man as a moral actor. These postulates cannot be established by theoretical reason's analysis of the world. But Kant did not conclude from this that the only remaining alternatives were determinism, materialism, and atheism. He attempted to reconstruct what he regarded as the important features of the Christian image of man that had been lost during the eighteenth century. By considering the moral dimension of human experience, Kant thought he could establish the rationality of belief in human freedom and immortality and of faith in a morally providential God. He saw man as a free moral actor who lives in a world ruled by a just, omniscient, and omnipotent God. Life in such a world is directed toward the progressive realization of a more virtuous existence. The reward for ardent moral striving is the enjoyment of a hope for future happiness bestowed by God. Kant believed that any person who reflected upon his innate moral awareness would be driven to agree with the human image he defined.

ORGANICISM

For many persons throughout the nineteenth century, Kant's image of man and his defense of religious belief in moral terms provided an adequate response to Enlightenment skepticism, materialism, and atheism. For others, however, these aspects of Kant's thought remained too embedded in eighteenth-century thinking to offer a persuasive rebuttal to the philosophical and religious problems posed by radical Enlightenment thinkers. Many argued that the gravity of the intellectual and spiritual crisis into which Christendom had fallen required nothing less than a thorough review of human self-understanding. In the area of religion, this formidable task was undertaken by Friedrich Schleiermacher (1768-1834). Schleiermacher is commonly regarded as the father of modern religious thought. The publication of his book entitled *On Religion: Speeches to Its Cultured Despisers* in 1799 marked the beginning of a new chapter in the intellectual history of the West.

The roots of Schleiermacher's thought, however, lie deep within an eighteenth-century tradition often overshadowed by rationalism—Pietism. In the years following Luther's death, the effort to define precisely the main tenets of Lutheran faith and to distinguish it from both Catholicism and Calvinism led to a form of Protestant scholasticism. Religious belief was effectively reduced to rational comprehension and intellectual assent. In the face of such austere formalism, the vitality of the inward faith of many persons withered. Pietism was largely a reaction to Lutheran scholasticism in which primacy was given to feeling or to immediate experience.[47] In his famous second speech on religion, Schleiermacher disclosed his Pietistic heritage when he insisted that throughout the eighteenth century both friends and foes of religious belief had misconstrued its most basic features. Nearly everyone had identified religion with either metaphysical knowledge or a cloak for morality. We have seen instances of the former position in Deism and an example of the latter viewpoint in Kant's writings. But Schleiermacher countered that religion is essentially a mode of feeling, rather than mere knowledge or moral activity.

> The sum total of religion is to feel that, in its highest unity, all that moves us in feeling is one; to feel that aught single and particular is only possible by means of this unity; to feel, that is to say, that our being and living is a being and living in and through God.[48]

By "feeling" Schleiermacher did not mean a momentary subjective emotion, but a state of consciousness that suffuses the entire personality. For Schleiermacher, religion is related more closely to the affective side of life than to human cognition or volition. Because an affection pervades one's whole life, it is more rudimentary than knowing or doing. Schleiermacher argued that the Enlightenment's emphasis on reason and morality had blinded people to the importance of human feelings. Any adequate image of man, he maintained, must do justice to the affective dimension of human experience.

Schleiermacher, however, sought to make precise what he meant by "feeling." Religious feeling is immediate; it is an experience that is prior to the separation between the self and the world that occurs in developed consciousness. Conscious knowing and doing are characterized by a polarity between self and other, between subject and object. The distinction between subject and object, in Schleiermacher's estimate, is not the most basic structure of experience. Prior to their separation, subject and object, self and other, are immediately related in an intimate union. This moment of unity between subject and object is religious feeling.

> Sense and object mingle and unite, then each returns to its place, and the object rent from sense is a perception, and you, rent from the object are for yourselves, a feeling. It is this earlier moment I mean, which you always experience yet never experience. The phenomenon of your life is just the result of its constant departure and return. It is scarcely in time at all, so swiftly it passes; it can scarcely be described, so little does it properly exist.[49]

By using evocative, sensual language, Schleiermacher tried to identify this experience more fully.

> Did I venture to compare it, seeing I cannot describe it, I would say it is fleeting and transparent as the vapour which the dew breathes on blossom and fruit, it is bashful and tender as a maiden's kiss, it is holy and fruitful as a bridal embrace. Nor is it merely like, it is all this. It is the first contact of the universal life with an individual. It fills no time and fashions nothing palpable. It is the holy wedlock of the Universe with the incarnated Reason for a creative, productive embrace. It is immediate, raised above all error and misunderstanding. You lie directly on the bosom of the infinite world. In that moment, you are its soul.[50]

In another important passage, Schleiermacher described this religious feeling in a way that suggests features distinguishing his image of man and notions of God and the world from views held by most eighteenth-century philosophers.

> The contemplation of the pious is the immediate consciousness of the universal existence of all finite things, in and through the Infinite, and of all temporal things in and through the Eternal. Religion is to seek this and find it in all that lives and moves, in all growth and change, in all doing and suffering. It is to have life and to know life in immediate feeling, only as such an existence in the Infinite and Eternal. Where this is found religion is satisfied, where it hides itself there is for her unrest and anguish, extremity and death. Wherefore it [religion] is a life in the infinite nature of the Whole, in the One and in the All, in God, having and possessing all things in God, and God in all. . . . In itself it is an affection, a revelation of the Infinite in the finite, God being seen in it and it in God.[51]

Schleiermacher's vision clashed sharply with the various images of God constructed throughout the eighteenth century. Whether as a deistic first cause who creates a mechanical world or as a just, omnipotent, and omniscient moral governor who watches over human actions, God was always depicted as outside, above, beyond, or beside the world. Schleiermacher found this view of God's relation to the world unacceptable. He rejected the emphasis on God's transcendence and stressed God's immanence or familiar presence in man's surroundings. In religious feeling, one realizes the "universal existence . . . of all temporal things in and through the Eternal." Or as he put it in a passage to which we have referred previously, "our being and living is a being and living in and through God." Schleiermacher's God is not somewhere above, beyond, or beside the world, but actually dwells in the universe as its creative source or ground of being. God and the world interpenetrate in the closest way possible. Just as the union of subject and object is more fundamental than their difference, so the unity of God and the world is more essential than their separation.

Schleiermacher's reappraisal of the relationship between God and the world was one of his greatest theological innovations. He did not feel comfortable with the traditional Christian image of a personal God for "we have an idea of the Highest Being, not as personally thinking and willing, but exalted above all personality, as the universal, productive, connecting necessity of all thought and existence."[52] The image of God as a person is too restrictive. As the ground of all reality, God is the creative source, not a particular instance, of personality. To imagine God as a person is to bind the divine and to segregate it from creation; it is to finitize the infinite. By the same token, the world itself cannot be a machine created by a transcendent God and ruled by immutable laws of mechanical necessity, as the Deists supposed. The cosmos resembles a vital, living body infused with creative power by the immanent presence of the divine. To Schleiermacher, the eighteenth-century notion of the world was static and stultifying, and he aimed to breathe life back into a universe that had been drained of mystery and vitality by the barren rationalism of the Enlightenment. The universe is an integrated whole, a totality, or his favorite image—a living organism. Schleiermacher's world was the world of Romantic poets such as Novalis, Wordsworth, and Coleridge; it was the world of the American transcendentalists such as Emerson and Thoreau. In many ways, Schleiermacher's shift from the mechanical to the organic image of the world marked the transition from the Enlightenment to the nineteenth century. Although anticipated in Kant's discussion of nature and art in the *Critique of Judgment* (1793), Schleiermacher's *Speeches* gave the first influential statement of the organic image.

The image of the organism intimates that all reality is interrelated in the closest possible way through God, creative source of everything that is. In religious experience, we realize that prior to separation and opposition, everything is integrated as an expression of a single creative power. In Schleiermacher's own terms, we apprehend "the existence of all finite things in and through the Infinite." This intuition of the unity of the universe arises only through religious experience. Schleiermacher posed a rhetorical question: "And if you see the world as a Whole, a Universe, can you do it otherwise than in God?"[53]

Schleiermacher's image of man takes each person as a particular and unrepeatable expression of the divine creative principle. The infinite expresses itself in the plentitude and variety of finite beings. Consequently, each person has an original, indissoluble relation to God. In a manner reminiscent of Leibniz's notion of monads, Schleiermacher claimed that each person mirrors the universe in a unique way. Through religious experience we gain an intuition of our identity with God and our connection to the rest of the world.

> You lie directly on the bosom of the infinite world. In that moment, you are its soul. Through one part of your nature you feel, as your own, all its powers and its endless life. In that moment, it is your body, you pervade, as your own, its muscles and members and your thinking and forecasting set its inmost nerves in motion. In this way, every living, original movement in your life is first received. Among the rest it is the source of every religious emotion.[54]

Significantly, Schleiermacher's image of man bore only faint likeness to the main contours of the Christian image defined in our third chapter. Nevertheless Schleiermacher, as so many authors before him, believed that his work sufficed as a defense of religious belief in the face of rising skepticism and atheism. But history has shown that Schleiermacher's ideas contained the seeds of the radical critiques of religion that emerged in the nineteenth century and are enthusiastically repeated in our own day. Between Schleiermacher's theology and these criticisms of religion, however, stands one of the most demanding thinkers in the history of philosophy—G. W. F. Hegel.

MAN AS AN HISTORICAL BEING

Perhaps no single thinker has had a greater impact on the intellectual, social, and political life of the twentieth century than Hegel. His colossal philosophical labors gave rise to movements as different as existentialist philosophy and literature, on the one hand, and Marxism on the other. Although his total philosophical system has been accepted by few, Hegel defined the terms in which his critics cast their arguments. By so doing, he set the course for most significant philosophical and theological reflection since his time.

At first glance, we notice what seem to be deep-seated differences between Schleiermacher and Hegel. Against Schleiermacher's emphasis on feeling and emotion, Hegel insisted that, above all, man is rational. He claimed that "man is explicitly man only in the form of developed and cultivated reason."[55] While Hegel admitted that religious conviction often is expressed in imprecise, sentimental terms, he believed this to be the result of the tendency of the religious imagination to issue in myths, images, and symbols. Careful philosophical thought must employ the clear and precise method of reason. When considering religious matters, the task of the philosopher is not to evoke pious feelings with emotional language, but to translate religious images into pure concepts. We might express Hegel's insight in a more contemporary idiom by suggesting that the philosopher of religion seeks to demythologize myths produced by religious believers. Such an undertaking usually presupposes that the mythological imagination is more primitive, and therefore less adequate, than mature rational reflection. Hegel shared this assumption, for he was persuaded that the process of rendering religious images and myths in pure conceptual terms results in a more adequate expression of the meaning intended by religious symbols. He regarded his philosophical system as a rational articulation of the Christian image of man and the world.

Nonetheless, Hegel's notion of reason differed substantially from the Enlightenment view of reason, and in this respect was not as much at odds with Schleiermacher's thought as it might at first appear. He highlighted his difference with the Enlightenment by drawing a distinction between "understanding" and "reason." Understanding is the analytical capacity by which we draw distinctions and establish oppositions. In Hegel's own words, "Thought, as *understanding,* sticks to fixed determination and to the distinction of one thing from another: every such limited abstract it treats as having a subsistence and being of its own."[56] For the understanding, each object or entity is defined in isolation from and in opposition to all other things. "It is the work of the understanding to analyze what is concrete, to distinguish and to define the moments of it, then to hold firmly to them and to abide by them."[57] Understanding never advances beyond an analysis of the world into its constituent parts. According to Hegel, what eighteenth-century philosophers called "reason" was, in fact, nothing more than understanding. Their world remained a collection of discrete and independent entities, associated in external and mechanical ways, like countless billiard balls bumping together on a table. Properly conceived, though, reason can be seen as the polar opposite of understanding. Whereas understanding dissects and differentiates, reason synthesizes and integrates. From the point of view of reason, everything concrete is a harmony of opposing and conflicting tendencies. To rest content with hard-and-fast distinctions, as the understanding does, is to abstract from concrete reality. For reason, "differences are posited not as exclusive, but as existing only in this mutual inclusion of one by the other."[58] Hegel called such reason "dialectical." "Dialectic" is the power of reason to grasp all things as mutually interdependent. The world forms a complex web in which every part is interrelated. The identity of any particular entity or person is a function of its position within this unified totality. The differences and oppositions stressed by understanding are only apparent and are overcome when we assume the all-encompassing perspective of dialectical reason. Thus Hegel agreed with Schleiermacher's image of the world as an organic whole. But he took issue with Schleiermacher on the point that this totality can be apprehended through feeling. Only reason, he held, can reveal the dialectical interconnection of all reality. Unless the world is grasped as an organic whole, it is fundamentally misunderstood.

For Hegel, one of the false dichotomies of the understanding is the separation of God and the world. God and the world dwell in or exist through each other; they are dialectically related. Hegel contended that Christianity first gave expression to the essential relationship between the infinite and the finite.

The heart of the Christian perspective is the incarnation—the claim that in Jesus, "man appears as God and God as man."[59] Through the assertion of God's incarnation in Jesus, "the unity of divine and human nature attains the stage of certainty . . . it receives the form of immediate sense-perception, of outward existence—in short, . . . this idea appears as seen and experienced in the world."[60] The incarnation "involves the truth that the divine and human natures are not implicitly different."[61] He explained this important point in more detail:

> This then is the explication of the meaning of reconciliation, that God is reconciled with the world, or rather that God has shown Himself to be by his very nature reconciled with the world, that what is human is not something alien to His nature, but that this otherness, this self-differen- tiation, finitude, as it is sometimes expressed, is a moment in God Himself, though, to be sure, it is a vanishing moment.[62]

The historical Christian faith, however, expresses the truth of the relation- ship between the infinite and the finite in an incomplete manner. The task of explicating the general truth implicit in the Christian symbol of God's incarna- tion in Jesus is left to what Hegel called "speculative" philosophy. According to the Christian myth, God becomes incarnate only in a particular individual at a definite moment in time. Philosophy discerns the general truth of the Christian vision. What Christianity claims for Jesus, philosophy asserts of the entire world. The incarnation is limited neither to one person nor a single moment. To the eyes of reason, the world as a whole appears as the self-manifestation of God. In short, dialectical reason synthesizes the infinite and the finite. With respect to Hegel's image of man, this argument means that each individual is a concrete expression of the infinite. God incarnates anew in every person. Hegel would agree completely with the God of William Blake's poem "Jerusalem" who proclaims:

> I am not a God afar off, I am a brother and
>   friend:
> Within your bosoms I reside, and you reside in
>   me. (4:19–20)

Such, in many ways, summarizes the gist of Hegel's difficult thought. But if Hegel had said no more than this, he would not have improved very much on Schleiermacher's own response to the Enlightenment. The genuine uniqueness of Hegel's image of man becomes fully apparent only when we add to these in- sights his profound appreciation of the significance of history.

Hegel's recognition of the importance of history for human self-under- standing is one of the greatest contributions of his philosophy. Throughout the Enlightenment, little attention was devoted to history. Eighteenth-century thinkers were more concerned with the universal type of man as a work of nature than with individual biographies and the drama of history. In all domains of inquiry, philosophers sought general laws or principles that particular things or events express. Eighteenth-century scientific thought exemplified this prejudice. Through the careful observation of the world, scientists attempted to discover invariable natural laws governing the cosmos. But the Enlightenment quest for universality was not limited to scientific inquiry. We also have seen it in the views of reason, morality, and religion that characterized this era. Most eighteenth-century philosophers believed reason to be universal. As the outer world is controlled by universal natural laws, so the inner world of the human mind is ruled by universal laws of reason. In other words, the minds of all persons share a common logical structure. In the realm of morality, it was argued that there are universal ethical principles that are recognizable by all rational beings. Finally, in the sphere of religion the search for universality was expressed in the effort to define a natural religion upon whose principles all historically particular religious traditions could agree.

While Hegel acknowledged the operation of universal laws in the world of nature, he was less convinced than his Enlightenment forebears about the universality of man's intellectual, moral, and religious life. He maintained that a person's historical situation strongly influences the way one thinks, acts, and believes. To a great extent, individuals are products of history. Moreover, the history in which they are all so deeply immersed is an evolutionary process in which each stage grows out of earlier stages and lays the foundation for historical developments yet to be realized. Hegel expressed this insight by calling history a dialectical process. No moment of history can be separated from its predecessors and successors.

Thus Hegel elaborated an image of man as an historical being. Human beings are involved in an ongoing historical process in which they are conditioned by what has gone before them and condition what comes after them. Our physical bodies, intellectual lives, moral codes, and religious beliefs are all outgrowths of historical evolution. Consequently we cannot claim for reason, morality, and religion the timeless universality the Enlightenment had sought. Hegel was not satisfied, however, with the simple assertion of the historical character of human existence. He attempted to demonstrate precisely the evolution of man's physical and mental life. Long before Darwin, Hegel sought to define the way in which man evolved from inorganic nature and lower forms of animal life. In his greatest work, *The Phenomenology of Spirit* (1807), Hegel tried to trace the exact course of man's conscious life from its earliest and most naïve form to its latest and most sophisticated manifestation. In other words he expanded themes suggested in the *Phenomenology* by detailing the history of aesthetics, religion, and philosophy. Throughout his system, Hegel elaborated a vision of the world as a gradually developing totality in which all members and epochs are dialectically interconnected.

The historical character of human life also applies to Christianity. Speculative philosophy, for Hegel, extends the Christian claim of God's incarnation from the particular person of Jesus to the whole world. But the world is a gradually developing historical process. Hence the incarnation is not a once-

and-for-all event, but is an ongoing process that takes place throughout world history. The entire history of the world is a progressive incarnation of God. Hegel believed that this incarnational process results in a more complete realization of the divine. World history itself is the means by which God reaches self-realization. In the language of Christian theology, "God thought of simply as the Father is not yet the True. . . . He is, on the contrary, Beginning and End; He is His own presupposition, He constitutes Himself His presupposition—this is simply another form of the fact of differentiation—He is the eternal Process."[63] Each phase of world history is an integral part of this "eternal process" of incarnation. Man can understand himself as a particular manifestation of the divine. An individual's personal history forms a chapter in the unfolding story of divine life. But man's role in this story is unique. Through man, history and hence God reach their consummation.

Hegel did not regard history as a random process. It is directed toward a specific goal that confers a unity and a rationale upon the whole course of world history. The end toward which history moves is the complete realization of the divine through the emergence of God's self-consciousness in man. Because of the intimate relation between God and the world, divine self-consciousness can develop only in world history. More specifically, through the long course of *human* reflection, God slowly reaches self-consciousness. Because the world is really the incarnation of God, man's knowledge of the world and of himself as a member of the world is at the same time God's knowledge of himself. Since self-consciousness is the proper end of man as well as of God, human fulfillment and God's complete self-realization coincide. Paul Tillich gives an illuminating summary of Hegel's complex image of man and of man's relation to God and the world.

> Here we have the whole vision of the world as a process of the self-actualization of the divine essences in time and space. Therefore, everything in its essential nature is the self-expression of the divine life. This world process goes through nature and through the various actualizations of spirit. In man's spirit, particularly in man's artistic, religious, and philosophical creativity, God finds himself as he essentially is. God does not find himself in himself, but he comes to himself, to what he essentially is, through the world process, and finally through man and through man's consciousness of God. Here we have the old mystical idea that in man's knowledge of God, God knows himself, and in man's love of God, God loves himself.[64]

Hegel imputed to his philosophical system an accurate and a complete expression of the basic elements of the Christian vision. But his attempted synthesis of religion and philosophy proved unstable. Hegel's successors found in his own work the tools with which to forge a criticism of his system. One of the most important features of this critique of Hegel is the radical attack of religion formulated by two of his most influential followers—Ludwig Feuerbach and Karl Marx.

THE DIVINITY OF MAN

We have already had occasion to discuss some of the outstanding features of the work of Feuerbach and Marx. In the first chapter of our study, we considered their contributions to our understanding of the way in which religion functions as a mirror of man. In this chapter we seek to explore the role their work has played in the breakdown of the Christian image.

Feuerbach's and Marx's critiques of religion depended heavily on arguments developed by Hegel. Feuerbach conceded that though many valuable ideas are suggested in Hegel's work, Hegel never fathomed the full implications of his argument for religious belief. According to Feuerbach, the conclusion to be drawn from Hegel's image of man and of man's relation to God is the death of God and the divinity of man. What Hegel had seen as a delicate dialectical interplay between God and the world, or more specifically between God and man, Feuerbach viewed as a simple identification of God and man.

> Such as are a man's thoughts and dispositions, such is his God; so much worth as a man has, so much and no more has his God. Consciousness of God is self-consciousness, knowledge of God is self-knowledge. By his God thou knowest the man, and by the man his God; the two are identical.[65]

As we noted in our first chapter, Feuerbach held that religion is the mirror in which man beholds his own image. But the image reflected in the mirror of religion always assumes a special shape. It is man's *ideal* image of himself. In a manner similar to d'Holbach, Feuerbach argued, "The divine being is nothing else than human being, or, rather, the human nature purified, freed from the limits of the individual man, made objective—i. e., contemplated and revered as another, a distinct being. All the attributes of the divine nature are therefore, attributes of human nature."[66] Man's actual existence always seems to limit and to restrict him in important ways. His goals are never reached; his dreams rarely come true. In this situation, man forms a picture of ideal, fully realized human nature, which he proceeds to deify. Man mistakes a product of his imagination for an actually existing divine being. To make matters worse, he bows down and worships the god he creates. By obeying this perfect being, man believes he can overcome the limitations he suffers. Feuerbach described the dynamics of this process with a term Freud later made famous—projection. "Man—this is the mystery of religion—projects his being into objectivity, and then again makes himself an object to this projected image of himself thus converted into a subject."[67] Through religious belief, man becomes the slave of a master of his own making. In Feuerbach's own words, "To enrich God, man must become poor; that God may be all, man must be nothing."[68]

The sincere believer, of course, is not aware of God as an enslaving product of his own imagination. He assumes there really is a God who can offer man a fuller existence. But, Feuerbach demanded, religious belief actually prevents man from attaining the fulfillment for which he longs and thus perpetuates human alienation. Man must see that the perfection he attributes to God actually represents an ideal form of existence that man himself can attain. The recognition of the illusory character of religious belief brings with it the awareness of man's boundless perfectibility. Man is potentially divine. By unearthing the roots of faith, Feuerbach thought he had opened the way for people to escape the bondage of religion and to progress toward perfection. All of Feuerbach's philosophical energies were centered on overthrowing the tyranny of religion.

> The purpose of my lectures as of my books is to transform theologians into anthropologists, lovers of God into lovers of man, candidates for the next world into students of this world, religious and political flunkeys of heavenly and earthly monarchs and lords into free, self-reliant citizens of earth.[69]

We should be able to detect significant parallels between Feuerbach and some of the radical representatives of the Enlightenment. For Feuerbach, as for certain eighteenth-century philosophers, the highest reality man can imagine is his own human nature. Religion is a self-incurred tutelage that must be overcome if man is to attain fulfillment. Man's affirmation of himself and his denial of God again are joined. Taken together, Enlightenment philosophers and Feuerbach form an important chapter in the story of the breakdown of the Christian image of man. But we must recognize the very different sources from which their similar conclusions sprang. In the face of the advances of modern science, many eighteenth-century thinkers attempted to defend continued religious belief by viewing God as a first cause who created the world and its laws. Having fabricated a smooth-running machine, little remained for God to do, and he withdrew from the world to his heavenly abode. With God so far removed from everyday affairs, it was a short step to the conclusion that God is an unnecessary hypothesis. As we have noted, this step was taken by eighteenth-century French atheists and materialists who regarded the world as governed by natural laws alone. In response to this form of atheism, nineteenth-century thinkers such as Schleiermacher and Hegel contended that God is not a distant first cause who is uninvolved in the world. To the contrary, they suggested that the infinite is immersed in the finite. God is so deeply involved in the ongoing course of the world that neither God nor the world can be considered apart from the other. To a thinker such as Feuerbach, the unity of God and the world, or the identity of God and man defined by Schleiermacher and Hegel, is so complete that continued belief in or talk about God is both superfluous and harmful. Thus God is "dead" to the world, for all practical purposes. But for Feuerbach and the radical tradition, the death of God should not be considered a tragedy; it leaves man on his own to master the world. The death of God is the liberation of man.

It is important to note that the breakdown of the Christian image in the nineteenth century was fomented by social and political forces to which the radical critiques of religion gave voice. During the latter part of the eighteenth century, a sudden increase in scientific and technical know-how gave rise to the so-called Industrial Revolution. Within the short span of sixteen years, England saw the introduction of the spinning machine (Richard Arkwright, 1768), an effective steam engine (James Watt, 1769), the spinning jenny (James Hargreaves, 1770), and the power loom (Edmund Cartwright, 1784). Such technological advances opened the way for the development of an economy based on large-scale industrial manufacturing. For some sectors of the population an actual increase in the standard of living accompanied these changes. There arose a confidence that man finally had acquired the power to dominate the natural order and to conquer troublesome adversities in his environment. The idea of inevitable historical progress, heretofore merely the unverified insight of certain philosophers, now seemed confirmed by historical events. This story, however, had another side. The new factories required a massive labor force. In hope of improving their lot, many people migrated from farms to urban manufacturing centers. But the dream quickly turned into a nightmare. In cities workers met unprecedented social and personal problems. The extraordinary influx of people created slums that were virtually uninhabitable. With unchecked industrial expansion, the quality of urban life deteriorated rapidly. Work itself often proved oppressive. Hours were long, working conditions poor, and wages very low. William Blake's "London" paints a vivid picture of the plight of the European factory worker during the Industrial Revolution.

> I wander through each chartered street,
>   Near where the chartered Thames does flow,
> And mark in every face I meet
>   Marks of weakness, marks of woe.
>
> In every cry of every Man,
>   In every Infant's cry of fear,
> In every voice, in every ban,
>   The mind-forged manacles I hear.
>
> How the Chimney-sweeper's cry
>   Every blackening Church appalls;
> And the hapless Soldier's sigh
>   Runs in blood down Palace walls.
>
> But most through midnight streets I hear
>   How the youthful Harlot's curse
> Blasts the new born Infant's tear,
>   And blights with plagues the Marriage hearse.

Philosophical departures in the years following the Enlightenment had not adequately addressed the social realities brought by the Industrial Revolution. Having personally experienced the horrors of nineteenth-century London, Karl

Marx set out to detect the source of the problem and to propose a cure for the disease. His understanding of religion formed an important part of his diagnosis. Marx concurred with many of Feuerbach's penetrating insights, as echoed in his famous statement: *"Man makes religion,* religion does not make man. And indeed religion is the self-consciousness and self-regard of man who has either not yet found or has already lost himself."[70] But Marx rebuked Feuerbach for not adequately answering the question of *why* man creates religion. "Feuerbach does not see, consequently, that 'religious feeling' is itself a social product and that the abstract individual he analyzes belongs to a particular form of society."[71] Marx held that the constructions of the religious imagination are products of distorted social arrangements. Writing from the London slums, he contended that the intolerable conditions in which many people are forced to live lead to the creation of an imaginary other-worldly realm of perfection in which the shortcomings of this life are surmounted. *"Religious* suffering is the *expression* of real suffering and at the same time the *protest* against real suffering. Religion is the sigh of the oppressed creature, the heart of a heartless world, as it is the spirit of spiritless conditions. It is the *opium* of the people."[72] Religious belief perpetuates inhuman social conditions. Drugged by the hope for other-worldly perfection, man becomes resigned to the deprivation and exploitation he suffers at the hands of an unjust society. From Marx's perspective, Feuerbach's failure to discern the social origin of religion blinded him to the way in which the enslaving chains of religion can be broken. Feuerbach thought that once man is convinced that he is the maker of religion, he will immediately discard religious faith. Marx argued, however, that there will be religion as long as there is a social need for it. The only way to overthrow religious belief is to transform the very world that compels religious belief. "The abolition of religion as people's *illusory* happiness is the demand for their *real* happiness. The demand to abandon illusions about their condition is a *demand to abandon a condition which requires illusions.* The criticism of religion is thus in *embryo a criticism of the vale of tears whose halo* is religion."[73] Marx's conclusion was that "the criticism of heaven turns into the criticism of the earth, the *criticism of religion* into the *criticism of law,* and the *criticism of theology* into the *criticism of politics."*[74] In Marx's socialist utopia, there will be no religion, because happiness in *this world* will be guaranteed by a just social order. Man's need for fulfillment can be accomplished in the mundane sphere of work and social relationships.

Feuerbach and Marx contributed more than any other thinkers to the abandonment of the Christian image of man. They maintained that the Christian picture of humanity as fallen creatures who live in a world ruled by a providential God is perverse. Religious faith does not make life meaningful, but leads to a deeper alienation, an alienation from one's essential humanity. Feuerbach and Marx constructed an image of man that directly opposed the Christian vision, an image we may term "humanistic." Man is not created by God; God is created by man. Moreover, the world is not governed by divine providence, but is a self-contained historical process ruled by immanent laws. Although in their present state human beings have not achieved their full potential, they can reach greater fulfillment through their own effort. The goal of the world historical process is *human,* rather than divine, self-realization. For Feuerbach and Marx, man will become truly human only when he "kicks the habit" of religion.

THE CORRUPTION OF HUMANITY

The optimism and self-confidence characteristic of Feuerbach's and Marx's versions of the human image dominated the remainder of the nineteenth century and the first decade of our century. Although not everyone was quite as enthusiastic about the human potential as Feuerbach, there remained a consensus that humanity's lot was improving and a more just social order emerging. Even theologians were touched by the spirit of the age. Toward the end of the nineteenth century, a movement named Liberalism arose in Protestant thought. Authors such as Albrecht Ritschl in Germany and Walter Rauschenbusch in America revived Kant's analysis of morality. The heart of the Christian message, they argued, is the notion of the Kingdom of God, conceived as an ethical commonwealth that is realized in history. Through moral striving, man can contribute to the dawning of this kingdom.

However, as the hopes of the Enlightenment were crushed by the brutal excesses of the French Revolution, so nineteenth- and early twentieth-century optimism and confidence were shattered by the First World War. In the face of the most widespread devastation and suffering in human history, the image of man as an infinitely perfectible being moving inexorably toward fulfillment seemed completely naïve and unrealistic. In response to the frightful turn of events that began on July 31, 1914, there was a revival of the Reformation image of man as a fallen sinner totally dependent upon God's grace. The publication of Swiss theologian Karl Barth's *The Epistle to the Romans* (1918) marked the beginning of a theological era known as neo-orthodoxy. With few notable exceptions, this movement overshadowed Western religious thought from 1918 through the late 1950s.

In *The Epistle to the Romans,* Barth returned to the work of a seminal nineteenth-century Danish philosopher who previously had gone virtually unnoticed—Søren Kierkegaard (1813–1855). Kierkegaard, like Feuerbach and Marx, was a critic of Hegel, though his complaints were along different lines. He did, however, agree with Feuerbach's contention that the real conclusion of Hegel's system was the death of God and the divinization of man. The nub of Kierkegaard's criticism was that Hegel's philosophy was not an accurate articulation of Christian faith, as Hegel had claimed, but was a misrepresentation of the most basic features of the Christian image of man, God, and the world. Humanity, Kierkegaard argued, is not an embodiment of the divine. Man is a corrupt sinner who has fallen as a result of the free exercise of his will. Between God and man there is an "infinite qualitative" abyss that human beings are unable to cross. God is the incorrupt, just, holy creator; man is a corrupt, unjust, sinful creature. Suffering under the burden of sin, individuals are gripped by anxiety, dread, and despair. The human image that Kierkegaard elaborated differs significantly from the pictures drawn by Hegel and Feuerbach. Consider the following passage:

> Just as the physician might say that there lives perhaps not one single man who is in perfect health, so one might say perhaps that there lives not one single man who after all is not to some extent in despair, in whose inmost parts there does not dwell a disquiet, a perturbation, a discord, an anxious dread of an unknown something, or of a something he does not even dare to make acquaintance with, dread of a possibility of life, or dread of himself, so that, after all, as physicians speak of a man going about with a disease in him, this man is going about and carrying a sickness of the spirit, which only rarely and in glimpses, by and with a dread which to him is inexplicable, gives evidence of its presence within.[75]

Through their own powers, human beings cannot overcome the despair and anxiety inflicted by sin. Kierkegaard argued that people depend upon God to help them resolve this dilemma. Developing the insights of Luther, he contended that in his incarnation in Jesus, God acts to forgive human sin and to abolish the dread and despair that haunt life. In his interpretation of the incarnation, Kierkegaard's deep differences with Hegel became evident.

> With the everlasting contemplation of world history and the history of the human race, with the everlasting talk about universal history and its significance, etc., people have become all too nimble in appropriating Christianity without more ado as a part of world-history, they have come to regard it as a matter of course that Christianity is a stage in the development of the human race. They have quite forgotten that the Christ's life on earth ... is sacred history, which must not be confounded with the history of the human race or of the world.[76]

Kierkegaard's view of the incarnation rested on two basic points that directly contradicted Hegel's position. The first we have already noted: the infinite qualitative abyss separating God and man. For Kierkegaard this meant that the religious assertion of God's incarnation is completely paradoxical. The paradox is deepened by his second point. Contrary to Hegel's conviction that the entire world historical process is the incarnation of God, God became incarnate only in a particular individual at a specific historical moment. Kierkegaard concluded that the incarnation is an absolute paradox—a fully contradictory coincidence of opposites. To the eye of reason, Jesus appears to be a man just like other men. That this particular, limited, finite person (a carpenter no less!) is at the same time the infinite, transcendent, holy God is the shipwreck of human reason. Kierkegaard maintained that there is nothing rational about the incarnation; the truth of the God-Man, as he called Jesus, cannot be expressed rationally. Indeed, the incarnation is a patent absurdity, an offense to reason.

> Offense has essentially to do with the composite term God and man, or with the God-Man. Speculation naturally had the notion that it "comprehended" the God-Man—this one can easily comprehend, for speculation in speculating about the God-Man leaves out temporal existence, contemporaneousness, and reality. . . . No, the *situation* is inseparable from the God-Man, the situation that an individual man who stands beside you is the God-Man. The God-Man is not the unity of God and mankind. . . . The God-Man is the unity of God and an individual man. That the human race is or should be akin to God is ancient paganism; but that an individual man is God is Christianity, and this individual man is the God-Man. There is neither in heaven, nor on earth, nor in the depths, nor in the aberrations of the most fantastic thinking, the possibility of a (humanly speaking) more insane combination.[77]

But how can a person possibly accept such an absurdity? Kierkegaard held that there is only one way: in the face of all rational evidence to the contrary, an individual must choose to believe that Jesus is the God-Man who forgives sins. Or, in Kierkegaard's celebrated phrase, a person must make a "leap of faith." From Kierkegaard's perspective, we can gain assurance that our sins are forgiven and hence conquer despair, doubt, and dread only by believing Jesus' absurd claim to be God.

Kierkegaard's reformulation of the Christian image of human existence was not aimed simply, or even primarily, at the leading philosophers and theologians of his day. He believed that the average person living in nineteenth-century Denmark had no understanding of the essential features of Christian belief. In large measure this was the result of the post-Reformation development of a state-related Danish church. Membership in the Christian community had become a matter of social custom and convenience, important only on certain ceremonial occasions such as birth, marriage, and death. Religious belief seemed to bear little relation to the daily lives of most people. This situation was exacerbated by clergymen who had become employees of the state and had lost all sense of the tension between Luther's two kingdoms—that of God and of Caesar. Rather than awakening individuals to the rigors of religious obligation, "secular" pastors tended to comfort and console people in their worldliness.

For Kierkegaard, such developments represented a betrayal of the most important aspects of Christianity. The alternative form of faith he proposed was a radicalized version of Lutheran Protestantism in which the life of the faithful individual becomes more, not less, difficult. As Kierkegaard wrote in his revealing journal,

> This [Christendom] is the enormous illusion which actually has abolished Christianity. One can get completely dizzy staring into the dreadful confusion of concepts which in this way has arisen with regard to what is Christian.

In brief, the confusion is this, but it is continued from generation to generation by millions upon millions: they enter into Christianity all wrong. Instead of entering as an individual, one comes along with the others. The others are Christians—*ergo*, I am, too, and am a Christian in the same sense as the others are.

It makes me think of old Socrates. He was concerned with what it is to be human, for in his age to be a human being was comparable to what it is to be a Christian nowadays. The individual *qua* individual was not a human being—but since the others are human beings, I am also.

But that confusion was still nothing compared to this one in Christendom, because being a Christian should be the most mature and most self-conscious decision.[78]

During the last years of his life, Kierkegaard turned his attention from philosophical and theological writing to an overt attack on the established Danish Lutheran church. As his critique became more penetrating and grew more violent, he encountered the increasing resistance of ecclesiastical officials, political representatives, and the general populace. Kierkegaard ended his life bitterly alienated from his society and thoroughly convinced of the necessity to appropriate the extraordinary image of human existence that he had articulated.

To Karl Barth, beginning his theological reflection during the First World War, Kierkegaard's image of man as a corrupt sinner tormented by doubt and anxiety seemed a more accurate form of the human image than the one presented by nineteenth-century authors such as Schleiermacher, Hegel, and Feuerbach. Barth too avowed that God is "Wholly Other,"[79] the "radically transcendent Creator and Lord of all things."[80] Man, by contrast, is a creature of God, who has fallen into sin and become totally corrupt. Nineteenth-century images of humanity as inherently one with God or as actually divine represented to Barth the epitome of prideful sin. Much of Barth's first major work was devoted to a description of the depths to which he believed the human race has fallen. Even more than his Reformation forebears, Barth was convinced of man's depravity. Fallen human beings can do absolutely nothing to right the wrongs they have committed. Barth argued that "measured by the standard of God the dignitaries of men forfeit their excellence and their serious importance—they become relative, and even the noblest human moral and spiritual attainments are seen to be what they really are—natural, of this world, profane, and 'materialistic.'"[81] World history is neither the progressive realization of the divine nor the gradual emergence of the Kingdom of God through man's moral activity. History is a chronicle of human transgression. God's relation to sinful man and his corrupt history is one of judgment.

The judgment of God is the end of history, not the beginning of a new, a second, epoch. By it history is not prolonged, but done away with. The difference between that which lies beyond the judgment and that which lies on this side of it is not relative but absolute: the two are separated absolutely. God speaks: and He is recognized as Judge.[82]

Barth embraced God's harsh judgment as an occasion for joy and not for despair. Through his condemnation of man's sin, God discloses his righteousness. With Luther, Calvin, and Kierkegaard, Barth proclaimed that

> The righteousness of God is His forgiveness, the radical alteration of the relationship between God and man which explains why, though human unrighteousness and ungodliness have brought the world to its present condition and are intolerable to Him, He nevertheless continues to name us His people in order that we may BE His people. . . . Unlike any other verdict, His verdict is creative: He pronounces us, His enemies, to be His friends.[83]

God reveals this forgiveness through the person of Jesus. Echoing Kierkegaard, Barth wrote that "in Jesus, revelation is a paradox," a "scandal"[84] to human reason. Consequently "to believe in Jesus is the most hazardous of all hazards."[85] Yet man's salvation depends upon his belief in this scandalous event. For Barth, however, man's sin so enslaves him that he cannot even believe in God's forgiving act in Jesus apart from divine assistance. Redemptive faith, he argued, comes only through God's grace.

For many people who lived through the carnage of the first half of the twentieth century, Kierkegaard's and Barth's efforts to resurrect the Christian image of man seemed to offer a viable perspective from which to interpret their experience. Theologians such as Rudolf Bultmann and Reinhold Niebuhr later developed themes suggested by Barth. Through the attempt to plumb the depths of human corruption, they sought to demonstrate humanity's abiding need for God's grace. But to others, the suffering born of two world wars told a different tale. This lesson forms the final chapter in our story of the broken image.

THE ANXIOUS SELF

> What are the roots that clutch, what branches grow
> Out of this stony rubbish? Son of man,
> You cannot say, or guess, for you know only
> A heap of broken images, where the sun beats,
> And the dead tree gives no shelter, the cricket no relief,
> And the dry stone no sound of water.[86]

"A heap of broken images." Rootless. "The Waste Land." So T. S. Eliot describes modern man's spiritual landscape. We have seen that Paul Tillich labels our time an era of meaninglessness in which there is a "universal breakdown of meaning. Twentieth-century man," he suggests, "has lost a meaningful world and a self which lives in meanings out of a spiritual center."[87] To many sensitive authors and artists, the horrors of our century have not revealed man's need for divine grace, but have demonstrated the utter collapse of the Christian image of man. How can a world in which millions die seemingly senseless deaths, they ask, be under the care of an omnipotent, providential God? Better to admit there is no God than to believe in a God who is either cruel or impotent.

Former Auschwitz prisoner Elie Wiesel probes the significance of wartime experience for religious belief when he recounts the execution of a young child and two adults who had been suspected of sabotage by their concentration camp guards.

> The SS seemed more preoccupied, more disturbed than usual.
>
> To hang a young boy in front of thousands of spectators was no light matter. The head of the camp read the verdict. All eyes were on the child. He was lividly pale, almost calm, biting his lips. The gallows threw its shadow over him. . . . The three victims mounted together onto the chairs. The three necks were placed at the same moment within the nooses. "Long live liberty!" cried the two adults.
>
> But the child was silent.
>
> "Where is God? Where is He?" Someone behind me asked.
>
> At a sign from the head of the camp, the three chairs tipped over. Total silence throughout the camp. On the horizon, the sun was setting.
>
> "Bare your heads!" yelled the head of the camp. His voice was raucous. We were weeping.
>
> "Cover your heads!"
>
> Then the march past began. The two adults were no longer alive. Their tongues hung swollen, blue-tinged. But the third rope was still moving; being so light, the child was still alive. . . . For more than half an hour he stayed there, struggling between life and death, dying in slow agony under our eyes. And we had to look him full in the face. He was still alive when I passed in front of him. His tongue was still red, his eyes not yet glazed. Behind me, I heard the same man asking: "Where is God now?" And I heard a voice within me answer him: "Where is He? Here He is—He is hanging here on this gallows."[88]

Twentieth-century man's response to the eclipse or the death of God is notably different from the reactions of his eighteenth- and nineteenth-century predecessors. Gone are the heady confidence and optimism of earlier times. Modern man knows too well the magnitude of human cruelty and depravity to believe humanity divine or infinitely perfectible. He finds Kierkegaard's image of man a more accurate reflection of the human condition than Feuerbach's deified humanity. As we have suggested, however, though many persons share Kierkegaard's diagnosis of man's illness, they cannot accept the cure he prescribes. They no longer are able to believe in a transcendent forgiving God who helps man overcome his corruption. Hence they are left with no remedy to the "sickness unto death," one of Kierkegaard's favorite phrases for despair. For such persons, the death of God brings a sense of despair and anxiety instead of emancipation and fulfillment. The world appears absurd and human life meaningless. Existentialism, the second major movement besides neo-orthodoxy spawned by Kierkegaard's thought, explores these dimensions of modern experience by drawing a graphic image of man as an anxious self.

Existentialism is a complex movement encompassing fields as diverse as philosophy, literature, and art. Running through all its forms, however, is the image of the human self as anxious, doubting, and despairing. Tillich points to the connection between the emergence of this variation of the human image and developments we have been considering throughout this chapter when he writes,

> The decisive event which underlies the search for meaning and the despair of it in the 20th century is the loss of God in the 19th century. Feuerbach explained God away in terms of the infinite desire of the human heart; Marx explained him away in terms of an ideological attempt to rise above given reality; Nietzsche as a weakening of the will to live. The result is the pronouncement "God is dead," and with him the whole system of values and meanings in which one lived.[89]

With the death of God, symbols that for so many centuries provided man with a way to envision the meaning of his life suddenly become empty. To existentialists, experience often seems senseless; history appears to be "a tale told by an idiot" with no point or purpose. Such a world thwarts human intentions and offers people no home. Like the anonymous villagers at the foot of Kafka's castle, modern man wanders aimlessly through a baffling and hostile world.

As we noted at the beginning of this chapter, Camus captures the absurdity of modern experience in this godless world. He reflects:

> I want everything to be explained to me or nothing. And the reason is impotent when it hears this cry from the heart. The mind aroused by this insistence seeks and finds nothing but contradictions and nonsense. What I fail to understand is non-sense. The world is peopled with such irrationals. The world itself, whose single meaning I do not understand, is but a vast irrational.[90]

Existentialist playwright Samuel Beckett describes the sense of self that emerges in this "vast irrational" world. "Infinite emptiness will be all around you, all the resurrected dead of all the ages wouldn't fill it, and there you'll be like a bit of grit in the middle of the steppe."[91] Such statements testify to the confusion and despair into which much of the Western world has been plunged as the result of the fragmentation of the Christian image of human existence.

THE ASIAN EXPERIENCE OF THE BROKEN IMAGE

Philosophers do not generally create the human images of their times; they reflect about them, interpret, and seek to clarify them. The images themselves emerge from the changing human experience and what it takes for granted as self-evident, sane, and insightful. From the experience of the machines of the Industrial Revolution emerged the more elaborate mechanical images of the French Enlightenment, as has been shown. From the experience of moral confusion that resulted from the breakdown of immemorial custom, as people moved from their home villages to city shops and factories, contrasted with the experience of brisk efficiency of the technological products and the accurate knowledge that produced and maintained them, came the image of moral law as universal and inexorable as gravity and inertia, which was the opening wedge of Kant's critical reflections. The philosophers whose creative work has just been traced were responding to social, intellectual, aesthetic, moral, and religious experiences with changing environments and styles of life. The vast coherent and integrative images of man and God, the kingdoms of earth and the Kingdom of Heaven, which so long had enabled humanity to feel at home in the world of God's creation, with the ministry of the Church and its sacraments ever at hand, were broken, shattered images, torn apart at their social roots. The philosophers were interpreting the meaning of what the people felt. Among the fundamental social changes that were modifying the experience of human beings in the eighteenth and nineteenth centuries was an increasingly global consciousness, a much more widespread awareness of the alien cultures of South and East Asia. Exploration, trade, military adventures, imperialism, colonialism, missionary enterprises to the "heathen" and scholarly inquiry into their literature, their languages, and their ways of viewing the world were also part of the human experience of this era. The works of many Americans and Europeans, among them Henry David Thoreau and Ralph Waldo Emerson, directly reflect this developing cosmopolitanism and awareness of Asian experience and provide an impact on the Western images themselves. However, it is not the impact of Asian upon Western ideas with which we are primarily concerned here, but a brief look at the parallel story of the breaking of the traditional images of the Asian religions that have been discussed in Chapters 4 and 5.

The Experience in India

The classical images that gave life orientation and meaning for Hindu society were so overwhelmingly comprehensive and adaptable that they could readily survive the rise and fall of dynasties, the introduction of some aspects of Western empirical science, and inevitable changes in the economic and social circumstances of persons. Even though the pace of change was slow, it was inexorable. The Moslem invasions and empires, from the eighth and surviving into the eighteenth century, disrupted the complex social order reflected in the classical caste system, as defined by the *Laws of Manu.* Neither Moslems, nor Christians, nor Buddhists had a place in the medieval system of caste hierarchy, although of course practical accommodations were always worked out to enable the society to continue to function. One result of these accommodations, however, was an increasing rigidity in the caste orders and some loss in flexibility and mutual respect which the classical system had provided. With the advent of British hegemony in much of India and the introduction of European science, business methods, industrialization, communications, and legal systems, many of the old stabilities of village-centered life were almost totally dissolved.

The scientific thought of the eighteenth and nineteenth centuries required relatively little adjustment in India. For one thing, scientific thinking directly affected very few people in Asia. For another, neither Newtonian physics nor Darwin's theory of evolution contradicted basic Hindu philosophy, which had always sought the universal laws of reality and presupposed immense cycles of evolving forms. The practical consequences of the Industrial Revolution were much more devastating. People were drawn from villages to cities, and there were organized according to the demands of industrial schedules and functions rather than the immemorial cycles of seed-time and harvest and divisions of labor. Wholly new vocations, opportunities, and demands rendered the old *dharma* system obsolete. Radically different responses to change appeared. Some people aggressively sought to westernize, to abandon old ways and to adopt new ones, while others withdrew ever more tightly into shells of resistance, creating new divisions among the people. An increasing population, with diminishing resources of space, goods, and self-respect; the usual vagaries of weather and crops; foreign, insensitive, sometimes brutal governmental authorities; intolerant religious communities; and frequent warfare, produced chaos, suffering, and disillusion on an unprecedented scale. For a time in the twentieth century these disintegrating tendencies were stemmed by the organization of the Indian freedom struggle. Under the leadership of Mohandas Gandhi and others during the 1920s and 1930s, rich and powerful symbols were drawn out of the Indian cultural treasury, the symbols of *Satyagraha*, truth-force, the irresistible energy that Gandhi believed lies in living for valid ideals, of *ahiṁsa*, nonviolence, the vision of a harmonious and fulfilling rather than an exploitative and demeaning caste system. These symbols helped to organize the successful struggle against British imperialism, but they also led to the bloody violence of the Moslem-Hindu partition and to an economic order that made India even less capable of competing successfully for international markets and economic development. Hindu thought was nourished by several innovative reformulations, but neither they nor any of the competing religious interpretations (for example, Christianity, Islam, Buddhism) were capable of attracting more than a small percentage of the population. Centuries of bureaucratic intrigue under alien authorities bore fruit in factionalism and corruption among lower governmental officials which the doctrinaire democratic socialism of the Congress Party has been impotent to overcome.

There have been several results of this fracturing of the religious traditions. One result has been the growth of disorder, rebellion, Marxist and Maoist revolutionary groups, disrespect for the symbols and institutions of tradition and established order. The fervor of these devotees of new images, whether of anarchy or of communism, produces an even more acute despair for those who shared only the certainty of loss. A second result has been a renaissance of intensively Hindu traditions, a widespread, but not widely organized, rebirth of the worship of Kṛṣṇa, and a renewed interest in devotion and mystical experience. A third result has been the emergence of new religious images. Most of these are eclectic and ironic. The Ramakrishna Missions radiate from the experience of a nineteenth-century Hindu mystic, Sri Ramakrishna. They teach consciousness of the universal divine reality. Some groups have developed modern social ethics within Hinduism, heavily dependent on the teachings of Christianity. Members of the Aurobindo Ashram, at Pondicherry, cooperate with the United Nations Educational, Scientific, and Cultural Organization in the building of a new international community dedicated to the cultivation of a *state of consciousness* favorable to a new world order of peace and brotherhood. Whether these new movements have long-range significance cannot be determined yet, but they are devoted to developing new images, based on the past spiritual insights of humanity and suitable for the new conditions of human existence.

Finally, it may be said that the hold of old traditions expressing the humane ideals is strong indeed. Despite all that the acids of modernity have done, many Hindus still observe *pūja* in their homes, participate gladly in festival occasions, worship and meditate in the temples, and honor the spiritual endeavor of holy men.

The Experience in China

For China the cataclysmic event that informs the contemporary situation has been the Communist revolution. All the religious traditions that we described—ancestor worship, Taoism, Confucianism, and Buddhism—have been declared to be enemies of the people. In their place the thought of Mao-Tse-Tung offers a vision of the future in a truly classless, peaceful, and prosperous society that will emerge from the energy, minds, and organization of the people led by the Communist state. They see the images of the archaic traditions as forming the basis of a "slave society." Although the government has not set out to annihilate those religious vestiges that remain, and, in fact, has preserved some religious monuments as historic relics, it does not encourage their growth and would undoubtedly resist energetically if any of them should appear to offer an image of life as compelling as that of the Communist state itself. We will not attempt to analyze the image of the Maoist state here, though one may wish to entertain the thought that it too is a religious image of humanity. Certainly there is much to suggest that even as Chairman Mao condemns Confucianism for its idealization of the past, he also does much to fulfill its image of the Superior Man, the gentleman-bureaucrat, who may safely regard his own feelings as the feelings of the people.

The Experience in Japan

Japan went through an historic convulsion in the late nineteenth and early twentieth centuries. Until the Meiji era (beginning in 1868), the influences most likely to produce cultural change in Japan were heavily suppressed. In the Meiji era and thereafter change was aggressively sought. The intellectual and social revolutions that occupied Europe and America for almost three hundred years were introduced to Japan in about seventy years. In addition, in mid-twentieth-century Japan set about creating a large colonial power base and then was compelled to surrender these ambitions. The result may well now be cultural rootlessness.

The Meiji era began when political authority was restored to the Emperor from the Tokugawa Shogun, or military authority, in whom political power had centered for more than seven hundred years. The Emperor opened Japan to the West and, in fact, sent delegations to Europe and America to bring back ideas for modernizing the social order. State-supported heavy industry, communications, and railways developed at the fastest rate in history. To support governmental authority there was a revitalization of Imperial Shinto, although it was arbitrarily defined as political and nationalistic rather than religious. These tendencies were accelerated and distorted by the new military clique that led Japan into World War II. Following the war this official Shinto was dismantled, but economic reconstruction went on as energetically and thoughtfully as before. Both traditional industries—such as fine china, lacquer ware, textiles, and trinkets—and new ones—such as electronics, automobiles, musical instruments, and synthetics—were rapidly developed. Cities were rebuilt. In spite of being confined to its home islands, Japan has become an economic world power. Hondas, coffee houses, rock music, and keeping up with inflation have become typical interests of the Japanese people. Many of the old traditions have little grip in this new age. Many persons have lost all significant touch with religious self-understanding. As might be expected, others have become fanatics for the same reasons. Much religious activity and tradition seem to have the appeal of museum artifacts—something to preserve, but not to take seriously for contemporary use. The most interesting reaction by far, however, has been the emergence of a steady stream of so-called new religions. Many of these are devoted primarily to earthly values, such as health, long life, prosperity, peace of mind, a sense of personal worth, happiness, and friendship. They borrow freely from Shinto, Buddhism, Christianity, and from popular psychology. Most have or have had charismatic founders, but several are securely into their second or third generation and are still thriving. They tend to be more group-oriented than traditional Buddhism or Shinto and to be quite evangelical in their approach to potential converts. But there are so many of these groups and their sacred symbols are still so very young that it would be hazardous indeed to forecast their future. A few were imported into the United States after World War II and have contributed to the new religious ferment in this country, which is discussed in the following chapter. It is impossible to know whether the fractured image of man can ever be restored in Asia, or whether the broken shell is releasing new life and new images to flourish in the dawning age.

FRAGMENTS

Throughout the past three hundred years considerable theological and philosophical ink has been spilled criticizing and defending the traditional religious images of man. Defenders of the image seem to have been fighting a losing battle, for critics gradually gain the upper hand. Finally the historical events of the twentieth century lend substance to eighteenth- and nineteenth-century critiques of religion. Under this ponderous weight, the traditional images of man shatter. But the broken image leads to the fragmentation of human existence. Without a mirror in which to behold himself, modern man no longer seems to know who he is. Doubt replaces certainty and confidence falls prey to growing anxiety. Frenetic economic and social activity and experimentation may be symptoms of this malaise rather than evidence of secure confidence in the victory of the secular over all images of transcendence. In concluding our story of the broken image, we are forced to ask whether man can long endure such an arid spiritual climate. Might not his unquenchable thirst for meaning lead to a further search for transcendence?

NOTES

1. Albert Camus, *The Myth of Sisyphus,* trans. J. O'Brien (New York: Alfred A. Knopf, 1955), p. 16.

2. Paul Tillich, *The Courage to Be* (New Haven, Conn.: Yale University Press, 1952), pp. 61, 139.

3. Peter Berger, *The Sacred Canopy* (Garden City, N.Y.: Doubleday & Company, 1969), p. 26.

4. Ibid., pp. 26–27.

5. Immanuel Kant, "What Is Enlightenment?" *On History,* trans. Lewis White Beck (New York: Bobbs-Merrill Company, 1963), p. 3. Reprinted by permission.

6. Paul Tillich, *Perspectives on 19th and 20th Century Protestant Theology,* ed. Carl Braaten (New York: Harper & Row, 1967), p. 31.

7. Ernst Cassirer, *The Philosophy of the Enlightenment,* trans. F. C. A. Koelin and J. P. Pettegrove (Princeton, N.J.: Princeton University Press, 1951), p. 141.

8. Alexander Pope, "Epitaph. Intended for Sir Isaac Newton, in Westminster Abbey."

9. Cassirer, *Philosophy of Enlightenment,* pp. 6–7.

10. See chap. 3, "The Forgiven Sinner," 112–19.

11. Voltaire, *Traité Métaphysique,* chaps. 3 and 5. Quoted by Cassirer, *Philosophy of Enlightenment,* p. 12.

12. Cassirer, *Philosophy of Enlightenment,* p. 6.

13. Ibid., p. 22.

14. Francis Oakley, "Christian Theology and the Newtonian Science: The Rise of the Concept of the Laws of Nature," in *Creation: The Impact of an Idea,* ed. D. O'Connor and F. Oakley (New York: Charles Scribner's Sons, 1969), p. 60.

15. Descartes, *Notes against a Programme, Oeuvres de Descartes,* ed. C. Adam and P. Tannery (Paris, 1897–1913), Vol. VIII B, pp. 358–59. Quoted by Frederick Copleston, *A History of Philosophy* Vol. 4 (New York: Image Books, 1963), p. 95.

16. John Locke, *An Essay Concerning Human Understanding,* Vol. I, ed. A. C. Fraser (Oxford: Clarendon Press, 1894), pp. 121–22.

17. Ibid., p. 124.

18. See chap. 3, "Nature and Supernature," pp. 104–9.

19. Locke, *Human Understanding,* Vol. II, p. 308.

20. Ibid., p. 309.

21. William Paley, *The Cosmological Argument,* ed. Donald R. Burrill (Garden City, N.Y.: Doubleday & Company, 1967), p. 166.

22. Ibid., p. 167.

23. Locke, *Human Understanding,* Vol. II, p. 412.

24. Ibid., p. 413.

25. Ibid., p. 416.

26. Ibid., p. 438.

27. John Locke, *The Reasonableness of Christianity,* ed. I. T. Ramsey (Stanford, Calif.: Stanford University Press, 1967), p. 61.

28. John Toland, "Christianity Not Mysterious," in *Religious Thought of the Eighteenth Century,* ed. J. M. Creed and J. S. Boys-Smith (Cambridge, Eng.: University Press, 1939), p. 20.

29. Ibid., p. 19.

30. Matthew Tindal, "Christianity as Old as Creation," in *Religious Thought of the Eighteenth Century* (Cambridge, Eng.: University Press, 1939), p. 36.

31. Robert R. Palmer, *Catholics and Unbelievers in Eighteenth Century France* (Princeton, N.J.: Princeton University Press, 1939, 1967) p. 8. Reprinted by permission.

32. Ibid., pp. 8–9.

33. Quoted in Lucien Goldmann, *The Philosophy of the Enlightenment,* trans. Henry Maas (Cambridge, Mass.: The MIT Press, 1973), p. 68.

34. Voltaire, *Philosophe de Newton,* I, *Oeuvres,* ed. Beauchot (Paris, 1828–1834). Quoted by Copleston, *A History of Philosophy,* Vol. 6, pt. I, p. 33.

35. Baron d'Holbach, *The System of Nature,* trans. H. D. Robinson (Boston: J. P. Mendum, 1889), p. 230.

36. Ibid., p. 280.

37. Ibid., p. 230.

38. *Les Philosophes: The Philosophers of the Enlightenment and Modern Democracy,* ed. N. L. Torrey (New York: Capricorn Books, 1960), p. 173.

39. David Hume, *A Treatise of Human Nature,* Vol. I, ed. T. H. Green and T. H. Grose (London: Longmans, Green and Cox, 1886), p. 311.

40. Ibid., p. 377.

41. Ibid., pp. 390–91.

42. David Hume, *Dialogues Concerning Natural Religion,* ed. H. D. Aiken (New York: Hafner Publishing Company, 1966), p. 23.

43. Ibid., p. 17.

44. Ibid., p. 25.

45. Immanuel Kant, *Lectures on Ethics,* trans. and ed. L. Infield (New York: Harper Torchbooks, 1963), p. 80.

46. Immanuel Kant, *Critique of Practical Reason,* trans. L. W. Beck (New York: Bobbs-Merrill Company, 1956), p. 3. Reprinted by permission.

47. The Pietistic movement in Germany was started by Philipp Jakob Spener

(1635–1705) and was promoted by August Hermann Francke (1663–1727). One of the consequences of this development was the renaissance of the Moravian Brethren under the direction of Count Nicolaus Ludwig von Zinzendorf (1700–1760). The Moravian Brethren influenced Schleiermacher quite strongly. It is important to note that similar revival movements surfaced in England and America during the eighteenth century. In England Methodism flourished under the watchful eye of John Wesley (1707–1788). In America the most important religious development of the eighteenth century was the Great Awakening, which began in New Jersey in 1726 and lasted over 50 years. The best known representative of the Great Awakening was Jonathan Edwards (1703–1758), whose account of the revival in Northampton, Massachusetts (in 1734–1735) entitled *A Faithful Narrative of the Surprising Work of God in the Conversion of Many Hundred Souls* remains an unsurpassed example of revivalist literature. Many persons whose lives were untouched by the philosophical and theological discussions of the Enlightenment were deeply influenced by the eighteenth-century religious revival.

48. Friedrich Schleiermacher, *On Religion: Speeches to its Cultured Despisers*, trans. J. Oman (New York: Harper Torchbooks), pp. 49–50.

49. Ibid., p. 43.

50. Ibid., p. 43.

51. Ibid., p. 36.

52. Ibid., p. 97.

53. Ibid., p. 94.

54. Ibid., pp. 43–44.

55. Hegel, *The Phenomenology of Mind*, trans. J. B. Baillie (New York: Harper Torchbooks, 1967), p. 83.

56. Hegel, *The Encyclopaedia of the Philosophical Sciences, Logic*, trans. W. Wallace (New York: Oxford University Press, 1968), paragraph 80.

57. Hegel, *Lectures on the Philosophy of Religion*, Vol. III, trans. E. B. Spiers and J. B. Sanderson (Atlantic Highlands, N.J.: Humanities Press, 1968), p. 204. Reprinted by permission of Humanities Press and George Allen & Unwin Ltd.

58. Ibid., p. 18.

59. Ibid., p. 73.

60. Ibid.

61. Ibid., p. 77.

62. Ibid., p. 99.

63. Ibid., pp. 12–13.

64. Tillich, *Perspectives*, p. 121.

65. Ludwig Feuerbach, *The Essence of Christianity*, trans. G. Eliot (New York: Harper Torchbooks, 1957), p. 12.

66. Ibid., p. 14.

67. Ibid., pp. 29–30.

68. Ibid., p. 26.

69. Ludwig Feuerbach, *Lectures on the Essence of Religion*, trans. R. Manheim (New York: Harper & Row, 1967), p. 23.

70. Karl Marx, *Writings of the Young Marx on Philosophy and Society*, ed. L. D. Easton and K. H. Guddat (Garden City, N.Y.: Doubleday & Company, 1967), p. 250.

71. Ibid., p. 402.

72. Ibid., p. 250.

73. Ibid.

74. Ibid., p. 251.

75. Søren Kierkegaard, *The Sickness unto Death,* trans. Walter Lowrie (Princeton, N.J.: Princeton University Press, 1970), p. 155. Reprinted by permission.

76. ——, *Training in Christianity,* trans. Walter Lowrie (Princeton, N.J.: Princeton University Press, 1967), p. 216. Reprinted by permission.

77. Ibid., pp. 83–84.

78. *Søren Kierkegaard's Journals and Papers,* trans. Howard and Edna Hong (Bloomington: Indiana University Press, 1967), no. 390.

79. Karl Barth, *The Epistle to the Romans,* trans. E. C. Hoskyns (New York: Oxford University Press, 1968), p. 49.

80. Ibid., p. 93.

81. Ibid., p. 77.

82. Ibid.

83. Ibid., p. 93.

84. Ibid., pp. 97–98, 99.

85. Ibid., p. 99.

86. T. S. Eliot, "The Waste Land," lines 19–24.

87. Paul Tillich, *Courage to Be,* p. 139.

88. Quoted by Thomas A. Indinopulos in "The Mystery of Suffering in the Art of Dostoevsky, Camus, Wiesel, and Grundwald," *Journal of the American Academy of Religion,* 43, 1 (March 1975), p. 59. Reprinted by permission of Farrar, Straus & Giroux, Inc.

89. Tillich, *Courage to Be,* p. 142.

90. Albert Camus, *The Myth of Sisyphus,* p. 20.

91. Samuel Beckett, *Endgame* (New York: Grove Press, 1958), p. 36.

FOR FURTHER READING

ALLISON, HENRY E., *Lessing and the Enlightenment.* Ann Arbor: University of Michigan Press, 1966. A study of the development of Lessing's theological and philosophical thought; a superb account of the eighteenth-century British, French, and German Enlightenment in a lengthy introductory chapter.

BARTH, KARL, *The Epistle to the Romans,* trans. E. D. Hoskyns. New York: Oxford University Press, 1968. Revolutionary analysis of Paul's Epistle to the Romans; launched the major theological movement of the twentieth century—neo-orthodoxy.

BAUMER, FRANKLIN L., *Religion and the Rise of Scepticism.* New York: Harcourt, Brace and World, 1960. Study of the emergence of modern scepticism, with special attention given to the influence of science on religious belief.

CAMUS, ALBERT, *The Fall,* trans. J. O'Brien. New York: Random House, 1956. One of the outstanding literary statements of the twentieth-century existentialist point of view; presents complex philosophical ideas in a readable and an engaging manner.

CASSIRER, ERNST, *The Philosophy of the Enlightenment,* trans. F. C. A. Koelin and J. P. Pettegrove. Princeton, N.J.: Princeton University Press, 1951. A penetrating study of the Enlightenment focusing on themes such as religion, law, society, and aesthetics; a difficult, though rewarding, book.

CRAGG, GERALD, *Reason and Authority in the Eighteenth Century.* Cambridge, Eng.: The University Press, 1964. Particularly helpful in tracing the interrelationship between social and ecclesiastical developments from the middle of the twelfth to the end of the eighteenth century.

FREI, HANS, *The Eclipse of Biblical Narrative.* New Haven, Conn.: Yale University Press, 1974. A masterful exploration of the development of nineteenth-century biblical hermeneutics.

GOLDMANN, LUCIEN, *The Philosophy of the Enlightenment: The Christian Burgess and the Enlightenment,* trans. Henry Maas. Cambridge, Mass.: The MIT Press, 1973. A novel interpretation of the impact of socioeconomic forces on Enlightenment thought by an eminent French Marxist.

HEGEL, G. W. F., *The Phenomenology of Mind,* trans. John Baillie. New York: Harper Torchbooks, 1967. The most important work of nineteenth-century German idealism; difficult, but has exercised tremendous influence on virtually all later philosophical and theological thought.

KANT, IMMANUEL, *Critique of Practical Reason,* trans. Lewis White Beck. New York: Bobbs-Merrill Company, 1956. Kant's effort to respond to Enlightenment critiques of religious belief by an investigation of moral action.

——, *Critique of Pure Reason,* trans. Norman Kemp Smith. New York: St. Martin's Press, 1965. Kant's major study of epistemology; a demanding work that sums up major currents of eighteenth-century thought and points toward nineteenth-century philosophical reflection.

KIERKEGAARD, SØREN, *Concluding Unscientific Postscript,* trans. David Swenson and Walter Lowrie. Princeton, N.J.: Princeton University Press, 1971. Kierkegaard's most extended critique of Hegel's philosophical system; identifies themes that play a major role in twentieth-century theology.

——, *Fear and Trembling*, trans. Walter Lowrie. Princeton, N.J.: Princeton University Press, 1973. The most engaging work of Kierkegaard's pseudonymous authorship; probably the best single volume introduction to his thought.

LESSING, GOTTHOLD, *Lessing's Theological Writings*, ed. Henry Chadwick. Stanford, Calif.: Stanford University Press, 1973. A brief, though useful, collection of Lessing's theological writings not otherwise available; long introduction especially helpful.

LÖWITH, KARL, *From Hegel to Nietzsche*, trans. D. E. Green. Garden City, N.Y.: Doubleday & Company, 1967. A lucid account of important post-Hegelian thinkers such as Feuerbach, Marx, Kierkegaard, and Nietzsche; identifies significant philosophical issues separating the major nineteenth-century schools of Hegelian interpretation.

MARX, KARL, *Writings of the Young Marx on Philosophy and Society*, trans. and ed. L. D. Easton and K. H. Guddat. Garden City, N.Y.: Doubleday & Company, 1967. An essential collection of writings that reveals the philosophical roots of Marx's economic theory; contains Marx's critiques of Hegel and Feuerbach and includes manuscripts in which his analysis of religion is developed in detail.

NIEBUHR, RICHARD R., *Resurrection and Historical Reason*. New York: Charles Scribner's Sons, 1957. An effort to show the nineteenth-century roots of contemporary biblical interpretation; combines historical analysis and constructive theological argumentation.

RASCHKE, CARL A., *Moral Action, God, and History in the Thought of Immanuel Kant*. Missoula, Montana: Scholars' Press, 1975. A detailed exegesis of Kant's analysis of the relationship between human action and religious belief.

SCHLEIERMACHER, FRIEDRICH, *On Religion: Speeches to Its Cultured Despisers*, trans. J. Oman. New York: Harper Torchbooks, 1958. The classic romantic statement concerning religious belief by the person commonly acknowledged to be the father of modern theology.

SCHWEITZER, ALBERT, *The Quest of the Historical Jesus*. New York: The Macmillan Company, 1964. A painstaking survey of the impact of modern historical inquiry on understandings of the figure of Jesus.

TAYLOR, MARK C., *Kierkegaard's Pseudonymous Authorship: A Study of Time and the Self*. Princeton, N.J.: Princeton University Press, 1975. A comprehensive study of pivotal issues developed in Kierkegaard's pseudonymous authorship; special attention given to Kierkegaard's relation to Hegel.

TILLICH, PAUL, *The Courage to Be*. New Haven, Conn.: Yale University Press, 1952. The clearest example of Tillich's effort to bring together insights of fields as diverse as theology, philosophy, psychology, and literature.

TROELTSCH, ERNST, *The Social Teaching of the Christian Churches*, 2 vols., trans. O. Wyon. New York: Harper Torchbooks, 1960. A pioneering work in the sociological approach to the study of religion; covers the development of Christian history from its earliest days through the nineteenth century; raises methodological issues that still merit serious consideration.

The Contemporary Social Crisis

and the New Forms of Transcendence

7

THE SEARCH FOR TRANSCENDENCE

In the previous chapter we examined how traditional religious images have splintered under the ponderous impact of modern science and secularization. Furthermore, we discussed the ways in which the period of Enlightenment, the advances of materialism, historicism, and rationalism throughout the nineteenth and twentieth centuries gave birth to a revaluation of the human condition. Many forward-looking intellectuals abandoned the venerable assumption that man inescapably requires religion for his day-to-day welfare, if not his eternal bliss. By the same token, many prophets and critics began to point to the absence of a genuine sense of God for a large segment of the population. But rather than decrying this turn of events, they acclaimed it as a sign of humanity's maturity and new appreciation of personal autonomy. Nietzsche rejoiced in this development, as we have seen, by minting a phrase that has grown into a rallying cry for secularists: "God is dead!" By the middle of our century even some Christian theologians and clergymen were applauding the German philosopher's verdict and adapting the theme themselves. Dietrich Bonhoeffer, a celebrated pastor and religious thinker martyred by the Nazis during the Second World War, wrote hopefully from his prison cell of the coming of a "religionless Christianity."[1] In the 1960s the so-called death of God movement swept through the popular press as well as the community of theological experts, thereby prompting *Time* magazine to inquire with the same prosaic detachment as it might look into voter preferences in the last election whether God had, *in fact,* passed on. The broken religious image of the new era had supposedly been discarded even by the proverbial middle Americans from Muncie and Peoria.

On the other hand, the triumph of the modern spirit has been marred by the devastation of two successive world wars, by brutal deportation and extermination of entire peoples for political purposes, by the collapse of long-standing institutions and a stupendous turnabout in social customs, moral beliefs, and life styles. The trauma of rapid, wholesale, and often violent change—what Alvin Toffler has aptly described as "future shock"—has precipitated for large segments of the population a loss of confidence in the blessings of modern culture.

> To survive, to avert what we have termed future shock, the individual must become infinitely more adaptable and capable than ever before. He must search out totally new ways to anchor himself, for all the old roots—religion, nation, community, family, or profession—are now shaking under the hurricane impact of the accelerative thrust. Before he can do so, however, he must understand in greater detail how the effects of acceleration penetrate his personal life, creep into his behavior and alter the quality of existence. He must, in other words, understand transience.[2]

This trauma often planted the seeds for various religious "revivals," especially in the United States, as happened immediately after the holocaust of 1939-1945, or in the wake of the Vietnam conflict less than a decade ago. Resisting the siren song of human progress and the tinsel promise of an easier and more abundant life for all, sizeable segments of a society rejected the coventional wisdom of their day and embarked on a search for new and more personally satisfying forms of life. Theoretically speaking, such is the process whereby a person's sense of self clashes with the definitions of reality that have heretofore been proffered by the social body to which one belongs. The upshot is the creation of an "alternative reality," which takes the place of what one's peers generally accept as genuine and true about the world. The sense of alternative reality leads to a new alignment of individual consciousness with the powers and mysteries of the universe.

In recent times this evolution of alternative reality, which at once yielded a wholly different human image, first manifested itself in the appearance of the "beat generation" of San Francisco, Hollywood, and Greenwich Village who traded the gospel of science and success for existentialism and Zen Buddhism. Later it surfaced again with the explosion of Eastern meditation cults, psychedelic drugs, and occultism. Gurus, apostles of mescaline and LSD, and flashy magicians and wizards replaced the staid apologists for the straight order of things. By the end of the last decade, those secularists who had eagerly awaited the surrender of revelation to reason were outmaneuvered by enthusiasts for the other dimension of experience. The premature burial of God, in a world dominated by social engineering and technology, was called off by the many who now sang of their growing thirst for transcendence.

William A. Johnson has characterized transcendence as "the presence of 'something above' or 'something beyond' or 'something more' than ordinary human experience."[3] In classical religious thought, "transcendence" was a term usually reserved for God, for the Creator of the Universe who lies above and beyond nature or modes of thought. But in the twentieth-century idiom the word has come to denote any *extraordinary* intuition, insight, feeling, or state of awareness. Transcendence therefore implies an order of reality located outside of the structures of conventional experience, and such a reality may properly be called "religious." Those who tout the joys and opportunities of secular life have always tended, of course, to depreciate the uncommon elements in daily life and therefore subordinate the purely religious interests of man to the claims of science and common sense. However, the mounting concern with transcendence reversed this order of priorities and brought a new delight in myth, magic, and mystical ecstasy. Paul Goodman, an eminent observer of the heaving cultural scene has dubbed this revival of long dormant religious sensibilities the "new reformation."[4]

Clearly, though, the new reach for transcendence has coincided with a crisis of the contemporary mind and spirit, with a sudden and intense shattering of the bedrock assumptions about the cosmos that have been second nature to men for generations. The outward symptoms of the crisis have been social and political—marches in the streets, the burning of ghettos, the machinations of government leaders, and the corruption of democratic politics through infamous scandals like Watergate. Yet the visible upheavals have both betrayed and hastened an ongoing reevaluation for many anonymous individuals of what is sensible, comprehensible, or *normal*. What Theodore Roszak labeled a "counterculture" sprung up during the 1960s, in many corners of society and at the same time spawned an unprecedented scheme of cognitive symbols. New perspectives on the human condition—for example, the emphasis on the sanctity of the individual as expressed in the saying, "do your own thing," the effort to locate man in a more subtle web of life forms as evidenced in the ecology movement—have taken root alongside new religious moods. Changes in religion have included a turn from institutional faith to private ecstasy, the rush to more primitive kinds of nature worship, vegetarianism, and witchcraft. By the same token, the impulse to radical political reform has generated a new interest in the utopia, in the creation of what are perceived as more humane life styles that serve as a counterpoise to "getting along" in the present socioeconomic system.

"Transcendence" thus implies a new consciousness, whether religious or political, that furnishes modes for restructuring the social order. Many latter-day revolutionaries, for instance, have talked with religious zeal about molding the "new man" who will be shriven of the old habits of competition with his fellows for material goods and of exploiting the world's resources solely for the sake of technological advancement. In consequence, yearning for transcendence has spawned a swarm of "political theologies" that look to the overhaul of society. The transformation of historical material existence through human intelligence and commitment replaces the conventional religious forms by which man has expressed himself and dealt with adversity.

We shall examine briefly the various instances in which the emerging images of transcendence give hint to a revaluation of the human image itself. The spectrum may well signal the close of one epoch and the beginning of a subsequent period, so far as religion and the human image are concerned.

THE WANING OF TRADITION
AND THE IMAGE OF THE "NEW"

Today's quest for transcendence, for new and unprecedented models of reality that stand in critical tension with the prevailing habits and values of modern culture, has proceeded apace with the loss of a sense of tradition for many people in our world. Observers of recent trends have been apt to categorize the dawning new era in terms of the "postindustrial," "post-Christian," "postmodern" age, and so on. Similarly, it may be said that we are now moving into a "posttraditional" age that underscores in a much larger manner the dividing line between the old and the new. It is the decline of tradition as a whole, including the symbol complexes, rituals, and behavioral roles that have constituted the familiar religious systems of the past, that perhaps illuminates the explosion of offbeat religious cults and sects as well as the various modes of experimentation with novel world views, strategies for action, and the mysteries of the mind.

The word "tradition" derives from the Latin *traditio* which means "to hand down." Traditions are those bodies of beliefs, concepts, pastimes, and rules of social etiquette that are handed down or passed on from generation to generation. Traditional religions subsist by means of the transmission of notions about God, worship, and morality from elders to their offspring. The child gradually learns and accepts the images of life that have been imprinted on him during his growing up as patterns for conducting his day-to-day affairs. Similarly, by assimilating these images he acquires a set of beliefs by which he can instruct his own sons and daughters as to what is true and real. Traditional cultures thus preserve or change very slowly certain standards or norms for experiencing the universe. The individual's own distinct preferences about how he feels or thinks, "this is the way it is," his personal impulses or fantasies, are subordinated to the definitions of reality urged on him by family and society. A priest or wise old grandmother drilling a young Catholic girl in the catechism, an Indian guru educating an adolescent boy from the Brahmin caste on the rigors and duties of his station in Hindu life, the child of pious Orthodox Jews enrolled in Hebrew school all typify the process according to which tradition maintains itself among diverse peoples.

On the other hand, in a posttraditional age the automatic transfer of ideas and images from older to younger, from established authorities to novices who have yet to appropriate the ways and lore of their ancestors, becomes difficult, if not impossible. Traditions, customary ways of seeing and doing things, grow suspect simply because they are traditions. No longer is the new regarded merely as a variation on former themes; it appears as a convulsive break with what has gone before. The transcendence of existing forms of life and sensibility bursts forth as a kind of ethical imperative. Gilbert Chesterton's memorable exhortation to "be wise, avoid the wild and new!" gives way to the sentiment for total change—"apocalyptic" as it is sometimes called—voiced by the anonymous writer of the Book of Revelation: "Behold, I make all things new."[5]

Alongside the wreckage of traditional loyalties, thoughts, and attitudes there takes place both an inversion of authority and a profound alteration of religious and cultural leadership. Gray hair and the counting of many years no more suffice as major criteria for gaining authority. Age is understood to guarantee not wisdom, but drooping faculties and falling "out of touch" with the times. Likewise, youth becomes a master image which many members of a society desire to emulate. The anthropologist Margaret Mead has characterized the split between traditional and posttraditional life forms as the difference between "post-figurative" and "pre-figurative" cultures.[6] Postfigurative or traditional orders are those that shape the individual personality according to stable cultural models and that provide consistent symbols and conceptual schemes for making sense out of human experience; such symbolic equipment remains in the custody of the older generations. Prefigurative orders, in contrast, are those that have abandoned an enduring system of cultural meanings and have left each rising generation to discover its own practical as well as sacred truths. In prefigurative cultures the young must decipher their experiences according to their own contrived codes. The cult of youth reigns supreme not only in clothing and life styles, but also in the formation of categories for interpreting events. As a result, the impetus for transcendence, for new values and experiences, tends to come primarily from among the young themselves. The practice of dabbling in mind-expanding drugs, such as mescaline and LSD, which create sensuous new vistas of awareness, revolutionary rhetoric and makeshift political programs, not to mention the flowering of exotic religious group and meditation techniques, all arise from the thirst among adolescents and young adults for a perspective on the world that is uniquely their own and disclosed through their own personal odysseys of trial and error. Postfigurative cultures hallow the past. Prefigurative cultures with their emphasis on transcendence eschew the past in order to unearth the treasures of the present. Therefore, it is hardly a coincidence that the children of the posttraditional era have been frequently criticized for having no interest in history, or that they have been wryly dubbed the "now generation." For in their eyes the insights and knowledge of earlier periods have lost their allure, if not their relevance. The tempo of change in the twentieth century has accelerated so fast that the images of prior generations have been made obsolete many times over. The posttraditional world is one in which change appears invariable, and hence the angle of vision on that world must be adjusted incessantly. Change, moreover, encourages a rush of new experiences which cannot be interpreted or evaluated according to time-honored criteria. The experience of the recurrently new becomes in itself a custom.

THE NEW USES OF EXPERIENCE

It is not surprising for an age whose watchwords are transcendence and anti-traditionalism that a completely new connotation is given to the term "experience." Traditional cultures always, of course, accorded worth to learning by experience, but the ultimate understanding that members of such cultures sought to attain was regarded as the product of long labors and perhaps suffering. Experience was something achieved slowly, with prolonged life, and its content was identified with the consciousness that people had realized under some guise or other in bygone days.

> Yet with great toil all that I can attain
> By long experience, and in learned schools . . . [7]

In other words, the accumulation of experience depends on the gradual socialization of the individual and his eventual recognition of the ways in which he can successfully perform his role to the approval of others. On the other hand, posttraditional man strives for experiences that do not necessarily have a common point of orientation. In his case experience must be dramatic and unrepeatable, unmediated by familiar forms of interpretation.

Experience thus passes from a set of *learned* perceptual habits acquired within every generation to a dazzling confrontation by the individual in his solitude with extraordinary panoramas of the spirit. All claims about the universe demand the test of immediate evidence, but evidence does not have to be within the public domain: it has only to be a private and intense conviction that something genuine has occurred. Kierkegaard's dictum that "truth is subjectivity" emerges as the principle by which both theories and conjectures are verified. Many a college student today will argue vehemently that if "you experience it as true," if the experience turns on flashing lights and tinkling bells, then it must be true. In this respect the model of experience for contemporary man borders on what might be called "ecstasy."

Harvey Seifert has defined ecstasy as "experiences of deep satisfaction and joy and well-being that are astonishingly intense and pervasive of the entire being."[8] Ecstasy consists in the transcendence of conventional views for the sake of what is personally engaging. Such colloquial expressions as "wow," "far out," or "out of sight" suggest the new rules for experience nowadays. Meaningful experience must have the abruptness of a thunderclap, the novelty of a chance encounter with an old acquaintance, the intensity of an orgasm. In the religious realm the new valuation of experience requires the discarding of collective dogmas and creeds as well as time-honored myths. All individuals become their own muses.

Alan Watts has commended all "religious experience" as a kind of "inspiration," as the wellspring of "spiritual genius."[9] Religion detaches itself from its social moorings and embarks on myriad mystic voyages into the unknown self. Indeed, the word "religion" itself, with all its ecclesiastical and formalistic overtones, is not frequently eschewed by devotees of new movements. For example, a disciple of the guru Maharaji—the teenage "Perfect Master" from India who has won quite a following in the United States of late—once remarked: "Ours is not a religion, but an *experience.*" The mysterious knowledge that the guru dispenses, according to another testimony, "can only be experienced, not fully described."[10] In fine, the esoteric experiential dimension of the new forms of transcendence overwhelms all appeals to public understanding. The self abandons the universe of meaning constructed by society and heads into a boundless expanse of inarticulate "cosmic" feelings and clouds of illumination. To use another metaphor drawn from modern existentialism, the self in contemporary culture finds itself "homeless" with no recognizable symbols or meanings to call its own.

THE HOMELESS MIND

The image of "homelessness," indeed, pervades contemporary discourse. The new transcendence rests upon a picture of humanity that implies the loss of a sense of place or rootage. The words of Bob Dylan's hit song of the mid-1960s capture this mood:

> How does it feel
> To be on your own
> With no direction home
> Like a complete unknown
> Like a rolling stone?[11]

In a recent best-selling book by Carlos Castaneda, *Journey to Ixtlan,* a similar message rings clear: the destiny of contemporary man lies in renunciation of all family and territorial ties, the abdication of all previous social roles and of personal identity, for the sake of a vagrant, spiritually isolated journey through a kaleidoscope of time and experience. Castaneda listens to a story told by Indian Don Genaro, a friend of his patron, the Yaqui Indian sorcerer, Don Juan. Don Genaro recounts how he spent many days on the road hunting for a way back to his hometown Ixtlan. But the tale ends with Don Genaro never reaching home. Don Genaro tells Castaneda that he will never get home, that he will always be traveling to Ixtlan.[12] The lesson of all homeward journeys in today's world, according to this parable, is that we have no home, no tradition left to which we can return. Contemporary man is on the one hand like the legendary

Greek hero Odysseus, who drifts from one enchanted isle to the next, yet who on the other hand has no Ithaca for which to set his sails.

As R. D. Laing puts it:

> Existence is a flame which constantly melts and recasts our theories. Existential thinking offers no security, no home for the homeless. It addresses no one except you and me. It finds its validation when, across the gulf of our idioms and styles, our mistakes, errings, and perversities, we find in the other's communication an experience of relationship established, lost, destroyed, or regained. We hope to share the experience of a relationship, but the only honest beginning, or even end, may be to share the experience of its absence.[13]

The new transcendence entails an image of man who is irredeemably an exile, a man without a country, a wandering Jew, a flying Dutchman, a depersonalized phantom whose only environment is the endless stream of change and becoming.

In a provocative work entitled *The Homeless Mind* Peter Berger has brilliantly analyzed the contemporary sense of being without place or stable identity in terms of the ongoing process of modernization.

> Modern identity is *peculiarly open*. While undoubtedly there are certain features of the individual that are more or less permanently stabilized at the conclusion of primary socialization, the modern individual is nevertheless peculiarly "unfinished" as he enters adult life. . . . Biography is thus apprehended both as a migration through different social worlds and as the successive realization of a number of possible identities.[14]

A similar appraisal of the contemporary human predicament comes from Robert Jay Lifton, who in an essay entitled "Protean Man" argues the thesis that the individual nowadays is incapable of sustaining a fixed concept of self. The self-image of the new person is akin to the mythical Greek figure Proteus, who can pass from one shape or form to another at will. Contemporary man is like a psychic chameleon who can modify his consciousness to fit his surroundings and his historical situation.[15] The homeless, formless mentality becomes a hothouse for the germination of new and occasionally bizarre expressions of the religious life. Tradition is seen as limiting man's radical openness and personal freedom. Only the spontaneous creation of fabulous, unchartered worlds of intuition and imagination, the dizzying delight in all that roils in the mind, regardless of its conscious or unconscious sources, is appropriate to the Protean type of humanity.

David Miller, a popular theological author, has gone so far as to proclaim the end of traditional "monotheistic" culture, which he roughly defines as not only our well-trodden allegiances to a single God, but also our closed system of morality and expectations as to what it means to be human. In the "new polytheism," which Miller praises as a more liberal and upbeat profile for the coming culture, man will be able to choose his divinities at will and live according to the values and experiences that they represent with unrestrained zest and freedom. In Miller's words,

> [The new polytheism] is . . . a matter of many potencies, many structures of meaning and being, all given to us in the reality of our everyday lives. We worship the Gods and Goddesses one at a time . . . but they are *all* at play in our culture and in our thinking and speaking about the deepest affairs of man in that culture.[16]

Religion will cease to be a domicile for the God of the fathers, but will become a sort of psychic "crash pad" through which the transient residents of the human soul can come and go as they please. The religion of the homeless mind that Miller and others describe feeds upon an all-encompassing temper of disaffection from traditional definitions of reality. Aiding and abetting the breakdown of long-cherished images and meanings, however, has been the influence of a very tangible, material force in the present society. That force has proven responsible for changing people's perceptions about the universe to a degree that has made possible the varieties of the new forms of transcendence. We are speaking, of course, about the impact of the drug culture and the manner in which it has drastically remolded many individuals' relationship to themselves and to other persons.

THE PSYCHEDELIC REVOLT: CHEMICAL TRANSCENDENCE

During the second half of the 1960s there flared across the United States and eventually in other Western nations a great interest in, and experimentation with, miscellaneous drugs or chemical substances that profoundly transform human consciousness. Socially prohibited and kept underground throughout earlier periods of Western history, the drug culture suddenly spewed forth and engulfed middle-class youth as well as some adults from all walks of life. LSD, mescaline, peyote, and "speed," along with marijuana and hashish, were no longer condemned as a devil's brew for criminal outcasts and escapists. Now they were celebrated enthusiastically by many who had tried them as the magic potion for society's salvation. The so-called high-priest of LSD, Timothy Leary, talked seriously about drugs as the new Western version of yoga. The garbled lyrics of rock music tunes, led by the Beatles, not too subtly suggested how popping a few milligrams of "acid" into the mouth could open passageways into the mind's deepest holy of holies. "Turn on" and "tune in" became slogans chimed with the fervor of the Salvation Army hymns of yesteryear.

Defenders of drug use have contended, sometimes quite extravagantly, that what are called "psychedelic" (literally, "mind-manifesting") substances have the power to induce states of mystical consciousness parallel to those found in the religions of the world. Some who, in the parlance of the period, succeeded in "blowing" their minds with psychedelics maintained that they had actually had a vision of God. Regardless of whatever religious or theological conclusions might be drawn from such claims, it is fair to say that the trances and sensations fostered by drugs did in some measure simulate authentic experiences of transcendence. Drug "highs" and "trips" succeeded in smashing the routine forms of everyday thinking and feeling. In a book, *The Doors of Perception,* which appeared a number of years before the drug craze, yet became a sort of manual of discipline for the new flights of mind-expansion, Aldous Huxley regarded his own use of mescaline as having cleansed his psyche of its conscious and unconscious fixations, thereby liberating it from the tyranny of ordinary thought habits and unlocking fantastic vistas of insight and amazement. In Huxley's words,

> all kinds of biologically useless things start to happen. In some cases there may be extra-sensory perceptions. Other persons discover a world of visionary beauty. To others again is revealed the glory, the infinite value and meaningfulness of naked existence, of the given, unconceptualized event.[17]

Of course, the diversity and individual oddities of reported drug experiences in no way matches the more symbolically structured forms of revelation or inner enlightenment that have occurred among the eminent representatives of traditional religion. Furthermore, the whirlpool of sound and light, the alternating tide of blissful and terrifying hallucinations that have frequently characterized many psychedelic ventures, turn out to be a far cry from the beatific vision portrayed by the saints of Christianity or the mindful serenity of the Hindu *samadhi.* In one sense the drug experience may be viewed as merely a process of bringing to the surface submerged unconscious fantasies and heightening the play of free-floating images by inhibiting the mind's ability to discriminate between external and internal events. From their extensive researches into psychedelic experiences Masters and Houston, for instance, have concluded that "mind-manifesting" drugs do little more than release suppressed memories of events, ideas, or sensations in an even more graphic form than were originally recorded at the conscious level. Enlarged and refined by the creative imagination, these "memory-traces," as Freud called them, unfold into a vivid cinema for the entertainment of the psyche.[18] There is also some evidence, according to their investigations, that the universal symbols or archetypes of religious experience, which according to Jungian psychology reside in the collective unconscious of all human organisms, are unleashed in the inward voyage of the person on drugs. However, the impressions and spectres that the drug-induced states of mind conjure up have such a fragile and fleeting quality that they correspond more directly to the spontaneous symbolizations that take place in dreams, or perhaps even in madness, than to the historic incidences of religious ecstasy.

As Claudio Naranjo has stated in a thoughtful summary of his work with mental disorders and chemical therapy, "a drug only makes an aspect of a person's psyche more manifest."[19] By the same token, Marlene Dobkin de Rios, an American anthropologist, has shown how in some primitive societies, such as the Indians of the Peruvian Amazon, drugs serve to cement the maturing individual's sense of cultural identity. Medicine men employ certain plants with hallucinogenic properties to teach young hunters about the secret lore of the animals they will have to pursue. Thus "accepting as one's own the values and interests of a social group can be greatly expedited by the use of plant hallucinogens in traditional society."[20] At any event, the drug experimentation does not transparently furnish new contexts for apprehending the ultimate meaning of life, but rather makes the mind more supple and responsive to its own inner promptings while enhancing the will to learn.

Nevertheless, drug use may very well take the individual up to the threshold of bona fide religious experience, to the portals of genuine transcendence. It may be for this reason that the drug epidemic of several years ago has now passed over into a religious revival of sorts. A large portion of current religious faddists will confess that they had heavily engaged in drug visions prior to joining a new sect or cult. A member of the Hare Krishna people once was quoted as saying that he could get a "much bigger and lasting high" by chanting the name of his Lord than by "dropping acid." While no measurable research has yet been completed concerning the affinity between former drug users and the new quest for transcendence, it is probably reasonable to assume that psychedelic and hallucinogenic substances act over time to "soften" the mind and make it receptive to unusual and more unworldly encounters. By destroying one's ingrained habits of perception and reflection, and by bringing into sharp focus those contents of the unconscious not previously apparent, the individual becomes aware of how changeable and arbitrary the world of his senses and imagination is. The dissolution of fixed forms leads to a thirst for some underlying and perhaps inexpressible unity of consciousness that transcends all finite feelings, attitudes, or ideas.

By the same token, the drug experience fosters what is possibly the most pervasive feature of mysticism and of other kinds of religious transcendence—the destruction of the tenacious ego, the surrender of personal identity. The effect of "depersonalization," that is, the corrosion of a strong sense of personal identity, has been described as a major consequence of drug taking. The petty, greedy, insecure, and jealous everyday self is exposed as a grand illusion, as a delicate bubble that bursts into a limitless and serene panorama of textures, shapes, colors, and noises. Alan Watts points up the connection between the drug consciousness and a dawning cosmic awareness:

> The mystical experience, whether induced by chemicals or other means, enables the individual to be so peculiarly open and sensitive to organic reality that the ego begins to be seen for the transparent abstraction that it is. In its place there arises (especially in the latter phases of the drug experience) a strong sensation of oneness with others.[21]

Through drugs the image of man as a creature whose mind and body is "homeless" finds its justification. However, the image of homelessness eventually gives place to a new perspective on the human condition—the view of man who has found a new home, that of the universe itself.

COSMIC CONSCIOUSNESS
AND THE NEW RELIGIONS

Perhaps the most significant trend within the remnants of the counterculture during the past few years has been the abandonment of drugs as a medium of ecstasy and the turn to varieties of yoga, meditation, and mystical or quasi-mystical religious paths. Despite the much publicized popularity of drugs in the 1960s, the younger generation has gradually become disenchanted with what Theodore Roszak caustically dubbed the "counterfeit infinity" of chemical transcendence. Many who either tried, dabbed in, or refrained from "blowing" their minds have now discerned not only the dangers but also the delusions of drug experiences. Although some drugs create an intense mood of quietude and expansiveness as well as providing new channels of insight and contemplation, they also foster an unnatural sense of reality that is neither consistent nor sure. The blissful "highs" of drug exploits must be revived repeatedly through the ingestion of an artificial agent. The beautiful and miraculous sights or sensations accompanying the average "trip" tend to seduce a person into a false belief in his own importance or invulnerability, as reported cases of young persons on LSD leaping out of second-story windows to their death below have underlined. In moments of rapture these unfortunates were convinced that they had magical powers and could even fly.

An analogy to the relationship between drugs and genuine transcendence may be found in the Zen notion of *makyo,* which literally means "from the devil." In the state of *makyo,* Zen trainees reportedly have fascinating hallucinations or experience unfamiliar states of mind which they mistake as *satori* or the goal of sudden enlightenment. They may hear heavenly voices, confront monstrous demons, or acquire a feeling of total mastery over their surroundings. Ever alert to this capacity for self-deception in his pupils, the Zen teacher will attempt to snap them out of such a state and prod them past this final obstacle to the ultimate peace of authentic *satori.* By and large the movement from the euphoria of drug "highs" to highly disciplined forms of religious exercise and devotion constitutes the overcoming of a temporary *makyo* phase among certain elements of our culture. It also suggests the continued relevance of help and guidance in the religious quest.

It is, of course, impossible here to catalogue or analyze all the different modes of religious transcendence that have taken shape of late. Yet one outstanding trait of the current religious ferment is evident. The new search for transcendence has turned, on the main, to Oriental or non-Christian styles of religious life and expression. In his book *The Road East* Harrison Pope, Jr. infers from his observations that, numerically speaking, "the current Eastern movement has far outstripped any previous episode in American history."[22] Although such a claim may be slightly exaggerated it does underscore the new importance of the Oriental way in the contemporary context. In another work, *Religious and Spiritual Groups in Modern America,* Robert Ellwood, Jr. links Asian-born meditational and devotional communities together with witchcraft, the occult, and sundry kinds of supernaturalism, all as part of a tradition of "alternative reality" that has affected Western culture in various times and places. Ellwood writes that the new religions "live in a monistic, mystic world full of occult initiatory laws. It is out of this stream that the world-view of modern cults comes. But because this option has never been entirely absent in Western history, we may call it the alternative reality tradition, meaning an alternative view and experience of reality."[23] Certainly the influence of magic and occultism has made itself felt in the past decade through a growing interest in the black arts, fortune telling, and Tarot cards, not to mention the brisk sales of paperback books on everything from Edgar Cayce to exorcism. But Eastern practices and wisdom seemingly have left a deeper impression on the lives of many young people today than the slick faddishness of the magical and demonic cults. The striking visibility, together with the billowing membership lists, of such groups as Divine Light, Meher Baba, Hare Krishna, Nichiren Shoshu Buddhism, and Transcendental Meditation attests to the far-reaching impact of the new Oriental spirituality. Even if, in terms of total following, they have still not come near to displacing the established religions of this country and the West, they nonetheless offer a tempting new model of reality that has generated enthusiasm in certain quarters. The formula for transcendence that these groups follow draws upon a mounting sense of the irrelevance and implausibility of the old religious forms among particular segments of society as well as a yearning for new values and experiences. We shall briefly enumerate several important elements of this formula.

The Rejection of Traditional Social Identity

Most, if not all, of the Occidental versions of the new Eastern religions seek to disengage the individual from his customary participation in the larger society into which he was born and brought up. While they do not encourage him to break completely with traditional social roles, at least in the sense of the occupation he holds, such religions succeed in tearing down his sense of identification with the personal goals dictated by his society. Peter Berger has pointed out that the "pluralization of life worlds in modern culture," the endless multiplication of possible careers and ways of doing things which a person may select throughout his journey from cradle to grave, results in a disintegration of traditional commitments to a single mode of living and, by extension, to all stable roles and responsibilities. In Berger's words:

Through most of human history, individuals lived in life-worlds that were more or less unified. This is not to deny that through the division of labor and other processes of institutional segmentation there have always been important differences in the life-worlds of different groups within the same society. Nevertheless, compared with modern societies, most earlier ones evinced a high degree of integration. Whatever the differences between various sectors of social life, these would "hang together" in an order of integrating meaning that includes them all. This integrating order was typically religious. For the individual this meant quite simply that the *same* integrative symbols permeated the various sectors of his everyday life. Whether with his family or at work or engaged in political processes or participating in festivity and ceremonial, the individual was always in the same "world." Unless he physically left his own society, he rarely, if ever, would have the feeling that a particular social situation took him out of this common life-world. The typical situation of individuals in a modern society is very different. Different sectors of their everyday life relate them to vastly different and often severely discrepant worlds of meaning and experience. Modern life is typically segmented to a very high degree, and it is important to understand that this segmentation (or, as we prefer to call it, pluralization) is not only manifest on the level of observable social conduct but also has important manifestations on the level of consciousness.[24]

In former periods, especially in traditional societies, not only was a person's role prescribed from childhood, but also his very universe of meaning was constructed around that role. A dizzying array of possible options for living did not exist. A farmer's son usually expected to go into farming and thus throughout his life retained the religious beliefs, moral principles, and common sense of the agrarian culture with which he was intimately involved. However, the loss of firm role expectations in the modern world has dropped upon the young adult the awesome burden of deciding who he wants to become as a person and at the same time removed most traditional guides for making such choices. The new religions manage to untie the Gordian knot of this role confusion. They claim that by "tapping" into the absolute, secret source of all life and being disclosed in cosmic awareness, a person can transcend the limitations of his historical and cultural situation while simultaneously securing a niche in society that is tentative, yet satisfying to him. A transcendental meditation poster, for example, quotes the Maharishi Mahesh Yogi as declaring that by reaching down for the universal "energy" that lies beneath all consciousness, you will be able to "choose what you want to be." Nichiren Shoshu maintains that rhythmic chanting of particular sacred syllables enables one to realize the best of what is potential within him. The new religions, then, provide a sort of spiritual "home away from home," a sense of location in some cosmic frame of reference that replaces the lost feeling of belonging within a concrete human community.

Naturalism

The new Eastern groups, supplying a recipe for cosmic participation, aim to abolish the traditional Western dichotomy between the self and the world, between the order of nature and the inventions of man. The current interest in ecology and the "back to nature" sentiment within the counterculture, as evidenced in the attraction to vegetarianism and organic foods, feeds directly into the appeal of the new religions. We have seen that traditional Eastern faiths, such as Hinduism, Buddhism, and Taoism, stress the apparent insignificance of man in light of the immensity of the natural world around him. The revolt in contemporary Western civilization against the excesses of industrialism and technology, against the consumer society and its ethic of material success, has found in the naturalistic orientation of Eastern religion a new font of inspiration.

The different forms of Buddhism, in particular, furnish a world-view compatible with this revolt. Not only does Buddhism preach the insubstantial character of the self, it also submits, especially in the Far Eastern traditions, that the person is nothing but the undifferentiated flow of existence itself. From this standpoint, man *is* the ongoing cosmic process. Hence, the end of human ambition and striving should be to cease ambition and striving altogether, to relinquish one's personal goals to the undefined course of life in its flow. Self and society are seen merely as fugitive manifestations of the stream of existence. The spiritually homeless individual, who is utterly alienated from the context of living he has always known, hence may very well find consolation and well-being in such an open-ended attitude about the universe.

The Flight from Time and History

Finally, the new Eastern religions bring to Occidental culture a wholly different standpoint concerning time and human history. Western religious myth and thought has always carried across the centuries a vital appreciation of change and the direction in which it is headed. At the core of the Judaeo-Christian image of man, as has been shown, lies a tacit drama of salvation—a "sacred history" that encompasses an account of the human race's sinful failing, the recurrent intervention of God in world affairs holding forth either the hand of mercy or the rod of wrath and judgment, the redemption of the righteous through faith and suffering, the purposeful march of events from paradise and fall to the coming of the Messiah and the final victory of eternity over time. Those religious philosophies that have seeped into Western thought currents and have promised a path of salvation above and beyond time and history are generally associated with the early Christian heresy of Gnosticism, which was discussed in Chapter 3. Nonetheless, the new Eastern religions depart significantly from the historical and progressive view of man in history and nudge closer to the Gnostic conception. They place their emphasis on the *ahistorical* and timeless truth that religious devotees are urged to discover by the discipline of meditation, by muffling the din of outside change and events. Unlike Judaism and Christianity, which teach that death, suffering, and evil can only be overcome by *living through* time and history in conformance with the will of God, the new forms of Eastern religion tell us that the key to unhappiness and misery consists primarily of a right understanding of our consciousness of time itself—our memory of past delights wrapped up with desire and anticipation of a rewarding future is what causes unrest. If, they say, we can learn to endure in, and accept with equanimity, the immediate present without thought for bygone pleasures or awaited triumphs, then we will no longer suffer the pangs of frustration or thwarted hopes. A latter-day Indian swami who has lectured extensively in the United States gives voice to this perspective. "To understand the Truth is to achieve the Truth," he writes.[25] Similarly,

> True, everybody has his better, but in my case, I know and feel that my conscious awareness of the ETERNAL NOW in me is my only better.[26]

Alan Watts underlines the same point.

> The whole problem of justifying nature, of trying to make life mean something in terms of the future, disappears utterly. Obviously, it all exists for this moment.[27]

For the new religions transcendence consists specifically of the elimination of the demands the ego makes on the world and others, *as well as* the loss of the sense of temporal succession in which the self accomplishes its goals and projects. Not history, but the transcendence of historical change lights the way to salvation.

The new religions' rejection of history in favor of the attainment of an eternal, cosmic consciousness is in keeping, moreover, with the current flight from tradition. The time-tested truths forged from the experience of dead generations are dismissed as meaningless. Only momentary, ecstatic illuminations have value for moderns who no longer look to the history books for guidance or to the prophets for glimmerings of a better tomorrow. There is, of course, a subtle irony in the fact that, whereas the Indian world-view from which many of the more recent faiths claim to reap their methods and insights springs from the cumulative wisdom of a traditional culture that treats innovation as merely a repetition of previous discoveries, the new religions concentrate almost exclusively on the inspiration of the instant. The symbols of the old Oriental paths conveniently express what is a uniquely Western venture into new forms of meaning. Transcendental meditation and Divine Light, for example, diverge boldly from any recognizable counterparts even in India today. Their social organization is adapted to an affluent, consumer society dominated by the mass media, and even their professed connections with traditional Hinduism are tenuous at best.

The new Eastern religions represent peculiar responses to a central crisis of culture in the Western world. We now turn to some other responses with language and strategies more naturally associated with the typical mentality of the Occident.

THE NEW DIONYSIANISM, RADICAL POLITICS, AND THE IMAGE OF LIBERATION

During the latter part of the 1960s the term "liberation" came to epitomize a broad range of radical ambitions and programs. The term, however, gradually assumed a more diffuse set of connotations than what it meant for social reformers and political activists. Liberation was understood as a general process of rescuing people from oppression, from harsh circumstances of life that prevented them from becoming fully human—in the areas of sexual expression, career goals, personal freedom, and participation in political and social institutions. The antitraditional mood of contemporary culture has contributed to a deep-rooted dissatisfaction among many individuals and groups with their lot. Thus many entrenched inequalities or accepted moral standards, such as male dominance or the virtues of thrift and hard work, that had been perennially taken for granted, were now perceived as instances of exploitation and oppression. The theme of transcendence came to be articulated in terms of the need for emancipating women, minorities, the aged, and homosexuals from their long-established roles in the social order. Within the context of liberation rhetoric there also arose a preoccupation with freeing the individual from himself, from old, encrusted attitudes about his body, his feelings, his very notion of what it means to be a person. Liberation, therefore, had both a psychic and social dimension, but in every case it implied transforming the established structures of knowing and doing in the world.

A major strand in this wider pattern of change went hand in hand with a drastic shift in social attitudes about human sexuality, with the broad acceptance of premarital sexual relations, the elevation of nudity as a public spectacle, and the glorification in art, cinema, and literature of the human body and raw sensuality. Though such a movement did not center in one particular group or social ideology, it came to attract the catch-all label of "the new Dionysianism." Dionysus, of course, was a god in Greek mythology whose cult gave free rein to the wildly emotional and orgiastic tendencies in people, especially women. During the late nineteenth century the philosopher Nietzsche spoke of the "Dionysian principle" in human life embodying everything irrational, unrestrained, and (to a certain extent) "mad." Against the Dionysian principle he opposed the "Apollonian," which represents what is rational, orderly, disciplined, and perhaps "civilized." The new Dionysians looked upon traditional social order—including sexual taboos, the ethic of deferred gratification, formal manners and etiquette, technology, and rationalism—as stifling man's true impulses. They conceived of man as a creature who cried out for liberation from the instinctual straitjacket that traditional culture had forced upon him. Transcendence consisted in the open, spontaneous expression of man's suppressed "natural" urgings.

As Sam Keen, a well-known spokesman for the new Dionysianism, phrased the issue:

> The Dionysian way exalts ecstasy over order, the id over the ego, being possessed over a possessive orientation, the creative chaos of freedom over the security of inherited patterns of social and psychological organization.[28]

Two words that encapsulated the mood of this movement were "fantasy" and "play." In 1969 the Christian theologian Harvey Cox wrote a very popular book called *Feast of Fools,* extolling the virtues of fantasy and whimsy, not simply as mechanisms for escaping the real world but as devices for creating alternative realities that fulfilled men's most intimate and irrepressible human longings. Cox upgraded fantasy to something more than the froth of idle daydreaming; fantasy would become a weapon of liberation. Cox wrote:

> [Fantasy] envisions new forms of social existence and it operates without first asking whether they are "possible." . . . It provides the images by which existing societies can be cracked open and recreated.[29]

By the same token, the spirit of "playfulness," the blithe celebration of personal caprices, inclinations, and unplanned little escapades, was hailed as an indispensable antidote to the serious and all-too-humdrum work of getting along in the larger social and economic system. The pursuit of play, like fantasy, according to this way of thinking, served chiefly to confound our cherished routines of looking at life and of dealing with its challenges. Play makes possible the consideration of previously unimagined or untried pictures of reality; it topples our "hang-ups" and prejudices. David Miller in *Gods and Games* explored the religious ramifications of play and fantasy. Miller asserted that these twin powers of the human psyche serve to free man from fossilized thinking, from pride and prejudice, from his own apathy.[30] In one crucial respect, the play orientation of the new Dionysianism derived from virtually the same human image that informed the new religions. The new Dionysians rejected the idea that the human animal could be standardized both in thought and deed. They depicted man as elastic, creative, and open to marvelous new possibilities of life. Alan Watts placed this image within a cosmic setting by drawing from Hindu myth the view of the universe itself as the never ending "play" or *lila* of God. This metaphysical position in itself has explicit meaning for the conduct of one's personal affairs. According to Watts,

> The fundamental dynamics of the universe is the game of hide-and-seek, lost-and-found, or peek-a-boo, the play of yes-and-no, positive-and-negative, up-and-down.[31]

This moral "responsibility" does not entail adherence to a rigorous code, but bending oneself to the supple rhythms of living. Transcendence is "playing God's game," so to speak, in the sense of ceaselessly fabricating new rules and ends for one's activity.

Concurrent with the rise of the new Dionysianism there developed a notion of transcendence as liberation from dehumanizing social conditions. In the main, this idea entailed a fundamental critique of capitalism and the overall status quo. One of the key sources of both the new Dionysian attitude and the nascent radical politics that adopted the latter view of transcendence was the social philosopher Herbert Marcuse (see also Chapter 1), who blended Marx and Freud into a systematic indictment of modern industrial civilization. In his lengthy work *Eros and Civilization* Marcuse argued that social repression of basic human instincts gives rise not only to unbalanced, sexually maladjusted men and women, but also to the general exploitation of workers in the capitalist economic system. Suppression of people's sexual energies, according to Marcuse, is an insidious social device for deflecting their attention from the normal quest for pleasure and personal satisfaction and making them more manageable as producers in factories and in offices. Thus repression of sexuality, fantasy, and play functions as an instrument by which certain classes of society can dominate others for the manufacture of wealth. Marcuse, like the new Dionysians, has regarded the free expression of the human body as helping restore the natural rights of the individual against the tyranny of the social order. But in contrast with the latter, Marcuse advocates a revolutionary reconstruction of objective social and economic conditions before the ultimate liberation of the person can be achieved. For Marcuse, the transcendence of the given state of affairs must occur as the consequence of collective action, not by the route of mysticism or through individual reveries and the tranquil enjoyment of fantasy worlds.

Marcuse's ideas, while not in themselves of a religious stripe, have nevertheless influenced certain theologians, either directly or indirectly. The theme of revolutionary transformation has taken on a religious aspect in the school of thought that has come to be known as "political theology" or, sometimes, "theology of hope." Such a school of thought assimilates the modern secular commitment to constant change to the Christian, messianic hope for the ultimate conquest of evil and suffering and the advent of a completely new order of things. Ernst Bloch, a German Marxist who considers himself (paradoxically) a "Christian atheist," has provided the theoretical foundation for the current political theologies in his book *Das Prinzip Hoffnung* ("The Principle of Hope"). In Bloch's view the kernel of the Christian faith is an uncompromising imperative to resist the powers of the existing world and to struggle continually for the improvement of the human race. Transcendence, therefore, does not mean simply an alteration of consciousness, but the advancing liberation of humanity from tangible forms of oppression and deprivation. Transcendence is the historical movement of man from the past into a more humane future. Another

German theologian with ties to the established churches, Jürgen Moltmann, has carefully redefined transcendence in this manner:

> The substantive "transcendence" means, then, the space ahead of us in the open future where historical transformations take place. This implies that future as transcendence can no longer be understood as quantitative extension and development of the present, but must denote qualitative transformation of the history which is experienced in conflicts.[32]

As with all models of transcendence discussed hitherto, the notion of transcendence as future excludes all allegiances to tradition and embodies an image of man who is forever navigating the winds and waves of change. The undertone of "homelessness" in the rhetoric of revolutionary transcendence is poignantly apparent in the following statement from an important document of contemporary radicalism—the manifesto of revolutionary student groups at the Sorbonne in Paris following the uprising of May, 1968. The students exhort other revolutionaries around the globe to "refuse the ideologies and utopias of total man which propose a goal, a stopping point, and which propose this in the name of progress only in order to refuse all the better our forward motion."[33] Transcendence requires an end to all definitive goals and visions of the human condition, both now and in the days to come. In this connection revolutionary ideology and its religious counterparts exhibit the image of the rootless, modern nomad. Like the devotees of the drug culture, the new Eastern religions, the new Dionysianism, the new political activists are clearly children of the posttraditional age.

THE CELEBRATION OF SELF:
THE INSTITUTIONALIZATION OF TRANSCENDENCE

Both political activism and the influence of the counterculture, however, have subsided in recent years, even though they have left lasting marks on our society. One still viable remnant of the cultural changes that came out of the 1960s is a diverse collection of popular psychological techniques and life philosophies that has come to be called the Human Potential Movement.

The Human Potential Movement, so called because it tends to emphasize various ways in which every individual can discover and cultivate the hidden potential within him, has had an impact both within and without Western religious communities, particularly in the United States. HPM combines an assortment of techniques in collective psychotherapy (such as those derived from "T-groups" or "encounter groups") with Eastern meditation skills and a concern with the free expression of a person's bodily feelings and sensations, as the New Dionysianism sought. Bound to no one rigid school of thought, HPM is secular and experimental. It does not claim to be a church, even though it has been practiced within the churches. It does not admit to having a religious outlook, even though it bears a close relationship with the new religious movements we have discussed. In short, HPM represents the distillation of many of the trends we have surveyed in this chapter. It constitutes an evolution of the style and attitudes of the counterculture into a method of living and experiencing that cuts across social and educational classes, although the price of enjoying its benefits has often made it a monopoly of affluent groups of people. HPM focuses radically on the art of "celebrating the self," as one spokesman for the movement has described it. It seeks to tap the "creative" sources of personal inspiration that are closed off by the moral standards, notions of truth and falsity, and expectations which all people, in the natural habit of trying to meet the demands of society, impose upon themselves. The HPM counsels avenues of finding personal happiness and satisfaction within one's own inner life and within oneself alone. Every person is encouraged to fabricate one's own universe, to fashion a realm of meaning that stands by itself and is not necessarily to be measured by external criteria. In fine, the movement glorifies the image of homelessness; it exalts the way of transcendence through the emancipation of the self from all fixed norms, values, and social aims.

John E. Biersdorf, director of the Institute for Advanced Pastoral Studies, has typified the Human Potential Movement as follows:

> People in the movement generally believe that what is most distinctive and important to know about human beings is not the learning patterns and mechanisms we share with rats or the stereotypical behavior of mental disturbances but the sensitivities, experiences, and achievements of the most loving and creative among us.[34]

The underlying assumption of the movement is that human nature is infinitely diverse and malleable. There is no universal or even cultural yardstick by which we can measure and evaluate human beings. Every individual is radically unique and deserves the opportunity to nurture and expand the latent talents with which he is endowed. The Human Potential Movement, in particular, draws upon the insights of the humanist psychoanalyst Abraham Maslow, who argued that the model of authentic humanity consists not in any lowest common denominator to which the life experiences and achievements of all persons can be reduced, but in the heights of individual and creative self-expression toward which each one in his own inimitable style may strive. Maslow talked about the attainment of "peak-experiences," which may be compared to religious experiences of transcendence, as the point at which man breaks out of his dependence on society and its definitions of reality. In the peak-experience the person becomes "self-actualized"; he energizes the drive to become a unique being within himself, which inevitably involves loneliness and separation from the comforting support of others. Maslow writes:

> The cognition of being . . . that occurs in peak-experiences tends to perceive external objects, the world, and individual people as more detached

from human concerns. Normally we perceive everything as relevant to human concerns and more particularly to our own private selfish concerns. In the peak-experiences, we become more detached, more objective, and are more able to perceive the world as if it were independent not only of the perceiver but even of human beings in general.[35]

In shedding his traditional social identity for the sake of a new understanding of himself, however, the individual does not necessarily plunge headlong into the chaos of spiritual uncertainty. He arrives at a distinctive sense of participation in the entire cosmos, in the totality of life and reality, which has come to be the sign of mystical awareness.

Following Maslow, the Human Potential Movement has endeavored to fashion techniques and to create the proper environment for individuals to realize their potential in this way. Unlike many previous experiments undertaken by the counterculture, however, the HPM does not strictly encourage the individual to adopt an eccentric way of living or to savage his mind with drugs. It undertakes to provide outlets for personal transcendence within the everyday world. Respectable businessmen as well as would-be gurus and social dropouts have enrolled in the programs that the numerous clinics and centers associated with the Human Potential Movement offer, the most prominent of which is the Esalen Institute in California. The results of the training and therapy they gain there, according to testimonies, are a fresh, new perspective on the importance of their lives as well as sustained awareness of a richer and deeper source of meaning that lies beyond getting and spending, working and worrying.

The Human Potential Movement exhorts individuals to abandon their obstinate allegiances to fixed ideas about themselves, inelastic moral codes, and habitual patterns of behavior. It constructs the image of man as protean or ever-changing, as a creature constantly making and remaking his character. Most concepts that people entertain about their own personality and about the nature of mortality, however, have a certain rigidity and therefore inhibit them from entering into the flux of life. Although man harbors the potential for creative transcendence of the limits that nature and society impose upon him, he tends more often than not to lapse into a routine and robotlike manner of experiencing the world and dealing with problems. The aim that the Human Potential Movement sets forth is to overcome this mechanical mode of existence. As Joel Latner, an exponent of Gestalt therapy, which figures heavily in the theory of the human potential movement, writes:

> Human nature is created again and again by each of us as we realize ourselves in the past. Even the natural structures can be modified, subsumed, and subverted in the course of living.[36]

Man's secure moorings are ripped away by the recognition and acceptance of both self and cosmos as a ceaseless process. The liberation of the self occurs when it no longer feels attached to the given conditions of its world, when it disentangles itself from the confining net of social commitments and obligations as well as the attributions of reality which it no longer cherishes. The Human Potential Movement denies the validity of any firm and sacred image of God or man, for both are merely mental constructs that draw attention away from the totality of all sensation and experience.

In this connection the HPM shares many of the traditional premises about life found in Eastern religions, though it does not cling to the conventional symbolism and rituals of those faiths. It represents a secular psychology with religious underpinnings. The movement's stress on tuning into immediate impressions and feelings in place of conscious thinking and reflection parallels in certain measure the popular interpretations of Zen Buddhism. As Robert Powell, a Western convert to Zen teachings, observes:

> Basically . . . all ideation is harmful because concepts hypnotize us into faulty perceptions and wrongful thinking. It divides the individual against himself and separates him from the rest of creation.[37]

By the same token, the Zen experience of transcendence blanks out consciousness of time, in which the self ordinarily moves and quests after its countless mundane and unsatisfiable goals. Zen advises man to give up living either for the past or the future and to celebrate what takes place within the self here and now. An echo of this instruction is heard in Latner's words: "Awareness is a happening in the present moment. All we can be aware of is what is happening now."[38] The nowness of experience is the window on reality. The Human Potential Movement insists that this experience can be had by everyone in the midst of their own humdrum worlds. Anyone, whether he is an insurance clerk or an Indian swami, is capable of living in the now. All he need do is listen to his own breath, rejoice in the fragile splendor of a flower by the roadside, or feel the sensuous pulses of his own body. He must revel in these sensations without attaching a value or a favorite conception of what they *mean* in some objective sense.

Such transcendence, therefore, provides a solution to the problem of moral and cultural rootlessness or the state of being "homeless." It supplies an ecstasy of self-discovery within the whirling vortex of contemporary social and historical change. Biersdorff declares, for instance, that "in this time of cultural confusion and change and of erosion of traditional religious beliefs, religion must exist as experience if it is to exist at all."[39] Earlier in this chapter we saw how personal experience for its own sake becomes the lodestar of meaning in a fragmented culture that has lost touch with its traditions. The Human Potential Movement has set about erecting institutional structures in which the free pursuit of such personal experiences can be carried forth. It is open to question, however, whether any durable fabric of culture and institutions can ever be woven within a movement that seeks to make relative and transient all models of human selfhood and society.

A RETURN TO TRADITION?

Throughout this text we have seen how religious symbols mirror the varying images of man in different periods and cultures. We have learned, too, how the image of man alternates in response to changing social, cultural, and psychological conditions of human existence. In the contemporary era, an acute crisis has arisen as a result of the loss of fixed meanings and symbols. On the other hand, the same era has, through different cultural and religious movements, generated an embryonic new image adequate to the homelessness and confusion of our times—the image of man without a star or rudder to steer him, the image of man in persistent search of the untested and undiscovered. Obviously, most of the examples of this image have been drawn from the experience of the late 1960s and early 1970s, an epoch of rapid change and upheaval throughout the world. The rate of change remains great, and certainly there still persists a climate of revolutionary anticipation and experimentation in many quarters of human culture. Yet in the same breath there is an increasing disenchantment with the cult of the new. In America, especially, the daily convulsions, riots, *avant-garde* trial balloons and outrageous life styles have abated considerably, and a mood of quietude, as well as nostalgia for the past, in some instances, has set in. Just as many people, according to Gallup polls, have tempered their former confidence and enthusiasm about the future, so they are also returning to many old ways and customs. Hair lengths get shorter; sexual mores become more conservative; aging gurus and revolutionaries find themselves without a clientele; the old work ethic becomes attractive again; family and group life begins to take precedence over free-wheeling individualism; the churches reverse the trend of the past decade toward attrition of members and level off in their following, if they do not in some cases increase. It may be that the image of the posttraditional age cannot in itself pass the test of time. It may be that the traditional images have not completely lost their vital spark, or at least their potential for revival and reinterpretation.

At any event, it is unlikely that religion and the human image that is contained within it will now freeze into some immutable pattern of meaning. History perennially yields the lesson that human events never stand still, that the future is always in the making. The broken image of modern culture and the desperate struggle for new forms of meaning that will suffice for the old may only be signs of a larger transition. Religions come and go, a period of uncertainty and disillusionment follows on the heels of accelerating change, but after a while new and more stable visions of the world and of reality start to take hold. Such was the story of the birth of the major religious traditions we have examined in this text. The story may now have come full circle. The new forms of transcendence constitute seeds perhaps for yet unmanifest human images, for new permutations in the understanding of the relationship between self, society, and cosmos. Some of these seeds will take root in the soil of ongoing experience. Others will rot beneath the ground. Despite the preoccupation of so much of the new spirituality with timelessness, it is time by which the worth and integrity of man's symbols and images of himself can be gauged. It is as simple as the old, familiar adage: "time will tell."

NOTES

1. See Dietrich Bonhoeffer, *Letters and Papers from Prison* (New York: The Macmillan Company, 1953).

2. Alvin Toffler, *Future Shock* (New York: Random House, 1970), p. 35.

3. William A. Johnson, *A Search for Transcendence* (New York: Harper & Row, 1974), p. 2.

4. Paul Goodman, "The New Reformation," *New York Times Magazine,* September 14, 1969, pp. 32–33.

5. Rev. 21:5. *RSV.*

6. See Margaret Mead, "The Future: Prefigurative Cultures and Unknown Children," in *The Futurists,* ed. Alvin Toffler (New York: Random House, 1972), pp. 27–50.

7. William Alexander, *The Tragedy of Croesus,* Act II, scene 1.

8. Harvey Seifert, *Reality and Ecstasy: A Religion for the Twenty-First Century* (Philadelphia: Westminster Press, 1974), p. 87.

9. Alan Watts, *The Meaning of Happiness* (New York: Harper & Row, 1968), pp. 40–41.

10. Charles Cameron, ed., *Who Is Guru Maharaji?* (New York: Bantam Books, 1973), p. 24.

11. Bob Dylan, "Like a Rollin' Stone," copyright Columbia Records, 1965.

12. Carlos Castaneda, *Journey to Ixtlan* (New York: Simon & Schuster, 1972).

13. R. D. Laing, *The Politics of Experience* (New York: Penguin Books, 1967), pp. 47–48.

14. Peter Berger, *The Homeless Mind* (New York: Random House, 1973), p. 77.

15. Robert Jay Lifton, "Protean Man," in *The Religious Situation* (Boston: Beacon Press, 1969), p. 816.

16. David Miller, *The New Polytheism* (New York: Harper & Row, 1974), p. 65.

17. Aldous Huxley, *The Doors of Perception* (New York: Harper & Row, 1956), p. 26.

18. See R. E. L. Masters and Jean Houston, *The Varieties of Psychedelic Experience* (New York: Dell Publishing Company, 1966).

19. Claudio Naranjo, *The Healing Journey* (New York: Random House, 1974), pp. 10–11.

20. Marlene Dobkin de Rios, "Cultural Persona in Drug-Induced Altered States of Consciousness," in *Social and Cultural Identity,* ed. Thomas K. Fitzgerald (Athens: The University of Georgia Press, 1974), p. 21.

21. Alan Watts, *The Joyous Cosmology* (New York: Random House, 1962), p. 97.

22. Harrison Pope, Jr., *The Road East* (Boston: Beacon Press, 1974), p. 20.

23. Robert Ellwood, *Religious and Spiritual Groups in Modern America* (Englewood Cliffs, N.J.: Prentice-Hall, Inc., 1973), p. 43.

24. Berger, *Homeless Mind,* pp. 64–65.

25. Sri Chinmoy Ghose, *Meditations: Food for the Soul* (New York: Harper & Row, 1971), p. 55.

26. Ibid., p. 72.

27. Alan Watts, *The Wisdom of Insecurity* (New York: Random House, 1951), p. 116.

28. Sam Keen, "Manifesto for a Dionysian Theology," *Cross Currents,* 19, no. 1 (Winter 1969), p. 41.

29. Harvey Cox, *Feast of Fools* (Cambridge, Mass.: Harvard University Press, 1969), pp. 82–83.

30. See David Miller, *Gods and Games* (New York: World Publishing Company, 1970).

31. Alan Watts, *Beyond Theology* (New York: Random House, 1964), p. 72.

32. Jürgen Moltmann, *Religion, Revolution, and the Future* (New York: Charles Scribner's Sons, 1969), p. 190.

33. "Appeal from the Sorbonne—June 13–14, 1968," in *The New Left Reader,* ed. Carl Oglesby (New York: Grove Press, 1969), p. 273.

34. John E. Biersdorf, "The Human Potential Movement and the Church," *Christianity and Crisis* (March 17, 1975), p. 55.

35. Alexander H. Maslow, *Religions, Values, and Peak-Experiences* (New York: The Viking Press, 1970), p. 61.

36. Joel Latner, *The Gestalt Therapy Book* (New York: Julian Press, 1973; Bantam, 1975), p. 29.

37 Robert Powell, *Zen and Reality* (New York: The Viking Press, 1975), p. 41.

38. Latner, *Gestalt Therapy,* p. 46.

39. Biersdorf, "Human Potential Movement," p. 58.

FOR FURTHER READING

BERGER, PETER, *The Homeless Mind*. New York: Random House, 1973. A provocative discussion by an important American sociologist of modern technological culture and its effects on individual consciousness.

CASTANEDA, CARLOS, *Journey to Ixtlan*. New York: Simon & Schuster, 1972. The third book in the series about an anthropologist's encounter with a Yaqui Indian sorcerer; contains many themes that resonate with the new religious quest for transcendence.

COX, HARVEY, *Feast of Fools*. New York: Harper & Row, 1970. A noted theologian's perspective on the relationship between religion and the spirit of "play," on fantasy and the utopian attitude.

ELLWOOD, ROBERT, *Religious and Spiritual Groups in Modern America*. Englewood Cliffs, N.J.: Prentice-Hall, Inc., 1973.

HUXLEY, ALDOUS, *The Doors of Perception*. New York: Harper & Row, 1956. A trail-blazing analysis of psychedelic drugs and their effects on normal perception; suggests an affinity between the drug experience and mysticism.

JOHNSON, WILLIAM A., *A Search for Transcendence*. New York: Harper & Row, 1974. An examination of the modern notion of transcendence in reference to the writings of such figures as Herbert Marcuse and R. D. Laing.

LAING, R. D., *The Politics of Experience*. New York: Ballantine Books, 1967.

LIFTON, ROBERT J., "Protean Man." *In the Religious Situation*. Boston: Beacon Press, 1969.

MASLOW, ABRAHAM, *Religion, Values, and Peak-Experiences*. New York: The Viking Press, 1970. A study of religion and personality structure with special consideration of mystical or "peak" experiences by one of the founders of humanistic psychology.

MILLER, DAVID, *Gods and Games*. New York: World Publishing Company, 1970. Another important book that sketches the fundamentals of a "theology of play."

——, *The New Polytheism*. New York: Harper & Row, 1974. Argues for the finality of the "death of God" and a return to polytheistic worship in the sense of a free exploration of the multiple psychic forces in man's unconscious.

MOLTMANN, JÜRGEN. *Religion, Revolution, and the Future*. New York: Charles Scribner's Sons, 1969. Regards the revolutionary attitude as a method of transcendence in the sense of its willingness to abolish the past and reach beyond into an unprecedented future.

POPE, HARRISON, JR., *The Road East*. Boston: Beacon Press, 1974. A casual inspection of some of the new Eastern religious movements in America today.

POWELL, ROBERT, *Zen and Reality*. New York: The Viking Press, 1975. A good elaboration of the philosophy and psychology behind Zen Buddhism with respect to its rejection of ordinary reality.

RICHARDSON, HERBERT, and DONALD CULTER, eds., *Transcendence*. Boston: Beacon Press, 1969. A somewhat dated, but still useful, collection of essays from the early period of religious discussion about the notion of transcendence.

262

TOFFLER, ALVIN, *Future Shock.* New York: Random House, 1970. The best-selling book by an editor of *Fortune* magazine on contemporary technology and change and its impact on institutions, values, and psychic health.

WATTS, ALAN, *The Meaning of Happiness.* New York: Harper & Row, 1968. A valuable introduction to the thoughts and reflections of perhaps the foremost apostle of Oriental religion and philosophy for Westerners.

Index

Knowledge, 204–5
    of God (*see* God, knowledge of)
    theory of, 191–92
Knowles, David, 112, 123*n*
Koan, 176
Kojiki, 171
Kṛṣṇa (*see* Gods, Hindu Krishna)
Kṣatriyas (Hindu), 136, 138, 141, 143
Kūkai, 173, 174

Laing, R. D., 17, 21*n*, 243, 260*n*
La Mettrie, Julien O. de, 198, 205
Lanternari, Vittorio, 17, 36*n*
Lao-Tzu, Book of the, 156, 160–62, 163, 169
Latner, Joel, 257, 261*n*
Law (*see Torah*)
Leary, Timothy, 244
Legitimation (*see* Religion)
Leibniz, Gottfried, 190, 210
Liberalism, 219
Liberation, 252–58
Lietzmann, Hans, 123*n*
Lifton, Robert J., 243, 260*n*
Lloyd, Charles, Jr., 36*n*
Locke, John, 191–95, 199, 203, 204, 231*n*
Lombard, Perer, 108
Lotus Sutras, 168, 173
Love, Torah subordinate to, 72
Loving-kindness, 69
Luckmann, Thomas, 5, 10, 36*n*
Lucretius, 32
Luke, Book of, 69, 78, 79
Luther, Martin, 112–17, 119, 175, 223
Lutheranism;
    Danish, 221–22
    German, 15
    scholasticism, 207

Ma'at (Egyptian), 51
Mahābhārata (Hinduism), 145, 146
Maharaji, Guru, 242
Mahāvīra, Vardhāmana, 142, 143
Makyo (Zen), 247
Man (*see also* Humanity)
    as autonomous, 187
    corruption of, 187, 219–23 (*see also* Sin)
    creation of, 47, 88
    as creature of God, 119
    divinity of, 215–19
    as exiled soul, 81–85

Man (*cont.*)
    goodness of, 187
    as historical being, 210–14
    in the image of God, 73–74, 89, 120
    maturity of, 187
    as moral actor, 203–6
    in relation to universe, 88
    as religious animal, 5
    as sinner, 45–48
    Man a Machine (de La Mettrie), 198, 205
Mana, 20
Mandāla (Hinduism, Buddhism), 137, 173
Manichaeism, 81, 83
Mantra (Hinduism), 137, 141, 145
Manu, Laws of (Hinduism), 136, 226
Mao-tse-tung, 228
Maoism, 227
Marcuse, Herbert, 17, 36*n*, 254
Martyrdom, 80
Marx, Karl, 7, 12–17, 18, 36, 40, 84, 109, 214–15, 218–19, 225, 232*n*
Marxism, 210, 227
Maskariputra, Gosāla, 142
Maslow, Abraham, 256, 261*n*
Master, The (Buddhism), 169–70
Masters, R. E. L., 31, 37*n*, 245, 260*n*
Materialism, 198–99, 206, 213, 216, 236
Matthew, Book of, 68–69, 98
Maya (Hinduism) 34
Mead, Margaret, 240, 260*n*
Mechanism, 190, 193
Meditation, 169, 173, 176, 240, 247, 251
Meiji era in Japan, 228–29
Memory, 99–100
Mencius, 165
Merton, Robert, 18, 37*n*
Messiah, 64, 69–70
Messianism, revolutionary, 17
Miller, David, 243, 253, 260*n*, 261*n*
Mind's Road to God (Bonaventure), 110, 123*n*
Moira (Greek), 43
Moksha (Hinduism), 142
Moltmann, Jurgen, 255, 261*n*
Monism (*see* Pantheism)
Moore, Charles A., ed., 37*n*, 181*n*, 182*n*
Morality, 34, 41, 205–6, 219
Moses, 46, 51–54
Mudra (Buddhism), 173
Muilenburg, James, 45, 66*n*
Mysticism, 29–31, 247
    Buddhism, 166
    Christian, 30, 109–12

Sacrifice, Chinese, 159–60
  Hinduism, 129, 141, 145, 159
  Roman, 79
Sages, Taoist, 160–62
Saichō, 173
Salvation, 169 (*see also* Nirvana)
Samsara (Hinduism), 133, 136, 148, 179,
  180 (*see also* Flow of life)
Saṁakāras (Hinduism), 136, 138, 140
Samuel, Book of, 57
Samurai (Japanese), 176–77, 178, 179
Sannyāsa (Hinduism), 137, 138
Sartre, Jean-Paul, 185
Sat-chit-ananda (Hinduism), 139
Satori (Zen Buddhism), 179, 180, 247
Satygraha (Hinduism), 227
Schleiermacher, Friedrich, 207–10, 212,
  216, 222, 232n
Scientific thought in 18th century, 189–91,
  213, 217
  pioneers, 188
Second coming of Christ (*see* Christ, second
  coming of)
Sects (*see* Cults)
Seifert, Harvey, 241, 260n
Sentences (Lombard), 108
Sexuality, 254
Shinran, 174, 175
Shintoism, 155, 170, 229
  cultural pattern, 171–72
  domestic rites, 171–72
  grand shrine of Ise, 170, 171
  imperial pattern, 171, 229
  spirits of reality, 172
Siddhartha (Hesse), 132
Sin, 45–48, 70–71, 120
  forgiveness of, 112–19, 223 (*see also*
    Faith, justification by)
  Hindu concept, 140
  original, 187
  Shinto concept, 172 (*see also* Evil; Man,
    corruption of; Suffering)
Sincerity, as Japanese virtue, 172
Singer, Milton, 150n
Smith, Adam, 190
Smith, Horace, 32
Social identity, 243
  traditional rejection of, 248–52
Sociology of Religion (Weber), 22
Soul:
  exiled, 81–85
  immortality of, 45, 206
  pre-existence, 96

Soul (*cont.*)
  synthesis of body and, 106
Southern, R. W., 103, 123n
Speeches (Schleiermacher), 209
Spirit, life in the, 71
Stoicism, 85, 86, 89
Streng, Frederick, 6, 36n
Sūdras (Hinduism), 136, 139
Suffering, 31–35, 185, 218
  Buddhist concept, 34, 143, 144
  Christian concept, 94–97, 251
  Gnostic concept, 83
  Hebrew concept, 60, 251
  Hindu concept, 34
  servant, 57–62, 70
Sukhāvati (Buddhism), 168
Suzuki, Daisetz T., 176, 182n
Symbolism of Evil (Ricoeur), 91, 121n
Symbols (*see* Religion; Religious images)
System of Nature (d'Holbach), 197, 231n

Taoism, 154, 155, 160–63, 166, 228
Tao-te-ching (see Lao-Tzu, Book of the)
Teaman and the Ruffian (Suzuki), 176
Ten Commandments, 46
Theodicy, 34–35
Theology:
  political, 238, 254
  systematic, 93–94
Thomas, Edward J., 150n
Tillich, Paul, 6, 18, 19, 32, 37n, 108, 113,
  123n, 185, 187, 214, 223, 225, 230n,
  232n, 233n
Timaeus (Plato), 85, 121n
Time, 59, 62–63
  cosmic, 102
  definition of, 99–100
  flight from, 250–52
Tindal, Matthew, 195, 231n
Toffler, Alvin, 237, 260n
Toland, John, 194, 231n
Torah, 42, 45–46, 48, 51, 57, 64, 71, 72
  Christ supersedes, 71–72
Torrey, N. L., 231n
Totem and Taboo (Freud), 15
Totem worship, 15–16, 20
Tradition:
  post traditional age, 239–40, 241, 251
  return to, 259–60
  waning of, 239–41
Transcendence, 5, 112, 209, 230
  chemical (*see* Psychedelic drugs)